The Medieval Town
1200–1540

Readers in Urban History
General Editors:
Peter Clark and David Reeder
The Centre for Urban History, Leicester University

THE MEDIEVAL TOWN
A Reader in English Urban History, 1200–1540
Edited by Richard Holt and Gervase Rosser

THE TUDOR AND STUART TOWN
A Reader in English Urban History, 1530–1688
Edited by Jonathan Barry

THE EIGHTEENTH-CENTURY TOWN
A Reader in English Urban History, 1688–1820
Edited by Peter Borsay

THE VICTORIAN CITY
A Reader in British Urban History, 1820–1914
Edited by R. J. Morris and R. Rodger

The English Medieval Town
A Reader in English Urban History
1200–1540

Edited by
Richard Holt and Gervase Rosser

LONGMAN
London and New York

Longman Group UK Limited
Longman House, Burnt Mill, Harlow,
Essex CM20 2JE, England
and Associated Companies throughout the world.

Published in the United States of America
by Longman Inc., New York

© Longman Group UK Limited 1990

All rights reserved; no part of this publication may be
reproduced, stored in a retrieval system, or transmitted in
any form or by any means, electronic, mechanical,
photocopying, recording, or otherwise without either
the prior written permission of the Publishers or a licence
permitting restricted copying in the United Kingdom issued
by the Copyright Licensing Agency Ltd, 33–34 Alfred Place,
London, WCIE 7DP.

First Published 1990

British Library Cataloguing in Publication Data
The medieval town: a reader in English urban
history 1200–1540. – (Readers in urban history).
  1. England. Towns, history
  I. Holt, Richard, *1948* June 22 –   II. Rosser, Gervase *1956* May 5 –
  III. Series
  942'. 009' 732

ISBN 0-582-05129-0 CSD
ISBN 0-582-05128-2 PPR

Library of Congress Cataloging-in-Publication Data

The medieval town: a reader in English urban history
  1200–1540 / edited by Richard Holt and Gervase Rosser.
      p.   cm.
    ISBN 0-582-05129-0. — ISBN 0-582-05128-2 (pbk.)
    1. Cities and towns, Medieval—England.   2. City and town life—
  England—History.   I. Holt, Richard, 1948–   II. Rosser,
  Gervase, 1956
  HT115.E54   1990
  307.76'0942'0902—dc20   89-49706
                                                                        CIP

R00976 67102

CHICAGO PUBLIC LIBRARY
CLEARING BRANCH
6423 W. 63RD PL.   60638

Set in Linotron 202 10/11pt Times Roman

Produced by Longman Singapore Publishers (Pte) Ltd.
Printed in Singapore

CONTENTS

Contents

ACKNOWLEDGEMENTS

We are grateful to the following for permission to reproduce articles:

Associated Book Publishers (UK) Ltd for 'Ceremony and the citizen' in *Crisis and Order in English Towns 1500–1700* edited by P. Clark and P. Slack (Routledge, 1972); Basil Blackwell Ltd for 'The first half-century of the borough of Stratford-upon-Avon' by E.M. Carus-Wilson in *Economic History Review*, 18 (1965); Bristol and Gloucestershire Archaeological Society and the author, R. A Holt, for 'Gloucester in the century after the Black Death' in *Transactions of the Bristol and Gloucestershire Archaeological Society*, 103 (1985); Council for British Archaeology and the author, Derek Keene, for 'Suburban growth' in *The Plans and Topography of Medieval Towns in England and Wales* edited by M. W. Barley (CBA Research Report 14, 1976); The Historical Association and the author, Caroline M. Barron, for 'Ralph Holland and the London radicals 1438–1444' in *A History of the North London Branch of the Historical Association, together with Essays in Honour of its Golden Jubilee* (London, 1970); Hodder and Stoughton Ltd for 'Craftsmen and the economy of London in the fourteenth century' by E. M. Veale in *Studies in London History Presented To Philip Edmund Jones* edited by A. E. J. Hollaender and W. Kellaway, copyright © 1969 Elspeth M. Veale; Leicester University Press, a division of Pinter Publishers, for 'Towns in societies: Medieval England' by R. H. Hilton in *Urban History Yearbook* (1982); The Past and Present Society and the author, R. H. Hilton, for 'Small town society in England before the Black Death' in *Past and Present: A Journal of Historical Studies*, 105 (November 1984), world copyright The Past and Present Society; Pontifical Institute of Medieval Studies for 'Commercial dominance of a medieval oligarchy' by M. Kowaleski in *Mediaeval Studies*, 46 (1984), © 1984 by the Pontifical Institute of Medieval Studies, Toronto; Royal Historical Society for 'Urban decline in late medieval England' by R. B. Dobson in *Transactions*

Acknowledgements

of the Royal Historical Society, 27 (1977), 'The English borough in the thirteenth century' by G. H. Martin in *Transactions of the Royal Historical Society*, 13 (1963) and 'The essence of medieval urban communities: The vill of Westminster 1200–1540' by A. G. Rosser in *Transactions of the Royal Historical Society*, 34 (1984).

Chapter One

INTRODUCTION: THE ENGLISH TOWN IN THE MIDDLE AGES

Richard Holt and Gervase Rosser

The period between the late twelfth century and the beginning of the sixteenth marked a distinct phase in the history of the English town. Within this long span of three centuries, wider economic and social developments brought about dramatic changes in urban life. The era opened, in a context of rapid population growth, with a rising trend of urban expansion and new town foundations; by the middle of the fourteenth century that trend was reversed, and within the contracted economy of England (as of Europe in general) after the arrival of the Black Death, towns inevitably contracted both in size and numbers. Nevertheless, the period is distinguished by an underlying continuity of the essential forms of urban life, which differed in important respects from those both of earlier and of later times. The purpose of this introduction, therefore, is to provide a working definition of the medieval town in England, and to establish the general context for the particular studies that follow.

The first point to emphasize is that most English towns of the late Middle Ages were small by the standards of the modern city, or indeed by those of the greater urban centres of medieval Flanders or Italy. The majority of English towns contained fewer than 1500 people. Even so, taking into account the numerous small towns established in England by the year 1300, the country should be seen as sharing in the urbanization that affected much of Europe in the twelfth and thirteenth centuries. Secondly, the medieval European town was not differentiated from the countryside to the same extent as towns in other times and places. The English town in particular was subject to the pervasive powers both of royal government and of society at large; the town's incorporation within the wider political and social framework was consolidated by legal and fiscal developments of the thirteenth century. The assimilation of urban to rural social structures was underlined by a further distinctive trait of the medieval English town, which was the relatively undeveloped nature of urban industry. The preponderance of domestic production in medieval industry rendered unnecessary the development of a large urban proletariat, with the result that social relations in

1

towns were not fundamentally different from those which pertained in the countryside. Finally, the social order of the English medieval town was pervaded by a set of religious beliefs which was given its definitive official form by churchmen in the thirteenth century, and which thereafter, until the Reformation, infused the language and the ritual of urban as of rural life. The sixteenth century witnessed the transformation of the medieval town in all of these fundamental respects. First, a new and unprecedented upsurge of population placed an intolerable strain upon social relations in towns as they had become defined in the late medieval period. Secondly, the successive stages of the Reformation removed the panoply of sacramental religion and ritual within which the social and political life of the towns had been played out during the preceding three centuries. The outcome, the early modern town, was in many ways a new social phenomenon.

For all their interest, published studies of towns during the period of the later Middle Ages have in the main been brief, with only rare attempts at synthesis. Alice Stopford Green's *Town Life in the Fifteenth Century*, a still inspiring masterpiece of social history published in 1894, has not yet been superseded by a work of equivalent length and depth of treatment. Susan Reynolds' recent survey, however, has brought a fresh clarity to all aspects of the subject, opening it up to the investigation of a new generation of students;[1] and the past two decades have been marked by the production of varied and creative work in this area. Consequently, the outlines of a new urban history are beginning to be discernible. The essays in this volume have been chosen to represent the vigour of recent work in the field, and the variety of methodological approaches to the subject currently being advocated and practised. Of itself, such a diverse collection of studies cannot amount to an integrated interpretation of their common theme. It should, however, indicate where the emphasis will lie in any future work of synthesis.

This is not to suggest that, prior to the current phase of interest, the English medieval town was neglected by historians. From the later Middle Ages onwards, antiquaries produced a host of local histories, works which individually can still contain much of value.[2] The turning of scholarly attention to general questions of medieval urban history, which occurred in the late nineteenth century, was prompted by specific contemporary concerns with the nature of English law, the origins of constitutional democracy, and the development of

---

1. S. Reynolds, *An Introduction to the History of English Medieval Towns* (Oxford, 1977).
2. See P. Clark, 'Visions of the urban community: Antiquarians and the English city before 1800', in D. Fraser and A. Sutcliffe (eds), *The Pursuit of Urban History* (London, 1983), 105–25.

capitalism: grand themes of history whose evolution various writers saw as bound up with the medieval town. F. W. Maitland, the principal founder of medieval urban history in England (though his work was by no means confined to towns), gave to this new field of study a specifically legal direction. Scholars of the next generation carried this further, and sharing a primary concern with constitutional niceties Mary Bateson, Adolphus Ballard, James Tait and others developed a perspective on towns narrower than that of Maitland himself. Tait's achievement was to bring to its culmination the study of the borough as a legal entity, defined by judicial independence and charters of privilege. Ironically the very thoroughness of his juridical researches, brought together in 1936 in *The Medieval English Borough,* gave the impression that he had exhausted the subject of the medieval town, which consequently remained largely neglected for the following quarter of a century.[3]

The narrow, legal definition of the chartered borough has tended to be taken all to readily as the model of the medieval town. The effect has been to exclude from view much of the full spectrum of urban life in the Middle Ages. The writer of the standard history of Birmingham, having examined the abundant evidence of economic life in this expanding market town, nevertheless concluded that it remained a village, an essentially agricultural settlement, throughout the medieval period. Having received no charter of urban liberties from its lord, it could not possibly have been a town.[4] More enlightened historians, meanwhile, have taken a broader view, well aware that the official legal framework provides at best a partial definition of medieval society, and that charters and constitutions are characteristic only of some towns at certain periods.

As an alternative to demonstrably inadequate legal definitions, attempts have been made – largely by sociologists – to provide a societal model of the town. Their success, however, has been limited, since they have failed to identify determinants of urban social organization which are confined exclusively to towns. The phenomena of industrialization, capitalism, or social segregation, for example, are not necessarily urban.[5] For historians, the positive lesson to be drawn from the literature of urban sociology is that the

---

3. See, principally, F. W. Maitland, *Township and Borough* (Cambridge, 1898); M. Bateson (ed.), *Borough Customs,* Selden Society, 18 (1904); 21 (1906); A. Ballard and J. Tait (eds), *British Borough Charters, 1216–1307* (Cambridge, 1923); J. Tait, *The Medieval English Borough* (Manchester, 1936).
4. C. Gill, *History of Birmingham,* vol. 1: *Manor and Borough to 1865* (Oxford, 1952), 12–26; and see R. A. Holt, *The Early History of the Town of Birmingham* (Dugdale Society Occasional Paper, Oxford, 1985), 2–3 and *passim.*
5. P. Saunders, *Sociology and the Urban Question* (London, 1981), provides a good critique of the literature of urban sociology.

town has never been an autonomous agent in society; indeed, on the contrary, it is always an integral part of society at large. Marx himself argued in this way, even while he recognized in the concentration of urban populations a catalyst of broader social changes. The point is made for the medieval town by Rodney Hilton (Ch. 2). So far from arriving like a strange cuckoo in the nest of medieval society, the town was a natural outgrowth and expression of existing social relations. This denial of urban autonomy has profound implications for the understanding of the social structure of medieval towns.

A definition of the medieval town needs, therefore, to take account of its assimilation to agrarian society. But it also had, undeniably, a distinct identity, which makes it a legitimate object of study. An acceptable working definition describes the town as a relatively dense and permanent concentration of residents engaged in a multiplicity of activities, a substantial proportion of which are non-agrarian. Furthermore, it was the heterogeneity of its composition, rather than the sheer weight of human numbers, that produced the distinctively urban character of the medieval town, since for this period at any rate it would be impossible to specify an absolute minimum size of an urban population. Diversity was accentuated by the fact that many town dwellers were non-natives, who lacked the shared experience of a common upbringing in a local environment. Only constant rural immigration could sustain population levels in the face of high urban mortality. The larger the town, the wider the catchment from which migrants came, and the greater the diversity of settlers. Diversity, indeed, was the fundamental characteristic of urban society in the Middle Ages; and it created social forms unknown in the countryside.

Three consequences, general and interrelated, followed from this. The first was tension or conflict within a population which incorporated such various, and often contradictory, interests; recorded clashes were perennial and sometimes violent. Secondly, interest groups formed, representing one set of ambitions or another. Factionalism and social strife were far from being purely urban phenomena, but the concentration of population intensified awareness both of common bonds within the group and of rival interests outside it. The third major result of the complexity and volatility of the urban population was the constant challenge to find ways of holding it together. That medieval towns survived at all, while yet, on occasion, accommodating significant adjustments in social organization, is testimony to the relative success of a range of responses to that challenge.

In the twelfth century the urban economy was still concentrated in a few centres, whose origins lay in the Anglo-Saxon period. The cities of Roman Britain had been abandoned after the breakdown of the Roman state in the fifth century. The new urban growths of the later Saxon and Viking periods, though in some cases for religious or strategic reasons located on the sites of former Roman towns, were different both in function and in form from the classical city. In early medieval England a number of different types of town coexisted, usually distinct from one another but occasionally found in combination. There was the royal estate centre; the trading emporium; the fortified site or *burh*; and the ecclesiastical focus of a religious cult. Over time, these roles tended to fuse in different combinations, a process that was complete by 1300. The later medieval town, whether large or small, was characterized by a greater homogeneity of basic functions than had been found in its early medieval predecessor.

The leading motive behind the wave of 'new town' foundations in the thirteenth century was commercial. As the national population expanded at an unprecedented rate, lords were presented with a clear economic incentive to speculate in the promotion of markets on their estates. In addition to obtaining royal market grants, many estate owners encouraged further economic development by inviting permanent residents to settle in the nascent market towns on preferential terms. The novelty of this pattern should not be exaggerated: such initiatives were certainly not unknown in earlier centuries. Moreover, while some of the thirteenth-century developments occupied virgin sites, many more were rather extensions of existing village settlements. Nevertheless, between the late twelfth and the late thirteenth centuries the number and scale of urban promotions reached hitherto unequalled levels, transforming the landscape of England in the process. Between 1200 and 1349 several thousand market grants were issued by the Crown, and while some of these represented confirmations of existing markets, collectively they represented a genuine expansion.[6] By no means every speculative venture succeeded. The hopefully named Newton, founded near Poole on the Dorset coast in 1286, seems never to have amounted to much more than the isolated farmhouse which it remains today, and this experience was not unique.[7] Other foundations enjoyed a brief life before vanishing again in the less favourable conditions of the fourteenth and fifteenth centuries. Caus, a twelfth-century creation in the Welsh Marches, amounted by 1300 to thirty-four burgages or house plots below the castle; yet within a generation of the first plague epidemic of 1348 decline had set in, and by the early sixteenth century the site was virtually aban-

---

6. R. H. Britnell, 'The proliferation of markets and fairs in England before 1349', *Economic History Review*, 2nd ser. 34 (1981), 209–21.
7. M. W. Beresford and J. K. St Joseph, *Medieval England from the Air* (Cambridge, 1957), 224–6.

doned.[8] In this way numerous small towns, like so many villages, were 'lost'. Nevertheless, despite the pruning which followed the over-expansion of the thirteenth century, a broad pattern of urban centres, large and small, was established by 1300 which continued in place until the end of the Middle Ages and beyond.

It is with reason that attention has already been drawn to the end of the medieval urban spectrum occupied by the smaller towns, for these were by far the most numerous category. By European standards, England boasted few large towns: indeed, London alone could be compared in scale with the greater cities of the Low Countries and northern Italy. The English capital probably contained 80 000 residents at its late thirteenth-century peak, a tally that would not be reached again, following the late medieval slump, until the 1580s.[9] After London, only Bristol and Norwich seem certain to have had populations of more than 10 000 at their maximum extent around 1300. Between the bench-marks of 10 000 and 5000 were bracketed about a dozen more provincial towns.[10] The precise rank-order of these towns varied; but throughout the later Middle Ages their number was concentrated in the south and east of the country. Since most of these relatively large urban centres (which included, in their respective heydays, Newcastle, York, Boston, Ipswich, Coventry, Salisbury and Exeter) owed much of their growth to international trade, their common location within easy access of the continental seaways was logical. But a more fundamental influence on the distribution of medieval towns of all sizes was the underlying pattern of human settlement. This was most dense in midland and southeastern England, in which zone it was natural that the greatest number of regional markets should be concentrated. Nevertheless, despite this weighting towards the south and east, the quantity and general distribution of England's smaller towns – in the early fourteenth century, perhaps 500 places each containing between a few hundred and 5000 inhabitants – meant that few people in this predominantly agrarian society lived more than a day's journey from an urban centre.

The economic functions of these various towns within the wider economy have been the object of increasing attention in recent years. It is no accident that a historian in the first place of rural society, Rodney Hilton, has most clearly drawn attention to the role of towns as centres of exchange. Here cash generated by the sale of rural produce in turn facilitated both the payment of rent to lords and the acquisition of manufactured goods. Richard Holt's study

---

8. *The Victoria County History of Shropshire*, vol. viii (London, 1986) 308–10.
9. ex inf. D. J. Keene; see *id.*, 'A new study of London before the Great Fire', *Urban History Yearbook* (1984), 18–19.
10. W. G. Hoskins, *Local History in England* (London, 1959),176–7.

(Ch. 8) shows how Gloucester served as the hub of a regional corn trade, which linked the town closely both with its rural hinterland and with greater markets further afield. Similarly, the evidence of debt relationships in fourteenth-century Exeter has been used to demonstrate the many ties which bound that city with suppliers of wool and consumers of fish in the villages of the surrounding countryside.[11] The economy of the English medieval town was at all times closely interdependent with agrarian production.

Although its market was central to the existence of every town, marketing never became an urban prerogative, nor indeed was it a guaranteed route to urban development. There were many country markets in the Middle Ages which failed to develop into viable towns, despite at times the best efforts of their lords. Around the marketplace a more or less extensive range of industrial services and manufactures needed to coalesce; for while the market may have attracted the peasant to the town, it was the range of specialized economic functions unavailable in the countryside that tempted him to spend what proportion of his money was not ear-marked for rent. And above the basic level of clothes and tools, the importers and the manufacturers of luxury wares drew an appreciable share of the rural surplus into the urban economy. This was true of all urban centres, great and small, although of course the diversity of the services offered increased with the size of the town. Stratford-upon-Avon in the thirteenth century, as described by Eleanora Carus-Wilson (Ch. 4), presented a spectrum typical of the smaller towns, including bakers and brewers and a handful of workers in the metal, leather and cloth trades. In London, at the other extreme, Elspeth Veale found (Ch. 7) almost 200 separately identified crafts, including that of making toggles for bootlaces.

While variety and specialization were characteristic of medieval urban industry, the scale of production remained small. Even those industries which in some towns purported to be organized within gilds were, at the level of production, located in the household. Consequently a very high proportion of urban populations was represented by living-in 'servants': apprentices and assistants in the family business. As many as one in four of Coventry's recorded population in the 1520s was made up of such servants, probably nearly all youths and children.[12] Moreover, no town could maintain more than a limited hold over a particular industry. While some industries – such as mining, pottery and tile making – remained predominantly rural throughout the Middle Ages, others shifted their

11. M. Kowaleski, 'Local markets and merchants in late fourteenth-century Exeter', Ph.D. thesis, University of Toronto (1982).
12. C. V. Phythian-Adams, *Desolation of a City: Coventry and the Urban Crisis of the Later Middle Ages* (Cambridge, 1979), 204ff., 221ff.

base as technological or jurisdictional constraints dictated. Holt's Gloucester exemplifies the early centre of cloth manufacture which, in the later medieval period, saw its production dwindle even as new centres, better situated geographically and less hampered by established patterns of production, grew up in the Cotswolds. Such newly developing places tended soon to become urban in their own right. But although the late Middle Ages witnessed the first signs of industrial activity, not only in the wool-manufacturing towns of the Cotswolds but also in those, such as Leeds and Halifax, of the Pennines, and again in the early metalworking centre of Birmingham, the medieval period knew nothing of the factory workforces and large capital investment in industry which would characterize towns of a later period. In 1540 the industrial city still lay far in the future.

Neither size of population nor scale of economic enterprise set the medieval English town apart from the countryside, but rather social and economic diversity. From the beginning, this diversity introduced major problems of organization. Geoffrey Martin's essay (Ch. 3) treats the early, heroic phase of development of the medieval urban constitution. What emerges from the records of the twelfth and thirteenth centuries is evidence of a great deal of experimentation, often in anticipation of the legitimating charters granted frequently after 1200 by impecunious monarchs and speculating lords. Although this period is served only patchily by surviving sources, it is clear that town dwellers never felt obliged to wait upon legal recognition before coordinating their efforts in a corporate response to urban problems. Typically, the leading inhabitants of Oxford, when requesting their first royal charter in 1191, claimed already to speak in the name of 'all the citizens'.[13] The urban communes of France and the Low Countries have attracted historians' attention for the force with which they campaigned for municipal liberties. But the collaborative achievements of English townspeople in this pre-legal, communal phase were no less remarkable for being in most cases non-violent.

By 1300 a political structure was generally in place in the larger towns, within which the legislative and executive rights that had been grudgingly granted were concentrated in the hands of a mercantile elite. This structure was not to be fundamentally altered in the later medieval period, although the element of formal representation – always restricted – would at times be broadened or narrowed in particular cases. A long-standing assumption that medieval urban government tended towards ever greater exclusiveness fits only some towns and not others. Late fourteenth-century Exeter, studied by Maryanne Kowaleski (Ch. 10), does display that

13. R. H. C. Davis, 'An Oxford charter of 1191 and the beginnings of municipal freedom', *Oxoniensia,* 33 (1968), 53–65.

pattern, but contrasting cases were cited long ago by Alice Stopford Green.[14] Control of urban government was always vested formally in a wealthy minority, but the ways in which that control was maintained merit closer consideration.

Political power was largely an expression of economic influence. Because of the small-scale and fragmented nature of the medieval urban economy, the merchants who generally predominated in urban government did not enjoy the concentrated power exercised by the factory master over his workforce in the later industrial town. Instead, the medieval urban merchant owed his prominence to his ability to control the supply of raw materials to the various crafts, and to the large profits which he derived from wholesale trade in luxury items and finished goods. The merchant's economic status, however, was not of itself a guarantee of effective power to govern the wider body of the townspeople. Since the mercantile class was never more than a small minority in urban society, wealth alone was not a practically sufficient basis of enforceable authority. One method of control widely adopted by the merchant rulers of the towns in the late Middle Ages was the establishment and supervision of craft organizations. These were a specialized form of a type of association encountered in many guises in the Middle Ages: the gild. While the craft-based gilds offered their members the sociable attractions of gilds or fraternities in general, in their economic role they served rather the interests of urban government. The craft organization was viewed by the wealthy merchants who ruled the towns as a means of controlling the industrial labour force, whether master craftsmen, journeymen or apprentices. In Hilton's words, the organized crafts were the 'industrial police' designed to enforce the policy of the ruling elite. In the twelfth century there existed independent gilds of clothworkers and other crafts in some of the larger towns, but by the early thirteenth century these had been suppressed or absorbed by the currently evolving borough authorities. Thereafter little is heard of the organized crafts until the fourteenth century. In the intervening period borough courts seem everywhere to have regulated working hours, wage rates and the length of apprenticeships. It was perhaps only when, after 1350, labour became scarce and a potential for artisan resistance was created, that urban rulers felt it prudent to exercise such controls indirectly. In the larger towns from the mid-fourteenth century there increasingly appeared trade combinations in which master craftsmen were compulsorily enrolled and from which they could be expelled if they broke the rules laid down by the wealthy men of their craft and ratified by the city government. The leading gildsmen, in

14. A. S. Green, *Town Life in the Fifteenth Century,* vol. ii (London, 1894), Chs. 11, 14.

return for the status of minor office, acted as the willing agents of the borough authorities. The system enabled insubordination to the urban authorities to be punished, in principle, by loss of livelihood.

The effectiveness in practice of the craft system as a means of urban government should not, however, be overestimated: its limitations were manifold. The administrations of the smaller towns rarely felt the need to introduce the system, and even in the larger centres it was generally applied only to crafts perceived as requiring a particular degree of control. Recent work has underlined Veale's conclusion (Ch. 7) that a great deal of craft activity in practice went unnoticed or unregulated.[15] The economic gilds have traditionally been seen by historians as reactionary checks on commercial enterprise, but this image is misleading. In the first place, the crafts themselves repeatedly proved capable of adapting to changed economic circumstances. The development in late medieval Coventry of the new craft of capping, which superseded in importance the old-established cloth trades, was effected within the framework of the gilds.[16] More importantly, the gilds' very lack of an effective monopolistic control over the urban economy left beyond their margins a significant zone of relatively ungoverned enterprise. In the suburbs and other areas outside the jurisdiction of the borough court, scope was left for a good deal of unregulated industrial and commercial activity.[17] In vain did the urban courts periodically attempt to clamp down on those who flaunted rules restricting trade to the paid-up body of the citizens: in a hopeless gesture of this kind the Norwich leet court in 1375 imposed fines for unlawful trading on Alice the wigmaker, Agnes the bookbinder, Andrew the lantern-maker, and John the silkman.[18]

The generally restricted functions of the organized crafts did not altogether prevent them, on occasion, from providing a focus for popular discontent. It is not surprising that independently created gilds of lesser artisans, such as that formed among the journeymen saddlers of London in 1383, tended to be quickly snuffed out by authority. But the complexity of urban society denied to town governments an unchallenged monopoly of power. Although formally unrepresentative of the urban population at large, urban councils were constantly exposed to the pressures of wider opinion. This was particularly likely to occur when rifts appeared within the

---

15. H. Swanson, 'The illusion of economic structure: craft guilds in late medieval English towns', *Past and Present*, 121 (1988), 29–48.
16. Phythian-Adams, *Desolation of a City*, 102, 144–6.
17. See e.g. G. Rosser, 'London and Westminster: The suburb in the urban economy in the later Middle Ages', in J. A. F. Thomson (ed.), *Towns and Townspeople in the Fifteenth Century* (Gloucester, 1988), 45–61.
18. W. Hudson (ed.), *Leet Jurisdiction in the City of Norwich during the XIIIth and XIVth Centuries*, Selden Society, 5 (1891), 66.

ruling elite. The attempt of either faction to mobilize wider support in such circumstances created a real, if unofficial, outlet for the popular voice. One such occasion has been described by Caroline Barron (Ch. 9). In the second quarter of the fifteenth century Ralph Holland, a tailor/draper, fought with the established oligarchy of drapers and other merchants. Holland's platform was an appeal for greater recognition of the crafts (including the tailors) in government. As a member both of the tailors' and of the drapers' guilds, Holland was well placed to campaign on behalf of the disadvantaged artisans. His great wealth made his own role ambiguous: to the governors of the city he appeared not as a popular champion but as a factious peer and rival, especially resented for his successful wooing of the craftsmen. But even though the tangible outcome of Holland's quarrel with the city government was limited, it provided a forum for the expression of the concerns of the crafts, and aired the principle of broader representation.

The craft organizations exemplify the delegation of responsibility for the day-to-day government of the town. Apart from the trade gilds, there existed in every town a system of petty officers, with local or specific duties: constables, ale tasters, scavengers or rubbish carters, and the like. Such minor offices represented a greater scope for participation in urban government than would appear from study of the city council alone. In daily practice, the particular neighbourhoods – the wards and parishes – of the town were to a large extent accountable for their own affairs. In London by the mid-thirteenth century, for example, it was the communities of the wards which were held responsible for knowing who were the mendicant poor in their districts.[19]

Beyond the official structures of urban government, other forms of association helped to give order to the diversity of medieval urban society. Among these, the most universally adaptable was the fraternity or gild. Unlike the economic gilds discussed above, the majority of these societies (called indiscriminately gilds or fraternities by contemporaries) was not specific to particular crafts, but represented instead the voluntary association of those living and working together in the town. Though not exclusively urban, fraternities multiplied especially in towns, whose diverse and mobile populations generated shifting social groups. The traffic of traders and other occasional visitors created a need for a body more flexibly defined than the parish, which might facilitate the integration both of diverse subscribers drawn from within the resident population itself, and of the respective urban and rural memberships. For many town-based gilds enrolled both local inhabitants and residents in the hinterland; the

19. M. Weinbaum (ed.), *The London Eyre of 1276*, London Record Society, 12 (1976), no. 25.

the hinterland; the latter doubtless had occasion to visit the town regularly, most likely for marketing purposes, and found in the gild a point of contact and an identity – signified by the fraternity badge or livery – within the otherwise potentially exclusive urban social environment. The annual feast, held in June, of a gild of St John at Walsall was typically attended by contingents of members from nearby Lichfield and from a number of other surrounding townships.[20] Membership of such a club held out not only the prospect of conviviality at the gild feast, but also guarantees of mutual support of a material kind. The medieval townsman's common experience of trading in markets away from home created a need for just this kind of solidarity: so the members of a Lincoln gild swore that in litigation before the market court of any town they would support one another, as guarantors and witnesses, 'as though they were children of the same parents'.[21] The gild evidently provided, within the rootless and shifting world of the town, a substitute for the natural supportive strength of the extended family which was more characteristic of the countryside. Further more, the gild offered varying levels of assistance in case of hardship, as well as functioning as a collective chantry, providing (at relatively low cost) the assurance of spiritual services in the form of intercessory masses, commonly celebrated by a gild priest. The range of their memberships confirms that, like the later nonconformist chapelries of industrial towns, the medieval urban gilds cut across the essentially immutable system of parishes, to meet more effectively the needs of a fluctuating society.[22]

In small towns, meanwhile, it was common for a single gild to assume prominence by claiming to represent the urban community. In this respect Westminster (Ch. 11) appears to have been typical of a numerous class of small urban centres which, precisely because they lacked legal recognition, sought an outlet for communal aspirations in the formation of a gild. The suspicion with which legitimate authority – the town's legal owner – regarded such behaviour accounts for a general lack of detailed surviving evidence on this theme; but a dominant gild seems often to have functioned in such cases as a surrogate government and a focus for urban identity. The typical catalyst for the formation of such a small town gild was some public work or practical necessity which was beyond the resources of the manorial administration. At Louth in Lincolnshire, the major local gild of the Virgin Mary in the late fifteenth century

20. Walsall Local History Centre, MS. 276/67.
21. Public Record Office, London, C47/41/143.
22. See also G. Rosser, 'Communities of parish and guild in the late Middle Ages', in S. J. Wright (ed.), *Parish, Church and People: Local Studies in Lay Religion, 1350–1750* (London, 1988,) 29–55.

engaged in the reparation of sea dikes and of the common sewer, managed a poorhouse, erected a gildhall, and made substantial contributions to the rebuilding of the extraordinary spire of the town's single parish church.[23] The regular meetings of such a gild could, moreover, serve as courts at which differences might be resolved and disunity before the lord's officials in the borough court be avoided.

The church represented always an ambivalent force for social integration in the medieval town. The Christian imperative of harmony was at different times both strengthened and undermined by the great range of ecclesiastical institutions encountered there. Parish churches were most numerous in the older towns: fifty in Norwich, double that number in the square mile of the city of London. The capital boasted in addition a cathedral and thirty-nine religious houses; on a smaller scale an equivalent diversity met the immigrant to lesser towns. This broad spectrum gave the townsman a choice of religious expression not offered to the country dweller. One index of that choice – patterns of benefaction – broadly suggests an early primary religious loyalty to major monastic houses where these existed, superseded in the late thirteenth and fourteenth centuries by a preference for the new friaries, which themselves lost ground in the late Middle Ages, when the parish churches were for most citizens the chief objects of attention. This schematization, though crude, may indicate a genuine increase in the desire of the urban laity directly to control matters of religion which affected them. The urban parishes appear themselves to have owed their origins, prior to 1200, to neighbourhood solidarities generated within a particular block or street; in the later Middle Ages the parish churches arguably became even more definitely the foci of local loyalties within the wider body of the town.[24] It was characteristic that the parishioners even of a tiny parish such as that of St Katherine Creechurch in London decided in 1530 to rebuild their church as a communal enterprise, raising funds by such means as the mounting of a stage play.[25] The cathedrals and great religious houses in the larger towns, meanwhile, were only too often the objects of material grievance. For while the territorial liberties attached to these ecclesiastical institutions survived (as they did generally until the sixteenth century, and in some cases even thereafter), the constitutional unity of the town embodied in the secular government was in practice compromised at every turn. The burgesses of Hereford

23. Licolnshire Archives Office, MS. Monson 7/1.
24. See in particular D. J. Keene, *Survey of Medieval Winchester*, Winchester Studies, II (Oxford, 1985), vol. i, 113, 127.
25. Corporation of London Record Office, City Letter Book O, fol. 164ʳ

in 1262 blockaded the cathedral clergy within their precinct;[26] a decade later Norwich cathedral was burned by a citizen mob.[27] In the mid-fifteenth century the mayor of Exeter inveighed against unlicensed trade in 'dishes, ornaments and jewels' conducted within the cathedral close and evidently serving clerical and pilgrim markets.[28] Yet on the whole the churchmen held fast jealously to their rights, once again frustrating the claims of the civic authorities to a monopoly of power. The church could be a divisive as well as a unifying presence in medieval urban society.

Town rulers attempted to contain the challenge of urban social divisions by stage-managing public rituals designed to reinforce the notions both of unity and hierarchy. Such dramatic festivities as the Coventry hocking, in which the women of the town chased and bound the men, or the midsummer bonfires lit in the London wards, were typical of many rural customs imported to the towns as self-conscious celebrations of the urban community. Charles Phythian-Adams' account of civic ceremonial in Coventry (Ch. 12) shows how these rituals operated in order to perpetuate the existing order. Some processions, such as those held in most towns on the feast of Corpus Christi, were organized according to strict social hierarchy; other dramatizations momentarily dissolved or inverted social differences, thereby relieving tension and, ultimately, re-affirming the *status quo*. On festal occasions notionally representative of 'the community of the town', the counterweights of fraternity and deference were nicely poised, before the vertical chain of authority was reimposed by the ruling council. To this account of civic ritual two observations may be added. First, the myths which provided the points of reference for ceremonial – like the stories of the Trojan foundation of London and Totnes, or of the Emperor Constantine's association with Colchester – were effective in this context for the very reason that familiarity with them was already shared by participants. Civic rulers who planned such ritual depended upon a substantial pre-existing community of outlook among the citizenry. Secondly, although civic myth and ritual was indeed orchestrated by urban government in order to manifest social

26. W. W. Capes (ed.), *Registrum Thome de Cantilupo*, Canterbury and York Society, ii (1907), 91–3; *Calendar of Patent Rolls, 1258–66*, 232; Public Record Office, London, JUST1/1191, mm. 3-4.
27. W. Rye, 'The riot between the monks and citizens of Norwich in 1272', *Norfolk Antiquarian Miscellany*, 2 (1880), 17–89; N. Tanner, *The church in Late Medieval Norwich, 1370–1532*, Pontifical Institute of Mediaeval Studies, Toronto, Studies and Texts, 66 (1984), 141–54.
28. S. A. Moore (ed.), *Letters and Papers of John Shillingford, Mayor of Exeter 1447–50*, Camden Society, 2nd ser. 2 (1871); M. E. Curtis, *Some Disputes between the City and the Cathedral Authorities of Exeter*, History of Exeter Research Group, Monograph no. 5 (Manchester, 1932).

unity within the hierarchy, this effect could not be guaranteed. Squabbles over precedence disrupted many a Corpus Christi day procession. The mythology of a shared history and identity served communitarian ideals by establishing a common language in which the true character of the town might be debated, but the interpretation that might be put upon it could not be predetermined. Thus all inhabitants of late medieval Coventry seem to have shared a common loyalty to the memory of Lady Godiva; yet while the city's governors cited her against royal intervention in the town, she was invoked by the poor commons against unjust assessment of civic taxes.[29] In this way ritual and myth could fuel division. But the fact that different participants were able to perceive the ritual differently also helps to explain the unifying force of civic ceremonial.

Urban ritual lent a passing dignity to the streets and open spaces of the town while, according to circumstances, public fountains flowed with wine, decorative carpets were hung from windows, and dramatic presentations of scriptural or historical themes were staged. The mundane reality of the urban environment, however, was insalubrious and unhealthy. The physical experience of urban life has only recently begun to attract the considered attention of historians, although quality of diet, clothing, housing and sanitary arrangements must have been of more immediate daily concern to townspeople than were borough charters or the political posturing of the elite. Standards of housing and nutrition depended largely on familial income, but other features of urban life – filth running in open ditches in the streets, fly-blown meat and stinking fish, contaminated and adulterated ale, polluted well-water, unspeakable privies, epidemic disease, casual interpersonal violence, disastrous fires – were experienced indiscriminately by all social classes.[30] The effects of industrial pollution in the crowded urban environment were reported by Londoners living near St Paul's Church in 1377: an armourer's forge was blamed for filling the neighbouring houses with smoke and of shaking their foundations, spoiling the wine in the cellars.[31] It is in the related fields of topography, archaeology and architecture that medieval urban history has made some of its most significant advances in recent years; these studies can help to recover the tangible experience of overcrowding, morbidity and social in-

---

29. Phythian-Adams, *Desolation of a City*, 171, 173–4; see also a forthcoming essay on civic myths and imagery by G. Rosser.
30. Some of these themes are discussed in E. M. Sabine, 'Butchering in medieval London', *Speculum*, 8 (1933), 335–53; id., 'Latrines and cesspools of medieval London', *Speculum*, 9 (1934), 303–21; D. J. Keene, 'Rubbish in medieval towns', in A. R. Hall and H. K. Kenward (eds), *Environmental Archaeology in an Urban Context*, Council for British Archaeology Research Report no. 43 (1982).
31. H. M. Chew and W. Kellaway (eds), *London Assize of Nuisance 1301–1431*, London Record Society, 10 (1984), 160–1.

equality in the towns of the Middle Ages. For example, although rich and poor townspeople were never physically far from one another, Derek Keene's essay (Ch. 6), which draws extensively on topographical evidence, characterizes the suburb particularly as a refuge of those weaker inhabitants who were both metaphorically and literally on the margins of urban society.

Keene's work on Winchester has shown most clearly how the topographical evidence contained in property deeds may be made to reveal demographic and social variations, not only across the urban area but also over time.[32] After urban populations had reached their peak density around 1300, detailed topographical study can reveal the stages of contraction in settlement, which by the mid-fifteenth century in Winchester and elsewhere had created open spaces where streets of houses had previously stood. Such comparative topographical studies as have been completed indicate a general buoyancy in urban populations during the second half of the fourteenth century (which in the context of epidemic disease can only be explained by increased immigration from the countryside) before contraction set in in the early 1400s. This evidence of relative population shifts is the more valuable given the notorious difficulty of establishing absolute population figures for medieval towns. Tax records, which in view of their complications have sometimes borne too heavy a weight of interpretation in the past, need to be supplemented wherever possible with evidence of numbers, size and relative value of urban properties at different periods.

Fresh local studies, drawing on topographical as well as other sources, should bring clarity to the now ageing debate on late medieval 'urban decline'. Of the types of evidence for the fifteenth century urban economy reviewed by Barrie Dobson (Ch. 13), the two most widely significant are rents and petitions. The already mentioned indications in urban rentals of a slump in population from the early fifteenth century find confirmation in contemporary petitions for remission of taxes addressed by numerous town councils to the Crown. Suspicions of special pleading in such petitions are largely dispelled by their circumstantial detail in some cases, by external proofs of their accuracy (as of the claim by the citizens of Winchester in 1440 that economic decay within the past fifty years had caused seventeen of their parish churches to fall into ruins) and by official acceptance of their verity on the part of royal officials. The general phenomenon of urban contraction, however, is in itself unremarkable, in view of the global reduction of population which marked the late Middle Ages. But historians have not always resisted the temptation to take the level of population as an index of prosperity, even though to do this is wholly misleading. It is

32. Keene, *Survey of Medieval Winchester,* 2 vols. (Oxford, 1985).

now generally recognized that the reduced population of the late medieval period may have enjoyed *greater* personal prosperity, as resources were spread more generously.[33] By the same token, the renewed increase in urban populations, which is variously documented from the late fifteenth or early sixteenth century onwards, should by no means be read as a sign of economic growth. The urban impoverishment recorded by commentators of the mid-sixteenth century was in general a different phenomenon from the recession lamented a hundred years before. From around 1500 town populations were swollen by the influx of unprecedented numbers of the rural poor, who increasingly strained the charitable and administrative resources of the urban communities. The desperate attempts by urban magistrates to contain this alarming and uneconomic growth are exemplified by an order of the mayor of Chester of 1539, which required a register of the urban poor to be compiled. Those entitled to beg were assigned specific wards in the city, within which householders were to be issued with lists of the authorized names, and were to give alms at their doors to no others.[34] The economic world of the mid-sixteenth century differed profoundly from that of the mid-fifteenth.

The role and performance of towns in the late Middle Ages needs further assessment in the light of changes in the wider economy. The picture of overall recession in the fifteenth century has been challenged with the proposition that this was, in certain respects, a time of economic growth. Certainly, some of the indicators of recession reflect no more than the inevitable reduction in the disposable incomes of the aristocracy. The other side of this coin was the successful resistance of agricultural tenants to their lords' demands, and the fall of land rents to levels lower than ever before. With land more readily available than it had been for centuries, this was a good time for many peasants, who increasingly resembled the yeoman farmers of later centuries. Even rural labourers enjoyed unprecedented prosperity, as their wages rose during a period of stable food prices. This, therefore, was a time of mixed fortunes, in town and country alike. The merchant supplier of luxury commodities – wine, spices, fine cloths – inevitably suffered a fall-off in the volume of trade, while on the other hand the urban craftsman manufacturing small luxury items – pewter vessels, leather goods, silver spoons – may have benefited from the increased spending power of a newly prosperous class of consumers. But as yet imperfectly understood is the extent to which the growth of rural industry affected urban commodity production; equally important is the question whether marketing patterns changed significantly during this period. Urban

33. C. Dyer, *Standards of Living in the Later Middle Ages* (Cambridge, 1989).
34. R. H. Morris, *Chester in the Plantagenet and Tudor Reigns* (Chester, n.d.), 355–6.

historians have been reluctant to broaden their vision to look at the wider economy of the fifteenth century; only by doing so will they be able to understand the ways in which the urban economy was coming under strain in the later Middle Ages, and why it was that certain sectors were becoming marginalized.

The evidence of fluctuating urban populations, and of both short- and long-term economic changes, raises once more the fundamental issue of tension and coherence in the town. Social conflict rooted in inequality, environmental problems attendant upon domestic over-crowding and industrial activity: these constantly threatened the viability of every town throughout the period. The reactions of townspeople, and their attempts to resolve such difficulties, run like a leitmotiv through the history of the medieval town between the thirteenth and the sixteenth centuries. The study of urban elites has helped to clarify not only the strengths but also the limitations of oligarchy (or, as some would have it, aristocracy) in the town;[35] for neither in the social nor in the economic sphere could town life be regulated effectively by the sole authority of the elected officials. A measure of self-imposed regulation can be observed, operating through the agencies of the parish and the fraternity. Here in-dividuals came together in groupings which were primarily social in character, and in which economic status, though doubtless not for-gotten, was not of overriding importance. A number of the essays in this volume, including those by Phythian-Adams and by Gervase Rosser, draw attention to processes whereby a wider body of townspeople came on occasion to participate in collective activity, of either a ritual or a practical kind. But how far, at such moments, could a shared sense of identity genuinely transcend social ine-qualities? Given the challenging realities of life in the medieval town, this is a question which, as much as any other raised by the authors represented here, will justify further investigation.

The essays gathered in this volume represent a fundamental trans-formation that has taken place over the past generation in the understanding of the medieval English town. Important conclusions have been reached with regard, for example, to urban social struc-ture, to the interrelation of town and countryside, and to the economic role of small towns. These essays indicate in addition part of the agenda for future research. This clearly must include the con-tinued assimilation of archaeological data, further study of the physical topography of the townscape, and systematic documentary work on the remarkably neglected theme of urban industries. Al-ready, however, the medieval town is a vastly more interesting place than it appeared only thirty years ago, and none the less so for being a great deal more varied and complex.

35. S. Reynolds, 'Medieval urban history and the history of political thought', *Urban History Yearbook* (1982), 14–23.

Chapter Two

TOWNS IN ENGLISH MEDIEVAL SOCIETY[1]

R. H. Hilton

from D. Reeder (ed.), *Urban History Yearbook: 1982* (Leicester, 1982)

Internationally respected as an analyst of social relationships in the medieval countryside, Rodney Hilton has recently turned to questions of urbanization, in particular to the contribution that towns and townsmen (and women) made to medieval society at large. In that sense he is not an urban historian: for him the medieval town, though a legitimate subject of research in itself, is not to be studied for its own sake. Town and country, he stresses, were inseparable – though we should not fall into the trap of believing that English town society merged indistinguishably into rural society. There was a distinct urban identity, born of the concentration of population and the diversity of manufacturing and service occupations, and consequently there existed distinct urban social forms and processes. But there was no essential antagonism between town and country. More importantly, medieval towns should not be regarded as a radically progressive force, helping to transform an economically and socially backward countryside. This is not to say that medieval economic life and social relations were unaffected by the existence of towns and townspeople; merely that the connection was not as dramatic nor as simple as has sometimes been claimed.

There is an old historical tradition which saw the towns in the middle ages as being an antagonistic element within the whole society which was seen – quite rightly of course – as being predominantly rural and agricultural. Put in more abstract terms the agrarian economy was seen as a natural economy and as such incompatible with the exchange economy of the towns. This simplistic vision could hardly stand the test of empirical investigation since clearly the urban and rural economies could not operate independently of each other. More sophisticated writers indeed saw the towns, not as an an-

---

1. Delivered as a lecture to the annual conference of the Urban History Group, University of Loughborough, 3 April 1981.

tagonistic element but as innovatory. The towns were literally responsible for a civilizing process. They sowed the seeds of the future in the not always receptive soil of feudal society.

This view of the medieval towns, as everyone knows, owes a lot to the work of Henri Pirenne and his followers. Pirenne was a fine historian and his work was enormously fruitful. After three quarters of a century and more his work on the towns of northern Europe is still essential reading, in spite of the sustained critique against him.

Although Pirenne can hardly be blamed for it, his interpretation of the rôle of the towns has supported a somewhat metaphysical perception of the rôle of towns in history, as if it appeared thousands of years back as an essence of urbanism which changed only in terms of size, performed the same function and propagated the same dynamic ethos whatever the nature of the whole society.

Such a conception is essentially unhistorical and belongs rather to certain trends in sociology. Historians naturally react against it, and some go too far. There has been, in England for instance, a tendency for some historians to overemphasize the rural aspects of the English medieval town, leading a deservedly famous French historian to go so far as to write of Salisbury in the fourteenth century as a 'rustic and pastoral city' – a city which, however, was sixth in ranking order of population in 1377 and may have had as many as 6500 inhabitants.

However, even if the reaction against the town as a metaphysical entity has sometimes gone too far, it points the way to a more balanced interpretation. We must look at the medieval town as one expression of feudal society and economy rather than as simply a contradictory element within it. I am not of course suggesting that feudal society did not contain contradictions, but that we must not assume that the town:country dichotomy explains those contradictions.

If we are to consider towns in feudal society it would seem reasonable first to define that society's principal characteristics, particularly in the three centuries after the Norman Conquest when our information is best and when there was considerable urban growth.[2] The economy was predominantly agrarian, probably 80 to 90 per cent of the population living in villages and hamlets. The vast bulk of this agricultural population worked within small units of production whose labour force was based on the family. Peasant society, as is well known, was not homogeneous, so the richer and even some of the middle strata would employ one or two wage

2. Not that late Anglo-Saxon England was under-urbanized compared with other states in north-western Europe. Domesday Book, which has no continental rival, shows this very well.

labourers, whose source would be primarily the always considerable though fluctuating population of small-holders.

The income which the ruling class, over whelmingly a landed aristocracy, derived from peasant society was mostly from rent, broadly defined so as to include the incidents of villeinage and the profits of private jurisdiction. At certain moments and on certain estates the profits of the demesne (worked partly at any rate by peasant labour services – another transfer of rent) were important but must not be exaggerated. Jurisdiction was, in this society, the main expression of social and political power. At the local and private level it was openly in the hands of the landowners. At the public level it was still in the hands of the nobility and the gentry, whether through the feudal patronage of the judges or, particularly in the fourteenth century, through the direct control of the Peace and Labourer sessions by the county gentry. The monarchical state itself exercised most of the power through jurisdiction. Its social and political rôle was to centralize and rationalize the landed interest.

The Church, that disseminator not merely of theological principles but of a coherent social ideology, had a guaranteed control over the mass of the population through its monopoly of the sacramental rituals and therefore of the route to salvation after death. But these sacramental rituals and these sermons preaching the right way of life were embedded in an organization which was also dominated socially and economically by a landed interest whose hierarchy in important respects mirrored the hierarchy of the feudal aristocracy.

The state, the Church and the whole of the landowning class had important and specialized consumption needs. The way of life that they led was an essential element in social cohesion; it was based on conspicuous consumption, and as luxury commodities became available they progressively became necessary symbols of status. Further expressions of status and, of course, practical need for vast bodies of retainers were secular buildings, such as castles and manor houses, matched on the ecclesiastical side by even bigger cathedrals, abbeys, collegiate and parish churches. Many of the buildings had a military function, and their costs were rivalled by the costs of equipment, men and horses diverted from productive labour into military expeditions. Nor must it be forgotten that from the eleventh to the fifteenth centuries the expenses of administration, as states came into being and grew, also considerably increased.

In spite of some direct victualling of landowners' households from their estates, all the expanding activities of the ruling aristocracy, the Church and the state required an ever increasing money income, the main constituent of which, given the structure of society and economy, was money rent. The agricultural producers therefore had to market their agricultural surplus, not only to get commodities which were not available in the villages, but to get cash to pay rents,

21

fines, amercements and tax. The provision of facilities for the sale of grain, malt and livestock was clearly a main function of the large numbers of village markets and seigneurial boroughs which multiplied in the twelfth and thirteenth centuries. Larger town markets were obviously locations, too, for the unloading of the surpluses of peasant cultivation, but they had an additional rôle, for it was here that money rent was *spent*. Wines, spices, fine cloths and armour were not to be found in the little local markets but in London, the provincial capitals, the big fairs, the ports and the county towns.

What was the level of urbanization in medieval English society? We have here a problem of documentation, not merely that our documents should give us an overview of the whole country, but that we should be able adequately to read their meaning. In spite of the fact that it was compiled after the devastating – and distorting – visitations of the bubonic plague it may be useful to concentrate on the 1377 Poll Tax. Compared with those of 1379 and 1380–1, this is not regarded as more than normally suspect on account of evasions. It gives us comparative population figures and we can be sure that these will reflect not so much a high urban mortality but a high rural immigration. Traditionally (i.e. going back to Thorold Rogers) the tendency has been to assume that the untaxed population below the age of 15 would have been one-third of the total. It is now argued, probably correctly, that we should use a multiplier nearer to 2 than 1.5 to account not merely for under-15s but for evaders. This would give us, at a guess, the capital city at 45 000 to 50 000; 4 towns between 8000 and 15 000; 8 between 5000 and 8000; and 27 between 2000 and 5000. This leaves us with, perhaps, 500 market towns between 500 and 2000 (and probably the bulk nearer 500 than 2000). These might well have contained half of England's urban population, and constitute a powerful argument for more research into towns of this sort.

In spite of the special features of the post Black Death statistics, the pattern is not all that different from the one that can be established from the 1334 lay subsidy return, based not on heads but on moveable goods. There are some shifts, of course, in the ranking order of individual towns, the main one being that of Coventry which moves up from 9 (with Salisbury) in 1334 to 3 in 1377. The *population* ranking order of Newcastle on Tyne, Yarmouth, Shrewsbury, Oxford and Ipswich fell noticeably from the *taxation* ranking order of 1334, but these shifts do not alter the impression that the observable pattern of urbanization in 1377 was not – as yet – fundamentally altered by the population collapse.

We must add another element to that of urbanization when we consider the rôle of the market in the feudal economy: that is, the village markets. As is well known, there was almost a headlong rush by lords, especially in the thirteenth century, to acquire charters for village markets which would allow them to cash in on direct and indirect market profits – as well as making it easier for tenants to acquire the cash needed to pay rent. These charters did not of course *create* markets, though as in the case of some seigneurial boroughs, some errors of judgement were made by over-ambitious lords. But even if some chartered markets did not altogether boom, we must assume that the lords who spent money acquiring the charters did so with some rational calculation and that the pattern of chartered markets does reflect the real pattern of rural trade. Their numbers, compared with established boroughs, large and small, are quite striking. I give a regional sample, which I think is fairly accurate, and also illustrates a contrasting relationship of boroughs and village markets between the East and West Midlands.

TABLE 1: Boroughs and village markets in the Midlands

County	Boroughs	Village Markets
Gloucestershire	29	30
Warwickshire	16	25
Leicestershire	5	29
Nottinghamshire	3	18

(medieval county boundaries)

Medieval, feudal society in England has many paradoxes but the apparent paradox in this pattern of marketing is very striking. We can be sure that a very large proportion of the total agricultural product never reached the market because it was either consumed within the peasant household economy[3] or (in the case of the demesne) within the seigneurial household. What did reach the market was sold in a way specific to this type of economy and society. Marketing was considerably decentralized, as is implied by the large number of urban and rural markets. The element of decentralization was further strengthened by the activities of itinerant traders, such as corn-mongers, who linked the villages and small market towns with the bigger areas of urban consumption. It is not easy to find documentation for these people outside the judicial records. Wool-mongers are better documented. They, too, strengthened .the decentralized element in marketing, in spite of some attempts at local monopoly by towns such as Leicester. The wool-mongers, how-ever, not only linked the producers with the bigger urban centres of cloth production, but with the overseas market.

---

3. We must not, of course, forget the informal market constituted by the buying and selling of goods between neighbours. But this was not sufficient to modify the picture of a peasantry providing its subsistence needs from its own holdings.

So, whatever the strength of the subsistence element in the economy, those who had goods to sell would not need to go far. This situation was reflected by the very great social importance (*not* eminence) of chapmen and merchants. The predominance of merchant over industrial capital has often been emphasized by economic historians but the pervasiveness of petty marketing down to village level also deserves emphasis. The huckster was not simply a target for satirists, seeking for symbols of greed (as in Langland's *Piers Plowman*) but omnipresent in this society. It is also worth remarking that Langland's Rose the regrater, the wife of Covetise, who 'hath holden hokkerye all hire lyf-tyme' is representative in another sense. At the small town and village level, retail trading, especially in victuals, was very much a woman's craft, as it was indeed on the streets of the capital and the bigger cities.

Marketing, then, was an essential element of the feudal economy and would be a process familiar to all. But if the market was present in the feudally dominated countryside, what correspondence was there in the city to the social and political structure of agrarian society? There were in fact important structural analogies. First, the basic unit of production in the towns resembled that of the countryside in certain important respects. The workshop was a small enterprise, as was the family holding. The labour force was based on the family. The place of work and the home largely coincided except in some highly specialized industrial centres – and even here it would be dangerous to overemphasize separation. This had important consequences for women, for whom 'housework' as the sole occupation could seldom be a reality. And where hired additional labour was found it was dispersed in ones, twos and threes and, in town as well as in country, tended to be domesticated.

The social stratification in the sphere of urban craft production was analogous too to the familiar social stratification of the peasantry, for to the rich, middling and poor peasants corresponded rich and poor masters, the latter often merging with the journeymen, just as the rural small-holders were often also hired labourers on demesnes or rich peasant holdings.

There is also an analogy to be drawn between the feudal landowner and the mercantile élite in the towns. In spite of the success achieved by the medieval aristocratic landowners in collecting a considerable income from their estates, there was always a distance between them and the peasant economy which was the foundation of their prosperity. That is to say, that although the estate administrators operating on behalf of the landowners were able to achieve some successes with the demesne economy, they never penetrated to the heart of peasant production. The peasant household economy was run by the peasants. It was in the nature of the small-scale family enterprise that even so intimately linked an outside force as the landlord was unable to direct its economic management. Is not the same thing broadly true of the small-scale enterprises in the towns? The artisan workshops? The retail traders? Powerful though the mercantile élites which dominated the governments of towns both large and small might seem to be, there was once again a distance between them and the artisan workshop which they could barely cross. It is true, of course, that urban governments came much nearer to controlling the industrial economy than did the landowners the rural economy. They used the craft organizations as a sort of municipal police, apparently determining the distribution of labour, the length of the working day, the remuneration of labour and various matters of production technology. But it is never certain to what extent they imposed their will or simply confirmed ordinances put forward by the leading craftsmen in the gilds. This of course has always been one of the more interesting problems of medieval urban politics for the historian to investigate.

The resemblances between the rural and urban structures are analogies rather than mirror images. Nevertheless they are sufficiently coherent to suggest that the constant flow of rural immigrants who sustained the demographically vulnerable urban populations would not by any means be entering an unfamiliar world as they stepped through the gates in the city walls. In any case, many of them must have been there before.

Those immigrants from the countryside where the feudal landed interest was dominant would in any case have found many other indications of a feudal presence. The medieval castle is by no means a purely rural phenomenon, even though in town it might be rather a symbol of the feudal state than of individual landowners. One may think in this respect of the Tower of London, and the royal or shrieval fortresses in Bristol, Nottingham, Norwich, Gloucester and Oxford. Even in big towns these fortresses could represent seigneurial rather than royal power – the Lancastrian castles, for instance, in Leicester and Lincoln; the Beauchamp castles in Warwick and Worcester. Such fortresses (royal as well as aristocratic) were, furthermore, very often placed within franchises outside urban jurisdiction, vividly illustrated by the financial accounts of the constables of Bristol Castle whose receipts even included levies on certain categories of Bristol craftsmen.

One of the features of English boroughs in Domesday Book was the large amount of urban property owned by the county nobility, and occupied by burgesses 'contributory' to rural manors. That presence seems to have diminished considerably after 1086 partly no doubt as a result of the transfer of secular property to the Church. At any rate, if we were to consider the rôle of the feudal landed interest in the towns it might be represented as much by the ecclesiastical institutions as by the castellans and garrisons of the royal and aristocratic castles. These ecclesiastical institutions were significant franchise holders and had sizeable enclaves within the areas of urban jurisdiction – jurisdictional powers which were, of course, supported by the ownership of real property. This ecclesiastical presence was inevitably felt in diocesan centres where cathedral chapters, bishops and archbishops had long established property and power – think only of York and Canterbury, of Lincoln, Winchester, Norwich, Worcester . . . and then the analogous power and property of religious houses, such as St Peter's Abbey in Gloucester, or the Benedictine Prior of Coventry with his partial functions as head of one of two chapters in the same diocese . . . And then, of course, these ecclesiastical lords often had specific commercial privileges such as the privilege of the St Giles Fair at Winchester, wielded by the Bishop, the fair controlled by the Benedictine Prior of St James in Bristol, the Abbey of Lenton's fair by Nottingham – privileges which could involve the suspension of normal urban trade during the period of the fair.

It is a commonplace, of course, that the lay nobility in northern Europe had no permanent dwelling places in cities as they did in Italy and southern France. The nobility and gentry, therefore, did not constitute such a permanent, visible, presence as the ecclesiastics.[4] Seigneurial power was not, however, absent even from some of the bigger towns. Leicester's lords, the earls of Leicester, then of Lancaster, held the town until the Duke of Lancaster became king in 1399. Warwick was the earl of Warwick's subject borough until the sixteenth century. The industrial suburb of Bristol, at Redcliffe, was, until the 1330s, the franchise of the Berkeleys. The earl of Chester and his Montalt successors were lords of more than half of Coventry until the middle of the thirteenth century when their part was bought by the Prior of the cathedral abbey, lord of the other part.

But these examples of the feudal presence in the larger towns, though significant, by no means indicate the total weight of the landed interest on urban society. We have to add the very considerable number of market towns which were seigneurial boroughs. Here there is no point in distinguishing lay from ecclesiastical lords. The latter (as the abbatial lords of the great cloth making town, Bury St Edmunds demonstrated) could take seigneurial domination as far as any baron. The seigneurial boroughs of both types constituted two-thirds of the total number of English boroughs. Given the high proportion of royal boroughs among the bigger towns this

---

4. But gentry occupation of urban dwellings would be an interesting subject to explore further.

means that private lords would possess many more than two-thirds of the market towns,[5] and would exercise more or less considerable control through the presence of their steward at the meetings of the portmoot.

Urban historians quite rightly stress the element of conflict in towns between seigneurial and burgess jurisdictions and show how the burgesses were fairly successful, by the fifteenth century, in buying out the seigneurial franchise holders. Nevertheless, the existence within medieval urban society, from great city to market town, of representatives of the feudal landed interest should at least remind us that towns were an essential and inseparable part of the wider society.

That society had, of course, another distinguishing feature which was not necessarily connected with the landed interest. So far the Church has been referred to as another feudal landowner. But of course it had a distinctive religious, cultural and ideological rôle, at least as strong in town as in the country – arguably much stronger. Some of the older towns had a very large number of parish churches: London, 110; Norwich, about 50; York, about 40; Lincoln, 46. Others had fewer: Gloucester, 10; Bristol, 7; Leicester, 3; Coventry 2. But these were increased by the churches of the religious orders, by chapels and by hospitals. For example, to Leicester's three parish churches, another nine ecclesiastical institutions should be added. There were in fact important religious manifestations thought to be specifically urban. The representatives of the four main mendicant orders found themselves mainly in the towns, partly of course because begging would be more successful in an area of dense population, partly because they developed something of a mission to the bourgeoisie. And although hospitals, religious gilds, chantries and schools were not necessarily only urban phenomena, they were particularly thick on urban ground. This strong ecclesiastical presence in town as well as in the countryside meant a homogenization of cultural attitudes throughout society, urban and rural. Once again we can suggest that the rural immigrant would not be entering an entirely alien world on coming to town.

Not entirely alien; we must not make the mistake of merging town and country when we insist that the medieval town must be understood as an integral part of feudal society. Even small towns of less than a thousand inhabitants were characterized by occupational heterogeneity, and contained a minority only of full time cultivators (as contrasted with some southern French and Mediter-

5. See the tables in the introduction to *English medieval boroughs: a handlist*, by M. Beresford and H. P. R. Finberg (1973), and *Urban History Yearbook* (1981), 59–61.

ranean towns). Towns were places where there was an advanced division of labour and greater craft skills than in the villages. The concentration of population was accompanied by specific forms of sociability and intellectual activity. The rhythm of work, though still affected by the seasons, was less so than in the countryside.

Nevertheless, even features which were evidently specific to urban society did not necessarily conflict with characteristic aspects of feudal society as a whole. The bourgeoisie, or rather the mercantile élite, did not find it difficult or painful to assimilate with the landed aristocracy. After all, the aristocracy was the major market for the high price goods in which the merchants dealt, so there was no fundamental clash of economic interest. It is a commonplace that well to do merchants invested in manorial property. The ceremony and largesse which is recognized as part of the aristocratic way of life had its counterpart in the conduct of urban rulers. The institutionalized recipients of that largesse were the craft fraternities and gilds, collectivities which grouped together the family based enterprises, as the village communities did the individual peasant households. Even the burgess privilege of toll-free access to the town market, which operated so clearly against rural interests, should be regarded as a specific form of medieval exclusiveness.

Medieval social theory preached the harmony of a society of inter-related orders, each occupied with its own rôle for the betterment of the whole. As Georges Duby has insisted, ideology is not a reflection of life but a scheme for influencing it.[6] The theory of orders was used to control social conflict by insisting on the legitimacy of inherited or (to a much lesser extent) acquired status. In practice the most serious conflict in feudal society which had to be controlled was that between peasants and landowners, but the tensions of urban society between mercantile ruling oligarchies and the organized crafts, between rich and poor craft masters, between masters and journeymen, also had to be faced. The ideology of status was put over as strongly in town as it was in the country, for the basic conflicts were within town and country, not between them.

6. *Les trois ordres ou l'imaginaire du féodalisme* (1978), 20. The American translation (*The Three Orders, feudal society imagined*) deforms this statement, pp. 8–9, *perhaps* by a printing error.

Chapter Three

THE ENGLISH BOROUGH IN THE THIRTEENTH CENTURY

G. H. Martin

Transactions of the Royal Historical Society, 13 (1963)

Since the first publication of Geoffrey Martin's essay, research (in particular by archaeologists) has underlined still more emphatically the complexity and sophistication of late Anglo-Saxon and early post-Conquest towns. The fact that the few surviving written records from this phase of urban history (Domesday Book above all) are primarily royal in origin may have caused an underestimation of the extent to which town societies were already, by the twelfth century, regulating their own affairs. Nevertheless this review of early borough records clearly demonstrates that the first appearance of such documents in the thirteenth century expresses a real change in the character of the places which generated them. In some cases a gild merchant – a common form of association with antecedents in the Saxon and more distant past – can be seen to have extended its responsibilities beyond the regulation of its own members; in others a distinct borough court or portmanmote undertook a public role. Martin draws attention to the way in which a substantial practical problem – as with defence or water supply – was often the catalyst for the formation of urban government. The practical concerns of the early borough communities, which are indicated in the custumals noted here, may be further explored in the texts of urban charters, of which a preliminary analysis was made by Mary Bateson in 1901. These first urban records merit close attention; though couched in the dry form of legal documents, they contain a great deal of vivid information about the life of towns in the thirteenth century and before.

The thirteenth century was a crucial time in the history of the English borough. It saw towns at the height of their prosperity before the calamities of depression and plague, and the last burst of town-making until the spas of the seventeenth century inaugurated our present urban society. It saw an apparent attempt by Edward I's government to define a hierarchy of towns, in which that which was not a borough would be seen plainly to be something else. It marks the time during which the continental commune was tamed and assimilated to English politics, and commune, gild and portmanmote fused together, in as many different ways as there were boroughs, to make the communities for which the Common Law had evolved the doctrine of incorporation. It also produced for us the first substantial quantity of original records written in the towns themselves, records which are from that time onward our principal source of information about municipal affairs. The purpose of this paper is to display the nature and scope of borough archives before 1300, both as a guide to the mass of material that survives from later centuries, and as a commentary upon the thirteenth-century borough. It is confined to those towns, such as the shire boroughs of Domesday Book, which may be presumed to have recruited their own clerks, and not, like the numerous enfranchised manorial towns of this time, to have had someone else provide them.

Besides its other distinctions, the thirteenth century has a special significance for historians: it marks the end of our authoritative history of the borough. The scientific study of municipal institutions, of the borough in general as opposed to individual boroughs, began early with Thomas Madox's *Firma Burgi* in 1726, but it was not until the end of the nineteenth century that professional historians were able to match the standards set by the harassed and impecunious Treasury clerk. In the meantime local historians wrote some excellent accounts of particular towns, but the gradual shift of interest to the publication of records, and their consequent and daunting growth, probably inhibited amateur enterprise as the nineteenth century passed. With the appearance of the First Report of the Royal Commission on Historical Manuscripts, in 1870, specimens of the towns' own records were made available for the first time on any large scale and helped to reawaken a general interest in municipal history. From Charles Gross's *Gild Merchant* (1890) to Adolphus Ballard's *British Borough Charters, 1042–1216* (1913), the study flourished marvellously, and in the years immediately before the First World War the borough seemed a lively and promising subject for enquiry.

After Ballard died in 1915 his work devolved upon James Tait, a scholar who had not been particularly associated with municipal history before the war, although as a young man he had demonstrated in a celebrated review the weaknesses of the two principal theories of Maitland's *Domesday Book and Beyond,* and had written, in *Medieval Manchester and the Beginning of Lancashire* (1904), a model essay upon a seignorial borough. Tait took up the charters with some reluctance, but he quickly responded to the problems that the subject set. In 1922, the year before *British Borough Charters, 1216–1307*, was published, he read a paper entitled 'The Study of Early Municipal History in England' to the British Academy. In it he surveyed the work already done, and sketched his hopes, and presumably his plans, for the future. Inevitably he commented upon 'a sort of fatality' that had waited upon his predecessors. Of the distinguished group of scholars working at the beginning of the century, Round alone was left, and Round had exercised his bitter acumen only occasionally upon municipal history. Maitland and Mary Bateson had both died in 1906; Charles Gross, after enlarging this country's debt to himself by his two remarkable bibliographies, died in 1909, Ballard six years later. Tait was undaunted by this ominous concatenation. He had taken up Ballard's work and his plan with some misgivings, but had worked them out in a satisfactory way; he now saw beyond the charters to a grander theme. The tone of his paper is strikingly confident; it is the work of a man who promises himself great things.

That buoyancy is missing from *The Medieval English Borough* (1936), the report upon his next fourteen years' labour. Its subtitle, 'Studies on its Origins and Constitutional History', is intended to dispel false hopes and its text does nothing to recruit them. The casual reader might well reflect that, if ever a subject were veiled in the decent obscurity of a learned language, then was English municipal history in 1936. The paper of 1922, which the casual reader is not likely to reach, makes a chastening epilogue to the work. Since 1936 there have been some notable additions to our knowledge of medieval towns, but the subject cannot be said to have flourished. And indeed, if Tait really failed to master it, then human ingenuity spent upon it is likely to be wasted, for Tait was a man of great learning, and breadth of mind, and uncommon patience: a scholar.

To say that, however, is only to spell out what the book's subtitle says succinctly. The subject is a difficult one, and Tait made it sound difficult; his book is not a failure, but it is necessarily incomplete. In the first place, the borough cannot be defined; there is no formula which defines all the kinds of community to which the terms *burh* and *burgus,* and between them, *port,* were applied from the time when the early English became articulate until the Tudor Poor Law hardened the pattern of local government. One can write a book upon such a subject, but the edges of its argument will be uncertain, and uncertainty may have unjustly a taint of misapprehension about it. In the second place, no matter how its limits are sketched, the history of the English borough demands a very large investigation. Any community that does not live solely by producing its own food – and that at least is a category into which every *burh, port,* and *burgus* must fall – is a complex and troublesome thing to apprehend, and the historian of the English borough in the Middle Ages can number his cares by scores, and if he will, by hundreds, before he begins to divide and analyse the material to which they lead him. And in the third place, that material, even for a history of the larger English boroughs that excludes London, is still imperfectly explored.

Tait's book would be a remarkable one even if these handicaps did not exist; its chosen limits are wide, and it would be difficult to frame a question within them that could not be answered from its text. Carl Stephenson's theories moved Tait to write the history of the Anglo-Saxon borough *de novo,* and the first six chapters of *The Medieval English Borough* set out the subject in a form that is not likely to be substantially altered. For the period after 1066 Tait was content to re-use the papers that he had published since 1922, but again he tells a story that is satisfyingly comprehensive, no matter what extra detail it might be asked to accommodate. Down to the thirteenth century we have at least a constitutional history of the borough with so much of its economic and social history as a proper understanding of what we call constitutional matters demands. It is after 1200 that the book's argument falls into self-sufficient parts.

Tait found himself unable to deal with two large topics: the jurisdiction of borough courts and the doctrine of incorporation. The second Martin Weinbaum had in hand; the first still waits, in a posture little changed since 1905, for someone to disentangle the pre-Conquest from the post-Conquest material in the borough custumals that Mary Bateson assembled. It was not simply for these reasons that Tait turned aside at that point. Weinbaum subsequently did for the theory of incorporation what he did for the later borough charters: he elucidated and expounded it in a rational way.[1] It is no denigration of his work to say that, if it were fitted into the interstices of Tait's later chapters, and if a similar exposition of burgal jurisdiction were added, there would still be many untidy holes in our borough history. *The Medieval English Borough* takes the story as far as it can be taken on the terms which Tait chose and which he managed so competently. Beyond 1200 there lie formidable problems, and a great mass of material which at present conceals the answers to them. Any means by which we can distinguish and explain the forces at work in the thirteenth century would be invaluable.

Charles Gross laid two mistaken, or misleading, emphases in his work: not an extravagant allowance for a lifetime of scholarship. Intent upon correcting the peculiarly English estimates of the gilds merchant, he confirmed another native notion of it, so that even M. Coornaert's arguments have not yet persuaded us that the gilds were, in terms of medieval European society, an entirely natural thing, a form of association as unselfconscious and irresistible as the

---

1. M. Weinbaum, *The Incorporation of Boroughs* (Manchester, 1937); *British Borough Charters, 1307–1660* (Cambridge, 1943).

committee is today.[2] In doing so, he underestimated the essential part that the gild played in fostering the nascent municipal community. And, again because of the strictness of his argument, he underestimated the weight of Henry II's hand while it rested upon the borough court, the portmanmote, and therefore the way in which the court rallied and the relative importance of the gild declined, when that dreadful presence gave way to the absentee Richard and the energetic, resourceful, but necessitous John.[3]

This important adjustment of the borough's principal institutions began in the late-twelfth century and extended into the thirteenth. Generally, although with some instructive exceptions, the portmanmote absorbed and redirected the political energies for which the gild merchant had previously offered the only legitimate outlet. The process was complicated by the coincidental excitement over the continental commune, an institution highly offensive to conservative tastes until it had been domesticated and naturalized. In the event the commune was tamed and suppressed very quickly, leaving little but the office of mayor and the sworn council behind it: powerful additions to the invigorated portmanmote, but no longer revolutionary institutions. This happened, and the later medieval borough took its long-enduring shape, within some two generations from Henry II's death.[4] Formal incorporation and its special patterns of government lay in the future, but their origins are found in the newly enfranchised borough community of the early-thirteenth century. Freed from the continual supervision of royal officers, and above all free to contrive their own surplus from the royal dues that they now handled, the burgesses of the great demesne boroughs turned to make the self-governing communities that the common lawyers rationalized and approved in the next two centuries.

A community of this kind needed a settled administration, a means of ordering its affairs that enabled it to fulfil its public obligations and to manage its private life efficiently. What mattered most was that the fee-farm should be paid when it was due, and that other charges, first tallages and later the Parliamentary taxes, should be met on demand, that the king's peace should be kept and justice done within the competence of the borough court. Besides these cares, the community had to be held together, its member's business furthered, and the costs of its modest public services defrayed. By the thirteenth century such an organization needed written records, and the survival of those records in increasing quantities is one of the factors that complicate the later history of the medieval borough.

2. E. Coornaert, 'Les ghildes médiévales', *Revue Historique*, cxcix (1948), pp. 22–55, 208–43.
3. J. Tait, *The Medieval English Borough* (Manchester, 1936), pp. 232–33.
4. Ibid., pp. 255–56.

As each town becomes articulate it has a right to be heard, and the municipal chorus of the fourteenth and fifteenth centuries is ragged but hearty, each of its many voices proclaiming the same theme in different words. The theme is an interesting one, but its origins are more interesting still. Because they are numerous, borough records have received only spasmodic attention, and little of that for their own sake. Their beginnings are mysterious, but their first appearance was highly significant: in an age when government was newly literate, the inception of regular written memoranda marked an important stage in a community's progress towards corporateness.

There are today eleven English boroughs, including London, which have preserved original administrative records from the period before 1272, and another eleven with records earlier in date than 1300. These are not large numbers, but they are remarkable enough, and they do not include towns like Northampton and Colchester which have later copies of earlier records or other evidence that they once possessed them. Moreover, the earliest town records now surviving are very early indeed, older by several years than the earliest bishops' registers, and, by a narrower margin, than the royal Chancery's enrolments of outgoing letters.

Historians of the borough have commented more readily upon the absence of early records than upon their presence. Tait said truly that the material for the twelfth century was 'deplorably scanty',[5] but on reflection we might rather wonder that there should be any at all. The existence of records before 1200, or even before the end of John's reign, pushes the period of what we might call experimental writing in the boroughs back to a time when writing was still not an indispensable part of public administration, and suggests in turn that the surviving material from the thirteenth century is likely to be the wreckage of a sophisticated system of archives, rather than the first indications of a practice that was not established and perfected until a much later time. They compare well, therefore, with the manorial accounts of the great monastic houses, which might, with their great store of documented titles, have been expected to outpace the towns in producing ordinary administrative memoranda.[6]

The earliest administrative records written and preserved in an English borough for its own purposes, and surviving there today, are the gild rolls of Leicester, the oldest of which dates from 1196. They are closely matched by the first gild rolls of Dublin, which also belong to the close of the twelfth century, although they cannot be

---

5. Tait, op. cit., p. 226.
6. See, e.g. E. Stone, 'Profit-and-Loss Accountancy at Norwich Cathedral Priory', *Trans. Roy. Hist. Soc.*, Fifth Series, xii (1962), pp. 25–26.

precisely dated, and they are younger than the oldest manuscript of the customs of Newcastle-upon-Tyne, but the Newcastle customs are now among the Chancery Miscellanea, while the rolls of the Leicester and Dublin gilds are in their original custody.[7] All these manuscripts are comfortably earlier than the oldest original records of the City of London, although there is evidence that London has lost material of this date. If, however, we consider only original texts, we are drawn into the thirteenth century. Shrewsbury has gild rolls that begin in 1209, and some twenty years later Wallingford can show taxation rolls from 1227 and court rolls from 1229.[8] Exeter has a custumal written about 1242, but no court rolls until 1264. Between these documents come the oldest enrolments of deeds in the hustings court of London, from 1252, the first court roll at Ipswich, from 1256, and the gild rolls of Totnes and Andover, beginning in 1261 and 1262 respectively.[9] Hereford has a solitary account roll of 1264, Canterbury an undated account of *c.* 1260, and Winchester a fragment of a roll of pleas written in 1270.[10] These complete the list for Henry III's reign; but some of the towns have other classes of records which are also earlier than 1272, such as the account rolls at Shrewsbury from 1256.

Besides these, there are eleven towns in which the surviving records begin between 1272 and 1300. Barnstaple has a fragmentary court roll of 1277, and Bridport a complete one of 1278; Fordwich has a roll of tenements sold in the borough, beginning in 1281.[11]

---

7. For Leicester, see *Records of the Borough of Leicester*, ed. Mary Bateson, i (Cambridge, 1899): *The Records of the Corporation of Leicester* (Leicester, 1956): G.H. Martin, 'The Origins of Borough Records', *Journal of the Society of Archivists*, ii, no. 4 (Oct. 1961). The Dublin rolls are printed and discussed in *Historic and Municipal Documents of Ireland, 1172–1320*, ed. J. T. Gilbert (Rolls Series, 1870), and the Newcastle customs in *Archaeologia Aeliana*, Fourth Series, i (1925), pp. 169–78.

8. *Calendar of the Shrewsbury Borough Records* (Shrewsbury, 1896): *Trans. Shropshire Archaeol. and Natural History Soc.*, Second Series, viii (1896), pp. 21–43: Hist. MSS Comm., *Sixth Report*, Appendix, Part I (Wallingford), pp. 572–77.

9. *The Anglo-Norman Custumal of Exeter*, ed. J. W. Schopp (History of Exeter Research Group, Monograph no. 2, 1925): Hist. MSS Comm., [*Report on the Records of the City of*] *Exeter* (1916). P. E. Jones and R. Smith, *A Guide to the Records in the Corporation of London Record Office* . . . (London, 1951). G. H. Martin, *The Early Court Rolls of the Borough of Ipswich* (Leicester, 1954). C. Gross, *The Gild Merchant* (Oxford, 1890), ii, pp. 3–12, 235–44 (Andover and Totnes); Hist. MSS Comm., *Third Report*, Appendix, p. 297 (Totnes).

10. Hist. MSS Comm., *Thirteenth Report*, Appendix iv (Hereford): Canterbury Corporation Archives, F/Z/2; J. S. Furley, *City Government of Winchester* . . . (Oxford, 1923). I am obliged to Dr William Urry for information about the records of Canterbury and Fordwich.

11. Hist. MSS Comm., *Ninth Report*, Part I, Appendix (Barnstaple), pp. 203–16. Bridport Borough Archives, no. 1465: the roll is for 6–7 Edw. I, not 2–3 Edw. I as in the manuscript calendar. Fordwich Archives (in Canterbury Cathedral Library), bundle 1, no. 121.

The first pentice court roll at Chester dates from 1282, and the first roll of registered deeds at Norwich from 1285. Oxford has a hustings court roll of 1292, Great Yarmouth's court rolls begin in 1293, and Cambridge has a single plea roll for 1294–95.[12] Reading has an account roll and King's Lynn a roll recording the assizes of bread for 1296, and Gloucester has a murage account for 1298.[13] If we close the reckoning at 1300, we exclude some boroughs, like Colchester, by a narrow margin, but we should have to advance it much further to include others, like Bristol and Carlisle, which are important and interesting but have suffered heavy losses in their early records. Most of these places, and perhaps all the larger Domesday boroughs, could be shown to have had their own records from 1300, if other kinds of evidence were adduced, and in the same way others could be moved back from Edward I's reign to Henry III's or even further. Bristol had a custumal drawn up before 1241, Northampton had one that was probably written in the 1190s; but both survive today only in later texts.[14] Cambridge now has only one thirteenth-century plea roll, but there were others in 1261, when they were produced before the justices in eyre, just as the Curia Regis rolls and other records of the central courts reveal the existence of coroners' rolls from an early date.[15] On the other hand, the records that have been lost can only be assessed effectively by reference to those which still exist, and the survivors, though a much reduced band, provide an invaluable commentary upon the borough's progress at a significant time.

The most obvious feature of the thirteenth-century and earlier records, apart from their concentration in the southern half of the country, is the primacy of the gild. The losses by accident and war

12. *Selected Rolls of the Chester City Courts*, ed. A. Hopkins (Chetham Soc., Third Series, ii, 1950), p. xv. *Munimenta Civitatis Oxonie*, ed. H. E. Salter (Oxford Hist. Soc., lxxi. 1917); the introduction discusses lost documents: Brian Twyne used hustings rolls from 1278. *Repertory of Deeds and Documents relating to Great Yarmouth* (Yarmouth, 1855); the earliest rolls of Edward I's reign have been lost since J. C. Jeaffreson reported on the borough in Hist. MSS Comm., *Ninth Report*, Part I, Appendix, pp. 299–324. *Cambridge Borough Documents*, ed. W. M. Palmer, i (Cambridge, 1931).
13. *Reading Records*, ed. J. M. Guilding, i (London, 1892), p. xiii. Hist. MSS Comm., *Eleventh Report*, Appendix, Part III, p. 210 (King's Lynn). W. H. Stevenson, *Calendar of the Records of the Corporation of Gloucester* (Gloucester, 1893), p. 456.
14. *Borough Customs*, ed. Mary Bateson, i (Selden Soc., 1904), pp. xx, xli–xlii.
15. P[ublic] R[ecord] O[ffice], Assize Roll no. 82. R. F. Hunniset, *The Medieval Coroner* (Cambridge, 1961), pp. 100–3. Norwich has a fifteenth-century text of the presentments to the justices in eyre in 1250, and Colchester once had records of inquests, the oldest of which seemed to Philip Morant to be as early as Richard I's or John's reign (*Records of the City of Norwich*, eds. W. Hudson and J. C. Tingey, i (Norwich, 1906) pp. 199–202; P. Morant, *History and Antiquities of Colchester* (Colchester, 1748), Book 2, p. 19, n. L).

at Newcastle and Carlisle have been matched by similar misfortunes all over the north of England, so that the surviving sparse indications have to remind us that the towns there may be credited with much less history, violence apart, than is their due. In the south, however, the early records are well distributed, and even when due allowance is made for the accidents of survival, they emphasize the importance of the gild merchant in a striking way. The examples of Leicester and Shrewsbury are reinforced by the Dublin rolls and by similar lists of gildsmen copied into the fourteenth-century Ipswich custumal, for the importance of the gild-register is that it implies a continuing series of records and not, as the custumal may be, a document compiled for a particular occasion. The lost Northampton custumal and the roll from Newcastle may indicate the presence of municipal clerks in those boroughs in the twelfth century, but they cannot by themselves prove that there was then a regular system of records. When the evidence of such a system does appear, it comes first from the gild merchant, not from the portmanmote, and although court rolls appear quite early at Wallingford, they are accompanied by elaborate taxation rolls that evidently owe nothing to the rather pinched memoranda of the borough court. If Dublin is included with the English boroughs, there are, down to the last decade of Henry III's reign, more gild rolls than other kinds of original records.

This pattern changes in the second half of the century, when the number of court rolls increases. In some instances they are specialized records of pleas or other business transacted in court, like the hustings rolls of London or the plea rolls of Cambridge, and in others bear undifferentiated entries as at Exeter, Ipswich or Bridport. From 1272 onwards a court roll is commonly the earliest record left in a borough, and often it is also the first of a long series. Despite what appears to be a later start, the court roll has a more varied history than the gild roll, and for that reason it has some claim to be the archetype of medieval borough records. The accounts and miscellaneous rolls that appear before 1300 have their own significance, but the subtle interaction of gild and portmanmote commands the borough's archival as well as its constitutional history.

The obvious questions to ask of these documents are: who wrote them and for what purpose? The answers present themselves less readily, but there are some indications to be gathered. Leicester's gild roll consists of eleven membranes of irregular widths of eight inches or less, and some fifteen feet long in all; its entries run from 1196 to 1233. The first membrane is ruled with a tabular grid in dry-point and has a list of sixty gildsmen and their payments under the heading: 'Isti intraverunt in gildam merchatoriam die festi beati Dionysii primo post adventum comitis in Angliam post deliberacionem suam de capcione sua in Francia' [i.e presumably 9

October 1196]. Each name is followed by the names of the entrant's pledges. The first twenty-eight entries are made in the neat, angular, hand that wrote the heading and that appears again lower in the column, but the record of payments and acquittance, like the occasional cancellation of entries, is in another hand. The gild merchant in Leicester was licensed by Robert, count of Meulan (1103–18), so there is no question of this roll being an inaugural register, despite the care with which the first entries are set out. Moreover, the amendments to the list, which are mainly notes of instalments of the entry fee paid, are made in a comparatively careless way. The roll is a working document, not a formal and ceremonial one. It also has a strong local flavour: of twenty-one years specified in the headings, fourteen were identified, as they cannot all be today, by reference to local events in Leicester or events with some special local interest – the release of Robert Fitz Parnell (1196), the death of Abbot Paul (? 1205), the dedication of St Nicholas's church (1220), or the capture of Damietta, where Saer de Quincy was killed (1220). Of the other seven dates, three are John's regnal years, two refer to the general interdict, one to the death of Emperor Henry VI in 1197, and the last to the death of William Marshal in 1219.

Leicester became a seignorial borough after the Conquest, and conversation at the castle echoed at the gild hall perhaps more readily than events in London. It was this tutelage, unusual in a town of Leicester's standing, that made the gild merchant so important to the townsmen and gave the gild a more commanding part there than in any of the other shire boroughs of Domesday Book. The second gild roll, now a bundle of twenty-one membranes, with entries running from 1234 to 1274, demonstrates the special relation of the gild and the borough community even more clearly than the first. The casual memoranda upon the first roll include a note upon the five great Midland fairs, for which a burgess was excused attendance at the portmanmote. Those on the second include a loan made *ad commodum ville* in 1239, payment for such public works as gates and bridges, and payments for presenting the new mayor to the earl and for negotiating the charters of 1255 and 1256 from Simon de Montfort and the king, which substituted primogeniture for ultimogeniture as the local rule of inheritance.[16] In another borough these would have been matters for the community, organized by the portmanmote. In Leicester they are not so much discharged by the gild as paid for by the gild. The haphazard nature of the entries show them to be incidental to the gild's principal business, which is to define, discipline, and further the interests of the merchant community, but the public demands upon the gild's dis-

16. *Records of the Borough of Leicester*, ed. Bateson, i, pp. 33, 61, 71, 74.

posable surplus make the gild a public body. There were more obvious forces at work: the burgesses did not hold the borough at fee-farm and the revenues of their portmanmote went to the earl; the gild was their most effective communal organization because it commanded the only income in the borough which was freely theirs. Moreover, the leading burgesses were the leading gildsmen; the alderman of the gild came to be the mayor of the borough, presided as mayor over the morning-speech and drew his expenses from the gild funds. The gild rolls illustrate this process and something more; by spending money upon municipal affairs the association takes on wider responsibilities. In 1271 the serjeant *de suburbio orientali* produced his pledges in full portmanmote to warrant his fidelity in office. By this time the portmanmote had its own rolls of pleas and estreats, but the serjeant's bond was entered upon the gild roll, and so were the pledges of the serjeant of the south ward at a later morning-speech.[17] The serjeants were officers of the borough court, and their pledges stand to protect the community from the consequences of their defalcation, but in Leicester the community that pays is the community of the gild, and the gild needs to know who the serjeants and their pledges may be.

The early stages of the transition from community to corporation are better illustrated in Leicester, where the normal process was impaired, than they are elsewhere. The burgesses made more rapid progress toward the impersonal Town, 'the Town which has rights and duties, the Town which owes and is owed money',[18] in their gild than they might have made in an unfettered portmanmote, and the records of the gild illuminate their way more distinctly than would the records of such a court. In other towns the gilds had a lighter burden to bear, but their earliest records are significant. Dublin and Shrewsbury had some similar problems, Dublin as a privileged settlement in a newly annexed territory, Shrewsbury as a border town, more secure than the Irish boroughs, but anxious enough. Medieval Dublin is now so lightly documented that its administrative history is obscure, but the survival and the form of the gild rolls show that the composition of its merchant community, the identity of its burgesses, were matters of prime importance. The 'Roll of names' records the gildsmen and their entrance fees; there are no casual memoranda as there are at Leicester, and the effect is that of a register rather than of an account or entry book. The Shrewsbury rolls have been less carefully preserved, but again they are concerned with admissions and payments rather than with business transacted.

The first roll at Shrewsbury consists of two membranes, sewn in

17. *Records of the Borough of Leicester*, ed. Bateson, i, pp. 110–11.
18. F. W. Maitland, *Township and Borough* (Cambridge, 1898), p. 80.

Exchequer style. The first membrane begins with an invocation, 'Sanctus Spiritus assit nobis', and then has something over 150 names, arranged in two subdivided columns. There is a general heading, 'De illis qui sunt in gilda mercanda in burgo Salopie et quorum patres prius non fuerunt in libertatibus gilde anno xj° regni regis Johannis et quorum finis est v sol. iiij*d*', which refers to the upper left-hand column of 31 names, each with a sum of 8*d* recorded against it. The lower left-hand column, containing 55 names, has the subheading 'De forinsecis qui intraverunt gildam et de finibus eorum'. The right-hand column has two subheadings, 'De illis qui primo intraverunt gildam', followed by nine names without payments against them, and 'Isti intravenerunt ad ultimam assisam primo', followed by more than fifty names, with a record of payments by instalments: 'dimidium marce; dabit ij*s*', and so on. The dorse has two columns of names, unheaded, in the same hand as the left-hand columns on the face. The second membrane records the fourth *assisa* of the grid in II John and has a subheading, 'De illis quorum patres fuerunt in gilda unde assisa de xxxij*d* apposita et pacaverunt iiij*d*'. Payments of 4*d*, some distinguished as primo and *secundo*, follow against 69 names. The dorse records the first *assisa* of 4 Henry III on 26 July 1220 and lists new admissions, without specifying payments. The remaining dated rolls from Henry III's reign have entries of a similar kind for 1232, 1239, 1242 and 1252 (three membranes), and 1268 (two membranes). That for 1252 has notes on the dorse of four cases of trespass, giving only the parties' names, but there is no record of any further proceedings.

Like the Dublin rolls, these lists are registers, and the first of them, with its pious introduction, looks like an early essay in record-keeping. The Shrewsbury gild was apparently not licensed by royal charter until 1227, and may not be much older than its records, but whatever its age it probably produced other less formal memoranda, rough jottings of accounts such as survive for a later period among the gild rolls of Totnes. At Shrewsbury, unlike Leicester, the gild's accounts were private rather than municipal, and have not survived, but for the same reason the borough kept elaborate accounts of its own, the remnants of which appear from 1249 onward. The first is an unusual fragment, a roll of assays from the mint, but the fullest are the murage and pavage accounts, which begin in 1256.[19] These are large rolls, the first, which has five membranes, being 7′ 6″ long by 5¼″ wide, with a year's weekly accounts cast on Sundays. Two *custodes muragii* are named in an incidental note, and two clerks, the first of whom, Richard Fitz Herbert, gave place to Henry *clericus* at the beginning of December 1256. The change is marked

19. Shrewsbury Borough Records, Box LXXVI, 2686 (assay roll); Box VIII, 302 ff. (murage accounts).

by a subheading, 'Hic incipit Henricus clericus scribere recepta et expensa muragii Salopie anno scilicet xlj', but on a later margin the hand changes again against the marginal note 'Hic incipit R. Pungh custodire muragium Salopie usque in posterum tocius istius rotuli', which may mean that Pungh acted as clerk as well as *custos*.

The accounts are very simple and record weekly receipts of about 20*s* from collectors at the town's three gates, which are spent regularly on the quarrymen's wages, the haulage of stone and building work on the English bridge. Extra charges include the master mason's fees, the smith's wages for repairs to the quarrying tools, and small sums for parchment. The chief interest of the documents lies in their form rather than in their repetitious contents. They represent a continuous record of public works, accounted for, not anonymously, but impersonally. Although the *custodes* were responsible for the sums that they handled, they did not render separate accounts; when the roll passed to a new clerk, he began his entries where his predecessor finished, in the middle of a membrane.[20] The document is a public record, not a private justification; it is, so to speak, itself part of the works for which the murage pays. And the borough not only employed the workmen directly, both on the quarry and the site, but provided their equipment at the quarry. The accounts include lists of 'hutensilia ville Salopie de quarrera', wedges, mattocks and picks, which are kept in good condition by the smith; not an impressive array, but an interesting example of communal property. It was by such modest means as this – chattels which the townsmen owned collectively, but which their employees used – as well as by the more exacting exercises demanded by the communal management of real property, that the medieval borough moved towards realizing, in Maitland's phrase, an 'its' which is not 'theirs'.

The earliest records at Wallingford fall between the dates of the gild rolls and the accounts at Shrewsbury. They begin with a *rotulus de pactionariis* of 1227, bearing a list of some 180 names each charged with a small sum, ranging from 2*d* to 2*s* 8*d*, and a note of its payment, usually by instalments.[21] The names are arranged by trades. The so-called tallage rolls,[22] which begin in 1229, are also

20. As late as 1537 the clerks of the mayor's court of London kept the rolls on which they were working in their own custody, and the city records have suffered accordingly (*Calendar of Letter-Books of the City of London, Letter-Book A*, ed. R. R. Sharpe (London, 1899), pp. iii–iv). At Worcester in the fifteenth century the town clerk was enjoined to make up the bailiffs' records and yearly acquittances in his own hand and to keep them 'for laufulle remembrance to be left to the said comynalte' (L. Toulmin Smith, *English Gilds* (E[arly] E[nglish] T[ext] S[ociety], xl, 1870), pp. 399–400).
21. Berkshire Records Office, W/FC/1.
22. Ibid., W/FT/1.

lists of names and small rents for tenements, probably arranged topographically. Both sets of rolls are written with exceptional care, on whitened parchment ruled with a grid. The records of the court, the burghmoot, which begin with an estreat roll in 1229, are more casually written. The first court roll, a single damaged membrane, is a record of courts hearing real and personal actions from July 1232 to the summer of 1233.[23] The cases are mainly of debt and slander, but there were two real actions in September 1232, for which the writs were copied onto the roll. There are also periodic notices of the assizes of bread and ale.

Besides this burghmoot roll, which is the first of a long series, there is a single membrane for the year 1232 headed 'Rotulus de captione terrarum in Wallingeford anno xvj regni regis Henrici filii regis Johannis'.[24] This has 33 undated and closely-written entries recording the gift and sale of lands and tenements in the borough. The transaction, which is described very tersely, is usually said to be witnessed by the court – *coram* or *teste* burgimoto – and there is no reference to any written deed. Whether deeds were exchanged or not, this was evidently an ancient function of the court, and one common enough to demand a record of its own. The burghmoot roll itself apparently covers a wide range of business, but there may have been other ancillary records like this roll and the roll of estreats.

An interesting feature of the 'rotuli de pactionariis' is a series of brief, but regular, general accounts on the dorse of each. The items, which amount to some thirty shillings each year, include trimestrial payments of 15*d* to Henry *clericus*, 'pro servicio suo', and occasional payments to three other clerks, Ralph, Robert and Clement. Parchment accounts only for an infrequent 2*d* or 3*d* in contrast to several shillings spent regularly on forage. Others sums are paid *servientibus de foro*, against the king's visits, and to messengers. These notes are presumably entered upon the company rolls as the records of the borough's principal source of revenue, and they appear to be the earliest domestic accounts of an English borough, being fifteen years earlier than the Shrewsbury murage accounts and more regular than the notes in the Leicester gild rolls.

The records of Wallingford are a good deal earlier than any comparable group elsewhere; for the next twenty-five years we find only fragments again. The Anglo-Norman custumal of Exeter is interesting as a text that can perhaps be attributed to a particular city-clerk, John Baubi,[25] but like other custumals it is a by-product of a literate administration, a statement of common practice and not a record of business done. It was apparently begun not later than 1242, and is

23. Ibid., W/JBe/1 (estreats); W/JBa/1 (burghmoot).
24. Ibid., W/RTa.
25. *Anglo-Norman Custumal of Exeter*, ed. Schopp, pp. 8–10.

therefore twenty-two years older than the first surviving court roll in the city. The intervening period covers the appearance of the oldest surviving administrative record of the City of London, the roll of deeds registered in the hustings court which now begins in 1252, and includes testaments from 1258. There is no heading to the roll, which is a straightforward record of the written deeds, rather than as at Wallingford the transactions themselves. It seems unlikely that this was the hustings court's first record, but there are now no plea rolls from the court until 1272.[26]

The first court roll at Ipswich dates from 1255 to 1256. The next is one for 1270–72, after which there is a nearly continuous series. The records of Ipswich are particularly interesting because we have some incidental contemporary information about them, and because they are the first court rolls in which we can watch the deliberate creation of an ancillary record.[27] In 1272 John le Blake, common clerk of the borough, decamped with various rolls of pleas and with the roll of the borough's customs called the Domesday. The custumal was not replaced until 1291, but early in the next century the customs were copied anew into a codex and other material added to them. Le Blake's default made the townsmen aware of their records and they took special notice of what remained to them. The fourteenth-century custumal contains an unusual and valuable account of the burgesses' proceedings when they received their first charter in 1200, said to be copied from a roll found in the common chest. Besides this record there are lists of gildsmen admitted between 1200 and Edward I's reign, which down to 1256 are taken from records now lost, and after that date are apparently copied from the surviving court rolls. It looks as though 1200 saw the beginning of regular written records in Ipswich, and that the earliest of them included gild rolls. Like the gild at Cambridge, the gild merchant at Ipswich seems to have languished as the enfranchised borough gained strength, and the apparent absorption of the gild roll by the portmanmote illustrates its decline.[28]

There were limits, however, to the business that could be accommodated in the portmanmote roll. In Edward I's reign separate rolls of personal actions or petty pleas appear, which at first record actions under the simple heading of *querele* [heard on] such and such a day, and much later develop into the rolls of a petty court. Then in the last years of the thirteenth century the clerk began to gather 'recognizances' of deeds registered in the portmanmote onto a single membrane of the court roll, and from 1307 to keep a separate roll of 'recognizances of free tenements' and testaments proved, which

26. *Guide to the Records . . . of London*, p. 64.
27. Martin, *Early Court Rolls . . . of Ipswich*, pp. 28–29.
28. Ibid, pp. 12–14.

within the next two decades bred a court of its own. The mayor's court roll of Exeter was divided in a similar way during the same period, but at Ipswich the process is quite explicit and the appearance of a 'petty court of recognizances', called into being by the roll, is a most unusual tribute to the power of the written word.

The gild and the portmanmote started on equal terms at Ipswich, and the portmanmote proved to be the more powerful institution. In towns that were smaller or overshadowed by formidable neighbours the gild was more likely to maintain its position and to produce a more elaborate and vigorous record. The gild rolls of Totnes and Andover date from 1260 and 1262 respectively. The first roll at Totnes has four membranes, five feet long in all, and runs from 1260 into Edward I's regin.[29] It is headed 'Rotulus gylde mercatorum Totton' tempore Ricardi filii Ade et Ricardi de Porta anno Domini mcc sexagessimo. Hec scripta sunt per manus Bartholomei capellani et clerici hujus fraternitatis qui est libertatis juratus.' The roll begins with a simple list of 200 names, but develops into an elaborate record of admissions, with details of the undertakings exacted from the candidates. It was also used for memoranda such as a note of the grant of a right of way in which the gild had no evident interest except as the town's governing body. Totnes, like Leicester, was a mediatized borough, and a small one. Andover enjoyed formal independence, but until the Weyhill fair became a national institution in the sixteenth century and the borough was incorporated, it was ruled by its gild merchant, and the gild rolls dominate the early borough archives. Like those at Totnes, they are chiefly concerned with carefully documented admissions, including disputes over admissions between heirs or other parties, and with recording the fines which were an important part of the gild's income.

The last decade of Henry III's reign produces, besides continuations of these and other records, the Exeter court rolls, the first accounts at Hereford, an early but undated account from Canterbury which probably belongs to this period, and the isolated roll of personal pleas at Winchester. Edward I's reign multiplies original records of all kinds, ranging from the comprehensive court rolls of Bridport to the carefully differentiated records of the city courts of Chester and Norwich, and of London itself. The earliest court roll at Great Yarmouth shows already in 1293 the grouping of particular kinds of business on separate membranes, and in particular the roll of letters despatched under the common seal that made the borough's records so distinctive in the next century. The only other new classes of documents that appear at this time are the assize-of-

---

29. *Trans. Devonshire Assoc.*, xii (1880), p. 183; Hist. MSS Comm., *Third Report*, Appendix, p. 343.

bread records at King's Lynn, distinguishing a class of business that at Bridport was still entered on the court roll, and the interesting customs rolls at Exeter, with a similar fragment at Ipswich which survives only as a tag on another roll.[30] By this time, however, borough records have begun to accumulate at such a rate that, except in a few unlucky towns (which include, by mischievous chance, Lincoln and York), some part of the municipal administration is continuously in view.

The records that do not appear among these survivors are as interesting as those that do. Although the compiler of the *Liber de Antiquis Legibus* of London, whose work lies just inside Edward I's reign, was able to make a list of mayors and sheriffs of the city from Fitz Ailwyn's time, consular tables do not seem to have been an inevitable, or at least a highly-prized, feature of early borough records.[31] The account of the borough-making at Ipswich, in 1200, names the first officers elected, but thereafter there seems to have been no record of the bailiffs' names until they became a feature of the court roll. On the Leicester gild roll some early entries are dated by the aldermen or chamberlains holding office, but there is no consistent attempt to record them. Similarly there are no chronicles, apart from the material used in the *Liber de Antiquis Legibus* and the anomalous document at Ipswich; they are for the most part a product of later centuries than the thirteenth, whilst cartularies do not appear at all. The absence of calendars, which were essential to efficient dating, is probably to be attributed to bigoted zeal after the Reformation; one survives at Fordwich, and Twyne saw a volume that contained 'a Calendar and a crucifix', presumably an illuminated calendar, among the Oxford city records.[32] There may be some others, but most have been lost. It would be possible with some labour to reconstruct them in part in some towns, but long runs of records would be needed to make the lists of feast days passably complete.

The calendars are likely to have been destroyed, the other classes

---

30. For the Yarmouth letter rolls, see Martin, *Early Court Rolls . . . of Ipswich*, p. 37. Not many early municipal letters have survived, but there is an interesting one at Lancaster sent by Northampton, *c.* 1200, in answer to an enquiry about the liberties of Northampton; see T. Pape, *The Charters of the City of Lancaster* (Lancaster, 1952), pp. 12–13. For the customs rolls, see Hist. MSS Comm., *Exeter*, p. 413, and Ipswich Borough Records, Great Court Rolls 29–31 Edw. I, m. 2.

31. Nor were they, apparently, on the Continent. The celebrated *Annales de Toulouse* derive from notices of consular elections that begin as late as 1295; see P. Wolff, *Histoire de Toulouse* (Toulouse, 1958), p. 13. M. Schneider implies that there were no regular tables in Metz before that time (Jean Schneider, *La ville de Metz aux XIIIe et XIVe siècles* (Nancy, 1950), p. 511; cf. p. 161).

32. *Archaeologia Cantiana*, xviii (1889), p. 92. *Munimenta Civitatis Oxonie*, ed. Salter, p. xii.

of missing documents were perhaps never very fully represented. What is left from the thirteenth century are the remnants of a substantial body of working documents, written in a business-like way for prosaic purposes. We are very imperfectly informed about their authors, the 'common clerks' and others who emerge dimly here and there. To whom, or to what, was the common clerk common?[33] Where was he educated and, in particular, where did he learn his law? Bartholomew the chaplain of the Totnes gild seems to have been an unusual figure;[34] there is no general evidence that the clerks were, in the ordinary sense, local clergy or that they looked to an ecclesiastical career. A number of early-thirteenth century deeds at Bath are witnessed by Reyner *aurifaber,* who is described in one, not very well written, as *scriptor gilde.*[35] Newcastle-upon-Tyne, which has lost almost all its medieval records, has kept deeds which reveal an apparent dynasty of common clerks in the thirteenth century: Adam of Newcastle, *c.* 1216–59, was succeeded by his son-in-law Bartholomew who was succeeded by his son Adam, from *c.* 1279 to 1300.[36] This was one means of recruitment. Elsewhere a kind of apprenticeship may have obtained, but not all such clerks were locally recruited if the presence of John of Colchester at Durham, and John of Dover at Bath, may be trusted.[37] If we knew more about these matters, we should know more than we do about medieval education and about the growth of the lay professions.

Private deeds are only one source of additional evidence about the early administration of boroughs, and that administration fills

33. *Clericus communis* (e.g. in Ricart's Calendar) seems to be the general medieval usage, although occasionally *clericus communitatis* is used, as of Roger de Scaddisdem at Leicester, *c.* 1280 (Leicester City Records BR II/8a/1). At Lincoln, *c.* 1230, there were two *clerici civitatis,* both called John and apparently equal in other respects (*Registrum Antiquissimum*, viii. ed. K. Major (Lincoln Record Soc, li, 1958), pp. 132, 198). It is difficult to say when the habit of using deputies began, but it may well have been early. The town clerk of Worcester was enjoined in 1467 to keep certain records and to attend to his business in person (L. Toulmin Smith, *English Gilds* (E.E.T.S., xl, 1870), pp. 399–400), but the common clerk of Bristol had a paid clerk (ibid., p. 423), Ricart, who called himself 'Toune clerk' in English and 'communis clericus' in Latin, refers to his assistant's official livery but not to a customary stipend (*The Maire of Bristowe is Kalendar*, ed. L. Toulmin Smith (Camden Soc., 1872), pp. 81–82).

34. Bartholomew the chaplain was made vicar of Totnes in 1269 (*Trans. Devonshire Assoc.,* xii, p. 183). By the fourteenth century gilds usually named a clerk amongst their officers (Smith, op. cit., *passim*). The Leicester gild merchant seems to have had two clerks; see above, p. 38.

35. C. W. Schickle, *Calendar of Ancient Deeds belonging to the Corporation of Bath* (Bath, 1921), pp. 3, 7.

36. *Early Deeds relating to Newcastle on Tyne* (Surtees Soc., cxxxvii. 1924), pp. 94, 171–72. For a contemporary regulation against such family connexions among the parochial *amanuenses* of Metz, see Schneider, op. cit., p. 163.

37. 'The Greenwell Deeds', *Archaeologia Æliana*, Fourth Series, iii (1927), p. 24; Schickle, op. cit., p. 28.

only one part, although an important part, of their history. The scope of the present survey could be largely extended by the inclusion of early records that survive in later texts, or which were noted or described before they were lost, but their accumulated evidence would be outweighed by other sources. The records of the royal Exchequer and of the central courts, the rolls of the justices itineranṭ, the Hundred Rolls, the rolls of letters patent and letters close, all contain a mass of information about the boroughs, about their relations with the king and with each other.[38]

The significance of the borough's own records in this period is of a different kind. Other sources are principally concerned with the forces that worked upon the town from the outside; their own archives reveal the townsmen as active rather than passive agents. The surviving originals show the towns not merely ordering their affairs in an effective way, but documenting them in a fashion that owes much less to external example than might be expected. The accidental loss of London's records before 1252 directs a proper share of attention to the provincial towns and displays their accomplishments without disparagement, for the earliest of their records stand up well to comparison, not only with bishops' registers, but with town records from the Continent.[39] The varied material that chance has preserved shows some striking characteristics. The chief impulse to record-keeping seems to have come, not from the borough court, the institution most concerned with the authorities outside, but from the gild, and seems to have been directed first to questions of membership and status, as well as naturally with finance. When court rolls appear, they are compiled with an eye to local and immediate purposes, and they are subdivided and developed at will. There is little or no trace of notarial influence in any of these documents; they are casual rather than formal, abstracts rather than *verbatim* records, and yet they are not tentative or experimental, but fair-written copies for reference. If they have not yet revealed as much about their authors as we might wish, they have a good deal to tell us about their purpose and effect. They were the mind and memory

---

38. The medieval chapters of the *Victoria County History, Yorkshire, The City of York* (1961), are an example of what can be done with material of this kind in default of ordinary municipal records.

39. Registers are only one test of professionalism, and a good deal can be said about bishops' chanceries before registers appear (C. R. Cheney, *English Bishops' Chanceries, 1100–1250* (Manchester, 1950), pp. 2–4). The history of towns on the Continent opens a very wide field for comparison, but in northern Europe their apparently superior evidences are often the product of their religious houses. The documents discussed in this paper are mostly earlier than the earliest town records in the northern Netherlands; see *De Oudste Stadsrekeningen van Dordrecht, 1284–1424*, ed. C. M. Dozy (The Hague, 1891). Even at Toulouse the magistrates' decisions were not formally registered before 1225, but were left in notaries' copies in private hands (Wolff, *Histoire de Toulouse*, p. 12).

of a community that was feeling its way toward corporate personality, and that achieved its purpose as much by their aid as by any means.

Editorial suggestions for further reading

Tait J. *The Medieval English Borough* (Manchester, 1936). M. Bateson (ed.), *Borough Customs*, Selden Society, 18 (1904), 21 (1906).

Martin G. 'Towns in Domesday Book', in P. H. Sawyer (ed.), *Domesday Book: A Reassessment* (London, 1985).

Chapter Four

THE FIRST HALF-CENTURY OF THE BOROUGH OF STRATFORD-UPON-AVON

E. M. Carus-Wilson

Economic History Review, 18 (1965)

> *This remains the classic account of one of the many 'new towns' promoted by lords on their estates in the twelfth and thirteenth centuries. Its publication had been shortly anticipated by M. W. Beresford's parallel study of urban speculative developments on the estates of the bishop of Winchester; and it was soon followed by the appearance, in 1967, of Beresford's* New Towns of the Middle Ages, *a survey of the whole subject. Beresford's gazetteer is now out of date – even his long lists give a far from complete tally of urban foundations – but the work remains valuable. Both Beresford and Carus-Wilson drew attention to the rich evidence contained in manorial records of the active interest of lords in urbanization, an interest which in the overwhelming majority of cases – as here at Stratford – was purely commercial. An index of the success of Stratford was the number of migrants who came to settle in the new town from villages up to sixteen miles away, a range of attraction which gives an idea of Stratford's regional importance. More recently, a sophisticated methodology for using locative surnames has been defined by Peter McClure, enabling comparative studies to be made of migration to different towns before 1350: since towns of higher status attracted immigrants from further afield than others, such analysis – which should be extended by future local case studies – can provide an approximate rank-order or hierarchy of towns. Stratford-upon-Avon would clearly come fairly low on such a scale; yet it was typical of an extensive network of small market towns covering the whole of England by 1300.*

Our knowledge of the medieval English borough, like that of the medieval manor, has been much influenced by the legal preoccupations of its first historians. Today we possess many learned studies of burgess status and burgage tenure, of borough 'customs', borough courts, and the law merchant, and many published collections of borough charters and custumals. But although some boroughs have

published large and varied selections from their records ranging far
beyond charters and custumals, we still know little of the social and
economic realities behind the legal formulas – of the origin of the
burgesses, for instance, of how they made their living, and of the
economic functions of urban communities in the life of the community as a whole. The prevailing approach to borough history, as
shown even in some of the best recent histories of English towns,
and in the general plan adopted by the *Victoria County History*, is
that of fragmentation, with separate sections on topographical, constitutional, and ecclesiastical developments, and in conclusion perhaps, quite unrelated to the rest, an isolated 'social and economic'
section, often anecdotal and much less scholarly in character. But
the inhabitants of the boroughs were not themselves thus fragmented. They were at one and the same time occupiers – and some
times builders – of houses and shops, suitors at the borough courts
and perhaps members of its governing body, and parishioners attending, regularly or irregularly, one of its churches; and for the
greater part of each week most of them were concerned with the
humdrum job of earning a living. In old age and retirement they
were, perhaps, founders of a chantry or inmates of a local hospital.
If we would understand any part of their history we must look at it as
a whole and be prepared to consider their ordinary avocations, commonplace as the subject may seem. Nowhere, probably, is our
ignorance greater than in the case of those smaller English
boroughs, founded after the Norman Conquest which are often
regarded as being distinguished from villages merely by the different
legal status of their inhabitants – a difference which seems sometimes to have neither purpose nor meaning. It may therefore be of
interest to look briefly at the formative period of one of them – one
which today is better known and more sought after by visitors from
all parts of the world than any other since it was Shakespeare's
birthplace.

The Domesday Survey of 1086 found no burgesses at Stratford-
on-Avon, but only a small rural settlement, as in early Saxon days,
close to the 'streetford' where the Roman road crossed the Avon.[1]
This settlement, however, would seem to have grown considerably
in the twenty years since the Norman Conquest. Both at the Conquest and in 1086 it formed part of an estate held by Wulfstan,
Bishop of Worcester, one of the few Saxon bishops who remained
in office under the new regime, and it continued to be held by his
successors until the sixteenth century. A monastery also had existed

1. O. E. 'Straetford', i.e. ford by which a Roman road crossed a river. All the
Stratfords are on Roman roads, and in this case the reference is to an important cross-road linking Fosse Way, via Stratford-on-Avon, with Ryknield Street
at Alcester

at Stratford in the late seventh century, but this had vanished utterly in the troubled times since then.[2]

On the bishop's manor of Stratford in 1086, according to Domesday Book,[3] there was demesne land with 3 ploughs, and 21 villeins, 7 bordars, and a priest with 28 ploughs between them. There was also a water-mill, whose annual value was reckoned as 10s and 1000 eels, and a considerable stretch of meadow land – five furlongs long and two furlongs broad. The whole manor was valued at £5 before and at the time of the Conquest, and at £25 twenty years later at the time of the survey. It would seem to have included then, as later, the hamlets of Shottery and Welcombe in addition to the settlement at Stratford itself.[4]

The countryside round Stratford was sharply diversified, for the Avon marks broadly the division between the wooded 'Arden' district to the north-west and the open 'Feldon' to the south-east. North-west of the river lay a region of woodland and scrub, as yet sparsely inhabited, extending beyond Henley-in-Arden into what came later to be known as the Forest of Arden, with vast stretches of virgin 'forest', scarcely as yet penetrated by the plough, reaching away to the northern boundaries of Warwickshire. Settlement in this region was mainly concentrated along the rivers, on the Avon's tributaries the Alne and the Arrow, and where these two met stood the little town of Alcester, indicating by its name its Roman origin; through it ran the Roman road which crossed the Avon at Stratford, bound for the salt-working centre of Droitwich. The valley of the Avon itself, with its rich, easily worked soils and its well-watered meadows, had long since been cleared and colonised. Some nine miles up the river above Stratford lay the Saxon borough of Warwick, founded as a defensive centre at the time of the Danish invasions; still a shire capital, headquarters of a royal sheriff, it was now resplendent with its new Norman castle. Below Stratford the river wound slowly on past Bidford, where it was crossed by a second Roman road bound for Alcester, into the broad open vale where stood the great Benedictine monastery of Evesham. South-east of the Avon the land rose gradually on to the open plateau of the Feldon, bounded by the steep northern slopes of the Cotswolds where, from the heights of Edgehill, a splendid panorama over the vale is unfolded. Already almost wholly cleared of woodland, the Feldon was even more thickly populated than the Avon valley.[5]

Potentially wealthy, with land well suited for corn-growing as well

---

2. Levi Fox, *The Borough Town of Stratford-upon-Avon* (1953), 15.
3. *Victoria County History of Warwickshire*, I, 302 b.
4. Ibid., III, ed. Ph. Styles (1945), 259–60, 264.
5. For the distribution of settlement at the time of Domesday see H. C. Darby and L. B. Terrett, *The Domesday Geography of Midland England* (1954).

as for pasturing sheep and cattle, the country round Stratford, more particularly the Arden woodland, was still at the time of Domesday an underdeveloped area. But a century later great changes had come over the scene. Everywhere there were signs of growing population and a more vigorous exploitation of the region's natural resources, of fresh penetration of the forest and more intensive cultivation of the old settlement lands. In Arden, for instance, new Norman landlords had carved out estates on what had once been waste, as did the Norman family who settled near the River Alne, calling the castle which they built 'the castle of the beautiful wilderness'*(Beaudesert)*.[6] New religious houses too, had been planted there. The Benedictines had founded a monastery at Alcester (1140) and a little nunnery at Wroxall (by 1135). The Cistercians had established houses for nuns at Pinley (*temp*. Henry I) and at Cook Hill (*circa* 1180), in addition to the much more important house for men at Bordesley (1138) which was actively concerned in farming the land from its many outlying granges such as Binton, Bidford, and Bearley in the immediate vicinity of Stratford. There were houses for Augustinian canons at Studley (post-1135) as well as at Warwick (pre-1123). At Wootton Wawen a small alien priory had been founded soon after the Norman Conquest by the Benedictine Abbey of St Peter de Castellion at Conches, and by the end of the twelfth century the Hospitallers had a house at Temple Grafton.[7]

Land-hungry peasants, also, were clearing woods and thickets, ploughing and cultivating the soil – and swelling manorial rent-rolls by payments for the new holdings they had won from the waste. Thus when the manor of Stratford was surveyed for the Bishop of Worcester a century after Domesday (in 1182) two tenants, Stigant and Stout, were reported to be paying 7*s*.8*d*. and two sextars of nuts each year for 'certain assarts' which they held.[8] These assarts were most probably some twelve miles distant in Lapworth parish[9] in the

6. *Victoria County History of Warwickshire*, III, *ut supra*, 45.

7. For the dates of these foundations see David Knowles and R. N. Hadcock, *Medieval Religious Houses in England and Wales* (1953), and for the Bordesley granges *V. C. H. Warwickshire*, III, *ut supra*, sub Binton Bidford, and Bearley.

8. *The Red Book of Worcester,* ed. Margery Hollings, Worcestershire Historical Society, 1934 (Parts I & II), 1939 (Part III), III, 260–262. The Red Book was compiled at the end of the thirteenth century and preserved among the cathedral archives till the time of George I, since when it has been lost. It is known to us through a transcript made, apparently very carefully, by William Thomas (1670–1738); preserved until recently at the Public Record Office among the records of the Ecclesiastical Commission, this transcript has now been returned to Worcester in accordance with the policy of dispersing the Ecclesiastical Commission records to the various dioceses.

9. Cf. the mention in a deed of 1197 of the house in Lapworth which Stigand the forester had occupied (Sir William Dugdale, *Antiquities of Warwickshire* (1730), 793).

Forest of Arden, in the Bishop's Wood (now 'Bushwood') which was appurtenant to his manor of Stratford and which may possibly be identified with 'Nuthurst' ('Hnuthyrste') – a woodland given to the bishop with Shottery in the eighth century.[10]

In areas of old settlement, too, population was evidently increasing. In the manor of Stratford, according to the Bishop's survey of 1182, the number of peasant landholders had nearly doubled since 1086; in addition to three cottars there were now some 42 villein tenants in Stratford, Shottery and Welcombe, holding between them 29 virgates apart from a few free tenants; three virgates were vacant.

Despite these signs of growth the manor of Stratford would appear still to have been wholly rural in character. Almost all the Bishop's tenants held in villeinage, and held the typical villein tenements of a virgate or half a virgate; about half of them held for a money rent of from 3*s*. to 4*s*. a virgate or from 1*s*. to 1*s*. 6*d*. a half virgate, and about half 'at works', owing three days labour each week on the lord's demesne in addition to a variety of other services and money payments. The manorial smith did all the necessary work on the demesne ploughs in return for his land, 'besides many other things as a grace'. There was still a manorial mill, now valued wholly in money at 36*s*. a year.[11]

Within a few years of this survey striking developments took place; Stratford became the scene of one of the many experiments made in the planning of new towns at the turn of the twelfth and thirteenth century. John de Coutances, Bishop of Worcester from 1196 to 1198, had not been long in office before he determined to found there a borough and market town. Doubtless he sensed the possibilities of this point at which the road striking off from the Fosse Way to Alcester and Droitwich crossed the river route between Evesham and Warwick; here, rather than at his neighbouring manor of Hampton, was the strategic site for a new town which might attract craftsmen and dealers and become a centre to meet the needs of the surrounding countryside, thus bringing added revenue to himself. On January 25th 1196 the Bishop obtained from King Richard I a charter for a weekly Thursday market at Stratford, thus securing the right to hold a market and to take for himself the profits accruing from it, such as rents for stalls and pitches, tolls on

10. Cf. Darby and Terrett, *ut supra*, 277 and V. C. H. Warwickshire III, *ut supra*, 261. Several other manors in the Avon and Feldon districts similarly held woodland some distance away in the Forest of Arden, as did Brailes, Wasperton and Wellesbourne (ibid. V. 168, 130. 112). These woodlands are, however, shown in the Domesday Woodlands map in Darby and Terrett (*ut supra* 292) not in the Forest but, somewhat misleadingly, in the manors to which they were appurtenant.
11. *The Red Book, ut supra*, 260–2, and 276–8 for definition of services, which are the same as for the manor of Hampton.

goods bought or sold, and dues for the use of standard measures. Markets had, indeed, been held in many places from time immemorial, by prescription rather than by charter, but more and more the Crown, ever seeking new sources of income, was insisting that the market was a royal prerogative, though one which could be conveyed, for a consideration, to a subject. If only for this reason it was as well to ask royal permission at the outset rather than to risk incurring a heavy fine later, or even the suppression of the market.[12] With his market rights assured, the Bishop formally created his borough, laying it out in uniform building plots, or 'burgages', to be held by burgage tenure at a money rent of 1s. a year, payable quarterly, in lieu of all services; at the same time he promised the 'burgesses' who should occupy them freedom from toll 'according to the custom of Breteuil'– the little Norman town whose customs were taken as the model for many of the new boroughs founded in England after the Conquest. Dugdale, writing his *Antiquities of Warwickshire* in 1730, had himself seen the original deed of foundation, now apparently no longer extant, in a cupboard among the episcopal archives at Worcester, and it is to him that we are indebted for our knowledge of it. He tells us, after describing the market charter, that the Bishop 'by his own deed, reciting the said charter of Richard, bestowed on his burgesses of Stratford (for by that name he calls them) the inheritance of their burgages, paying yearly for each of them to himself and his successors 12d. for all services at four times of the year viz. Michaelmas, the Nativity of Christ, Easter, and the Nativity of St John the Baptist, to each of which burgages he thereby allowed three perches and a half in breadth and twelve perches in length, that they should be free of toll for ever according to the custom of Bristol [sic],[13] excommunicating all those persons who should presume to make violation of these their privileges'. All this, Dugdale adds, the next bishop confirmed, while at the end of King John's reign (in 1214) Bishop Walter Grey obtained the grant of a fair on the eve of the Trinity to continue for two days.[14]

What success attended the Bishop's venture? How many burgages came into being? Who took them up? And how did the burgesses make their living? Who, in fact, was prepared to pay 1s. a year for

12. For the great increase in chartered markets at this time see G. H. Tupling, 'Markets and fairs in medieval Lancashire', *Essays in Honour of James Tait* (1933).
13. 'Bristoll' should no doubt be 'Breteuil'; see M. Bateson, 'The Laws of Breteuil', *English Historical Review*, XV (1900), 513. The date of the market charter is that given in Dugdale.
14. Dugdale, *ut supra*, 680, quoting in each case '*ex autog. in Armario Wigorn. Episc.*', and Charter Roll 16 John, m. 7.

a mere quarter acre of land,[15] when a whole virgate (perhaps some 30 acres of arable, with rights in meadow, wood, and pasture) could be had for 3*s.* or 4*s.*? What was the relation of the new borough to the old manor? By good fortune answers, even if not complete answers, to these and many other questions can be obtained from a remarkably detailed survey made half a century after the founding of the borough for one of John de Coutances' successors, Bishop Walter de Cantilupe, in the fifteenth year of his pontificate, i.e. in 1251–52. The original survey, like that of 1182, has disappeared, and it is known to us by a transcript which is to be found bound up with a variety of other documents printed by Sir Thomas Phillipps at his Middle Hill Press between 1840 and 1850.[16] Presumably the original itself was once among Sir Thomas Phillipps' papers; just possibly it may even yet be traced.

The transformation that had come over the Bishop's estate at Stratford during the first half of the thirteenth century is at once here apparent. For the survey of 1251–52 is divided into two distinct parts, each with its heading, separately, but similarly, dated, and each with its concluding, but totally different, list of jurors who had sworn to its veracity. The first part is entitled 'Extent of the Manor of Old Stratford' (*Extenta Manerii de Veteri Stratford*); the second, 'Extent of the Borough of Stratford' (*Extenta Burgi de Stratford*).[17] In the first part comes an account of the Bishops' demesne lands – arable (220½ acres), meadow, woodland, pasture, mills and fisheries, followed by a list of tenants holding by knight service, of free tenants, customary tenants, and cottars; there are sub-headings for Shottery and Welcombe, as in the preceding survey, and there is a new one for Lapworth, where there had evidently been further forest clearance since six tenants (one described as 'le wodeward') now held assarts there, paying 24*s* 6*d.* a year. Altogether some 70 tenants are listed in this section – a considerable increase since 1182. Between 50 and 60 of them were customary tenants holding in villeinage the typical virgate, half virgate, or occasionally quarter virgate. Appended to the name of the first customary tenant is a long and detailed account of what was due for each virgate. The

---

15. Not half an acre as in Levi Fox, ut supra, 36.
16. British Museum Tab. 436 b.y (10): *Sir Thomas Phillips Tracts: Topography and Genealogy 2: Hampshire-Warwickshire*, Middle Hill Press *c.* 1840–50, unpaged. Reprinted in *The Red Book, ut supra*, 471–97.
17. The whole survey had sometimes been erroneously referred to simply as '*Extenta Manerii de Veteri Stratford*', e.g. by Philip Styles in *V. C. H. Warwickshire III, ut supra*, 221–2, 247, even when the second part is being quoted. Levi Fox also twice refers to it as a 'survey of the manor' when quoting the second part, though once he speaks of it as 'a survey of Stratford (*Extenta Burgi de Stratford*) made for Bishop Walter de Cantilupe in the year 1252' (op. cit. 17, 34, 68). Both authors date the survey 1252.

services were many and onerous. For each virgate the villeins owed one day's work a week from Michaelmas to June 24th, and four days, with one man to assist, from June 24th to Michaelmas, in addition to a multitude of other miscellaneous dues and services and a money rent of 2*s*.11*d*. a year. Should the lord not wish to exact labour services he could, at his pleasure, take in lieu a money rent only; this was now fixed at 8*s*. a virgate, i.e. at about twice the level of that of 1182 – a significant pointer to the pressure of population on land; in addition to this the tenant was still liable for various tolls and other customary payments. There was still a manorial smith, holding half a virgate in return for work on two ploughs and another piece of land for work on a third plough. Here then is the traditional 'classic manor', with demesne and villein services, appropriately called from this time on '*Old* Stratford' – a name which has puzzled some historians.[18]

In sharp antithesis to 'The Manor of Old Stratford' stands that new creation 'The Borough of Stratford'. The second part of the survey – *Extenta Burgi de Stratford* – consists of a single long list of the names of 'burgesses', with the holding of each and the annual rent due. Appended to the first name, that of Robert le Tanur, is a detailed account of the conditions of tenure. They are simple indeed compared with those of the customary tenants on the manor. Robert le Tanur is described as holding one burgage (*burgagium*) by service of 12*d*., payable quarterly at Christmas, Easter, the Nativity of St John the Baptist, and Michaelmas; and he owes suit 'to the court of the borough' (*ad curiam burgi*) at the three lawmoots, i.e. at the first court after Michaelmas, the feast of St Hilary, and Hock Day[19] respectively, and at other times when summoned. At the end of the list is a note to the effect that all the 'burgesses' named (*omnes supradicti burgenses*) owe the same suit to the court of the borough, and in the same manner, as Robert le Tanur. The length of the list is impressive. It contains the names of no less than 234 tenants,[20] holding between them some 250 burgages, 54 pieces of ground (*placea* or *placea terrae*), 14 shopa (*solda*), 10 stalls (*stalla*), 2 ovens (*furnum*), and 2 dyepans (*tinctorium*). Only two of these

18. See, e.g. the section on Stratford-upon-Avon by Philip Styles in *V. C. H. Warwickshire*, III, *ut supra*, 221. Mr Styles notes that the term 'Old Stratford' is first mentioned in the 13th century survey, while in that of 1182 'the manor is described simply as Stratford'; he suggests, however, that the term 'was probably used to distinguish the chief manor from the various sub-manors which by then had been formed out of it'. Mary Bateson was nearer the truth when she wrote, over sixty years ago, 'Old Stratford may well have been the original 'old' town', and 'Stratford-on-Avon seems to have been cut out of Old Stratford' (Mary Bateson, *ut supra*, 340).
19. The second Tuesday after Easter.
20. One of the names in the list of 'burgesses' is that of 'the Altar of the Blessed Mary'; all the others are those of persons.

names occur also in the survey of the manor. Hence it is apparent that the total number of the Bishop's tenants in Stratford, manor and borough, now exceeded 300 – a sixfold increase in half a century, and that a new and quite distinct community had come into existence in the borough: a community (if we measure by the number of tenants holding directly from the Bishop) more than three times as large as that of the manor, though this too had much increased since 1182. The total population of the borough may well, at a very conservative estimate, have been in the region of a thousand, thus perhaps approximating to that of Warwick, and exceeding that of Worcester, at the time of Domesday. The Bishop's bold enterprise had been amply rewarded; his burgages had proved a most attractive proposition.

The survey of 1251–52 thus makes it abundantly clear that Bishop John de Countances had partitioned his estate, cutting out of it a portion to be known henceforth as the Borough of Stratford, with its uniform burgage tenements held for a money rent only, and its separate borough court, while the remainder continued as the manor of Old Stratford with its villein tenants liable for their labour services, tolls, and other dues, and its separate court of the manor. The borough was not coextensive with the manor – the total holdings of the burgesses amounted only to some 60–70 acres; nor had the bishop's villeins been converted wholesale into burgesses, as has sometimes been suggested.[21]

In doing this the Bishop was only following the fashion of his day. As Mary Bateson noticed long ago in those penetrating and suggestive articles which in fact contain much more than a discussion of the problem of the laws of Breteuil, many of the boroughs founded at this time 'look as if they had been cut out of townships'. And she observes that this is probably what happened at Stratford.[22] In a similar manner Hugh de Gondeville (*circa* 1180–84) created a little borough not far from Stratford that came to be called 'Chipping' (or 'market') Campden to distinguish it from the manor.[23] So, too, Maurice Paynell carved a borough out of his manor of Leeds in 1207, with thirty building plots on each side of a wide street leading up from the Aire crossing, on the outskirts of the existing village.[24] What remained of the old rural manor with its fields, pastures, meadows, and dwellings was sometimes distinguished from the borough by the suffix 'Old', as at Stratford, while sometimes it, or the borough, acquired a wholly different name; thus at Tavistock

21. E.g. by Levi Fox, op. cit.,16.
22. See p. 56, note 18.
23. P. C. Rushen, *Chipping Campden* (undated) pp. 2, 3, 16.
24. G. Woledge, 'The Medieval Borough of Leeds', *Thoresby Society Miscellany*, XXXVII, Pt. III (1944), 288 *et seq.*

the Abbot's new borough retained the name of Tavistock (as it could hardly fail to do since it was apparently on the actual site of the original vill), and what remained of the manor was called after his demesne farm – 'the manor of Hurdwick'.[25]

The very large number of burgage holders at Stratford makes it evident that the great majority of them cannot have sprung from families already on the manor. Whence then had they come? On this problem, too, much can be learnt from the survey of 1251–2. It is, of course, true that not all those described as burgesses and holding burgage tenements were necessarily themselves resident in Stratford. No doubt here as elsewhere an active market had developed in burgages and some must have been held merely as investments. Nevertheless, though strictly speaking the list tells us only who were the tenants holding burgages 'in chief' from the Bishop, not who were the occupants of the burgages, it would be unreasonable not to regard it as reflecting to a considerable degree the composition and character of the new community. What then can it tell us of the origin of the immigrants? Virtually all the burgesses are described, as the tenants of 1182 were not, by both a Christian name and a second name. More than a third of the second names are place names preceded by '*de*', and almost all of the places prove to be within 16 miles of Stratford. While it is likely that those few Stratford burgesses who were called after places further afield than this had not come directly thence, in the case of the great majority of place names it would seem probable that we have in fact the name of the place from which the burgess himself, or his father, or just possibly his grandfather, had come. If this is so, then we have here a very fair sample of the origin of the immigrants.

A detailed analysis of the list shows that 82 burgesses have place surnames, and that if we exclude names such as 'de la Grave', 'de la Waude', 'de Bosco', 57 different places occur, some of them more than once. We may identify at least 47 of these places with a fair degree of certainty; 26 of them prove to be (as the crow flies) within 6 miles of Stratford, 31 within 8 miles, 33 within 10 miles, 37 within 12 miles, 40 within 14 miles, 42 within 16 miles, and only 5 outside the 16 mile radius (Figure 1). Most of the ten places which cannot be certainly identified are probably close to Stratford, for several of the names are those of small hamlets like Greenhill, Sydenham, and Wike, of which there are more than one in the immediate vicinity. It is noticeable that none of the burgesses were called after the two ancient boroughs in the immediate neighbourhood of Stratford – Warwick (8 miles away) and Alcester (7 miles away). These towns were no doubt attracting immigrants themselves, as perhaps were

25. H. P. R. Finberg, 'The Borough of Tavistock: its origin and early history', W. G. Hoskins and H. P. R. Finberg, *Devonshire Studies* (1952), 176.

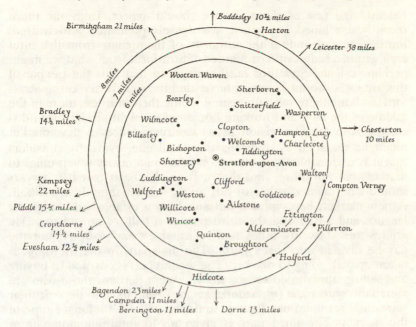

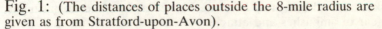

Fig. 1: (The distances of places outside the 8-mile radius are given as from Stratford-upon-Avon).

those villages within a few miles of Stratford which had gained market charters by the mid-thirteenth century, like Bidford (1220), Henley-in-Arden (1220), Kineton (1220), Aston Cantlow (1227), Snitterfield (1242), and Wellesbourne Hastings (1246). Of all these only Snitterfield appears among the Stratford surnames.[26] Indeed within the 16 miles radius the only market towns to appear in the list of surnames are Evesham and Chipping Campden.[27] Outside the 16 miles radius we can identify among the surnames Kempsey (22 miles), Birmingham (22), Bagendon (32),[28] Leicester (38) and possibly Southwell (69),[29] while one of the burgesses appears to have been Irish in Origin ('le Yreis').

Judging then from our sample of place surnames it would appear that some 90 per cent of those who took up Stratford burgages came from little villages and hamlets within a 16 mile radius; most of them were from ancient settlement areas in the Avon valley and in the

26. It is just possible that 'Wells' may represent Wellesbourne Hastings.
27. If 'Campden' may be identified as Chipping Campden.
28. Probably the correct identification of 'Bagingedone', which is found as 'Bagingedon' in the thirteenth century.
29. 'Suwelle'.

Feldon, and few of them, as we should expect, from the more recently developed and much less densely populated Arden area. Further, it is clear that the majority of them came from the rural area within a radius of 6 or 8 miles of Stratford, from what we might perhaps call the Stratford market area, in that it is the people of this area who would regularly have used the weekly market at Stratford, walking there in the morning, doing their business there in the middle of the day, and walking home before nightfall. Bracton, discussing with legal precision in what circumstances a new market might be regarded as injurious to an old one, evidently considers that it is reasonable for a man to expect to go nearly seven miles to market, but not more, and that it is on this basis that the lawyers should determine whether or not a new market should be allowed. A new market, he says, is a nuisance if it is established 'within six leagues and a half and the third part of a half' of an old one. He argues thus: 'Twenty miles is a reasonable "day" (*dieta*). Let the day be divided into three parts. The first part, in the morning, is taken up with going to market. The second part is devoted to buying and selling; this should suffice for all except perhaps those who are merchants with stalls (*mercatores stallati*), who have to deposit their wares and set them out for sale and who will need a longer time in the market. The third part is given up to returning home from market, and all this must be done in the daytime and not at night, for fear of ambushes and attacks by robbers, so that all shall be in safety.'[30] In other words, a man would not normally wish to deal with a market more than 6–7 miles from home. Within this distance he could be sure of getting there and back by daylight, even in the shortest days of winter. Two markets on the same day 13 or 14 miles apart would therefore scarcely be in competition with each other, for each would draw its regular customers from a different area. There was in fact no other Thursday market within 20 miles of Stratford, except for one which was granted to Feckenham in 1237, and this was moved to a Saturday in 1253.

What had lured these many immigrants into the Bishop's new borough? It is clear that they cannot have come as agricultural colonists for, as we have seen, they had no holdings in the fields; and though a burgess might keep pigs and poultry, and perhaps a cow, and grow fruit and vegetables on what was left of his quarter-acre burgage after a house had been built on it, to pay rent at 4s. an acre for such a purpose was scarcely a tempting proposition. Here again the survey of 1251–2 is illuminating. A first reading of the list of borough tenants after that of tenants on the manor at once gives

---

30. Bracton, *De Legibus*, ed. Geo. E. Woodbine (Newhaven: Yale University Press, 4 vols. 1915–1942), III, 198, (f.235b). If Bracton's 'league' is here a two-mile league, as it seems to be, he suggests that a new market would be a nuisance if established within 13⅓ miles.

the impression of a community of traders and artisans, in sharp contrast to that of the manor. Out of all the 234 burgesses 64 have occupational surnames compounded (unless they are in Latin) of 'the' or '*le*' with a word descriptive of a trade or profession. At this date these surnames must almost always, if not invariably, indicate the occupation of the burgess himself or at least that of one of his immediate forbears. Here, surely, we have a very fair sample of the trades practised by Stratford burgesses within half a century of the borough's foundation.

Most of the occupational names are those of artisans, and of such artisans as would be concerned with supplying the essential goods and services required by Stratford and the rural 'market area' round it. None suggests the production of luxury goods – there is no sign of a goldsmith, for example – and no one trade is more prominent than the others, which suggests that there was little if any specialisation in one particular product for sale over a wider area. Stratford, in fact, was a very ordinary market town.

Most prominent are what might be called the clothing trades – those concerned with leather working and cloth working, for both of which the raw material was ready to hand in the hides and wool produced from the sheep and cattle in the surrounding countryside. Six burgesses are described as tanners (*le tanur*) and while some of them appear to be wealthy men, like Richard le Tanur holding 4 burgages, 2 half burgages and a piece of ground, some are of more modest means, holding only a half or quarter burgage. Two are described as shoemakers (*sutor*), and the Stratford glovemakers, famous in the sixteenth century, not only because Shakespeare's father was a glover, were already in evidence, for there are two burgesses called *le waunter*. A *parmentarius*, too, probably worked in skins. Clothmaking is represented by two men described as weavers (*textor, le webbe*); two as fullers (*fullo, le fulur*); and three as dyers (*tinctor*). There are three tailors (*le tailleur*) concerned, no doubt, with making up, altering, and selling clothes new and secondhand. That fulling and dyeing were carried on in Stratford is also shown by the mention of a fulling-mill in the survey of the manor, and of two dyepans (*tinctoria*) in the survey of the borough, held at rents of 3*d*. and 2*d*. respectively by two men who each have in addition a half burgage. Thus Stratford could supply clothing of all sorts, including shoes and gloves.

Different kinds of metal-working are indicated by three men called whitesmith (*albus faber*), two of whom share a shop (*solda*) while the other holds four burgages and two half burgages; by two men called smith (*faber*), and one called locksmith ('Adam the Lokiere'). Woodworking and the building trades are represented by one carpenter (*carpentarius*), three tilers (*le teler*), four coopers ('cooper', *le cuverer, le cupere*), and one wheelwright (*rotarius*).

Among the less common productive industries there are already signs of the oil-making that gave its name to Ely Street in the surname, occurring twice, of 'Ylger' or 'Ylgier'; there was an oil mill ('ullemylle') in Ely Street at least by the early fifteenth century,[31] and perhaps these oil-makers were using nuts from the Bishop's wood. There is also a woman rope-maker, 'Alice the roperes'.[32]

The food trades are represented by one man called butcher (*le fleshmonger*), one called baker (*le furner*), one called cook (*cocus*), and two called miller (*molendinarius*). There is also mention of two ovens for which rents of 1s. and 1s. 6d. were paid. The mills, as we have seen, were still a part of the manor, not the borough, and instead of the one mill ('*molendinum*') worth 36s. mentioned in 1182 there were now four mills – three for grinding corn in one building, and one fullingmill ('*molendinum fulerez*') in another; the four were farmed out at £13. 6*s*. 8*d*.

That entertainment was not lacking in Stratford even in its early days is suggested by the surname 'le Piper' and by 'Iseude Jugleur', and among miscellaneous trades and professions mentioned are those of butler (*le buteiller, pincerna*), beadle (*le bedel*), chamberlain (*camerarius*), doctor (*medicus*), clerk (*clericus*), parson (*persona*), palmer (*le palmer*), carter (*carectarius*), and farrier (*marescallus*).

It is impossible to be certain whether *le mercer* implies a general merchant or, more narrowly, one trading in mercery, but general merchants no doubt there were, dealing in all manner of commodities, among those with family or place names. By 1270 at least there was at any rate one grocer, William le Spicer, and one skinner, William Pelliparius, who probably dealt in skins as well as making them up.[33]

The striking contrast between these burgess names – the majority compounded of place-names or occupational names – and those of the manorial tenants further emphasises the distinction between the two communities: the one rural and ancient, with its roots stretching far back into the past; the other urban and modern, composed of diverse folk drawn together from many places. The manorial tenants have, it is true, surnames, as most of them had not in 1182, when many were just plain Alured, Eynulf, Frewin, Teodulf and so forth, though if the name was a common one they were often further described as, for instance, 'William son of Lothair' was distinguished

31. *V. C. H. Warwickshire*. III, *ut supra*, 222.
32. The ropemakers had their stalls in Bridge Street in the 17th century, ibid., 237. That Alice was not alone in following this occupation may be seen from the mention of Walter the ropemaker (*cordarius*) in a deed of *c*. 1235 relating to land in High Street, F. C. Wellstood, Calendar of Medieval Records belonging to the Mayor and Corporation of Stratford-upon-Avon (1941, unpublished manuscript in the custody of the Shakespeare Birthplace Trustees).
33. Calendar of Medieval Records, *ut supra* note 2, deeds of *circa* 1270.

from 'William son of Hereward', and 'Adam son of Tinbert' from 'Adam de Shottery'. But at least a third of the 70 manorial tenants listed in 1251–2 were called after one or other parent, as were 'Alured son of Eynulf' and 'Thomas son of Cicely', while in the borough only three out of 233 were so described. Only eight (six of them free tenants) had surnames compounded of place-names. Only seven (or ten if we include the reeve, the hayward and the wood-ward) had occupational surnames; three of these – a weaver (*le webbe*), a fisherman (*piscator*), and a clerk (*clericus*), were cottars; the remainder include the manorial smith, a second weaver, a second fisherman ('the fissere'), and a falconer (*le faukoner*), each with half or quarter acre holdings. Some were known by nicknames like 'Fayrher', 'le Large', or 'the Newman', while a very few have what seem to be established family names, as had Adam Mogge and Alice Bardolf – whose family must surely still have been there in Shakespeare's day. This is very different from the borough, where those with no established family name – some two-thirds of the whole – were almost invariably called after either a place or a trade; in so new a community parentage was of little account. Thus the borough was distinguished from the manor not only by the legal differences associated with burgage tenure, burgess status, and a borough court, but also by its almost completely different personnel and economic functions. A wholly new urban settlement had grown up along side the village; its people were mainly immigrants recruited from the surrounding countryside, and they lived primarily not by agriculture but by trade and industry.

The commercial and industrial character of the borough is also shown by the mention here and there in the survey of a shop (*solda*) or a stall (*stalla*). There were altogether 14 shops (*soldae*). For some a rent of 1*s.* a year was payable, for others 8*d.* or 4*d.*, whereas for each of ten stalls no more than 2*d.* was charged. Whatever the precise meaning of the word *solda* at this time, it clearly implied something more substantial than a mere movable stall or the site on which one could be erected. Such stalls would be used not only by Stratford people but by outside folk – Bracton's *mercatores stallati*, who, when they came to market, needed to set out their wares on a stand, unlike the dealers in sheep and cattle, corn and wool.[34]

If neither 'shop' nor 'stall' can be precisely defined, we are more fortunate in the case of 'burgage'. As we have seen, when the Bishop created his borough he planned a wholly new town and laid it out in uniform building plots, allowing to each 'burgage' 3½ per-ches in breadth and 12 perches in length. Each burgage thus had a frontage of almost 60 feet and stretched back nearly 200 feet from the street, giving an area of 1270½ square yards, or rather more

34. Cf. supra, p. 60.

than a quarter of an acre. In thus standardising his building sites the Bishop was conforming to the general practice of those who founded new boroughs, though the actual size varied from borough to borough. The street frontage of the Stratford plots, for instance, was slightly wider than that allotted by Maurice Paynell for his borough at Leeds.[35]

With a site of this magnitude a tenant would have space enough, should he also have the means and the inclination, to erect a house comparable to many of the modest manor houses then going up in England, with an entrance passage and several rooms – including a hall – on the ground floor facing the street, and perhaps other buildings round a garden or courtyard behind. A fourteenth-century burgess house of this description can still be seen not far from Stratford at Chipping Campden; it was built by the wool merchant William Grevel, and was even more extensive than one on a Stratford burgage could have been, but then Grevel was 'the flower of the wool merchants of all England' in his day.[36]

Doubtless only the wealthiest burgesses in Stratford, as in Chipping Campden, could have afforded houses of anything like this size. Burgages, however, with their wide frontages, lent themselves readily to subdivision into two, three, or four dwellings, each with its own front door on the street. Perhaps at Stratford there was some such rule as at Preston in Lancashire, that a tenant could qualify as being of burgess status provided he held a street frontage of at least 12 feet;[37] even this would give room for the building of quite a sizeable town house, particularly if it had more than the two storeys which was all that most manor houses of the period achieved. Many a wealthy merchant in England's leading commercial cities was content with such a frontage. In the High Street at Bristol, for instance, the Chesters' house, rebuilt in the fifteenth century, had a width of only 10 feet 5 inches, but this allowed for a shop on the ground floor, a hall over it with an oriel window, a chamber on the second floor, also with an oriel window, and yet another chamber above this, while the house stretched back behind the street nearly 20 feet.[38] But even in Bristol not all streets were as built up as the ancient and congested High Street. In suburbs such as Redcliffe merchants' houses were more rural in character, with a generous

35. Woledge, *ut supra* p. 57, note 24, 293–4. The street frontages allotted to burgages in newly-created boroughs varied from 1 to 4 perches, or even more, while the depth of the burgages varied from 5 to as many as 24 perches. The plots were usually, but not invariably, uniform within a single borough.
36. See the inscription on his brass at Chipping Campden. On the planning of town houses see W. A. Pantin, 'Medieval English Town-House Plans', *Medieval Archaeology*, VI–VII (1962–3).
37. M. Bateson, *ut supra* p. 50, note I. 503.
38. E. M. Carus-Wilson, *Medieval Merchant Venturers* (1954), 76.

allowance of ground and a lofty open-roofed hall and other buildings grouped around a courtyard. Such was the house to which the Canynges family in the fifteenth century added a new and up-to-date wing fifty feet long, with four bay-windows.[39] The spacious lay-out of Stratford clearly made it possible to build houses of this kind when a whole burgage was retained in the hands of one man, and even the centre of the town must always have been as well provided with trees and gardens as it was in Shakespeare's day.

How then were the Stratford burgages distributed in 1251–2? As we have seen, there were altogether 234 'burgesses' holding between them some 250 burgages, besides shops, stalls, 'places', ovens and dyepans. Inevitably there were inequalities of wealth, even among the burgesses, let alone among the many servants, apprentices and mere labourers who could not aspire to burgess status, and whose very names are unknown to us. Yet few considerable concentrations of property appear in the survey. The largest burgage holder was Richard de Bagendon holding 'many burgages and places' and paying a rent of 18*s.*, equivalent to 18 burgages. Next in importance was Richard Warner, holding 5 burgages, 8 half-burgages, 5 shops, a stall, a place, and a share in an oven held jointly with Rosa Manning; Rosa held also 5 burgages and 2 half-burgages. Almost as important were Richard de Pydele holding 4 burgages, 4 half-burgages, and 2 stalls; John the Whitesmith with 4 burgages and 2 half-burgages, and Richard the Tanner with 4 burgages, 2 half-burgages and a place; 29 other burgesses held from 2 to 4 burgages each. Of the remaining burgesses, 66 held single burgages, in some cases sharing one with another burgess; 67 held half a burgage each, again in some cases sharing with another; two held two-thirds of a burgage each; five one-third each ; and one a quarter of a burgage. Some held only a place, a shop or two, or a stall. Thus the majority of the burgesses held only a single burgage or less.

It is noteworthy that more than two-thirds of the original burgages remained undivided in 1251–2, and that most of the rest were split only into half. Indeed many whole or half burgages remained intact long after then, and even at the present day the Bishop's building plots may still be traced on a $1/2500$ ordnance survey map or by perambulating the streets of his borough; their outlines are unmistakable. Such is the site of Mason's Court in Rother Street, now split into two tenements. From the existing building on this site – a half-timbered building which certainly goes back to the fifteenth century – a good idea may be obtained of the lay-out and character of one of the larger burgess houses of Stratford in the middle ages. Along the street frontage this house has a central hall of one 14-foot bay, originally open from ground to roof, with a through passage cut

39. Ibid., 75.

off one end of it, leading to the courtyard behind, a south wing on one side of the hall about 12 feet wide, and a north wing on the other side of two 13½ feet bays, making a total frontage of about 53 feet.[40]

Other Stratford houses also still perpetuate the outlines of the original burgages as, for example, does 'The Five Gables' in Chapel Street (formerly Corn Street), with its five approximately 12-foot bays, making a frontage of some 60 feet. The Shakespeare Hotel next door, with which it is now incorporated, is also about 60 feet wide – i.e. the width allowed by Bishop for one of his burgage plots (Figure 2). Adjoining the Shakespeare Hotel, at the corner of Chapel Street and Sheep Street, the modern Town Hall occupies the site of yet another burgage, once owned by Hugh Clopton, younger son of the lord of the manor of Clopton, close to Stratford, who made his fortune as a Merchant Adventurer and was chosen Lord Mayor of London in 1491. At the other end of Chapel Street, on the corner of Walker Street, we can still discern the burgage plot on which Hugh built for himself that 'praty house of brike and tymbar'– New Place – which so attracted Shakespeare a century later that he bought it and made it his home.

As we may trace the outlines of the Bishop's burgages in Stratford today, and gain some impression of their size and form, so too we may trace the outlines of the streets he planned, noting as we do so how broad and spacious they were; the principal ones were 50–60 feet wide, or even more (see Figure 2). Bridge Street, leading up from the great bridge over the Avon, was as much as 90 feet at its widest, but this was the main shopping street, as was Bridge Street at Leeds. Down the centre of it was a block of shops – or perhaps originally stalls which were gradually converted into more permanent structures.[41] This was known as Middlerow, and it is here, and here alone, that shops are mentioned in surviving thirteenth century deeds. Sometimes the goods on sale there are also mentioned; thus we hear of the shops where meat was sold, or salt, or honey.[42] After Middlerow the street forked, dividing into the road leading towards Henley-in-Arden (Henley Street) and that leading to Alcester and thence to Worcester (Wood Street).

South of Bridge Street three roads branched off at right angles parallel to each other and to the river (Figure 2), while two cross-roads running east and west, parallel to Bridge Street, divided the space between them into four nearly rectangular blocks or *insulae*

40. *Victoria County History of Warwickshire*, III, *ut supra*, 230. Mason's Court is illustrated in Levi Fox, op. cit., Plate following p. 96. The great fires of 1594, 1595, and 1614 destroyed most of Stratford's medieval timbered buildings.
41. Cf. W. G. Hoskins, *Local History in England* (1959), 85, quoting Stow's *Survey of London*.
42. Calendar of Medieval Records, *ut supra*; deeds of *c.* 1260, 1275, 1285, etc.

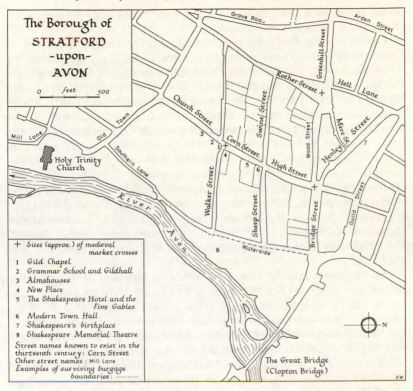

Fig. 2: *The Borough of Stratford-upon-Avon, from Ordnance Survey map as revised in 1938.*
(The area round the parish church of Holy Trinity, including most of Southern Lane and Old Town, was outside the borough until 1879: the borough's northern boundary ran from the river at Clopton Bridge along Guild Street, and its western boundary along Arden Street and Grove Road. Beyond, on each side, were the common fields).

as they would have been called by Roman planners. Indeed in the symmetry of their lay-out the thirteenth century town-planners were emulating their classical predecessors. Bridge Street and the two cross-roads parallel to it were nearly 400 feet distant from one another, thus giving room for the burgages, each of which, as we have seen, stretched back 12 perches (nearly 200 feet) from the

67

street front. Still today a clear demarcation line half way between these cross-roads is readily apparent.

Deeds now in the possession of the Mayor and Corporation of Stratford reveal that many of these streets still carry the names by which they were known in the thirteenth century, as for example do Bridge Street, High Street, Henley Street, Mere Street, Greenhill Street, Rother Street (i.e. the street where cattle were sold), Sheep Street – 'the street where sheep are sold',[43] and Church Street which leads away from the borough towards Old Stratford and the parish church of Holy Trinity.[44] The present Ely Street was then Swine Street or 'the street where pigs are sold',[45] Windsor Street was Hell Lane;[46] Chapel Street was originally Corn Street, where corn was sold;[47] while Chapel Lane was Walker Street – the street of the walkers, i.e. fullers, down which ran a brook that flowed into the Avon close to the present memorial theatre; later evidence records a walk-mill (i.e. fulling-mill) at the bottom of this street.[48] We read also in the thirteenth century of a street where hay was sold.[49]

As in most medieval towns, whether in England or on the continent, the fullers at Stratford tended to congregate together in one street where a supply of clear, fresh water was available near by, and where its use could be regulated. Otherwise there was comparatively little localisation of industry. Marketing, on the other hand, was highly localised, and instead of one general market-place a town of the size of Stratford set aside special places for the sale of the chief products brought in to the market, such as corn, hay, sheep, cattle, or pigs, as we may see from these thirteenth-century street names. In course of time at least three market crosses were erected; one – the High Cross, at the junction of Bridge Street and High Street, another – the White Cross, at the junction of Corn Street and Walker Street, and a third in Rother Street.[50] Thus on a

---

43. Ibid., a deed of *c.* 1260 refers to a tenement in 'Sheep Street' ('Scep strete'), and one of *c.* 1270 to a messuage *'in vico ubi bydentes venduntur'*
44. Ibid,. e.g. a deed of *c.* 1272.
45. Ibid, a deed of *c.* 1270 records a messuage *'in vico ubi porci venduntur'*, while a grant confirmed in 1277 speaks of 'Swynistret'. For the change of name from Swine Street to Ely Street see *supra*, p. 62.
46. Ibid., e.g. deeds of *c.* 1294, 1297/8
47. Ibid., e.g. deeds of *c.* 1265, *c.* 1270, *c.* 1285; for the change of name see *infra* p. 69.
   Ibid., grant confirmed in 1277; for the book see *Victoria County History of Warwickshire*, III, at *supra*, p. 222; for the fulling-mill see E. I. Fripp, *Shakepeare's Stratford* (1928), 42.
49. Calendar of Medieval Records, *ut supra*, deed of *c.* 1270.
50. *Victoria County History of Warwickshire*, III, *ut supra*, 222; the White Cross is mentioned in a thirteenth-century deed (Calendar, *ut supra*, deed of *c.* 1275), as is 'the street where hay is sold' (ibid *c.* 1270)

Thursday market day almost every corner of the borough must have been full of activity.

The 'great bridge' over the Avon, on the site of the ancient ford, had certainly been built by the early thirteenth century, if not before then, for in 1235 we hear of a house on the bridge and of a bridge keeper – 'Richard the Bridge-keeper'.[51] But as yet it was only a timber structure. Leland, after describing the 'sumptuose' 14-arch stone bridge and its stone causeway over the marshy land, built at the close of the fifteenth century by Hugh Clopton, and still one of the glories of Stratford today, remarks that before this time there was only 'a poore bridge of tymber, and no causey to come to it; whereby many poore folkys and othar refusyd to cum to Stratford when Avon was up, or coming thithar stood in jeopardy of lyfe'.[52]

Stratford's celebrated gild buildings at the corner of Church Street and Walker Street (now Chapel Lane) – the chapel of the Holy Cross, the grammar school and the guildhall that became the centre of the borough's government, date only from the end of the middle ages, but they replace earlier gild buildings. Part of the structure of the chapel is almost certainly thirteenth-century, going back at least to the time when Bishop Giffard granted a licence (in 1269) for building a chapel and a hospital of the Holy Cross.[53] And that the gild or fraternity of the Holy Cross, together with the hospital, had come into existence within half a century of the founding of the borough is clearly shown by two deeds now in the possession of the corporation. One, of about 1235, records a grant of lands 'to the Hospital of Jesus Christ and the Holy Cross of Stratford'; the other, attributed to the early thirteenth century, states that 'William Wade of Stratford' (one of the burgesses in the 1251–2 survey) granted the rent from a house in Henley Street 'to the Fraternity of the Holy Cross, for the souls of himself and his ancestors'.[54] A later roll of grants confirmed by Edward I in 1277 shows that many other burgesses listed in the 1251–2 survey gave lands, houses, or rents to the Fraternity, as John Whitesmith (holder of 4 burgages and 2 half-burgages) gave the rent of a piece of ground 'whereon Robert Billesley built a solar', between the land of John and Robert (holder of 1 burgage and 1 half-burgage).[55]

Thus within half a century of the borough's creation a new and vigorous community had developed, recruited from the surrounding

51. *Victoria County History of Warwickshire*, III, *ut supra*, 224, quoting a deed of 1235.
52. *The Itinenary of John Leland*, ed. Lucy Toulmin Smith, II (1908), 49–50, cf. 27.
53. *Victoria County History of Warwickshire*, III, *ut Supra*, 247, 276.
54. Calendar of Medieval Records, *ut supra*, deed of *c*. 1235 and of the early thirteenth century.
55. Ibid., grant confirmed in 1277.

countryside, for which it provided goods and services and a convenient market centre, and united in a fraternity which watched over the interests of its members in this world and the next. The earliest extant ordinances of the gild or fraternity of the Holy Cross, dating from 1269, come to us from ecclesiastical sources. They therefore reveal nothing of the part it must have played then, as it certainly did later, in the ordinary secular affairs of the borough. But they do tell us of its religious and charitable activities, such as were properly associated with the term fraternity, for these came within the jurisdiction of the church. Thus we learn of the chapel, where masses were to be said for the souls of all the faithful departed, as well as for those of members and their ancestors, and of the hospital with its common dormitory, refectory, and infirmary; here aid was to be given not only to needy brothers and sisters of the fraternity and to poor priests of the diocese, but also to 'the poor of the town'.[56] Stratford-upon-Avon had created its own welfare services. Perhaps its school also had already been established, though positive evidence of this dates only from the late thirteenth century.[57]

Editorial suggestions for further reading

Beresford M. W. 'The six new towns of the bishops of Winchester, 1200–1255', *Medieval Archaeology*, 3 (1959), 187–215.

Beresford M. W. *The New Towns of the Middle Ages* (Leicester, 1967).

McClure P. 'Patterns of migration in the later Middle Ages: the evidence of English place names', *Economic History Review*, 2nd ser., 32 (1979), 167–82.

---

56. J. Harvey Bloom, *The Register of the Gild of the Holy Cross, The Blessed Mary and St John the Baptist of Stratford-upon-Avon* (1907), v.
57. Levi Fox, op. cit. 88.

Chapter Five

SMALL TOWN SOCIETY IN ENGLAND BEFORE THE BLACK DEATH[1]

R. H. Hilton

Past and Present, no. 105 (1984)

The many market towns of medieval England, less well docu-
mented than the larger centres, are in consequence relatively little
known. The unusually abundant court records of the borough of
Halesowen yield a picture of life in one of these smaller towns.
Social structure in the medieval town is sometimes presented as a
static model; preferable is the approach exemplified here, in which
urban society is observed through the dynamic interrelationships of
its constituent elements. This approach has the merit of giving due
attention to such processes as the developing relationship between
lord and burgesses, the gradual assimilation of immigrants, or the
rise of a craftsman's family to office-holding status. To recognize
such processes is not, of course, to deny the existence of clear social
distinctions. Hilton draws attention in particular to tensions on the
margins of society manifested in criminal behaviour involving
recent immigrants to the town: outsiders were always suspects. Yet
evidence is presented also of collective endeavours by the town com-
munity: evidence which suggests that, from time to time, social
differences were overcome by the perceived need for common ac-
tion. In fact, however, Hilton does not develop here the theoretical
analysis for which he has called in his other article reprinted above
(Ch. 2). Further comparative study of small town society will
elucidate the processes touched on in this essay.

Charles Phythian-Adams recently observed that we need to be
reminded that in the pre-industrial English town the poor 'might represent almost a third of an urban parish's population and that these
people were every bit as much townsmen as the "middling sort"'.

1. This article develops in much greater detail some of the themes already sketched
   in my 'Lords, Burgesses and Hucksters', *Past and Present*, no. 97 (Nov.1982).
   Inevitably there is some repetition, but it is hoped not so much as to make this
   offering irrelevant.

He was referring to late sixteenth-century Warwick, but the comment would be valid for earlier periods, especially in a similar context of population pressure.[2] The nature of the documentation of the medieval town tends to focus our attention on the recognized classes – the mercantile élites, the organized crafts with their masters, apprentices and journeymen, the middling traders and the food processors. Bronislaw Geremek has shown us, for medieval Paris, how much of urban existence was not contained within these accepted structures. Paris, of course, was unique, with its large population of students and unbeneficed and alienated clergymen; but the London records contain enough hints of an impoverished and criminalized underworld to support Geremek's general argument.[3]

The problem also exists at the level of urban life represented by small towns with populations of 1000 or less – a substantial proportion of the total urban population. This we will attempt to illustrate. But one might also suggest that in spite of much writing about them, often of a rather antiquarian character, small towns tend to be a marginal element in the writing of urban history, almost analogous to the neglected marginal population of the big cities.

Small town records are very diverse in character, in some cases almost non-existent. For the most part they consist of charters of foundation, or grants of privilege, occasional surveys and rentals, property deeds and some information about chantries and religious gilds. Where the lord of the town happens to be a monastery or other ecclesiastical owner, there may be a well-kept cartulary with useful material about the town. The Evesham Abbey cartularies contain surveys and property deeds which illustrate the history of the borough of Evesham from the late twelfth century; and these are reinforced by similar material in the abbey chronicle. The bishop of Worcester's borough of Stratford-upon-Avon has a mid-thirteenth-century survey, well exploited by E. M. Carus-Wilson for defining its role in the regional economy; and for its later history there are the property deeds and accounts of the Holy Cross Gild of the fourteenth and fifteenth centuries. One of the earliest well-presented collections of documents for a small town was R. H. Gretton's *Burford Records*, but again mostly consisting of charters and property deeds for this interesting Oxfordshire borough. For High Wycombe

2. In *Midland Hist*, viii (1983), p. 175, reviewing A. L. Beier in Peter Clark (ed.), *Country Towns in Pre-Industrial England* (Leicester, 1981).
3. Bromslaw Geremek, *Les marginaux parisiens aux XIVe et XVe siecles*, trans. D. Beauvois (Paris, 1976); one need go no further than the *Calendar of Plea and Memoranda Rolls of the City of London*, ed. A. H. Thomas, 2 vols. (Cambridge, 1926–9) for evidence about the London marginals.

we have a slightly different insight into small town life with its collection of ordinances.[4]

This type of material can, if one is fortunate, be reinforced by materials from national records, such as the pre-1334 lay subsidy returns, the later poll tax returns and the early sixteenth-century subsidies. But there can be little doubt that continuous series of records of borough courts would be likely to provide the best information covering a wide social spread. For the evidences already mentioned – surveys, charters and deeds – inevitably inform us primarily about the better off members of these urban communities. There is, of course, the possibility that the court records might also reflect mainly the doings of the better off. But if leet jurisdiction and proceedings against breaches of the assize of bread and ale (as well as of other foodstuffs) are included, the social groups covered are immediately widened. However, even where they are, the results can still be somewhat disappointing, as in the case of the Henley Assembly Books which do not begin until the fifteenth century.[5]

Small town society is therefore less well understood than that of the manor and village. The accounts, extents and especially the court records of the medieval English manor are unique in Europe. Pioneers like Maitland and Vinogradoff laid the foundations for a remarkable tradition of agrarian history. Perhaps the full interest of the court rolls themselves, as providing a continuous, year-in-year-out record of individuals, was not fully appreciated by the pioneers. Yet the published work of the Toronto school and more recently of Zvi Razi has shown how remarkable an insight into village life can be derived from a detailed analysis of the manorial court rolls, even when, as in the case of Halesowen studied by Razi, there is virtually no ancillary manorial or estate documentation.[6]

Seigneurial boroughs (mostly 'small towns') can, by the accident of survival among estate records, sometimes present us with an opportunity for the same sort of examination of small urban communities as has been done for the manor and village. At this

4. R. H. Hilton, 'The Small Town and Urbanization: Evesham in the Middle Ages', *Midland Hist.*, vii (1982); R. H. Hilton, *A Medieval Society: The West Midlands at the End of the Thirteenth Century* (London, 1966; repr. Past and Present Pubns., Cambridge, 1983), pp. 190–2; E. M. Carus-Wilson, 'The First Half-Century of the Borough of Stratford-upon-Avon', *Econ. Hist.* Rev., 2nd ser., xviii (1965); R. H. Gretton, *Burford Records: A study in Minor Town Government* (Oxford, 1920); *The First Ledger Book of High Wycombe*, ed. R. W. Greaves (Buckinghamshire Rec. Soc., xi, Welwyn Garden City, 1956).

5. *Henley Borough Records: Assembly Books, 1395–1543*, ed. P. M. Briers (Oxfordshire Rec. Soc., xli, Oxford, 1956).

6. Z. Razi, *Life, Marriage and Death in a Medieval Parish: Economy, Society and Demography in Halesowen, 1270–1400* (Past and Present Pubns., Cambridge, 1980) is primarily a demographic study of the manor of Halesowen. It is not concerned with the borough.

point we must put on one side J. A. Raftis's attempt to establish the well-documented ancient demesne manor of Godmanchester as a 'small town model'. As a reviewer has correctly noted, this analysis of a community 'largely dependent on agriculture', in which the author ignores the role of the market, makes the application of such a model more than doubtful.[7] Much earlier, H. G. Wood used the borough court records of Tamworth (straddling Staffordshire and Warwickshire) in an attempt to illustrate its fourteenth and fifteenth-century history, but unfortunately not pursuing the matter very far.[8] The present author has made some investigation of the earl of Gloucester's (later earl of Stafford's) borough of Thornbury, near Bristol. These records, though more detailed than those of Tamworth, are unfortunately by no means so continuous. They begin only in 1324, sixty years or so after the borough's foundation, and cover only four full and two partial years before the Black Death. They improve in the late fourteenth and fifteenth centuries and naturally offer important information for the period of supposed urban decline. This period is also interestingly illuminated for Newmarket by Peter May, who makes good use of an unfortunately short run of market court records (1399–1413), backed up by the evidence of detailed fifteenth-century account rolls.[9]

How useful, then, would be an opportunity to look at a small town in a period of urban growth and of population pressure analogous to that of the sixteenth century. This is, in fact, provided by the borough of Halesowen, a mid-thirteenth-century foundation set within an already well-documented manor whose boundaries coincided with a large parish containing a dozen hamlets. Halesowen was in Shropshire from the twelfth to the nineteenth centuries, when it was transferred to Worcestershire (1844). It was part of the wooded Birmingham plateau and (in the thirteenth and fourteenth centuries) already connected by trading relations with the other growing small town of Birmingham. It was also near to the Stour and Severn valleys and was in contact with the trading route which went from Coventry through Bromsgrove and Droitwich to Worcester. This northern part of the west midlands region illustrates a

---

7. J. A. Raftis, *A Small Town in Medieval England: Godmanchester, 1278–1400* (Toronto, 1980). This work by the inspirer of the Toronto school concentrates on family and custom. The review referred to is by J. M. Cooper in *History*, lxviii (1983), pp. 499–500. For a critique of the methods of the Toronto school, see Z. Razi, 'The Toronto School's Reconstitution of Medieval Peasant Society: A Critical View', *Past and Present*, no. 85 (Nov. 1979).

8. H. G. Wood, *Medieval Tamworth* (Tamworth, 1972)

9. The Thornbury borough court rolls are deposited in the Staffordshire County Record Office, Stafford. See R. H. Hilton, 'Towns in English Feudal Society', in *Class Conflict and the Crisis of Feudalism* (London, 1984); Hilton, 'Lords, Burgesses and Hucksters'; P. May, *Newmarket Medieval and Tudor* (King's Lynn, 1982).

process of urban growth between the eleventh and the fourteenth centuries. The county towns of Worcester and Warwick were, of course, already well established at the beginning of the process, as were some smaller centres, such as Winchcombe and Droitwich. Coventry, in the thirteenth century, was rapidly overtaking them all. But a significant constellation of smaller market towns, in north Gloucestershire, Warwickshire and Worcestershire, from the Avon valley to the Birmingham plateau, makes its appearance. In all there were about twenty-five, the majority of which were founded or sponsored by lay and ecclesiastical lords in the thirteenth century. They were clearly a response to a combination of factors operating in the rural economy – an improvement in productivity, a considerable increase in population, an increased demand for manufactured commodities by agricultural producers and, very important, an increasing demand for rent and tax in money by lords and the state.

There is, however, a problem about this urbanization process which is worth posing. Was there a continuum between the clearly urban places – ports, industrial towns, county and cathedral centres – and the agricultural villages where the majority of the population produced their own means of subsistence – and that of the rest of society as well – so that town shades off into country, especially at the smaller end of the urban spectrum? The presence of cultivators in towns, as well as of craftsmen and traders in villages can, of course, be convincingly documented. Nevertheless it would seem that the recognition of a qualitative difference between village and town is essential for a clear understanding of late medieval society as a whole. Even quite small places can be recognized as urban by one fundamental feature differentiating them from the village – that they were peopled by a majority of men and women who did not produce, totally, their own subsistence, but were engaged primarily in manufacture, food processing and (mainly retail) trade. Certain institutional features were normally, though not inevitably, linked with such an economy – freedom of tenure and status, privileged access to the market, some administrative and even jurisdictional autonomy, as implied by borough status. The institutional features could be acquired through the purchase of a charter, by or for a community which was already urbanized in the sense mentioned; or the process of urbanization could be precipitated and certainly encouraged by the prior acquisition of the institutional features. We will examine Halesowen in the light of these considerations.

The records of the Halesowen borough (or hundred) court are almost the only source of any significance which remain for the borough.[10] They are parallel to, but never confused with, the

10. They are in the city of Birmingham Reference Library. The borough or hundred court rolls begin in December 1272, BRL 346512. The pre-Black Death rolls

manorial court records and run from 1272 to the sixteenth century. There is a ten-year gap after 1282, but otherwise only short occasional breaks of a year or so. The court should, in theory, have been held every three weeks. In fact it was held at most monthly. There were two 'great' courts a year for the view of frankpledge, and an occasional 'pie powder court' (*curia pulentis*) for settling disputes between normal court sessions, usually arising at fairs and markets. The records are as full as those of most manorial courts with one important exception. The absence of customary tenure meant that there was no necessary recording of the surrenders and reissues of land, including surrender at the tenant's death. This diminishes the use of borough court records for demographic purposes, since burgage tenure normally escaped seigneurial control and record. Otherwise the Halesowen court records contain details of litigation about debt, trespass and broken contract; presentments of offenders for a wide variety of offences, against the peace, against the lord's interests, and so forth; presentments of breaches of the assize of bread and ale, as well as meat; land transactions recorded in some abundance, though not as frequently (for the reasons stated) as in the manorial court; admissions to burgage tenure, burgess privileges and shorter-term enjoyments of urban liberties by stall-holders and other temporary traders. Regrettable though it is that the court rolls are virtually the only source of information, it is nevertheless interesting to see how much can be extracted from this single source.

Other advantages of the court roll evidence for the period considered here (1272–1349) are as follows. In general it is useful to have a rich source for a period notable as one of considerable population pressure on scarce resources, as well as, seemingly, of considerable market activity. Halesowen also has the advantage of typicality. It is difficult to estimate its population precisely but with about six hundred inhabitants and a market function for the surrounding – quite small – rural hinterland, it must have been similar to many other market towns.

More particularly, it is useful to have the detailed records of a seigneurial borough so soon after its foundation. This was not a 'planted' town. It seems likely that a pre-urban settlement existed

analysed in this article run through to BRL 346605. Given the multiplicity of references to the rolls in this article, I have given the year in which each episode occurs without further footnote references to the rolls. A possible borough court roll entry of 1275 has been printed in the Worcester Historical Society edition of the manor rolls: *Court Rolls of the Manor of Hales, 1270–1307*, ed. J. Amphlett, S. G. Hamilton and R. A. Wilson, 3 vols. (Worcs. Hist. Soc., Worcester, 1910–33), i, p. 19. For other sources for the history of Halesowen, see the *Descriptive Catalogue of the Charters and Muniments of the Lyttelton Family* ed. I. H. Jeayes (London, 1893).

as early as the eleventh century, and that there was a market and fair in the 1220s. But the grant by the Premonstratensian abbey of Halesowen, probably in the late 1260s, of such of the privileges of the borough of Hereford as the future burgesses of Halesowen would like to adopt, obviously triggered off a new phase of development, even though they did not set up a gild merchant as at Hereford.[11] Another specific feature of Halesowen was the nature of its lord. The abbey, though not in the town itself, was less than a mile from the town centre. More important, the town was entirely surrounded by the manorial property of the abbey, from which came many of the town's new settlers. The abbey was not an easy landlord. Already in the 1270s it was engaged in conflict with its rural tenants. It seems to have been extremely reluctant to admit, for the townspeople, the implications of these privileges which it had itself granted.[12]

Before considering the pre-Black Death society of Halesowen borough it is essential to attempt some description of its economic base. Most of those who settled down as resident burgesses came from the hamlets of the manor and may still have had land in those places. This is a very delicate matter, given the uncertainty of the identification of persons with the same surnames, whether of place-name origin or occupational. A preliminary comparison of the data of the borough court rolls with that of the manor suggests that only 17 per cent of the burgesses had manorial land.[13] However, there is adequate evidence in the borough court rolls and in some surviving land deeds of the existence of arable land within the boundaries of the borough, portions of which were held by some burgesses. 'Cleyfurlong' is an area occasionally mentioned, as are 'Heyfeld', 'Wyteleyefeld' and some other pieces. The portions involved did not usually exceed five selions, and although transactions in real property are numerous, they usually concern messuages, burgages, curtilages and the like – though it should be mentioned that arable land was sometimes held by burgage tenure. Many burgesses, as one would expect, kept animals, not only horses, which were common, but sheep and swine which frequently trespassed on the lord's

11. The Halesowen borough, market and fair charters were already noted in T. R. Nash, *Collections for the History and Antiquities of Worcestershire*, 2 vols. (London, 1781–99), i, pp. 514–15; see also *V. C. H. Worcestershire*, iii, p. 141; *Descriptive Catalogue of the Charters and Muniments of the Lyttleton Family*, ed. Jeayes, no. 27. The components of the Hereford charter of 1215 will be found in *British Borough Charters, 1042–1216*, ed. A. Ballard (Cambridge, 1913), *passim*.

12. G. C. Homans drew attention to the bad relations between the abbots of Halesowen and their manorial tenants in his *English Villagers of the Thirteenth Century* (Cambridge, Mass., 1941; repr. New York, 1960).

13. I have to thank Dr Z. Razi for checking my borough court index against his own manor court index to obtain this figure.

land, even though the burgesses had the right of common pasture in the manor, outside the demesne enclosures. Other indications of the rural environment are the frequent prosecutions for sheaf-stealing and fence-breaking, no doubt for fuel. Sheaf-stealers were often women and children from families resident in the borough. The grain by which they were tempted would, as like as not, be on the other side of the ditch separating their urban curtilages from the manorial arable. There is no indication that this provoked conflict between town and manor.

The essence of Halesowen's economy was not land cultivation but the market. It was to seek access to the market which brought men and women into Halesowen in the (often realized) hope of settling down as residents. The charter of Hereford had stated that only members of the gild merchant could engage in trade (*mercandisum*) in the city and its suburbs. As already mentioned, there was no such gild in Halesowen, but access to the market, toll free, was specifically stated as the liberty accompanying burgage tenure, the payment of stallage or, quite simply, the purchase of the 'liberty of the borough', the latter usually acquired on an annual basis. In the first three decades of the court record, the liberty is frequently referred to without its precise implications being spelt out. By the first decade of the fourteenth century the conditions are stated more precisely. The right to follow a craft is given, for example, to a smith, to a glover, to a dyer; others are given the right to trade. By the 1320s the grant of the liberty is stated as being the right to buy and to sell all merchandise without impediment, as other burgesses do.

The commodities bought and sold in the market have to be deduced mainly from court litigation as in cases of debt and unjust detention. As is well known, these can be remarkably unrevealing. A debt plea can be initiated and terminated without either the amount of the debt or the reason for the debt being revealed. The Halesowen material is, however, by no means as baffling as in many similar records. Reasons for the debt and the sums involved, and where appropriate the goods bought or sold, are often given. The conclusion for the whole of the pre-Black Death period is clear. The main commodities sold were grain (especially oats), malt and livestock, the typical commodities of a rural market and not dissimilar from the commodities found in an analysis of the less good court rolls of Thornbury.

As the burgess community was established, as short-term stallagers and buyers of the liberty increased in number, the need was felt for various services. Most important was the supply of foodstuffs, which in an era of a predominantly carbohydrate diet (at any rate for the poor and middling element) consisted mainly of bread and ale, supplemented by some meat and fish. The supply of processed foodstuffs came from two main sources: first, the bakers and the brewers (and some bread and ale retailers), and secondly the cooks, the owners of what in effect were take-away shops. The most professional of these people, in Halesowen as elsewhere, seem to have been the bakers. We know about the bakers because of the operation of the assize of bread which was stringently enforced by the wardens of the assize, as they presented bakers selling short-weight or inadequately baked loaves. The presentments suggest that there was only a small number of full-time bakers in Halesowen, not more than four or five at one time. They were usually male. The existence of the cooks is mainly indicated by their occupational surname, supported by indications that they were buying grain, livestock and poultry. Brewers were numerous, numbers up to twenty-five or so being presented by the ale-tasters, either for breaking the assize or for brewing weak or red ale. It was clearly a part-time occupation for householders mainly engaged in other trades. Only a minority of those presented at court were women, though references to *bratriatrices* (as in national legislation) suggest that it was normally assumed that the actual brewers, as distinct from those presented – heads of households – would be female. Brewers, then, were distinct from such one-trade professionals as the bakers, and probably also the butchers. This contrast between those engaged in only one occupation and those with several should not be over-emphasized – bakers sometimes brewed, indeed most households of whatever occupation did so.[14]

The food processors probably mainly served the urban community. There were also industrial craftsmen who may well have supplied the surrounding countryside as well as the town. Apart from occupational surnames, which should be examined critically, there is plenty of court roll evidence for craftsmen, in litigation, amercements and ordinances. The most numerous craftsmen and women were in the textile and leather trades. Woollen cloth was spun, woven, fulled and dyed, but it would appear that the manufacture of linen cloth was more important. The preparation of flax was one of those occupations, almost like brewing, which people undertook who were involved in other trades. The evidence for this is mainly in the frequent presentments in the court of those who

14. There was a considerable increase in the proportion of women presented for brewing after the Black Death. Already by the 1370s, men presented for brewing were a very small minority. It is difficult to conclude whether this represented a significant shift in the sex of the actual brewers or a change in presentment procedure. My assumption that women had always provided the majority of the actual brewers suggests the latter. For bakers and brewers in general, see R. H. Hilton, 'Pain et cervoise dans les villes anglaises au moyen âge', in *L' approvisionnement des villes de l'Europe occidentale. Cinquièmes journées internationales d'histoire, 1983* (Auch, 1985).

soaked flax in the lord's vivaries. Tanning and making leather goods was almost as important as cloth-making. Judging by a court record of 1274, giving a fortnight's respite to 'all men' of the borough in the sale of hides/leather (*coreum*), the craft would seem to have been widespread, although specialization is later evident. The abbey had its own tannery and in 1300–1 tried to keep the number of tanners down so as to limit competition. Nevertheless there was a substantial family of tanners (surnamed 'Barker') as well as two or three others allowed to practise the trade. Secondary leather workers were mainly shoemakers and glovers. Fewer in numbers than those in the textile and leather trades were metal workers (shoe smiths, ordinary smiths, ironmongers), wood workers (carpenters, turners, a wheelwright), masons and tailors. We may finally refer briefly to another occupational category, very difficult to pin down – that is, servants of one sort or another (*serviens, famula, famulus, ancilla, garcio*) or employees of a temporary nature. All in all there are remarkably few references, and of these a fifth are to abbey servants or servants of outsiders. No doubt the record does not reflect their full presence. Nevertheless one suspects that the trading households were normally based on a family labour force, only occasionally reinforced by one or two servants.

This brief sketch of the Halesowen urban economy, intended as a background to a consideration of social relations in the seven recorded decades before 1349, may be concluded with two observations. First, although the economic life was, as normal in medieval society, based on the household, these households tended to be multi-occupational, with few exceptions such as the closely controlled bakers. The principal by-occupations were brewing and flax-soaking, perhaps a reflection of a sexual division of labour in the household. There would also be, for some households, cultivation and the raising of poultry and animals. The second point to be noted is, as one ought to expect in a market town, an increasing role of money and exchange. Quite apart from records of debt in which the nature of the transaction is described – delay in paying for specified goods, non-payment of wages – the number of debt cases in which money only is specified increase almost eightfold between the 1270s and the 1340s. These are difficult to interpret. The sums involved range from 3d. to 20s. They may, in some cases, be evidence of actual money loans, sometimes stated as a *mutuum*, but most often, no doubt, they were cases of delayed payment and so may serve as indications of a considerable extension of credit, due to an increase in trade, and not yet to a shortage of coin.

There is nothing unexpected about this small town economy, but a study of the social dimension reveals interesting and not often well-documented features of small town life. What were the social consequences of the creation of a seigneurial borough? In view of the apparent collapse of the market network between the fourteenth and the sixteenth centuries,[15] one might wonder whether some of the new boroughs, created in what seems to have been an epoch of seigneurial euphoria about the possibilities of cashing in on developing trade, would ever in practice get off the ground. Would they attract newcomers? Would stable burgess communities establish themselves? We must not, however, misunderstand the disappearance of markets in the period after the Black Death. Most of the west midlands medieval market towns were still active in the sixteenth century. It was the village markets which were most vulnerable – more than half of them disappeared.

Halesowen seems to have been very successful – perhaps more successful than the lord of the town had hoped. The early years, as reflected through the applications for burgess privileges recorded in the court rolls, saw considerable pressure by would-be settlers (1272–82). Pressure slackened somewhat between 1293 and 1303, intensified again between 1303 and 1312, slackened again in the next decade and resumed with some force after 1322 and especially in the decade before the Black Death. Although no mention of burgage plots or burgage tenure is to be found in the Hereford charter of 1215, in which one may presume the Halesowen burgesses would find their model customs, burgage tenure was in existence (in Halesowen) by 1278 – and was of course a familiar institution in most towns. In that year the jurors of the court reported that a certain Alice, future wife of Richard Wygge, discussed the purchase of a burgage with the abbot, but seemingly handed the negotiations over to Richard once she became contracted to him. References to burgage holdings at this early stage do not refer specifically to linked trading privileges, although this might be implied later when Edith of Tewenhale, in 1294, acquired a messuage already built on and enclosed by Thomas Steynulf. She is said to have got this in perpetuity for herself and her heirs *in liberate burgagii*, not, as in other cases, in *liberate burgi*. It is possible that the privileges of the borough had to be specifically granted at the same time that the burgage was acquired. In 1318, for instance, the whole court stated that if an outsider bought a burgage he was not to trade or use the liberty until he had the lord's permission (*gratum domini abbatis fecerit*). Geoffrey of Essex's first appearance in the record is when, in 1323, he bought a messuage, a garden and a path to Trolleswelle from John le Keu (cook) of Horeburn to hold in free burgage, with the liberty of the town.

It is clear from the earliest of the court records that the 'liberty of the town or borough' was more often bought independently of

15. See A. Everitt, 'The Marketing of Agricultural Produce', in *The Agrarian History of England and Wales*, iv, 1500–1640, ed. Joan Thirsk (Cambridge, 1966), pp. 466 ff.

tenurial considerations. At the Easter court of 1276 Nicholas le Yonge, a butcher (who twenty-five years later was to claim that he had been a burgess for thirty-eight years), paid 4d. for a year's enjoyment of the liberty. We also find that a variable fine is paid for the first acquisition of the liberty (ranging from 6d. to 2s.) with varying subsequent annual payments (2d., 4d., a pound of wax). In 1281 Agnes, the widow of Geoffrey le Seriaunt, paid 20s. for having used the liberty without permission; but this large sum brought her also permission to use it freely in the future. This means of acquiring trading rights continued, side by side with similar acquisitions when land was obtained, during the whole period. Another and increasingly popular mode of entry into the trading community was to pay stallage. The earliest court roll reference is to William Fayter in 1293, who took seisin of a stall once belonging to a smith (Nicholas Faber), for 3d. a year, paying an entry fine of 12d., including the use of the liberty. From then on, stallage becomes a regular payment, though at varying rates, presumably including an element of the rent for the space on which to set up a stall.   .

These buyers of burgages, of stallage or of the liberty, constituted the legal trading community. Whether immigrants or existing residents, they were certainly pressing to get these privileges from the earliest recorded period. But they were by no means the only ones hurrying into the town. The earliest court sessions recorded suggest that the new borough also attracted what were evidently considered by the lord – and no doubt by the established families – as disreputable elements. The presentment by the jurors in the first session, of December 1272, well illustrates this concern. Two resident women and one man were accused of giving lodging (*ospitant*) to evil (*pravos*) men, against the will of the lord, so the jurors believed (*ut credunt*); in the house of another man, three badly behaved women were lodging, and must leave if unable to find sure pledges; another man was lodging two badly behaved males, who were to be expelled; a married couple was lodging a woman, who was to be removed; and another man was accused of lodging a woman who had already been banned. Names of these illegal immigrants are sometimes given, but not always, and reference is sometimes made to their arrival without a precise count of those concerned being given. One third of the presentments between 1293 and 1349 refer to 'strangers' or 'ill-doers' without giving name or sex. Numbers of people are therefore incalculable, though one can count how many actual presentments of offences were made. A further problem is that a change in terminology occurs after the early years. The term *ospitare* is replaced by *recipere*, which in some cases could imply not so much giving lodgings as receiving thieves or other offenders. Another problem involved in making calculations is that the intentions of the immigrants – or entrants – is unknown. Did they hope to settle or only to spend a few days buying and selling?

The evidence is, therefore, not easily quantifiable, but it is clear that women may have formed the majority of illegal immigrants or entrants. Between 1272 and 1349 there were some two hundred presentments of residents lodging or receiving these persons. Between 1272 and 1282 about 65 per cent of those whose sex can be determined were women. Between 1293 and 1349 about 75 per cent were women. This fits in with the picture we how have of a very strong female element among retail traders in the medieval town – the possibilities of trading were obviously what brought in most of the immigrants.[16] These illegal entrants of both sexes sometimes remained and became legally recognized residents, though not without ups and downs. Richard Ordrich, whom the jurors in 1298 thought unsuitable to remain in the town unless he found pledges for good conduct, did in fact find such and paid 4d. for the right to trade. Accusations of being a homicide and a receiver of thieves were made against him and in 1300 he and his wife were ordered out of town. However, since he was accused of setting up a latrine (*cloaca*) by the stream shortly afterwards, he is likely to have still been resident. In fact the following year he hired a stall and was then ordered out again for not behaving honestly to his neighbours. But he was still quarrelling with them in 1308, and had been doing so continuously over matters which testify to his residence in the borough.

Three sisters from Illey, a nearby hamlet, illustrate similarly chequered female careers . Alice was already identified as an illegal immigrant in 1281 and was regularly in trouble until 1315. Her sister Cristina (probably much younger) appears in 1298, paying for the use of the liberty, but like Alice was a fence-breaker. An attempt was made in 1311 to query her status in the borough and it is clear that she was suspected of shady dealings, like selling flour with illicit measures; conspiring with three other women to keep goods for sale from neighbours, presumably so as to push prices up; forestalling marketable goods, no doubt for the same reason. Their sister Juliana had a similar career. She was accused in 1298 of trading without a licence and then paid 2d. a year for the liberty. She too was a forestaller, sold ale in false measures and did some baking. In 1301 she had to pay the lord 12d. for being deflowered, an indication of the lord's unwillingness to recognize the freedom of those who had paid to use the liberty of the borough. It is of some interest that an inquisition in 1365 concerning an inheritance reveals that Juliana had

16. R. H. Hilton, 'Women Traders in Medieval England', in *Class Conflict and the Crisis of Feudalism*. As I show in this article, there was a strong female element among retail traders even in large, old-established towns. They were unable to break into the gild-dominated crafts, though even here wives and daughters probably played a bigger role than has been generally recognized.

a daughter Margery by Thomas le Couper, 'conceived outside matrimony' (*extra legem matrimonii procreata*). In 1317 Margery, described as the daughter of Thomas le Couper, was received (having stolen sheaves) by her mother Juliana. It is characteristic of Halesowen that we discover that Cristina of Illey had two sons. No husband is mentioned, though five men in the record with the surname 'Illey' could have fulfilled that role.

Another woman, Margery Turgis, resembled Cristina of Illey in the ambiguity of her relationships with men. She was attacked in 1310 by Philip Sley, a very dubious character, as we shall see. Sley was presented for having drawn her blood and she apparently took refuge with Alice le Herl. Both of these women were then expelled. Nevertheless in the following years Margery took on lease a cottage from Thomas Garding. She and another woman, tenant of a similarly leased cottage, were accused of causing danger from their fires (something with which the jurors of the borough were much concerned). She seems to have remained in the borough until 1342, her last court reference being to a break-in (*hamsokn*) at her house. She was clearly unpopular – several people unjustly raise the hue against her and she obtained 20s. damages from Richard Aleyn and his mother against whom she, in turn, had justly raised the hue. She was several times declared unfit to stay in the town, including an order in 1315 when she and her sons (probably Nicholas and Richard who briefly appear later) were ordered out. There is no mention of a husband, though in 1315 she was briefly received by a John Turgis. Her unhappy career continued. She returned to the town, even (so it was hinted) being received by the lord. She brewed, was involved in fights and was successful in suing two women who had taken some of her chattels. In 1335 she raised the hue justly against six named persons, who (judging by their other references) seem to have been young rowdies.

By the early fourteenth century, Halesowen society may have achieved some stability. Lacking any surveys, it is difficult to be sure about the numbers of residents, for clearly many persons who appear in the court records were visitors to the market, mostly from villages in the immediate vicinity but some from markets further afield, especially Birmingham. The total number of people named in the court record as engaged in some form of activity (other than acting as essoins or pledges) was 311 between 1272 and 1282, and 1716 between 1293 and 1349. About 35 per cent were women (a smaller proportion than that of female immigrants). The proportion of residents to total numbers in the record is in the region of 40 to 50 per cent.

Within this resident population it is possible to identify some hundred established families – those, that is, who can be established by a substantial number of entries in the record. Of these, about eighty can be given genealogies – that is, family interrelationships over two or more generations can be established. There are pitfalls of course, of which the most serious is that of confusing families of the same surname, whether occupational or of place-name origin. It should again be stressed that the possibility of family reconstitution is much more remote than in manors where most tenants held by customary tenure. Apart from the absence of consistent record of the deaths of burgage tenants, there are no indications of entry into tithing which sometimes allows calculations, from manorial documents, of life-spans. Nevertheless to be able to pin down, even if rather roughly, the established families is of considerable importance.

A minor feature of the history of these established families is of some interest. It has already been mentioned that there were many active women in the town and that some appear to have had children without any link with a father being noticeable. A certain Mable Walters appears in the record in 1280, finding a pledge so that she could have the freedom of the borough. The next two decades see her brewing ale, dealing a little in land and being involved in minor fracas with neighbours. She had two daughters, Margery and Cristina, who alternatively used the surnames 'daughter of Mable (or Mawe)' and 'Walters'. Margery was the most active. She was a frequent brewstress and dealt in small quantities of land from 1298 until 1322. In 1302 she married Robert Marmion, a mason, who took seisin of Margery's tenement. At this point he disappears from the record, having only made one previous appearance, when he hit Richard the Hayward in Mable Walter's house. Another set of prominent women was the wife Agnes and the five daughters of Henry Medicus (or Leche). Henry was fairly active, including being a juror from 1272 until his death eight years later. Agnes disappears after 1302, having had occasional clashes with neighbours and been presented for soaking flax and stealing grain . . . Her daughter Margaret was active, unruly and quarrelsome with her neighbours. She was a stall-holder and frequently threatened with expulsion. Her sister Scholastica was of a similar nature, quarrelsome and a frequent brewstress. Juliana and Clarice seldom appear, but Mathilda brewed and baked. She had a daughter, and a son who was a notorious night-walker. There is no mention of Mathilda's husband. She retains her mother's surname throughout. Phases in family history such as these were of course rare, as one would expect in a society where all positions of control were in male hands. What is remarkable is that there were so many women whose activity was on their own behalf rather than simply reflecting their association with father or husband.

If this society had, despite evidence of some fluidity, achieved stability, the evidence for this may be the establishment of a steady élite, effectively ruling the borough under the watchful eye of the lord and, as we shall see, characterized by somewhat different levels of conduct from those outside their ranks. The problem of the definition of an élite poses itself. The court evidence is not of such a nature as to permit calculations of relative wealth. The 1327 subsidy return, which does not separate manor from borough, is not helpful, other than to suggest that in so far as they can be separated out, more manorial taxpayers were in the higher tax brackets than those from the borough.[17] However, holding the position of juror was evidently of crucial importance. It normally led to nomination to the offices of bailiff and ale-taster, and less frequently to that of 'cachepol' or collector of monies (from tolls, fines, amercements and so on), for the post of cachepol often *preceded* selection for jury service. More important, it was the jurors, chosen once or twice a year, who presented offenders (other than those against the assize of bread and ale), made judgements on contentious issues, stated custom and, no doubt, were the inspirers of those decisions and ordinances whose origins were attributed to the 'court' or to the 'community'. Inevitably the jurors would have to present offences against the lord's interests or property. But they also, in the choice of what offences or offenders to present, would articulate the interests, indeed the mores, of the established members of the trading community.

As one would expect, the jurors were mainly drawn from the established families mentioned above. Between 1293 and 1349 there were 125 jurors. Only twelve of the established families did not contribute to this list. This does suggest an element of stabilization. On the other hand, 43 per cent of the jurors served for three years or less. And even long-serving jurors could cease performing their role many years before disappearing from the record. Explicit reasons are not given for short tenure of the post, though there are some hints of reluctance on the part of some jurors. The lord, or his steward, could also be unwilling to accept certain persons.

The assertiveness of the lord has been mentioned. I have elsewhere quoted examples of his unwillingness to accept the full freedom of the burgesses and of the townspeople's response.[18] The pressures varied from time to time. Between the 1270s and the 1290s the lord was demanding labour services, sometimes as a punishment for an offence (such as trespassing on the demesne meadow, brewing bad ale, baking light bread, illegal fishing), but sometimes as a condition for staying in town. This strange demand for labour services slackened off in the late 1290s, possibly for economic reasons. Then

---

17. 'The Shropshire Lay Subsidy Roll of 1327', *Shropshire Archaeol. and Natural Hist. Soc. Trans.*, 3rd ser., v (1905).
18. Hilton, 'Lords, Burgesses and Hucksters'.

other demands normally connected with villeinage appear. In 1294 a man had to pay to marry a burgess and to get the liberty; in the same year another man paid 12d. to marry a woman holding land in the borough who was described as a neif. In 1299, 12d. was again demanded of a fuller who wanted to enter the borough and marry a local resident. By the early years of the fourteenth century, residents enjoying the freedom of the borough were being identified as neifs so that their chattels could be appropriated or extra levies demanded from them. From the 1320s the pressure slackens, but the lord is now, in effect, demanding heriots on the deaths of some tenants. These are described as 'principals' and in one case justified as being from a parishioner, though the term 'mortuary' is not used. Significantly, the servile term 'heriot' is sometimes written down and then deleted to be substituted by 'principal'.

The abrasive behaviour of the Premonstratensian lord of Halesowen produced hostile comments from the burgesses, beginning already in 1293 and continuing, off and on, until the second decade of the fourteenth century, after which hostility was not expressed – at any rate in such a way as to provoke court proceedings. But what about relationships among the burgess and residential families? How can we know about these, beyond the purely economic relationships entered into when land and commodities were bought and sold?

The nature of judicial records is such that conflict is inevitably over-emphasized as one concentrates one's attention on individuals. One might get the impression of warring families and a fragmented community. But the same record also shows common action, first by the jurors but often specifically by the court and the community.This terminology could conceal the imposition of the lord's will on the borough or the imposition of the will of the richer burgesses on the rest of the community. No doubt these pressures existed. Nevertheless there are sufficient indications that the community and the court, acting through the jurors and even the officials, were articulating common needs. This is shown throughout the period in, for example, the frequent sanitary ordinances, as against dyers, butchers, tanners and others polluting the streams. Others include very detailed elaborations of the assize of ale, such as the repeated requirement that female maltsters should dry malt properly for the benefit of the brewers. A similar concern is shown for the quality, not merely the weight, of bread. It could also be said that the exclusion of undesirable outsiders revealed a common – if selfish – concern.

The evidence for conflict is considerable, though the various categories of that evidence are uneven in detail. The least detailed are the presentments of the raising of hue and cry. Here, A is simply reported as having raised a just or unjust hue against B; or quite often a hue between A and B is presented, the only indication as to the guilty party being the imposition of an amercement. The great majority of hue and cry cases state no details. In the rare cases where detail is given, it can range between hue being raised because some form of violence is committed to a neighbours' squabble about the shifting of a dung-heap. So presentments of the hue tell us rather little though it is of some interest that hue is quite often raised within the family, between husbands and wives or between brothers and sisters. Cases of assault, *hamsokn* and bloodshed are often more specific, though not as fully described as one would wish. They sometimes, but not always, led to the raising of the hue. Then there are various presentments for misconduct, short of violence, which again are by no means always specified, but could be for illicit trading and therefore not involve interpersonal conflict. Finally an interesting type of misdemeanour is contumely, vituperation, personal abuse. Details are not always given, but when the abusive words are reported they do give some indication of what were considered to be local standards of behaviour.

Presentments of interpersonal violence in the borough court exclude felonies, which would be presented before the king's justices, operating under such commissions as Gaol Delivery. They do not, therefore, provide a complete measure of reported violence. Nevertheless in spite of the brevity of description ('A shed the blood of B; C assaulted D; E broke into F's house') an analysis shows some interesting results. In spite of the fact that one can suspect that the young were prone to violent behaviour, there was surprisingly little gang violence: only 4 out of 17 cases of interpersonal violence between 1272 and 1282 involved groups of three or more; 2 out of 33 cases between 1293 and 1303; 2 (the same gang) out of 46 cases between 1312 and 1322; and – to jump a few years – 4 out of 93 cases in the decades before the Black Death. It might be expected that violence in that hard decade, 1312 to 1322, would show an increase over the previous periods – but then the amount of violence between 1339 and 1349 was double that of the hard decade. This could hardly reflect economic difficulties comparable to those of the famine years, but could very well have been the consequence of increased immigration and intensified market activity.

Another interesting aspect of these figures is that of the sex of the aggressors. As we have seen, although the women of the borough shared most of the legal, social and political disabilities of their sex in medieval society in general, there are grounds for supposing them to be quite self-assertive, a reflection of their importance in retail trade. This self-assertiveness was very little reflected in personal violence. About 15 per cent of the aggressors in violence cases in the decade analysed were women: 10 per cent in 1272–82 and 1339–49; but 15 per cent in 1293–1303; and 35 per cent in the hard decade, 1312–22. Women were frequently the victims of men; men rarely the victims of women.

Women's principal form of aggression was vituperation, though in absolute terms men were presented as often as women for this offence. Yet we are given much more detail in the record about what women actually said as compared with men. In an early case of defamation by a man, no details are given. At the Easter court of 1276 there was a neighbours' quarrel between the Mercers and the Smiths (Fabers). John the Mercer, the court was told, defamed Nicholas Faber and his wife; Nicholas hit him and broke the fence between their holdings; Mercer's wife spoiled the mantle of Agnes of Hales to spite Nicholas Faber – Agnes presumably being at the Fabers' house. When details are given in other cases, the abuse frequently referred to sexual matters. It was inevitable that in abusing the Premonstratensian canons their celibacy should be questioned, as was alleged against Margery, wife of Nicholas Sutor (shoemaker) in 1279, who was said to have referred to the cellarer's and the canons' relationships with women. The favourite form of abuse was for women to be called whores (*meretrices*). Whether the word meant, to those who shouted the accusation, a person who engaged in extra-marital sexual activity or who did so for payment is not clear. The former would seem to be implied in a presentment in 1282 of Roger Wyte or his *meretrix*, suspected of taking hose from somebody's house, though half a century later the word *concubina* was used. This may simply have been a change in terminology. On the other hand, the implication of prostitution may have been intended by Margery la Leche in 1300 when she called the wife of Nicholas Sutor a whore – 'or if she were not married she would have been one'. Guilt in this case brought Margery la Leche to the pillory.

Whatever might be the precise implication of the word *meretrix*, it was frequently used as a term of abuse, mostly by women, occasionally by men. In 1297, Thomas le Fleccher (arrow-maker) called the wife of Henry Baker a whore, as a result of which she beat him and tore his clothes. Thomas did not learn his lesson. Four years later he was brought up in court for calling Henry Trolli's wife a whore and manhandling her. Additional abusive suggestions were sometimes made, as in 1302 when Juliana of Shirlet called Agnes, wife of William the skinner, a thief, a whore and a 'wych', or when, in 1305, Margery of Hulle called Juliana, wife of John, son of Juliana, a whore and a thief. The sexual element in abuse is further illustrated in 1302, when Scholacia la Leche was accused of saying that John the Tanner was of the stature and nature of a woman. Non-sexual abuse (in so far as words are reported) was rare, as when, in 1306, Nicholas Sutor called Richard Broun a robber and a ribald. For some reason, presentments of abuse end in the late 1330s. The last such before the Black Death was in 1338, when Juliana of Halen assaulted Agnes of Halen, calling her a whore and other contumelies.

What was the reason for this concern for sexual or marital rectitude? The ecclesiastical elevation of chastity as woman's most outstanding virtue may be considered as a background factor, but it is more likely that married respectability rather than virginity would have been most present in people's mind. Were women abused as 'whores' because the term was deeply shocking, more so than other swear-words? Or was the word used in effect for the opposite reason, namely that sexual laxity was by no means uncommon? We have seen that women heads of household were not unusual in medieval Halesowen, or at any rate that their legal husbands were but shadowy figures. A report to the court in 1342 makes it clear that rules excluding bastards and their children from inheritance operated in Halesowen. And in general we know that peasant and small town marriages, even though legal, were much more informal affairs than was once thought.[19] All this could add up to a sensitivity to extra-marital sex which could partly manifest itself in vituperative accusations.

The figures quoted to illustrate the varying incidence of interpersonal violence at different periods do not reveal very much. Was violence generalized among all social groups? Or was there a social stratum which was more inclined than others to violent behaviour?

The prominent members of the families whom we can assume to be the most affluent in the borough were seldom, sometimes never, involved in violent quarrels with their neighbours. This is not unexpected. They were the people who ruled the town, not simply on behalf of the lord, but for their own benefit. Being in control of the administrative and legal apparatus, they did not need to be violent to achieve their ends. The division of functions in the servicing of the market may have precluded violence in pursuit of economic aims. This does not mean that they escaped presentment for offences: they baked light-weight bread, brewed weak ale, soaked flax in the lord's vivaries. If they did get involved in violent acts it tended to be when they were beginning their careers – youthful self-assertion in a period before they were obliged to take on responsibilities?

The tanner Ranulph Barker, who died in 1347, first appears in the record in 1306, guilty of bloodshed, and he was a juror by 1311;

19. M. M. Sheehan, 'The Formation and Stability of Marriage in Fourteenth century England: Evidence of an Ely Register', *Mediaeval Studies*, xxxiii (1971); R. H. Helmholz, *Marriage Litigation in Medieval England* (Cambridge, 1974).

but apart from a quarrel with his brother Henry, after which he had to pledge in court not to molest him, the rest of his career was lacking in any other than minor offences (flax, ale). Henry, the son of John Knyt (or Knyst), dead by 1313, traded from a stall, was a householder and occasionally a juror. He first appears in 1293, when he was ordered out of town for stealing a hen. In 1294 he became the victim, not the perpetrator, of violence. Margery, the daughter of Mable Walter, whom we have already met, came to him with a message from Cristina, the daughter of Robert the Cook (a juror and a borough official with no record of violence), asking him to meet her at night in her father's barn. There, waiting to beat him up, was William Norreys (later married to Cristina), who broke his arm. The jury said that Henry Knyt was not a tavern haunter or night-walker (*tabernarius sive nocturnagium*). His attacker, who was later given land by Cristina's father, presumably on marriage, is also not found involved in any subsequent violence. John Gachard, a carpenter, who disappears from the record in 1342 (and may have retired from work in 1322 when he surrendered his tenement to his son), was regularly a juror from 1298. He too was involved in violence and bloodshed early in his career (1293), but was only involved once subsequently in a fight with another carpenter. This pattern of abstention from violence, if not from minor offences and shady dealings, is repeated in the biographies of more than two dozen well-to-do Halesowen burgesses.

The evidence of the court records inevitably, as suggested above, emphasizes violent or delinquent behaviour – delinquent in terms of the standards of the lord and the leading burgesses. Nevertheless it is useful, as far as possible, to locate this behaviour in terms of social status. A large number of persons enter the court record only once or twice because of minor offences against the lord, of which sheaf-stealing and fence-breaking were the most frequent. These were non-residents who happened to be dealt with in the borough court. And, as already indicated, a large number of persons, especially females, were presented as illegal immigrants and removed from the town, even though no offence was alleged. Some obtained pledges for good conduct and remained, to be absorbed eventually into the community of traders. There was also a sort of sub-criminal element, sometimes totally marginalized, though not infrequently occupying some sort of residential accommodation and attempting to find work or trade locally. And clearly there were also what one might term 'marginalized' members of otherwise established families who for much of their lives seem to stagger from one fracas to another.

An example of a violent man who managed to remain in the borough, with no apparent residence, for a surprisingly long time was Philip Sley. He appears in 1305 accused of assaulting with an axe a servant of Lady Agnes de Somery of Weoley, whom he chased around the streets of the borough. In 1307 he and two others are presented as vagrants (*vagastes*) who threaten men at night, causing fear. He was twice presented in the following year for quarrelling and in 1309 for bad conduct at night time. In 1310, strangely, having shed the blood of that other shady character, Margery Turgis, he was received first by the carpenter John Gachard and then by the vicar, although by then he had been ordered out of town. He found pledges for good conduct, but was quickly presented again for bad conduct. After several quarrels and a hue justly raised against him, he disappears from the scene. Another violent person who managed to install himself, apparently more firmly, was William Malinsone, who in 1293 was presented for diverting a stream as well as fighting with John Gachard. In 1298 he was presented for beating his sister and repeated these bloody quarrels several times over the next eleven years until he was expelled in 1311, though he must have returned two years later to have his blood shed by Thomas le Seriaunt. Malinsone was not homeless, as Sley apparently was. In 1301 he leased a stall to another suspicious character, Richard Ordrich (mentioned above), and in 1306 he leased a messuage place for six years, also to Ordrich, with licence to build on it.

Some members of otherwise 'respectable' families behaved badly. John, brother of the juror and official Henry le Barun, was presented for threatening people with his knife in 1298 and until 1311 did not appear in court other than for violent behaviour, especially against women. But in 1318 his brother gave him a tenement; he acquired the liberty of the borough; became cachepol in 1323 and only once shed blood (in 1326) before his last appearance in 1340. This John le Baron seems to have prolonged the violent behaviour of younger members of established families rather longer than most. Much of the violent behaviour came from members of families who did not make it into the ruling élite. It is difficult, if not impossible, to decide whether this was because their unlawful behaviour made them unacceptable or whether exclusion from the ranks of the decision makers provoked them into violent modes of exercising their will.

William le Wyte, of a non-élite family, was said to have reported rumours of a discussion among a group of leading burgesses. They were said to have been slandered by Richard Tinctor (the dyer), and the rumours came from Nicholas Faber (the smith). Both Richard Tinctor and Nicholas Faber were in fact members of the ruling group. After some trouble, Nicholas had to admit that he spread these rumours, indicating rifts within the élite. It is of interest that the veil over inner quarrels was revealed by William le Wyte, whose general conduct reveals the obstreperous behaviour of the excluded. He was probably a relative of Roger le Wyte, who appears in various violent episodes between 1272 and 1282 and whose holding escheated into the lord's hands because he was indicted as a felon. William first appears in the court in 1312, when he was presented for breaking down the wall of Roger's former holding, which the lord had let out to others. William was a typical small town trader engaged in a diversity of occupations – stock-dealing (sheep and cattle), occasional baking of bread, dealing in flax, land sales. But above all he was a violent man, especially in the first recorded years, when he beat people and shed blood. Even later, in the 1330s, a woman raises the hue against him; he is charged with bloodshed; and in 1344 with breaking into a house along with two other unruly characters.

Similar careers can be delineated in the case of other individuals. There were also whole families whose members were engaged in delinquent activities. James Hall (de Aula) and his wife Alice had a house in the town in 1307. Alice brewed at home in contempt of orders against her dating back to 1303. Both became notorious from about 1307 as receivers of malefactors; both had to find pledges for their good conduct. They eventually surrendered their property to the lord, and abjured the borough in 1318 – though they were then illegally received by John Tinctor, John of Haslebury and Mathilda la Baxtere. The first two of these were relatively 'respectable', although Mathilda, a long time resident, was not. James and Alice Hall had a daughter and a son (John and Alice), both of whom had to find pledges for good conduct in 1316 because of previous bad behaviour. A less prominent 'bad' family were the Bondes. Thomas Bonde, in 1296, was discovered selling flour by false measures; he and his family stole grain; broke fences; his son Thomas, during a quarrel with Isabel, daughter of Isabel Walreven, hit her. His daughters Cristina and Agnes had several convictions for stealing timber and grain; in 1311 Agnes was declared unfit to stay in the town unless she found pledges for her conduct – which she did, and continued with her hedgebreaking and sheaf-stealing.

Other, and even less well-endowed, families had similar careers – the atte Broks, the Boudons, the Burminghams, the Curteys, the atte Heaths, the Notwyks, the Turners. The Wygge family is worth a little further elaboration, although their interrelationships are a little obscure. The fullest recorded is Robert, son of Isabel. He seems to have been the butt of a group of youths from the better-off families (John, son of Thomas Tinctor; William Sutor; Thomas in le Hem; Thomas of Pircote). In 1297 they pushed him through Ralph of Warwick's window as a joke. Perhaps this was a form of unofficial retribution for Robert's theft of a small quantity of wool, kept concealed by Isolda, wife of William the shepherd. He wanted to sell it but did not succeed in doing so, and it was eventually returned to its owner. Robert's career continued with more stealing (of grain) and with several fights between 1301 and 1307 in which he shed blood. In 1307 he was summoned for contempt of the lord and for assault, but did not appear. His pledges for good conduct tried to deny that they were such. They were unsuccessful and were ordered to produce him, but he had disappeared, apparently for good.

He was only one of many Wygges. The next best recorded was John, probably a relative, who between 1298 and 1312 appears as a host to malefactors and wandering hucksters (such as Isabel of Brocton, the old-clothes dealer). He brewed and was presented for putting up a sign outside his house without being a burgess. He regularized his position by paying stallage and continued to brew. His wife, apart from having bought clothes from Isabel of Brocton, only appears again for having beaten the wife of Stephen the tailor. Other female Wygges also appear briefly and in dubious activities. Agatha and her daughter Margery (husband not named) were guilty in a case of hue and cry. Agatha also brewed bad ale. Cristina, not otherwise identifiable except as a 'Wygge', was expelled from the town in 1316, though she appears as an illegal lodger two years later. John's daughter Emma also appears, but as a victim, her house having been broken into by Walter Carpenter, who beat her.

Finally it is worth mentioning the Mauncel family, which makes a curious though brief appearance. There were four brothers – Nicholas, Thomas, Walter and William. In 1316 Nicholas was found guilty in a fracas involving bloodshed against Robert and Roger le Prus (who only appear otherwise as bloodshedders). Nicholas was respited at the request of the lord of Somery. Was he his retainer? Was the family related to the gentry Maunsells of Gloucestershire? They behaved like a hired gang, for three years later William, Nicholas and Thomas Mauncel, supported by Thomas and John ate Lude, John Elyot and William Wawe (a local baker), followed a certain John ate Oldenshulle to the house of Sarra ate Pole, broke the doors and windows and took Sarra's goods and chattels. Sarra naturally raised the hue and cry and in the subsequent presentment evidence was presented of considerable blood-shedding, involving, so it would seem, others who joined in the fight against the Mauncels. Sarra was herself a receiver of outsiders and a regular brewer (and flax-soaker) between 1315 and 1329. The ate Poles were a well-established family, though Sarra's relationship to them is obscure. She had a daughter, but a husband is not mentioned. John ate Oldenshulle may have had two sons, Richard and Robert; and there was a Thomas of that name. All appear mainly in contexts of bloodshed. However, Thomas of Oldenshulle was presented in 1349 for using the liberty without licence, so he may have been a resident; and an Elias Mauncel was presented in 1326 for receiving malefactors, so he too must have been a resident. In other words, the quarrel was not simply an affair between outsiders and may be seen to reflect in extreme form the less respectable aspect of Halesowen borough life.

The information about lives and attitudes in this small town is too fragmentary to provide information which will indicate general social attitudes, apart from obvious indications of hostility to outsiders, sensitivity to sexual behaviour and possibly a disrespect for hierarchy arising from the fluidity of the social structure and hostility to a hard lord. It would be too much to expect the court to inform us about the influence of religion. The Premonstratensian canons, as lords of the town, never appear in such a way as to indicate any respect for them. The town was in the diocese of Worcester, but there is little of interest in the bishops' registers and there are no records of the church courts surviving. The vicar of the town (and parish) church of St Mary in Halesowen is a shadowy figure, but it would appear that the church was the home of a chantry of St Mary. It is first referred to in 1307, when two quarrelling women, Cristina and Alice Chapeleyn, were ordered to pay 2s. to the light of St Mary if their quarrel continued. There had already been in 1281 an endowment of 4d. a year to the church (together with 4d. to the abbey church) in the will of Philip of Wyllinghurst, for an anniversary for himself and his wife Alice to be paid for from his hereditary holding. By 1332 the chantry of St Mary is mentioned, for in this year the lord granted to it a house and a curtilage to be held by the chantry chaplain. Six other clergy are mentioned in the record, but only on one or two occasions each. One of them, Thomas the clerk, was once a juror. Curiously the cleric who is mentioned most was the rector of Old Swinford, a parish to the west of Halesowen, whose church was three and a half miles from the centre of the town where this rector lived. He had acquired a tenement on High Street next to the market (*forum venalium*) in 1305, once held by Henry Tinctor. The deed recording this transfer gives more detail than the court record, to the effect that the property was held in joint possession with his god-daughter Alice of Willishamstede and with Simon of Harwedene and his sister Beatrice. [20] Simon does not appear in the court record, but it is clear that the rector, Alice and Beatrice lived together with a servant called Isabel. The lord gave them extra land to increase the curtilage of the original tenement and, in 1309, some arable land in Cleyfurlong. At the same time the rector's tenure was established as a free burgage. He is still referred to in 1327, when he defaulted from his suit of court.

All this does not amount to much of an ecclesiastical presence. There was no house of friars, so the town fails one supposed test of

20. *Descriptive Catalogue of the Charters and Muniments of the Lyttleton Family*, ed. Jeayes, no. 97.

urbanization,[21] and, more important, it did not experience the presence of a more sympathetic representative of the church than was the abbey. All the more weight therefore must be given to the record of the borough court. This is indeed remarkable in its detail. It leaves no doubt that Halesowen was genuinely urban, even if at the bottom of a presumed scale of urbanization. It was genuinely a borough, even though it had to fight to maintain that status against its own creator. Primarily a trading community focused on its market, it was decidedly jealous of its rights, against all comers. And yet, being a possession of the abbey, its separate existence as an urban entity was virtually ignored by outside authority. The manor was the unit for the assessment of subsidies, into which for this purpose the borough was merged. While the other small towns of Shropshire (Bridgenorth and Ludlow) made presentments before the royal justices itinerant as boroughs, Halesowen's jury of presentment was that of the manor. Pleas of the crown involving borough residents were mingled with those concerning only people from the villages in the manor.[22] Were it not for the separate court record, a remarkable example of small town existence at a crucial period of urban growth would be unnoticed.

Editorial suggestions for further reading

Hilton R. H., 'The small town as part of peasant society', in his *The English Peasantry in the Later Middle Ages* (Oxford, 1975).

Hilton R. H., 'Lords, burgesses and hucksters', *Past and Present*, 97 (1982), 3–15.

Hilton R. H., 'Medieval market towns and simple commodity production', *Past and Present*, 109 (1985), 3–23.

Hammer C. I., 'Patterns of homicide in a medieval university town: fourteenth century Oxford', *Past and Present*, 78 (1978), 3–23.

21. J. Le Goff, 'Ordres mendiants et urbanisation dans la France médiévale: état de l'enquete'. *Annales. E. S. C.*, xxv (1970)
22. Cf. Public Record Office, London, Just. I, 739, containing pleas of the crown and gaol delivery proceedings in Shropshire for Michaelmas 1272. *The Roll of the Shropshire Eyre of 1256*, ed. A. Harding (Selden Soc., xcvi, London, 1981) is of doubtful relevance here as the borough may not have been founded.

Chapter Six

SUBURBAN GROWTH

D. J. Keene

from M. W. Barley (ed.), *The Plans and Topography of Medieval Towns in England and Wales* (Council for British Archaeology Research Report 14, 1976)

The boundaries of the greater towns – delineated by walls or ditches – rarely coincided with the less precise line of economic and social reality, which truly marked the boundary between town and countryside. For most towns had suburbs outside their walls, settlements which were sometimes legally part of the town, though often they were not. As Derek Keene emphasizes, they evolved from an early date, and they could be very large: more than half of a town's population might live outside its walls. Keene here describes suburbs as 'the growing edges of the town', and examines their origins, their structure, and some of the specialist functions that took place outside town walls, such as cattle markets and horse fairs; but there was more to them than this. The character of the suburb was different from that of the town. These were not the quiet havens of genteel respectability that the suburbs of the modern town would be; they were distinctly a fringe development, inhabited by people who were marginal in more than one sense of the word. Christopher Dyer has drawn attention to the suburban settlements recorded in Domesday Book: often substantial colonies of cottagers dwelling outside town limits, working as labourers and growing garden crops to take advantage of the ready local market for fresh food. The poor, who were to be found in every part of the medieval town, gathered particularly here. In the Gloucester suburbs in the fifteenth century one-fifth of the tenants were women – no doubt widows; a sure sign that this was an impoverished social group. In addition to the poor, suburbs were favoured by a small number of the very wealthy who did not depend upon constant proximity to the marketplace and who found sites for spacious, airy and private residences on the fringe of the town. The juxtaposition of the very rich and the very poor was an important and distinctive feature of the medieval and early modern suburb. Where a suburb was under a different jurisdiction from the borough, inevitably there would be an unofficial, toll-free market. Craftsmen's wages would here not be subject to regulation by the borough court, and there would be no irksome borough taxation to pay. Not surprisingly, the suburb might be resented by those within the walls, who refused to see it as part of the urban community: at Hereford in the thirteenth century the citizens resolved that in time of war and other immediate danger the town gates should be shut against the suburban poor. Having contributed nothing towards the heavy cost of building and maintaining the defences, they were now to realize that they could expect none of the benefits.

The growth of the mercantile suburb in relation to a pre-urban nucleus is one of the dominant themes in speculation on the emergence of towns in northern Europe.[1] The concept may be applied to many of the smaller and to a few of the larger towns of medieval England. To contemporaries, however, *suburbium* denoted a settlement which was in some sense additional to an existing town; a suburb could only be defined as such when the original urban area was enclosed with a wall, a bank, or other limiting feature. As in classical usage, suburban meant extra-mural. The extended classical usage by which the term 'suburb' was applied to an extensive rural territory around a town, or to a separate town within the orbit of a great urban centre was also current in medieval England. Thus 10th century Winchester was surrounded by a *terra suburbana quae undique adiacet civitati* extending up to 8 km (5 miles) from the walls and Torksey could be described as a suburb of Lincoln.[2] This paper will be confined to those built-up areas adjacent to the walled town. This is not to say that areas of similar character did not occur towards the limits of towns which were not enclosed or where settlement did not extend beyond the walls.

Suburbs were the growing edges of the town. In the period of the middle ages for which detailed documentary evidence survives, they were the areas of a town's most recent growth and may even have been continuing to expand. Suburbs may thus reveal something of the ways in which towns were formed and of their evolution from rural settlements. Their expansion will usually provide a chronological guide to the growth of the town. Their final extent, related to that of the original enclosure, will be a key to understanding the regional status of a town in its early years, and the changes in status which may have accompanied later expansion. Bristol and Northampton are cases where suburban growth strikingly reflects this latter aspect of their histories.

1. F. L. Ganshof, *Etude sur le Développement des Villes entre Loire et Rhin au Moyen Age* (Paris, 1943).
2. M. Biddle (ed.), *Winchester in the Early Middle Ages: an Edition and Discussion of the Winton Domesday*, Winchester Studies, I (Oxford, 1976), 256–9; J. W. F. Hill, *Medieval Lincoln* (Cambridge, 1948), 186.

Approach roads and the gates through which they entered the walled area dictated the forms of suburban growth. The earliest suburban settlements perhaps clustered immediately outside town gates and may have spread along the lanes which ran round the outside of the town defences. Records of houses which have encroached on to the town ditch, as at Canterbury by the later 11th century and at Winchester by the early 12th century, may provide early evidence for these developments.[3] Churches standing just outside town gates, of which nearly every substantial medieval town has at least one example, were presumably established to serve these settlements. They would also have served travellers at both ends of their journeys, and so could count on a substantial revenue in addition to that drawn from their parishioners. At Winchester the earliest recorded foundation of a parish church was that of St Martin immediately outside West Gate, dedicated in 934-*c*. 939.[4] For Hereford we may use the evidence of the extra-mural churches to propose a chronology for the development of the northern suburb in the 11th century. The pattern of parish boundaries suggests that All Saints, just outside the entry through the primary enclosure, was the earlier of the two churches within the later north wall.[5] Since the other church, St Peter's, is recorded in 1085, All Saints is likely to have been a pre-Conquest foundation. Its existence thus reinforces the archaeological evidence for a suburban settlement outside the north gate of Hereford in the late Saxon period.[6]

A market place was often the focus of activity immediately outside the gate. This might be formed on an irregular site at the junction of the roads approaching the gate, as at the church of All Saints outside the presumed entry to the Danish Borough of Stamford.[7] The market place in the corresponding position at Northampton has a more regular form, but could have developed in the same way with the minimum of disturbance to existing territorial interests on waste land beside the approach roads and the extra-mural lane. The long rectangular suburban market place appears to have been a later development, and is most strikingly exemplified by St Giles's, Oxford. Here, the laying out of a wide street in the ill-defined area where two roads merged may have been accom-

3. *Liber Censualis Vocatus Domesday Book*, eds. A. Farley and H. Ellis (London, 1783–1816), 1, 2; Biddle (ed.), *Winchester in the Early Middle Ages*, 274.
4. Ibid., 329–30.
5. M. D. Lobel (ed.) *Historic Towns: Maps and Plans of Towns and Cities in the British Isles, with Historical Commentaries from Earliest Times to 1800*, Vol. 1 (Oxford, 1969), 'The Liberty of Hereford'.
6. P. Rahtz, 'Hereford', *Current Archaeology*, 9 (1968), 242–6.
7. W. G. Hoskins, *Local History in England* (London, 1959), 87; A. Rogers, 'Parish Boundaries and Urban History: Two Case Studies', *J. Brit. Archaeol. Assoc.*, 3rd. ser., 35 (1972), 56–63.

panied by the foundation of a second church to serve a suburb which had expanded well beyond its original nucleus near the church of St Mary Magdalen by North Gate.[8] A similar development may be detected in the plan of Northampton, where the church of St Giles stands at the far end of a broad strip of land extending east between two converging roads from the church of All Saints in the market place. In the later middle ages this area was closely associated with Northampton fair and the community of burgesses.[9] The new borough casually referred to in 1086 may have been based on this linear growth, rather than the whole of the area enclosed by the later walls.[10] At Hereford the dry level site provided by the gravel terrace and the direction imposed by the road from Worcester caused the linear market place which emerged in the late 11th century to be sited along the street outside and parallel to the defences, rather than at right-angles to it. The similarly situated Broad Streets of Stamford and Oxford gained the width which enabled them to function as market places by encroachment on the town ditch.[11]

8. H. M. Cam, *Liberties and Communities in Medieval England* (London, 1944), 121.
9. Victoria History of the Country of Northampton, Vol. III (London, 1930), 7–8.
10. *Domesday Book*, 219.
11. Hoskins, *Local History in England*, 87.

A note on the figures

The plans which accompany this paper (Figures 1–9) are intended to demonstrate the extent of suburban development in relation to the original enclosed area of ten English medieval towns. In each case there are shown the lines of town walls which may reasonably be supposed to have been in use at any period during the middle ages. Precinct walls are not shown, except where they supplanted the town walls entirely. Suburban parish churches are shown in order to provide some measure of the extent and chronology of suburban growth. Any attempt to represent parish churches within the original enclosure would have cluttered the plans unnecessarily and obscured the relationship between the street pattern within the walls and the pattern without. On the other hand, religious houses and hospitals both within and without the walls are shown, since the overall pattern of their distribution often indicates the conscious choice of a suburban site. These plans are not intended as representations of the ten towns but as graphical demonstrations of some of the processes of their suburban growth.

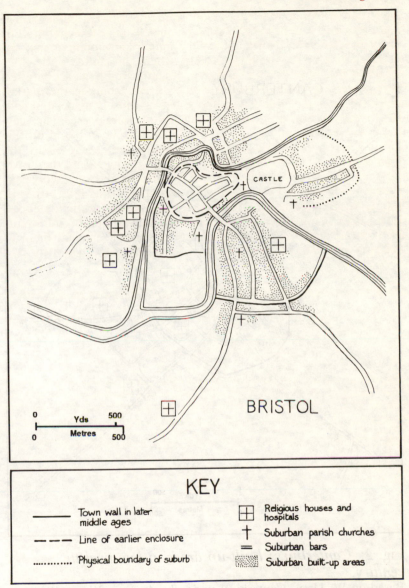

Fig. 1: *Bristol: built-up areas in later Middle Ages*.
Based on Speed (1610); H. A. Cronne ed., *Bristol Charters 1378–1499* (1946); and C. D. Ross ed., *Cartulary of St Mark's Hospital Bristol* (1959).

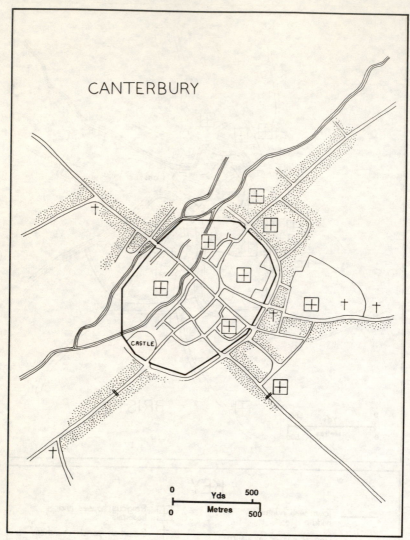

Fig. 2: *Canterbury: built-up areas in late twelfth century.*
Based on W. Urry, *Canterbury under the Angevin Kings* (1967); and Speed (1610).

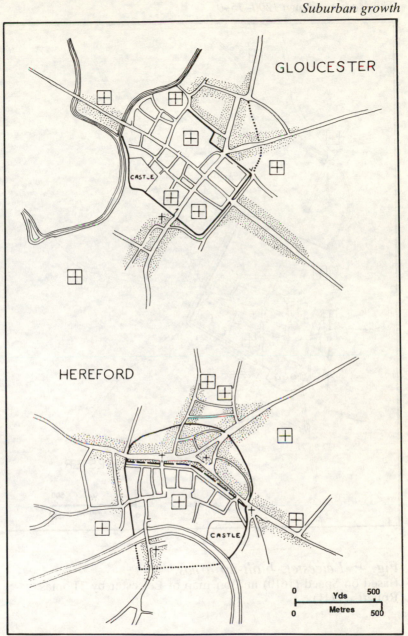

Fig. 3: *Gloucester and Hereford: medieval built-up areas.*
Based on M. D. Lobel, *Historic Towns and Cities in the British Isles, with Historical commentaries from Earliest Times to 1800,* Vol 1 (1969)

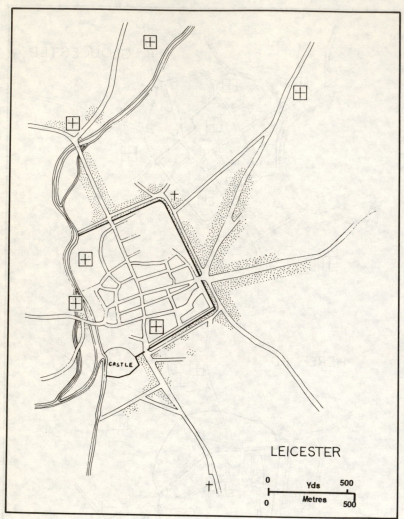

Fig. 4: *Leicester: built-up areas.*
Based on Speed (1610) and on map of Leicester by Thomas
Roberts (1741).

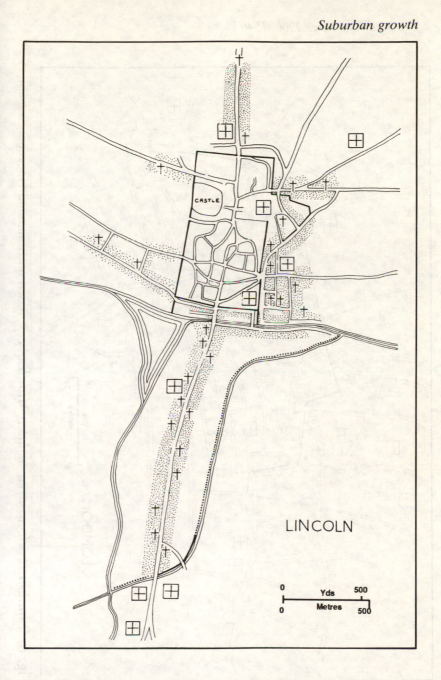

Fig. 5: *Lincoln: medieval built-up area.*
Based on Hill, *Medieval Lincoln* (1948) and Speed (1610).

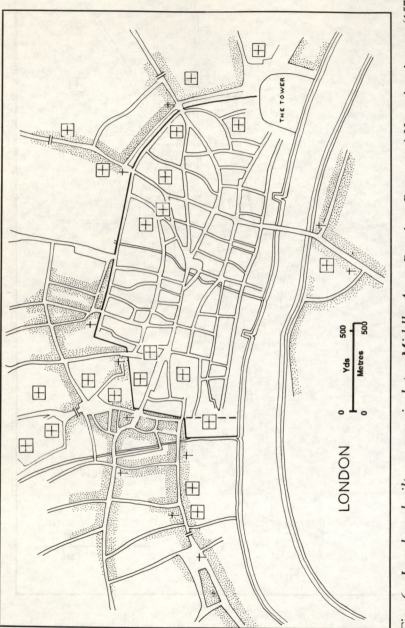

Fig. 6: *London: built-up area in later Middle Ages. Based on Braun and Hogenberg's map (1572).*

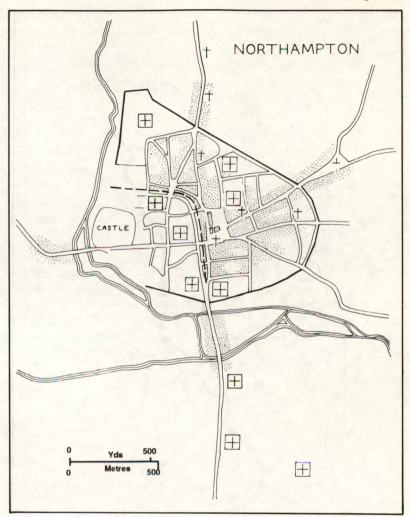

Fig. 7: *Northampton: built-up areas in later Middle Ages.*
Based on Speed (1610)

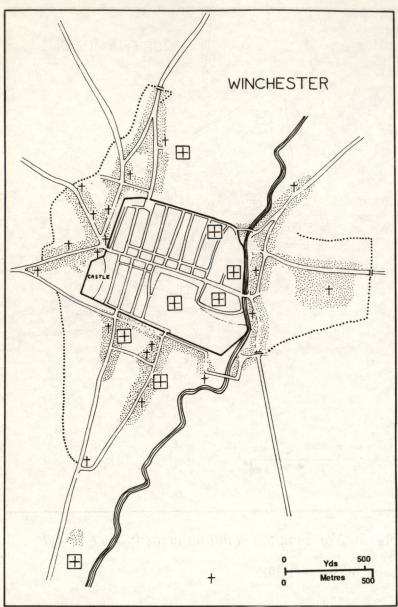

WINCHESTER

CASTLE

Fig. 8: *Winchester: built-up area in mid-12th century.*
Based on M. Biddle ed., *Winchester in the early Middle Ages*
(1976), *passim*, except for the site of St Giles's fair, which is
represented as in *c.* 1250 (Keene, *Survey of Medieval Winchester*
(1985)).

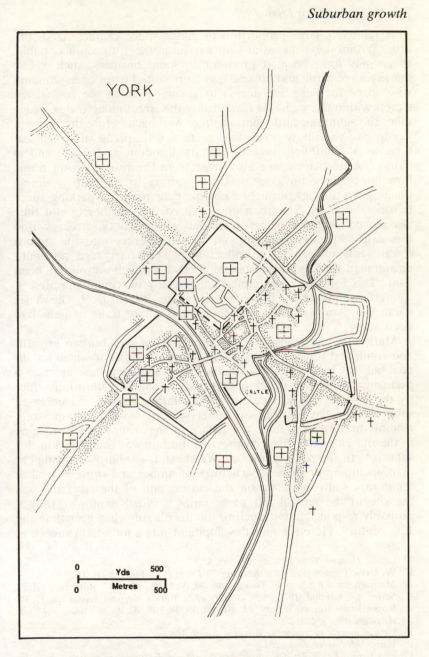

Fig. 9: *York: built-up area in later Middle Ages.*
Based on A. Raine, *Medieval York* (1955) and Speed (1610).

A relatively large proportion of public space characterized suburbs. Within the walls, as at Caernarvon in the 13th century, public space may have been at premium.[12] Some business, such as the marketing of cattle and horses, was more suited to an open situation with space for pens and access to grazing than to the constricted streets within the walls. At Canterbury the street name *Rithercheape* takes the suburban cattle market there well back before the Norman Conquest.[13] Similarly horse fairs were a widespread suburban feature, as at Smithfield in 12th century London, at Bristol, and at York.[14] A need for space also arose from the restriction on traffic flow imposed by town gates. Carts waiting to pay toll or simply queuing up to pass through a narrow gate required parking space outside the walls. Suburban approach roads, whether or not they also served as market places, were thus wider than the streets within the walls, and often opened out from the entry into the suburb towards the town gate. A collection of stationary carts no doubt encouraged trading on the spot in goods for which no toll had been paid. This form of commercial activity may be commemorated at Canterbury in the suburban street name *Wincheap*.[15] The York name Bootham indicates a further stage where stalls or pens had been set up.[16]

Marketing and transport were key factors in suburban growth, and combined to their fullest effect in those towns at which an annual fair was held. Troyes in Champagne is a notable case in which a permanent suburban development was associated with a fair. Here by the end of the 12th century a regularly planned and enclosed suburb had been laid out on either side of a wide market street leading directly away from the palace of the counts of Champagne in the old city. The main business of the fair was transacted in this suburb.[17] In the same period at Winchester a suburb of rectilinear plan, including permanent structures of timber and stone as well as temporary stalls, grew up on the eastern hill of the city, and was the site of the annual fair of St Giles.[18] Northampton's fair was probably responsible for much of the town's suburban growth in the 12th century. Here the new development was a long-term sucess: at

12. Lobel, *Historic Towns,* 'Caernarvon', 4.
13. W. Urry, *Canterbury under the Angevin Kings* (London, 1967), 203.
14. *Materials for the history of Thomas Becket,* Vol. III, ed. J. C. Robertson (Rolls Series, 67, London, 1877), 6; *Cartulary of St Mark's Hospital Bristol,* ed. C. D. Ross (Bristol Record Society, 21, Bristol, 1959), 108; A. Raine, *Mediaeval York* (London, 1955), 270–2.
15. Urry, *Canterbury under the Angevin Kings,* 108.
16. Raine, *Mediaeval York,* 261.
17. E. Chapin, *Les Villes des Foires de Champagne des Origines au début du XIVe Siècle* (Bibliothèque de l'Ecole des Hautes Etudes, section des Sciences Historiques et Philologiques, 268, Paris, 1937), 108–20.
18. Biddle (ed.), *Winchester in the Early Middle Ages,* 286–8.

Winchester the site of the fair was virtually denuded of buildings by 1400.[19]

The suburbs themselves usually preserved an image of those features which had moulded their development. By identifying this image we can sometimes reconstruct the situation before the suburbs grew. Suburban roads may indicate the relative importance of different approaches to the town at an early date. The road pattern to the north and west of the walled area of Winchester suggests that in the period before the late 9th century the Roman north gate was blocked, and that traffic from the north entered the city through West Gate along the dominant east-west axis.[20] This was an important precondition for the early suburban growth of Winchester. Land boundaries and patterns of tenure and jurisdiction often provide a basis for a chronology of suburban growth. Urry has been able to show how house plots outside Canterbury were formed, presumably in sucessive stages, out of individual fields butting on to the suburban street.[21] A 10th century rural estate boundary can be used to show how the urban area of Winchester expanded to the north of the city between then and *c*. 1110. The 12th century pattern of land tenure suggests that the southern and eastern suburbs encroached on the ecclesiastical estates outside the city in the same way. By contrast, the settlement outside West Gate was the only one of the suburbs of Winchester where there were tenements in the royal fee, and so appears to have been part of the urban area from an early date.[22] This pattern of land tenure led to the emergence of two parallel jurisdictions in Winchester, and such divisions of authority were a typical feature of many suburbs. At Bristol the suburbs of Redcliffe and Billeswick within the manor of Bedminster and of Temple Fee were the subject of a prolonged battle of jurisdictions, which was only resolved by the redefinition of the urban area and its elevation to county status in 1373.[23] Cam has shown that the suburb of St Giles, Oxford, was a similar though less clear-cut case. In 1419 the jury spoke truer than they knew when they stated that the town of Oxford had no suburb except that outside the south gate, for it is in the area to the south of the later walled borough that archaeological evidence for the earliest settlement in medieval Oxford has recently been discovered.[24] Very early settlement patterns may be reflected in the extent of later liberties.

19. D. J. Keene, *Survey of Medieval Winchester*, Part I, Winchester Studies II, (Oxford, 1985).
20. Biddle (ed.), *Winchester in the Early Middle Ages*, 261.
21. Urry, *Canterbury under the Angevin Kings*, 188.
22. Biddle (ed.), *Winchester in the Early Middle Ages*, 265.
23. *Bristol Charters 1378–1499*, ed. H. A. Cronne (Bristol Record Society, 11, Bristol, 1946), 31–41.
24. Cam, (1963) *Liberties and Communities in Mediaeval England*, 117; T. G. Hassall, 'Excavations at Oxford, 1971', *Oxoniensa*, 37 (1972), 143–5 .

By the later 12th century the built-up area of many towns extended several hundred yards beyond their walls. There is a real possibility that such suburbs engulfed detached hamlets or encouraged a concentration of a scattered farming population along the main roads leading to the town. Within the suburbs themselves there may well be traces of these pre-urban settlements. A particular question concerns towns of Roman origin, and the possibility that certain suburban churches may have originated in the service of hamlets of the sub-Roman period, as has recently been demonstrated for Mainz.[25] There are sufficient examples of proximity between Roman or Dark Age cemeteries and suburban churches in England to suppose that eventually a similar connection may in some case be proved.

The built-up area of most suburbs consisted of either a single ribbon development or a more compact grouping of houses around several roads converging on a town gate or river crossing. The most striking English example of the former is the Lincoln suburb of Wigford, which by 1100 extended for nearly a mile to the south of the city along the north-south axis which dominates the movement of land traffic in the Lincoln area.[26] As its name implies, Wigford conforms to the classic German concept of the *wik*, the street of traders.[27] Linear suburbs of nearly so great an extent were not uncommon. In the second half of the 12th century houses extended for half a mile beyond the walls outside North Gate and Worth Gate at Canterbury, and some years earlier houses extended a similar distance to the north and south of Winchester.[28] At the same period, a continuous and busy suburb extended 2 miles west of London.[29] Here the attraction of the palace of Westminster encouraged ribbon development. Stourbridge fair perhaps acted as a similar magnet for the one populous suburb of 13th century Cambridge, which extended towards Barnwell.[30] Where there was no such special attraction linear suburbs of this type appear to have been most characteristic of the major long-distance routes approaching a town. The more compact suburbs around converging streets perhaps more easily became fully part of the town. Northampton is the outstanding case. The western suburb of Winchester, apparently fully built-up by *c.* 1110 and with its conspicuously heterogeneous tenure and high rents, was easily the most prosperous of the four suburbs of the

25. K. Weidemann, 'Die Topographie von Mainz in der Romerzeit und dem fruhen Mittelalter', *Jahrbuch des Romisch-Germanischen Zentralmuseums Mainz*, 15 (1968).
26. Hill, *Medieval Lincoln*, 35–6.
27. H. Planitz, *Die deutsche Stadt im Mittelalter*, (Graz, 2nd. ed. 1965), 65–70.
28. Biddle (ed.), *Winchester in the Early Middle Ages*, 266–7.
29. Robertson, *Materials for the History of Thomas Becket*, 3.
30. F. W. Maitland, *Township and Borough* (Cambridge, 1898, repr. 1964), 148–9.
31. Biddle (ed.), *Winchester in the Early Middle Ages*, 265, 375–82.

city.[31] At Gloucester a suburb of similar form grew up around two roads leading out of the north gate, perhaps as early as the 11th century.[32] The prosperous Bristol suburb of Redcliffe and Temple Fee appears to have been formed by a deliberate modification of the two roads approaching Bristol bridge so as to allow for the creation of a third suburban street between them.

That progressive enlargement of a town's defences to include its growing suburbs, which is usually thought to be characteristic of continental cities, is not rare in England. Between the 11th and the 13th centuries such widely differing towns as York, Bristol, Northampton, Nottingham, Hereford, and Stamford underwent this process. These developments did not match the scale of expansion at Paris, Cologne, Ghent, or Bruges, but of all English towns only London belonged to that group of perhaps fewer than ten in northwest Europe which were of this order of size and prosperity. Nor was the need for fully developed suburban defences so marked in England. Many English suburbs were probably protected by a ditch and earth bank of which little trace now remains. Place-names sometimes provide a clue to the existence of such defences. *Erdberi* in 12th century Winchester was an area within the bank and ditch of the western suburb.[33] *Baggeberi,* outside the north gate of Canterbury, and perhaps Sidbury on the south side of Worcester, may have denoted less substantial enclosures.[34] A defensive line enclosing the north suburb of Gloucester may be indicated by a ditch of running water with an adjacent lane whose public characters were defined by their respective names, the 'king's water' and the 'king's way'.[35] The Wigford suburb of Lincoln was defended in a similar fashion and the vulnerable point of entry at its south end was given additional strength by the construction of two stone bars and a length of stone wall.[36] At least three of the entries to the Winchester suburbs gained extra protection from the parish churches situated immediately inside the suburban boundaries.[37] Bars almost universally marked the suburban limits. In their simplest form they may have been capable of keeping out little more than stray animals, but the example of Lincoln shows that they could develop into substantial structures.

The definition of a boundary was sometimes followed by secondary suburban growth. To the citizens of 14th century York the

32. Lobel (ed.), *Historic Towns,* 'Gloucester', 3.
33. Biddle (ed.), *Winchester in the Early Middle Ages,* 237.
34. Urry, *Canterbury under the Angevin Kings;* A. Mawer and F. M. Stenton, *The Place Names of Worcestershire* (English Place-Name Soc., 4, Cambridge, 1927), 22.
35. Lobel (ed.), *Historic Towns,* 'Gloucester', 8.
36. Hill, *Medieval Lincoln,* 162.
37. Biddle (ed.), *Winchester in the Early Middle Ages,* 264–5.

suburb on the south side of the Ouse was not the transpontine development of Bishophill, which had been included within the city's main line of defence by the early 12th century, but the straggling line of houses outside Micklegate.[38] The north suburb of Gloucester was still recognized as a suburb in the 13th century, but beyond the outer north gate there had emerged further rows of suburban houses known as the Newland.[39] In some towns considerations of defence may have meant that the physical boundaries of the suburbs were laid out short of the actual extent of houses in the same way as the more outlying parts of a built-up area were sometimes excluded from a walled enclosure when it was first created.

When one examines the evidence for the chronology of suburban growth, the most striking feature is the early date at which it appears to have achieved its maximum extent. If the 13th was the century of the new towns, the 11th and 12th centuries were the period of greatest growth in the old-established centres. The defended suburbs of York were at their largest by the middle of the 12th century, and the important suburb of Bishophill was a largely pre-Conquest development.[40] Growth beyond these limits is not well documented but may already have been extensive by 1200. During the reign of Henry I houses probably extended further from the walls of Winchester than they were to again until after the coming of the railway. The same is probably true for Canterbury. Bristol's greatest suburban development took place in the 12th century and the limits of its medieval built-up area were probably achieved before 1300.[41] In few, if any, English towns do the suburbs appear to have expanded after this date. In most they probably contracted. By the time of our earliest town maps substantial parts of the medieval suburbs had merged into the countryside out of which they had been formed.

Many of the inhabitants of a medieval English town thus lived outside its walls. As late as the 1520s about a quarter of the population of Exeter lived in its suburbs.[42] The proportion was nearly twice as much at Winchester in the same period. Shortly before the Black Death at least a third of the population of Winchester lived in two of its four suburbs. In 1148, when the intra-mural population of the city had probably just passed its peak, 37% of the properties recorded in the survey of that year lay outside the walls and the

38. J. H. Harvey, 'Bishophill and the Church of York', *Yorkshire Archaeol. Jnl.*, 41 (1963–66), 387, 391.
39. Lobel (ed.), *Historic Towns*, 'Gloucester', 8.
40. *City of York*, II: The Defences (Royal Commission on Historic Monuments, London, 1972), 7–9.
41. Ross, *Cartulary of St Mark's Hospital Bristol*, xxxv–vi.
42. W. T. MacCaffrey, *Exeter, 1540–1640* (Cambridge, Mass., and London, 1958), 13.

suburban population was probably higher than at any later period in the middle ages.[43] In the reign of John the assessors of the aid for the Irish expedition reckoned that the wealth of the men of Redcliffe and Temple Fee exceeded by half that of the men of Bristol.[44]

In these circumstances it is not surprising that the commercial and social centre sometimes shifted away from the original settlement into the principal suburb. Lincoln, Hereford, Northampton, and Leicester may be taken as representative of different stages in this evolution. Its eleven churches and its great extent testify to the early prosperity of Wigford, but it was always subordinate in commerce, density of population, and municipal importance to the lower city of Lincoln on the north bank of the river Witham. If the two main roads which approach Lincoln from the south had converged on High Bridge rather than a point a mile to the south of the city, and a wider well-drained area had been available for settlement south of the river, the development of Lincoln may more closely have resembled that of Cambridge. At Hereford and Northampton, the extra-mural market place quickly became the commercial centre of the town and was subsequently the seat of municipal authority. Both suburban developments were soon encompassed within an extended enclosure, and at Northampton the main London road appears to have been re-routed to lead directly to the new town centre.[45] The parallel development at Leicester was only completed in the 16th and 17th centuries and so was not enclosed with a wall. Here the commercial nucleus shifted from within the walls to the market area outside the east gate in the most populous of the medieval suburbs. The London road was attracted away from the south gate and henceforward followed an extra-mural route direct to the new centre. The East Gate area became the focus of the modern expansion of Leicester.[46]

The distinctive character of those suburbs which remained suburban was reflected in their topography, their buildings, and their social and occupational structures. On average the inhabitants of the suburbs were poorer than those within the walls and there was less of that intermingling of rich and poor which was common in the central area of a medieval town.[47] A floating population of the des-

---

43. Biddle (ed.), *Winchester in the Early Middle Ages,* 377; Keene, *Survey of Medieval Winchester.*

44. *The Great Roll of the Pipe for the Twelfth Year of King John,* ed. C. F. Slade (Pipe Roll Soc., 64, NS 26, London, 1951), 143–4.

45. F. Lee, 'A New Theory on the Origins and Early Growth of Northampton', *Archaeol. J.* , 110 (1953), 164–74.

46. C. J. Billson, *Mediaeval Leicester* (Leicester, 1920), 20–1; *Victoria History of the Country of Leicester,* Vol IV, 'The City of Leicester; (London, 1958), 52–3; A. M. Everitt, 'Leicester and its Markets: The Seventeenth Century' in A. E. Brown (ed.), *The Growth of Leicester* (Leicester, 1970), 39–45.

47. MacCaffrey, *Exeter, 1540–1640,* 248.

titute may have also been typical: medieval Winchester had two Beggar Streets and a *Paillardestwychene* outside its walls. Suburban housing reflected this poverty: in 1417 the northern suburb of Winchester had a higher proportion of cottages in its stock of dwellings that most areas within the walls.[48] Rows of simple two-storey dwellings dating from the 15th to the 17th centuries, and of a uniformity startling by comparison with the diversity of structures within the walls, survived in the suburbs of a number of towns until the demolitions of the mid-20th century.[49] Speculative housing of this type is recorded in the suburbs of Winchester by the early 12th century.

Of all suburban trades, that of blacksmith was probably most characteristic. Smiths are recorded immediately outside the gates of Canterbury and Winchester in the 12th century and they occupied this position throughout the middle ages.[50] This emphasizes the fundamental importance which the servicing of transport has always had in town life. Significantly, smiths are among the earliest of all tradesmen to be recorded in the urban context.[51] Potting was a distinctively suburban trade, perhaps because of the availability of raw material as well as the greater risk of fire within the walls. One of the best documented suburban colonies of potters was that outside the west gate of Dublin.[52] Tanners and fullers were probably attracted to the suburbs by the ready water supply and the open space available for the drying of cloth rather than any intrinsic advantages of extra-mural life, although attempts were sometimes made to banish noisome leather-making processes to the suburbs.[53] Fullers, engaged in a trade which involved the coordination of several processes, would probably require the headquarters of their business to be situated near the commercial centre of the town. At Gloucester there was a Fullers' Street within the walls as well as 'fullers' land' outside near the river Severn.[54] Many suburbs had a

48. D. J. Keene, *Some Aspects of the History, Topography and Archaeology of the North-Eastern Part of the Medieval City of Winchester with Special Reference to the Brooks Area* (Unpublished D. Phil. thesis, Oxford, 1972), 85.
49. S. R. Jones and J. T. Smith, 'The Wealden Houses in Warwicks. and their Significance', *Trans. Birmingham and Warwicks. Archaeol. Soc.*, 79 (1960–61), 24–35; H J. Dyos, *The Study of Urban History* (London, 1968), 162 and plate 5.
50. Urry, *Canterbury under the Angevin Kings*, 12, 131; Biddle (ed.), *Winchester in the Early Middle Ages*, 434.
51. Biddle, ibid.; M. Tikhomirow, *The Towns of Ancient Russia* (Moscow, 1959), 73–4.
52. *Register of the Hospital of St. John the Baptist without the New Gate, Dublin*, ed. E. St J. Brooks (Coimisiún Láimscribhinní Na h'Eireann, Dublin, 1936), viii and *passim*.
53. *Memoranda de Parliamento*, ed. F. W. Maitland (Rolls Series, 98, London, 1893), 47.
54. Lobel (ed.), *Historic Towns*, 'Gloucester', 8; W. H. Stevenson, *Calendar of the Records of the Corporation of Gloucester* (Gloucester, 1893), 87.

marked agricultural aspect: the cornfield and pastures close to its walls were the pride of at least one 12th century Londoner. At this period corn was grown actually within the suburban defences of Winchester.[55] Some of the suburban inhabitants were no doubt engaged full-time in farm work, while others diversified their domestic economies with part-time agricultural employment. Small plots of pasture, orchards, and in the 16th century hop gardens and saffron plots were common in between and behind the suburban houses. Earlier in the Middle Ages there were suburban vineyards in the south of England.[56]

The availability of spacious sites for town houses was perhaps the main reason why, at major royal and administrative centres such as London and Winchester, magnates who visited the town from time to time acquired tenements or had lodgings in the suburbs. Throughout the middle ages the western suburbs of London were noted for their aristocratic and ecclesiastical residences set back behind the rows of smaller houses on the street frontages.[57] At Winchester similar houses were probably falling into decay by 1200.[58] A few suburbs were conspicuous for the wealth of their ordinary inhabitants, and this engendered a special sense of identity in the suburban community. The great gild of St Mary was an independent social nucleus for the men of the Wigford suburb at Lincoln, and at Winchester the Easter Gild of the men outside West Gate performed the same function.[59]

Space was also the main consideration in the siting of extra-mural institutions. Religious houses founded in towns after 1100 nearly always had a suburban site at the edge of the built-up area. Rare exceptions to this rule, such as the priory of Holy Trinity by Aldgate in London, can usually be shown to have been sited in the least densely occupied part of the walled area. A suburban situation enabled a proper conventual enclosure to be established with the minimum of disturbance to existing property interests. There is little evidence that such foundations stimulated suburban growth, although the existence of a religious house a little way from the town as at Leicester might encourage a straggle of ribbon development, and the presence of a religious house outside a contracting town might halt the decay of the particular suburb where it lay. Religious houses appear rather to have provided an effective limit to suburban

55. Biddle (ed.), *Winchester in the Early Middle Ages*, 265.
56. Biddle (ed.), *Winchester in the Early Middle Ages*, 135; Urry, *Canterbury under the Angevin Kings*, 205–6.
57. C. L. Kingsford, 'Bath Inn or Arundel House', *Archaeologia*, 72, 2nd ser. 22 (1922), 243–77; 'Essex House, formerly Leicester House and Exeter Inn,' *Archaeologia*, 73, 2nd ser. 23 (1923), 1–54.
58. Biddle (ed.), *Winchester in the Early Middle Ages*, 389–92.
59. Hill, *Medieval Lincoln*, 162–5; Biddle (ed.), *Winchester in the Early Middle Ages*, 427.

expansion. By their occupation of valuable frontage and the restriction on movement imposed by their precincts they may even have hindered commercial activity. St Mary's Abbey at York may have had this effect on the settlement outside Bootham Bar.

The Friars' mission, however, was to the urban population. The Black Friars and the Grey Friars at least seem to have tried to establish themselves as far into the built-up area as possible. Their convents were often within the walls, in contrast to those of the lesser mendicant orders, in particular those of the eremetical Carmelites. Hospitals were characteristically suburban institutions. General hospitals, such as Lanfranc's foundation at Canterbury, were usually close to the walls and were integrated with the community. Leper hospitals, of which most larger towns had at least one by the reign of Henry II, were set apart at a considerable distance from the walls and were rarely incorporated into the built-up area. Travellers approaching a town would have had another reminder of mortality some way from its walls, for the gallows were usually sited at the limits of the urban jurisdiction. Closer to the walls at nine provincial towns and the capital there were the cemeteries of the Jews.[60]

For every town where suburbs may be identified we must ask the questions: when did this development begin, what was its maximum extent, and when was this achieved? The answers will illuminate not only the history of the individual town but also the changing structure of the hierarchy of English towns in the middle ages, for in suburban growth we have something very like a measure of the rate of a town's expansion or decline. The evidence for suburban topography is often even sparser and more intractable than that for the town within the walls. We must therefore be prepared to extract everything possible from place-names, field and road patterns, liberty and parish boundaries, as well as from written historical records. But often only archaeological evidence will be able to tell us the extent and intensity of human habitation outside the walls and the nature and date of suburban boundaries. in the suburban context above all, concrete knowledge of our medieval towns can frequently be sought only with the spade.

60. M. B. Honeybourne, 'The Pre-Expulsion Cemetery of the Jews in London', *Trans. of the Jewish Hist. Soc. of England,* 20 (1959–61), 145–59.

Editorial suggestions for further reading

Biddle, M. (ed.), *Winchester in the Early Middle Ages,* Winchester Studies, I (Oxford, 1976).

Keene, D. *Survey of Medieval Winchester,* Winchester Studies, II (Oxford, 1985).

Geremek, B. *The Margins of Society in Late Medieval Paris,* trans. J. Birrell (Cambridge, 1988).

Dyer, C. Towns and cottages in eleventh-century England', in H. Mayr-Harting and R. I. Moore (eds.), *Studies in Medieval History presented to R. H. C. Davies* (London, 1985), pp. 91–106.

Chapter Seven

CRAFTSMEN AND THE ECONOMY OF LONDON IN THE FOURTEENTH CENTURY[1]

E. M. Veale

from A. E. J. Hollaender and W. Kellaway (eds.), *Studies in London History presented to Philip Edmund Jones* (Leicester, 1969)

> *A popular image of the craftsman in the medieval town, engaged upon his particular trade under the close supervison of a controlling gild system, is dispelled by this study of manufacturing industry in London. The prestige of the major London gilds or livery companies has distorted our perception of the economic life of the capital. In reality London, by far the largest city in England, boasted an enormous variety of specialisms, many unregulated by formal gild control. Here we read of feather-mongers and seal-engravers, wimplers and linen-armourers – often highly skilled men and women who were at the same time sufficiently versatile to pursue more than one craft. When by the end of the medieval period citizenship of London could be acquired only through gild membership, entailing enrolment in one of the livery companies, a citizen would carry an occupational designation which frequently bore little relationship to how he actually made his living. The relationship between the craft organizations and municipal authority calls for further study. It is clear that informal craft associations pre-existed their legitimation and formal incorporation into city government. Arguably they continued to serve the interests of their members, while at the same time they provided the city governors with a convenient means of control. Craftswomen, briefly illustrated here, are given fuller treatment in the recent work of Swanson and Goldberg, cited under Editorial suggestions for further reading on page 140.*

Historians interested in the economic development of fourteenth-century London have tended hitherto to direct their attention towards its role as a great port and distributive centre, and their

---

1. I should like to thank Dr A. R. Bridbury for invaluable help in connection with this paper, which also owes much to ideas discussed in a seminar at the London School of Economics led by him and Miss O. Coleman.

particular concern has been with mercantile activities of all sorts. But the reverse side of the coin, the role of Londoners in providing supplies and services for those attracted to the City, whether as permanent inhabitants or temporary residents, and the impact of changes in their requirements on her industrial and commercial development has been little studied. We should like to have answers, however partial and tentative they have to be, to a number of important questions. Could London craftsmen satisfy the requirements of exacting customers drawn from the City's wealthy and sophisticated society? Or were the bulk of the luxury goods acquired of foreign origin? Or were they manufactured by Londoners from materials of foreign origin? To what extent were men from the provinces, or from particular areas, whether great lay or ecclesiastical magnates or humbler traders, accustomed to turn to London craftsmen for work they required, and were there fields in which Londoners seem to have been particularly expert? What was the effect of the concentration of an increasing range of governmental activity in the capital and the size of its transient population? How important a contribution to London's economy was the need to supply the vast range of services required – food, accommodation, transport, clerical and domestic help, etc.? What changes took place during the century in London's industrial development? It was not, for instance, to be expected that the City's economy should develop during the middle years of the century unaffected by the efforts which went into the prosecution of the war with France. How important was this? I propose in this brief paper – which excludes for convenience the question of food supplies – to consider some of the preliminary problems and suggest lines for further study.

London's medieval records are unrivalled in their number and variety. Some are efficiently calendared and annotated, some in print, some still in manuscript. They have been consulted by scholars for a multitude of purposes, and information drawn from them has been used, often out of context, to illustrate a great variety of themes. No one, however, has yet attempted to write an account of the economic development of late medieval London. The most helpful studies available are studies of the London gilds.

Yet the concentration by so many writers on the history of the London gilds has had much to do with obscuring the study of the certainly complex economy of late medieval London. The very strength of the sentiments felt towards their companies by their members today, as much as in the nineteenth century and the middle ages, has contributed to this, as often they alone have been in a position to commission and finance contributions to the history of London. Inevitably these have taken the form of histories of individual livery companies. This means that groups of Londoners, not of necessity bound by common economic interests, have been studied in isolation, and the history of institutions which became inextricably interwoven with political and social developments have been investigated rather than the history of particular trades. Then, too, such histories give not only a partial but a distorted picture of the City's economy since only freemen were members of the gilds, in themselves only a small proportion of the population of the London area, both City and suburbs. Nor can it be assumed that all freemen exercising a particular craft formed one of the associations we call gilds. Thus much is concealed by this approach to the history of the economy of the City. On the one hand the versatility of the skilled medieval craftsman is obscured, as well as the existence of small groups of specialists; on the other hand groups of freemen who felt no necessity of independent organization are overlooked, as are the many workmen in the City who, although rarely freemen, contributed services which were essential to the functioning of City life.

It is not easy to shake oneself free of this preoccupation with London freemen and their gilds. Yet unless this can be done no overall picture of London industry can possibly be reconstructed. It will be helpful first, therefore, to analyse more thoroughly the limitations of this particular approach to the history of London.

Citizenship carried valuable privileges which Londoners fought hard to protect, and freemen constituted, therefore, a privileged caste to which admission was jealously guarded. Can we discover the size of this group or analyse its structure? Unfortunately, where York, for instance, has registers of freemen from 1272 to 1509,[2] the registers kept by the chamberlain of London for the medieval period no longer exist. The names of those admitted to the freedom during the years 1309-12 – 253 by apprenticeship and 656 by redemption – were also entered in one of the City's Letter Books and therefore survive.[3] These entries cover too short a period and reflect too troubled a period in London politics to be susceptible to analysis on the lines required. However, the names of those admitted have survived and over 120 occupations are represented.

More valuable information about fourteenth-century freemen is derived from assessments for subsidies which exist in part for the years 1292, 1319 and 1332.[4] While the occupations of taxpayers are only rarely stated, the great wealth of London records for this period makes identification of many of them possible, although of necessity such identification is more often conjectural than certain. Assess-

2. Analysed by E. Miller, 'Medieval York' in *V.C.H. City of York* (1961), 43, 114–16.
3. C[alendar of] L[etter] B[ook]D, 35–179; *C[alendar of] P[lea and] M[emoranda] R[olls], 1364–81*, pp. 1–1vi.
4. Printed in *Two Early London Subsidy Rolls*, ed. E. Ekwall (Lund, 1951) and M. Curtis, 'The London Lay Subsidy of 1332', *Finance and Trade under Edward III*, ed. G. Unwin (1918).

ments for 1292 survive for only twelve wards; discrepancies between the names of those taxed in 1319 and 1332 mean that neither list can be used on its own. Some taxpayers of 1319 were presumably elderly and dead before 1332; others were recently established in 1332; some who had goods worth 6s. 8d. in 1319 were excluded by the higher minimum figure of 10s. in 1332. But Ekwall has shown that whereas the numbers taxed in both years in some wards were more or less the same, the names of those taxed differed greatly: only 25 of the 72 taxpayers in Tower in 1319 were also taxed in 1332; only 21 of the 73 taxed in Cordwainer; 14 or 15 of the 76 or 77 taxed in Queenhithe, and 7 of the 40 in Aldersgate.[5] There were thus also many who were taxed in 1332 but not in 1319. Ekwall concluded that there were many people in London whose possessions were just at or below those of the taxable minimum and who, while liable for taxation one year, were exempt another. Moreover, rough and ready methods of assessment, inaccurate information and evasion certainly contributed to the difficulties in a city the size of London. There was confusion in London for some time over which people should be taxed. In 1292 some men who paid were not freemen; in 1319 two men had their assessments cancelled because they were not freemen.[6] Presumably it became customary as levies on movables lost their novelty to assume that only freemen were liable. But identification of freemen can have been no easy task in the early fourteenth century. London citizens had already for several decades fought hard to protect their ancient privileges against the relentless pressures of a constant influx of other English and alien immigrants, and procedures for controlling admissions to the freedom were clarified by the charter granted to the City by Edward II in 1319.[7] How long it took to strengthen and develop the existing machinery we do not know. No doubt identification of London freemen became progressively easier as the fourteenth century passed, although the regulation of admissions probably functioned much less efficiently than we like to think.[8]

Early fourteenth-century taxpayers, then, were freemen who owned goods worth the taxable minimum or above, and may be estimated at the 2000 or more heads of households who paid the subsidies of 1319 and 1332. But there is no doubt that they represented only a small proportion of the working population of the London area. Ekwall estimated the total population of the City at

---

5. *Two Early London Subsidy Rolls*, 78.
6. Ibid., 88.
7. G. A. Williams, *Medieval London* (1963), 264–84.
8. e.g. H. T. Riley, *Memorials of London and London Life, 1276–1419* (1868), 474–5. Individuals could be asked to produce their certificates of admission: ibid., 597; *Cal. London Possessory Assizes*, ed. H. M. Chew (London Record Soc., i. 1965), no. 114.

not far short of 40 000.[9] He worked out possible figures for citizen households, including family, wards, servants and apprentices; noted evidence for those with property below the taxable minimum; listed those excluded – the clergy and others who served St Paul's, the 110 parish churches and a number of other ecclesiastical and monastic establishments; the moneyers, the colonies of alien merchants, and the households of magnates who maintained a London home; the judges and royal and other officials. Finally he vividly illustrated the possible numbers of the City's underworld by reminding us that in 1318 Robert de Lincoln left a bequest of one penny for each of 2000 poor people, and that in 1322 the crowd swarming round the gate of the Blackfriars when alms were distributed was so vast that over fifty people were trampled to death.

The very poor may escape us altogether and we are perforce concerned only with magnates, clerics and aliens as consumers. But we are vitally interested in one group of those not taxed whose economic importance it is only too easy to underestimate. It consisted of those freemen whose possessions, after deduction of goods exempted, were valued at figures at or below the taxable minimum, and tradesmen and craftsmen who were not freemen.[10] We have already been advised in general terms of the numbers of *foreigns:* A. H. Thomas suggested that for every adult freeman there were three men who were not free.[11] Ekwall drew attention to a list of tradesmen – tailors, upholders, hosiers, skinners – summoned in 1321 for selling their wares at the evening fairs held on Cornhill and in Cheapside.[12] A number came from the poorer areas just outside the city wall, and one from Kingston. Many may be difficult to identify elsewhere because of confusion over surnames. But seventy-four men and sixteen women, mostly wives working with their husbands, were summoned, of whom about a dozen can be traced as taxpayers of 1319.[13] Yet the men involved were far from being humble craftsmen turning naturally to street selling as their only outlet into retail trade. They were able to appeal for support to the king and a royal writ of 1323 ordered the mayor and aldermen to allow them to sell their goods according to their ancient rights.[14] They were, in this writ, described as *mediocris populi* or people of middle condition in the City, in itself an important and healthy

9. *Two Early London Subsidy Rolls,* 71–81. Williams, op. cit., 315–17, agrees with this estimate and discusses other figures which have been proposed.
10. J. F. Willard, *Parliamentary Taxes on Personal Property, 1290–1334* (Cambridge, Mass., 1934), 79–80. In addition to garments for husband and wife, their bed, a valuable ring, buckle, girdle, and drinking cup, it seems to have been usual to exempt the goods required for the earning of a living.
11. *C.P.M.R., 1364–81*, p. lxii.
12. *Two Early London Subsidy Rolls,* 78.
13. *C.L.B.E,* 156–9.
14. *C.P.M.R., 1323–64,* 1.

reminder that many who were considered of middle status were not liable to taxation either because they were not freemen or because they were too poor. But ultimately only detailed research on members of allied trades effectively spotlights the size of this group. For instance, 147 skinners were named in the London records between 1330 and 1350; only sixty of them paid the subsidy in 1332.[15] We may assume that a number passed their days unnoticed by the authorities, and that, if we include the tawyers who dressed the skins, perhaps more than two-thirds of the men working in the fur trade belonged to this category. Some were prosperous dealers who worked from their homes or sold in the streets and markets, who contrived to evade the responsibilities of a citizenship whose advantages had little attraction for them;[16] others formed the pool of both skilled and semi-skilled labour on which the merchants depended. Conditions varied from handicraft to handicraft, but we are working in the dark until more research has been done. London records for the fourteenth century yield a surprisingly rich harvest, if also a vexing number of problems, for those with the patience to search them with this subject in mind.

It was the freemen of the City of London who formed the associations known as gilds. Before we can discover the extent to which this form of organization was adopted by London craftsmen, some definitions are essential. The group of freemen exercising a particular craft was known as a mistery or *officium,* and after the struggles of the late thirteenth century it was to become municipal policy to delegate to this group the responsibility for certain functions previously handled by the municipality itself: admissions to the freedom and apprenticeships.[17] In a number of trades, particularly those which contained a high proportion of merchants, there was already an association in existence which could take over these functions. These associations were the fraternities, founded to provide opportunities for social and religious activities, which in some cases had already been used as pressure groups for political and economic purposes in the late thirteenth and early fourteenth centuries. They then depended on the Church rather than on secular authority for protection and for their sanctions, and it was this link with the Church which gave the fraternities their particular character throughout the middle ages. From the 1320s, however, mistery and fraternity grew together, and the authority of the association, strengthened by royal or municipal recognition, came to depend both on common economic interests and on the social cohesion of

15. E. M. Veale, *English Fur Trade in the Later Middle Ages* (1966), 116 and n.
16. Cf. the cardmaker who, in 1365, although a freeman, found it to his advantage to plead as a *foreign, C.P.M.R., 1364–81,* 24.
17. I summarize here some of the comments made in *English Fur Trade,* 101-16 where references will be found.

the group involved. These are the associations, drawing their strength from several roots, which we may rightly call gilds. It was these organized misteries which were to acquire additional powers when recognized as the corporate bodies known as livery companies, and which were to establish themselves within the framework of the constitution of the City. Thus while in the mid-fourteenth century a freeman was admitted by his fellow craftsmen, by the early sixteenth century membership of one of the particular associations known as livery companies was the essential preliminary to citizenship. During the intervening years it was customary to label an individual not only with the term 'citizen' but with the name of the group which had sponsored his admission. Occupational ascriptions came to mean no more than gild and company membership, which might or might not provide some indication of occupation. The great variety of activities of the City's freemen was, as it were, drawn superficially within a straitjacket which served to channel political and social aspirations and helped to solve some of the problems of municipal control of trade.

Unfortunately the sources available for the fourteenth century, which is obviously the most interesting period in the history of the gilds in connection with the subject under review, rarely permit us to distinguish their constituent elements. We cannot assume that because there is no evidence of a fraternity among the members of a particular mistery one did not exist. The minstrels' fraternity, for instance, only came to light, like many others, when they made their return in response to the inquiry into fraternities in 1389. The ordinances of this fraternity, dated 1350, reveal, however, the solely charitable nature of their association.[18] Nor can we assume that because a mistery did not produce ordinances for recognition by the municipality for the supervision of its members and the goods they made there was no organization at work. But I suggest that among the many crafts exercised by freemen there were a large number to which we can certainly attribute a degree of organization, a smaller number where organization was minimal and spasmodic, and that in others there may have been no association at all. I put forward these conclusions with some hesitation since they can only be fully explored in the light of circumstances within particular groups of allied trades.

We may assume that the members of the majority of the fifty-one misteries given the right to elect to the common council in 1377 were united in some form of association.[19] The powerful mercantile groups had received royal charters, and all but half a dozen misteries

---

18. H. A. F. Crewdson, *The Worshipful Company of Musicians* (1950), 13–14, 79–81.
19. *C.L.B.H*, 59; *C.P.M.R., 1364–81*, 243.

had already presented ordinances for confirmation or were shortly to do so. In some cases we know by chance of the existence of a fraternity. The painters, for instance, who chose masters in 1328, had a fraternity dedicated to St Luke in St Giles' Cripplegate, the area where many of them lived;[20] the cutlers, of whose fraternity linked with the Charterhouse we know from the enquiry of 1389, elected masters in 1328 and presented ordinances in 1344 and 1380.[21] But what was the position among the many other groups of craftsmen active in London at the time?

Before we can try to answer this question there are a number of perplexing problems to be solved. Particular crafts have to be identified under their various names. Since the names of over 180 trades are to be found in the London records, and even contemporaries made mistakes,[22] it is scarcely surprising that we are easily confused. Are the *quilters* or quilt-makers of the fourteenth century to be identified as the *stuffers* in a list of crafts of 1422?[23] If not, what were the *stuffers* doing? Then changes in the activities associated with a particular craft have to be followed across the period. The upholder of the early fourteenth century, for instance, whose chief interest was in the sale of second-hand clothing, was not the same man as the upholder of the late fifteenth century whose chief interest was in bedding and who was to be the predecessor of the modern upholsterer. Such problems call for more than the study of linguistic derivations; again, only research into the activities of groups of allied crafts will supply answers. Work, for instance, on the role of different groups within the leather trades made it possible to draw the distinction which Riley, Sharpe and Unwin failed to appreciate between the whittawyers, who dressed leather skins with alum, and the tawyers or greytawyers who dressed fur skins for the skinners.

The fullest contemporary list of London crafts was that compiled by the Brewers' clerk in 1422.[24] Both Unwin and Thomas assumed that the 111 crafts named were organized in some way, even if some had private associations unrecognized by secular authority, since the clerk stated that he had made the list 'in case it may in any wise profit the hall and Company of Brewers'.[25] But I suggest rather that the Brewers' clerk was doing exactly what he said he was doing:

20. *C.L.B.E*, 233; G. Unwin, *Gilds and Companies of London* (3rd ed., 1938), 107.
21. Ibid.; Riley, *Memorials,* 217, 438. Details of the fraternities of the London whittawyers, barbers, cutlers and glovers, who sent in returns in 1389, will be found in H. F. Westlake, *Parish Gilds of Mediaeval England* (1919), 187–8.
22. Riley, *Memorials,* 474–5: a York cutler found he had joined the bladers (cornmongers) instead of, presumably, the bladesmiths.
23. e.g. *C.L.B.D*, 49; Unwin, *Gilds and Companies*, 167, 370.
24. Unwin, *Gilds and Companies*, 167, 370.
25. Unwin, *Gilds and Companies*, 88.; *C.P.M.R., 1364-81*, xxxvi.

making a list 'of the names of all the crafts exercised in London from of old and still continuing'. He was not an expert, he used names he was not always familiar with, and he tried to be comprehensive. But he overlooked important trades like the masons and fusters which had been among the fifty-one misteries of 1377, and others like the coopers and bladesmiths who had presented ordinances before 1422, as well as other crafts we know were exercised in the fourteenth century. This conclusion is strengthened by his inclusion of the *burlesters* or *birlesters* about whom very little indeed is known although as hucksters or poor men and women who carried food, particularly fish, about the streets for sale, they were no doubt very familiar to contemporaries.[26] Few, if any of them, can have been freemen, and their inclusion, together with that of the basketmakers, many of whom we know to have been *foreigns*,[27] indicates that he was not attempting to list organized bodies of freemen. In the case of some of the occupations he named it seems reasonable to suppose that the joint activities of the craftsmen concerned had, in the mid-fourteenth century, been limited to the functions delegated to them by the municipality, handling admissions and apprenticeships. But a decree of 1364 ordered them to elect and present to be sworn masters who should supervise their fellow craftsmen and the goods they made or sold.[28] This decree certainly stimulated institutional development in some trades. Some not only presented masters but also formulated ordinances and secured municipal approval for them. This implies the existence of some form of association, and even among the lesser misteries such as the barbers, evidence survives of the social and religious activities sponsored by fraternities as well as the supervision of a trade.[29]

But it seems probable that a surprising number of misteries named by the Brewers' clerk and others he omitted continued to carry out their municipal responsibilities in a much more casual and haphazard fashion. Some were slow indeed to obey the decree of 1364, although it made sufficient impact for the limners, writers of text letter and those who bound and sold books to refer to it when they jointly presented masters in 1403.[30] The galochemakers were not supervised in 1400,[31] and the braziers admitted that they had not been in the habit of electing masters when they presented their ordinances in 1416.[32] The latoners presented masters in 1416, 1417, 1423, 1428 and 1432, but seem on no other occasion to have found

26. *C.L.B.G*, 123, n. 6.
27. *C.L.B.L*, 37.
28. Letter Book G, f. 135v; *C.P.M.R., 1364–81*, 13, n. 2.
29. Westlake, op. cit., 187.
30. Riley, *Memorials*, 557.
31. Ibid., 554–5. Galoches were wooden-soled sandals.
32. Riley, *Memorials*, 624–7.

joint action before the municipal authorities necessary.[33] The fellmongers, parchmyners, bookbinders, paternostrers,[34] jewellers, organ-makers, quilters, mirrorers, feathermongers and seal-engravers never troubled either to present masters or to formulate ordinances. Presumably they were able to handle their joint problems in a completely informal way.

The corporate activities of some other misteries came to light for the first time after the City's decision in 1487 that unauthorized ordinances were to be cancelled,[35] and soon afterwards ordinances, of which the original date is therefore unknown, were hurriedly brought in by a large number of misteries.[36] Among those to appear for the first time, such as the greytawyers and the marbelers, it is perhaps most interesting to look more closely at the netmakers and the *corsours* or horse dealers, both of which were included by the Brewers' clerk in his list. The netmakers were admitting freemen in 1400 when one man whom they had admitted was allowed to transfer to the salters, a far more socially acceptable group, on the grounds that he exercised that trade.[37] Their ordinances were very brief and give no hint of common social or religious activities: two wardens were to be elected, no member was to take an apprentice if not presented and approved, or put *foreigns* to work without permission.[38] The ordinances of the corsours, formulated only in 1488, were even briefer: they agreed to choose their wardens on a particular day, to pay 4d. each, and a fine of 4d. if they failed to attend.[39] They shared with the drovers a common interest in the cleanliness of Smithfield, and this appears to have been their only other joint concern.[40] Can we infer the existence in such cases of any effective association which we can describe as a gild?

Further investigation of those groups of craftsmen of whose joint activities there is little or no evidence will no doubt shed some light on this problem. Some were obviously highly skilled men whose specialist skills were such that their economic interests were rarely threatened. They may have satisfied their social needs through some parish fraternity or a fraternity associated with a more powerful trade as did the more prosperous fellmongers, tawyers and upholders who joined the skinners' fraternity dedicated to Corpus

33. *C.L.B.L*, 173, 186; *C.L.B.K*, 29, 98, 149. The name appears in various forms.
34. Sharpe, followed by Unwin, listed the beaders among the 25 misteries who elected masters in 1328. This name is not a version of *bedemakers* but is, judging from the men involved, a mistake for bladers, or cornmongers, *C.L.B.E*, 233.
35. *C.L.B.L*, 246.
36. Ibid., *passim*. The Letter Book itself should be consulted for these ordinances.
37. *C.L.B.I*, 13.
38. *C.L.B.L*, 254.
39. Ibid., 265.
40. Riley, *Memorials*, 366. See also p. 597 where a cutler lost the freedom after having been admitted by the corsours.

Christi.[41] No regular visitor to the Public Record Office can fail to appreciate the importance of the parchmyners or parchment-makers and yet we know very little about them. They seem to have sold their wares through the haberdashers: possibly few were freemen.[42]

Since the size of the groups concerned must have had much to do with the degree of organization required it is instructive to look closely at one mistery, the botellers, or makers of leather bottles, of whose activities more is known and whose numbers we know as a result of the chance which involved them with so powerful a man as Sir William Windsor, husband of Alice Perrers. They first obeyed the City's decree of 1364 in 1373 when they agreed to be ruled by two or three of their members, presented two men who were sworn as masters, and resolved that each boteller should put his mark on his bottles.[43] Their representatives were sometimes associated with those of other leather crafts in assaying leather, as in 1378 and 1412, and they presented masters in 1377, 1378, 1380, 1423, 1424, 1427 and 1428.[44] It is obvious that two men, William Carlil and Thomas Torold, were behind the activities of the 1370s and 1380s. It was they who were masters for much of the time and who were called in as arbitrators when, owing to some defective bottles, Sir William Windsor lost the 180 gallons of wine he had taken with him to France. During the long dispute over the settlement of this case it transpired that 'the whole mistery' consisted of only seven men and the culprit himself, who, judging from his complaints, was not a freeman.[45] Elections of masters, dealing with admissions, apprenticeships and occasional crises, can have required no organization in groups of this size; joint action does not imply the continuous existence of any association for social and religious purposes. Exact numbers are rarely available, although we know there were forty-one fullers in 1376,[46] one of the misteries important enough to elect to the common council in 1377. Possibly there may have been only a dozen or twenty freemen in a considerable number of misteries.

The greater number of the men in some trades were probably *foreigns*, with only a sprinkling of freemen among them, and there were a few crafts dominated by women such as the throwing of silk. Men who did unskilled labour such as lime-burning and many who provided services were rarely freemen. The work of corn, salt and coal meters and porters was regulated by the authorities in the

---

41. Veale, op. cit., 115, 186.
42. Riley, *Memorials*, 423; *Register of John of Gaunt, 1379–83*, ed. E. C. Lodge and R. Somerville (Camden 3rd ser., lvi – lvii, 1937), 259.
43. *C.L.B.G*, 317.
44. Riley, *Memorials*, 420–1; *C.L.B.I*, 100; *C.L.B.H*, 63, 96, 133; *C.L.B.K*, 15, 30, 77, 97.
45. *C.P.M.R, 1381–1412*, 77–8.
46. Riley, *Memorials*, 400.

late thirteenth century, and their fellowship was believed to date from time immemorial, but virtually nothing is known of their society until the sixteenth century.[47] Others, too, played an important role in city life: drovers, watermen, lightermen, carters, hackneymen who let horses for hire, *traventers* who let carts for hire, and launderers who waited until 1960 to found their gild but who even in the fourteenth century included specialists such as *kercheflavenders*.[48]

If we leave institutions aside and try to probe further into the activities of different craftsmen we will probably find that the versatility of the London workman was as remarkable as the range of interests shown by its merchants. But while the London records themselves provide an invaluable backcloth against which the craftsmen can be studied, they provide only a partial picture of Londoners at work, particularly as the character of the material entered in the Letter Books changes during the century. For more information we must search further afield into records of commissions executed and purchases made, as well as into surviving examples of medieval craftsmanship. The value of archaeological and artistic sources for the student of medieval London is not to be ignored but it is obviously limited; surviving accounts, inventories and wills are biased in that they reflect chiefly governmental activity or the interests of the wealthier private consumer. But nevertheless, provided a group of allied trades is studied in these extensive sources, still relatively unexplored from this standpoint, some interesting light should be shed on the network of relationships which bound them, the particular contribution of Londoners and the area they served, and the range of skills of individual craftsmen.

There can be no doubt that as well as those already mentioned such as the mirrorers, there were individuals in fourteenth-century London who specialized within a relatively narrow field. Robert Leg, for instance, was an *ageletmakere,* a man technically concerned only with the making of the metal tags of shoelaces, although it is obvious from the attempt in 1365 of a wiredrawer, presumably the supplier of his raw materials, to monopolize his output that he was in fact making shoelaces as well as their tags.[49] Roger Hackesalt and Robert de Shilyngtone, in a petition of 1353, stated that they did not know nor had ever used any other craft but that of 'workers in wood for saddles' and that if they were hampered in any way both the fusters who made the saddle bows and the saddlers who finished

47. W. M. Stern, *Porters of London* (1960), 12, 82–4.
48. *C.P.M.R., 1381–1412*, 214.
49. *C.P.M.R., 1364–81*, 13. Usually the chapemakers made small metal objects such as these tags, shoebuckles, clasps for gowns and shoes, chains, ginger graters etc., *C.L.B.L,* 64.

and sold them would suffer.[50] What exactly were they doing? They were presumably a couple of woodmongers who had found it paid them to concentrate on securing from estates such as that of the abbey of St Albans, from one of whose parks came oak for the rafters of Westminster Hall,[51] the particular timber required and to prepare it for sale to the fusters who as joiners did the more specialized work on it. Similarly, among men and women who made clothes small groups of specialists seem to have existed: *wimplers, callers, camiser* and *cambister* or shirtmakers, paltokmakers, linen-armourers who made the tunics worn under armour, and, at the end of the century, *shapers* and *shepsters* or cutters-out.[52] Work closely associated with this was the making of tents and pavilions, usually of cloth, serge, worsted and fustian, and miscellaneous items such as banners and hangings. Edward III's tentmaker, *pavillonarius*, from at least 1331 to 1343, was John de Yakeslee, a Londoner with an impressive mansion on Cornhill.[53] We know, too, that when Edward of Carnarvon required tents in 1303 for his expedition to Scotland, a team of sixty-three tentmakers was set to work in Holborn on the great hall with six posts, a chamber for the prince himself, and another twenty-six tents.[54]

But while there may be evidence here of specialization it is more probable that the Londoner with a particular skill could and did make use of it in a number of different contexts and might therefore be described in different ways. Linen-armourers, for instance, may also have made bedding; since references to tentmakers are so rare in the London records, they may also have made tents.[55] Their close association with the tailors – they were all members of the fraternity of St John the Baptist in the late thirteenth century – strengthens this assumption, and it is worth noting that Yakeslee's home was to become the Merchant Taylors' Hall.[56] Then a glover was essentially a man skilled in the making of fine leather goods. We should expect to find him selling gloves as was John de Stanton in 1396 – he had 134 pairs in stock – but the inventory of the contents of his shop shows that he was equally interested in the making of purses. He

50. *Calendar of Letters, 1350–70*, ed. R. R. Sharpe (1885), nos. 111–12.
51. *History of the King's Works*, ed. H. M. Colvin, i (1963), 529.
52. e.g. *C.L.B.A*, 22; *C.L.B.D*, 38; *Calendar of Coroners' Rolls*, ed. R. R. Sharpe (1913), 183; *C.P.M.R.*, 1364–81, 232; *C.P.M.R., 1413–37*, 208; *C.L.B.I*, 283.
53. Riley, *Memorials,* 184; P.R.O. Exchequer, King's Remembrancer, Accounts Various, 389/14.
54. H. Johnstone, *Edward of Carnarvon, 1284–1307* (1946), 87.
55. John de Colonia, the king's *armourer or armator* in the 1330s and 1340s, was making beds, mending and making clothes and embroideries, F. Devon, *Issues of the Exchequer* (1837), 144, 145; Exch. K.R. Accounts Various, 389/14. The staff of the Great Wardrobe, however, usually included a tailor, a linen–armourer and a tentmaker, ibid., 397/16.
56. Stow, *Survey of London* (1908), i. 181–2, ii. 192.

had 118 purses, of six different types, for sale, and, as well as leather points or laces and miscellaneous skins, also possessed twenty-four patterns for purses.[57]

A far better known example of a craftsman with a wide range of interests is Henry Yevele. Perhaps few Londoners in the building trades achieved a similar reputation, the result of outstanding artistic abilities combined with business skill. The printed calendars to the Corporation records provide us with only the scantiest hints of his career, but the extensive research which has been carried out in recent years in building accounts by L. F. Salzman, J. H. Harvey, H. M. Colvin and R. A. Brown has helped to produce a much fuller account not only of his contribution to the architectural history of the period but, what is of great value to us, of his role as a London businessman.[58] He was presumably a skilled mason when he left his home county, settled in London and took up the freedom in 1353. After some work for the Black Prince he was appointed in 1360 'disposer' of the King's works of masonry, and from then until his death in about 1400 he was constantly in the royal service. Of his private contracts less is known, but it seems very likely that he was acting in a supervisory capacity to Westminster Abbey and Canterbury Cathedral, helping the London Charterhouse, and that he worked at the Savoy Palace and Hertford Castle for John of Gaunt. However, the income which made it possible for him slowly to acquire property in eleven City parishes and an estate in Southwark was derived not only from fees for the various services he rendered to what was undoubtedly a wide circle of clients but from the profits of his City workshops. He had built, before 1381, workshops on a plot of land leased from the dean and chapter of St Paul's, and his business seems to have combined the work of builder's merchant and monumental mason. At various times, for instance, he supplied Flanders tiles, plaster of Paris, and lead and stone for different royal building projects, and worked on the tombs of Cardinal Langham, Richard II, and Queen Anne. It is possible, too, that the famous Neville screen of Durham Cathedral, of whose packing and despatch from London we have a number of details,[59] was made in Yevele's workshop: in style it is similar to the tomb of Blanche of Lancaster. Tombs for both Blanche and her husband, John of Gaunt, buried in Old St Paul's, and therefore known to us only through a Hollar engraving, were made by Yevele, at an estimated cost of £486. Yevele worked chiefly in stone, but these tombs were of alabaster,

57. P.R.O. Chancery, Extents on Debts, 46/17.
58. L. F. Salzman, *Building in England to 1540* (1952); *History of the King's Works*, i–ii. The following details of Yevele's career are taken from the fullest accounts written by J. H. Harvey, 'Henry Yevele Reconsidered', *Archaeological Journal*, cviii (1951) and *English Mediaeval Architects* (1954), 312–20.
59. Salzman, *Building in England*, 395.

and he referred to his stocks of marble in his will. Did he employ a marbler or alabasterer or did his masons also work on materials other than stone? It seems possible, too, that the alabaster effigies of William of Windsor and Blanche of the Tower, two of Edward III's children who died in infancy and were buried in Westminster Abbey, may have been made in this workshop.[60] While Nottingham may have been the chief centre for the production of the alabaster ware for which England became famous, there were certainly alabasterers at work in London throughout the fourteenth century.

It is more remarkable, however, to find a reference in Yevele's will to his stock of latten, the alloy of copper and other metals of which many small objects and such articles as monumental brasses and lecterns were made.[61] In his position it was no doubt a matter of convenience to be able to supply such items and it is interesting to find that the nature of his business presumably led a stone-mason into employing a metal-worker. It is not easy to discover who made the brasses by which it became increasingly fashionable to be commemorated in the fourteenth century.[62] While the finest were certainly imported, it seems probable that there were central workshops, possibly of some size, for the production of those of cheaper quality. J. P. C. Kent, by analysing the characteristic elements of military effigies, suggests that two major firms, probably based in London, were producing brasses in the second half of the fourteenth century, working from standard patterns to which small modifications were gradually made, thus producing a succession of types.[63] One workshop, he suggests, was active from the mid-fourteenth century or earlier until about 1410, and its brasses, poorly drawn but finely engraved, were distributed, with a few exceptions, throughout the home counties. Another workshop which began work about the same time was producing brasses with livelier figures and distributing them more widely. We need not despair of finding documentary evidence to illustrate further the work of what may have been either a small body of specialist craftsmen or a group of metal-workers who could turn their hands to several tasks. The best known London brass-worker of this period, John Orchard, described as a *latoner*, about whom the printed Corporation records say nothing, was responsible for the execution of several royal commissions.

60. J. D. Tanner, 'Tombs of Royal Babies in Westminster Abbey', *Journal of the Brit. Archaeological Ass.*, 3rd ser., xvi (1953), 34–5.
61. C. C. Oman, 'Medieval brass lecterns in England', *Archaeological Journal*, lxxxvii (1930); H. F. Owen Evans, 'Latten lecterns', Monumental Brass Soc., *Trans.* ix (1962), 375.
62. e.g. as early as 1352 a London hosier asked that a brass be set in his tomb, *Cal. Wills*, i. 656–8.
63. J. P. C. Kent, 'Monumental brasses: a new classification of military effigies', *Journal of the Brit. Archaeological Ass.*, 3rd ser., xii (1949), 70–8, 94–5.

In 1369 he supplied a weather vane for the roof of the kitchen at Eltham Palace, and later, in 1376, six copper angels for the white marble tomb made by Jean de Liège for Queen Philippa.[64] The two Londoners, however, who worked from 1395 to 1399 in two houses in the parish of St Alban Wood Street on the fine gilt bronze effigies of Richard II and Anne which rest upon their tomb, were described as coppersmiths.[65] Besides latoners and coppersmiths, there were others working in non-ferrous metals such as braziers, pewterers, sealmakers or seal-engravers and goldsmiths who do not appear to have specialized, at least in the fourteenth century, in the making of particular items.[66] Thus it was William Torel, a London goldsmith, who, using the casting techniques of the bell-founder, was responsible for the bronze effigies in Westminster Abbey of Edward I's father and wife, Henry III and Queen Eleanor;[67] William de Keyles, goldsmith, engraved superb seals of silver and gold for Queen Margaret in 1299.[68] The priory of Holy Trinity sought the services of Richard de Wymbissh, potter, in 1312 when a second bell, weighing 2820 pounds, to ring in tune with the greater bell he had already made for the church, was required.[69] Thus while potters may have spent much of their time making brass pots and founders, according to their ordinances of 1365,[70] spurs, buckles, stirrups, lavers and candlesticks, it is obvious from this and other commissions that there were workshops or foundries capable of doing much more skilful work than that which they normally did.

Some of this work was concentrated in the Aldgate area, where William de Aldgate, brazier, was making and supplying cannon to the royal officials at the Tower between 1353 and 1360,[71] and where

---

64. *History of the King's Works*, ii. 933; i. 486. For fuller details see W. St. John Hope, 'On the early working of alabaster in England', *Archaeological Journal*, lxi (1904), 223–4. Orchard's name has also been associated with the exquisite miniature effigies of Edward III's children which stand in the niches of his tomb but Colvin has not found any documentary evidence for the construction of the tomb, carried out sometime after 1386: *History of the King's Works*, i. 487. Tanner, op. cit., 35, n. 1, points out that in the original roll Orchard was described as *lantoner*.

65. The contract is printed in full in *Chaucer's World*, comp. E. Rickert (New York, 1948), 416–17, and other details will be found in J. H. Harvey, 'The Wilton Diptych – a re-examination', *Archaeologia*, xcviii (1961), 8, n. 6. The men were paid £400 for the work and a further £300 for the gilding.

66. L. Stone, *Sculpture in Britain: the Middle Ages* (1955), 263, n. 29, suggests that seal-engravers may have made brasses. See also pp. 177–86.

67. H. J. Plenderleith and H. Maryon, 'The Royal bronze effigies in Westminster Abbey', *Antiquaries Journal*, xxxix (1959), 87–8.

68. One is reproduced in L. F. Salzman, *English Industries of the Middle Ages* (1923), 132. Cf. Devon, *Issues of the Exchequer*, 201.

69. Riley, *Memorials*, 100.

70. *C.L.B.G*, 194–5 and Riley, op. cit., 512.

71. T. F. Tout, 'Firearms in England in the Fourteenth Century', *Collected Papers*, ii. (1934), 249.

William Wodeward, founder, was both casting bells and making cannon in Richard II's reign.[72] Bell-founding was localized there at least as early as 1298 when Belyeters Lane had already received its name,[73] and it was there that some famous bells were cast such as Edward Westminster, which Stow tells us could be heard in the City on calm days.[74] This was one of three bells made by John Bellyeter of Aldgate for the clocks set up in the clock tower at Westminster, 1365–7, at the castle of Queenborough and at the manor of King's Langley. For the three bells, John Bellyeter was paid £246 16s. 8d., i.e. for 13 228 pounds at a rate of 4d. a lb.[75] The bell for the earliest mechanical striking clock to be set up in England, that at Windsor Castle in 1351, was also transported from Aldgate, possibly from the same workshop, at a cost of 6s. 8d. to Baynard's Castle and then by water to Windsor for 4s. The clock itself, iron plates to support the bell, brass pulleys, copper and other wire, cords and a hammer, as well as other miscellaneous items were brought from London; but the three men, one of whom was 'master of the clock', who were paid at the rate of 6d. a day for six and a half weeks for setting up the clock and its striking mechanism, were Italians.[76]

It was in Aldgate, too, that John Brampton, glazier, lived and presumably had his workshop.[77] As he worked for the king from 1349 until sometime after 1383, it is possible, as with Henry Yevele, to reconstruct something of his career.[78] He was probably a young man in 1351 when he worked as one of a team of glaziers on the windows of St Stephen's Chapel, Westminster. He was breaking and laying glass on the painting tables at 6d. a day.[79] Shortly afterwards he was working on the same site on panels for windows at Windsor Castle.[80] Over twenty years later, in 1378, he had reached the height of his career when he was appointed the first king's glazier, and in that year spent over a month in charge of work being carried out at the manor of Woodstock at 1s. a day.[81] Royal commissions across

72. Ibid., 248–9, 252–3; Salzman, *English Industries,* 151; a representative for Port-soken, *C.P.M.R., 1381–1412,* 55.
73. *Cal. Wills,* i. 134.
74. Stow, *Survey,* ii. 121–2, 379–80.
75. R. A. Brown, 'King Edward's clocks', *Antiquaries Journal,* xxxix (1959), 284.
76. Ibid, 285; the accounts are printed in full by W. H. St. John Hope, *Windsor Castle: an architectural history* (1913), i. 152–3, 166–7.
77. *C.P.M.R., 1364–81,* 87.
78. *History of the King's Works,* i. 226.
79. Salzman, 'The Glazing of St. Stephen's Chapel, Westminster'. *Journal of the British Society of Master Glass-Painters* (1926), 32. The master glaziers who designed the figures received 1s. a day, those who painted the glass 7d. a day.
80. Salzman, 'Medieval Glazing Accounts', *Jnl. Brit. Soc. Master Glass-Painters* (1928), 120, 188.
81. *History of the King's Works,* i. 189, 226; *Jnl. Brit. Soc. Master Glass-Painters* (1928), 191.

the intervening years leave no doubt that, like Yevele, he had a London workshop where the glazing was designed and manufactured. Glass, usually white with coloured borders of flowers or falcons and the royal arms, was supplied by the foot for Windsor Castle, Hadleigh, the Tower, Westminster, Sheppey Castle, Sheen, Havering and for a bathroom where hot water appears to have been laid on at King's Langley.[82] The scale of his business and of those who worked with him or for him is indicated by some of the sums involved – over £122 for glass for Windsor in 1363 and 1364, and £75 13s. 9d. for Sheppey in 1365.[83] It was in London, too, that the windows for the chapel in Nottingham Castle, for the Castle of Morende, Northants., and for the choir at King's Langley were made.[84] His standing in the mistery was recognized by his election as warden in 1373.[85] His prosperity – we know he owned, among other things, houses and a horse in 1364[86] – must also have owed much to his private clients, and when we remember that Sir Roger Ellis's house in Paternoster Row, rebuilt in 1389/90, had eighty-seven windows, there was no doubt plenty of work available.[87] Study of the accounts of the repair of the Bridge House properties in the City might shed further light on this subject, and indeed on Brampton's career.

Of the size and organization of these workshops little is at present known. The largest staff noted in the London records were the eighteen men maintained by a pewterer,[88] but as will have been noticed very little indication of the above activities is provided by the printed London records, and further research in other sources may prove helpful. What is certain is that in this area, the wards of Aldgate and Portsoken – the suburb which had grown up outside the Wall and which stretched almost from Bishopsgate to the river – there were plenty of opportunities for relatively unskilled work. Portsoken had only forty-three taxpayers in 1319, of whom possibly five were potters, and twenty-three in 1332 – potters, a drover, butchers, brewers and fruiterers.[89] These numbers suggest a population with a high proportion of men who were either poor

82. *Jnl. Brit. Soc. Master Glass-Painters* (1928), 189–191: *History of the King's Works,* ii. 974.
83. *Jnl. Brit. Soc. Master Glass-Painters* (1928), 189.
84. Ibid., 190.
85. *C.L.B.G*, 309. Others elected as masters of the mistery like Henry Stannerne, William Papelwyk and John Geddyng also worked on royal commissions.
86. *C.P.M.R.*, 1364–81, 2, 13, 87. Bequests he received from his sister-in-law indicate his standard of living: *Cal. Wills,* ii. 214.
87. P. E. Jones, 'Some Bridge House Properties', *Journal of the Brit. Archaeological Ass.,* 3rd ser., xvi (1953), 72.
88. S. L. Thrupp, *Merchant Class of Medieval London* (Chicago, 1948), 9: 1456. Another pewterer had 12 workers, ibid.
89. *Two Early London Subsidy Rolls*, 85, 252–4; Curtis, op. cit., 76–7.

freemen or not freemen at all, many of them probably little more than labourers. Metal workers like the braziers, whose ordinances imply that only one of the four categories of men employed were fully trained and skilled men, no doubt drew heavily on these sources of labour.[90] Proximity to the Tower, too, may have helped to provide casual employment in this area as the war with France brought increasing demands for supplies of all sorts. While a small permanent staff was maintained at the Tower, which served as a depot for bows, arrows, timber, canvas and rope despatched from different parts of the country, there were numerous odd jobs to be done in the Tower itself such as making covers for crossbows, corselets for archers, quivers and boxes for carrying arrows and armour, and painting ships and shields for ships.[91]

The extent of Edward III's military and building operations and the work already done on available sources has made it possible to draw together some of the more accessible information relevant to some aspects of London's economy in the fourteenth century and suggest lines for further study. But there is a wealth of material in similar sources from which such subjects as the making of ecclesiastical vestments, clothes, bedding, cushions and hangings of different kinds may be studied.[92] Men and women from all levels of London society, not only craftsmen who practised a wide variety of skills but English and Italian merchants who financed the luxury trade, catered for the important market in these goods. Since no single aspect of the work on textiles, English or imported, can profitably be studied in isolation, this is a wide subject for study. A preliminary survey, however, makes it difficult to agree with A. H. Thomas's conclusion that 'apart from plate and jewellery most of the articles of luxury in London were of foreign production'.[93] For instance, some of the finest products of English craftsmanship in the middle ages were the ecclesiastical vestments and other articles embroidered in gold and silks in the style known as *opus anglicanum* in which an important export trade developed. A casual reference by Matthew Paris for the year 1246, and some early fourteenth-century commissions leave us in no doubt that Londoners were closely involved

90. Riley, *Memorials*, 624–7.
91. H. J. Hewitt, *Organisation of War under Edward III* (1966), 65–73.
92. References to a number of these sources and an indication of their value will be found in M. K. Dale, 'Women in the textile industries and trade in 15th–century England', unpublished M. A. Thesis, University of London, 1929 and Veale, *English Fur Trade*.
93. A. H. Thomas, 'Sidelights on Medieval London Life', *Journal of the Brit. Archaeological Ass.*, 3rd ser., ii (1937), 112. *Cf.* J. Evans, *English Art, 1307–1461* (1949), 92–3, 203.
94. A. G. I. Christie, *English Medieval Embroidery* (1938), 2; Riley, *Memorials*, 52, 60, 65.

in this.[94] Mrs Christie, whose superbly illustrated book, *English Medieval Embroidery*, is the chief study of the subject, concluded that, judging from surviving examples, the quality of the work declined after about the mid-fourteenth century.[95] This may be true of the work done on ecclesiastical vestments and may reflect the more secular interests of the period. But the increasingly general use of the fine imported textiles for clothes and bed-hangings and the enthusiasm for decoration characteristic of people of all classes provided work of a different kind for the London broderers, of which inevitably only rare examples have survived. Edward III's delight in fine craftsmanship and love of comfort, illustrated by his extravagant expenditure on his favourite homes, particularly those within easy reach of London, were also reflected in their furnishings: he slept in a bed with hangings of green velvet, embroidered in gold with sea sirens and bearing a shield with the arms of England and Hainault.[96] Robert Ascombe, one of the leading London broderers, worked for the fashion-loving Richard II,[97] and Peter Swan was, from his London base, responsible for the coordination of the work of ten designers, 45 men, and 30 women on a great variety of articles for Henry IV which contributed to the brilliance and splendour of the court.[98]

London was far and away England's greatest medieval city; it stood at the heart of a network of communications both regional and international; it could stand comparison in size and range of economic activity with many a European city. The story of her economic development in the later middle ages is not an easy subject to investigate – the sources, while plentiful, are scattered and elusive and often difficult to interpret – but it is sad indeed that this is a field to which so few people have been attracted. We cannot hope for a general survey until more detailed research has been carried out: then we may look forward to the major study which the importance of the subject demands.

94. Christie, op. cit., 28.
96. Christie, op. cit., 36.
97. Ibid., 37; *C.L.B.H*, 43.
98. Dale, op. cit., 109–13.

Editorial suggestions for further reading

Goldberg, P. J. P. 'Women in fifteenth century town life', in J. A. F. Thomson (ed.), *Towns and Townspeople in the Fifteenth Century* (Gloucester, 1988), 107–28.

Swanson, H. 'The illusion of economic structure: craft guilds in late medieval English towns', *Past and Present*, 121 (1988), 29–48.

Swanson, H. *Medieval Artisans: An Urban Class in Later Medieval England* (Oxford, 1989).

Blair, J. and Ramsay, N. (eds), *Medieval Industries* (forthcoming).

Chapter Eight

GLOUCESTER IN THE CENTURY AFTER THE BLACK DEATH

Richard Holt

Transactions of the Bristol and Gloucestershire Archaeological Society, 103 (1985)

This article presents a general view of the society and economy of a major provincial town in the later Middle Ages. Richard Holt's study of Gloucester illustrates the importance of placing any town firmly in the context of its locality: not only in a regional hierarchy of towns and markets, but also as the centre of an integrated local economy of town and village. That the peasants of the hinterland marketed their products through Gloucester may be expected; more revealing is the evidence that village brewers and bakers supplied the town on a regular basis, that neighbouring small towns produced a proportion of its industrial raw materials, and that Gloucester was the main market for the high quality fish caught in the Severn. Gloucester's merchants met the local gentry's demand for luxury goods, while its lawyers provided legal support – an expensive service in any age. Holt's essay underlines the need for further work which will integrate the evidence of urban and rural records within a given region. One such recent study is that of Britnell on Colchester, cited in the editorial suggestions for further reading on page 159.

The century after 1350 saw great economic and social change in the English countryside which would, in the course of time, lead to a transformation in the pattern of agricultural production, with a consequent revolution in social relationships. The factor associated with this process of change was the dramatic collapse of the population that accompanied the initial outbreaks of bubonic plague, whilst a further factor was the failure of the population level to recover; indeed the population lowpoint in England was not 1350 but probably 1450, and it was only after a long period of stagnation that we see evidence of population increase by 1500.[1]

The towns, as integral parts of the feudal economy and society,

---

1. J. Hatcher, *Plague, Population and the English Economy 1348–1530* (1977), 69.

were not immune from such long-term upheaval, although through their ability to attract large numbers of immigrants from the countryside their levels of population remained for a long while fairly stable. By the end of the century after the Black Death, however, as their traditional roles were becoming less important in the face of the new economic conditions, few major towns were able to maintain their levels of wealth.[2] In this respect Gloucester, as a very typical middle-ranking town, was no exception. The revival of its population after the Black Death was to be relatively short-lived, as the symptoms of its economic decline became apparent by 1450.

The Black Death came to Gloucester in the spring of 1349. Hearing of the appalling effects of the plague on Bristol, the burgesses of Gloucester attempted to seal themselves off, but to no avail.[3] The death-rate in the town, as elsewhere, was no doubt hideously high: at Lanthony Priory, on the edge of Gloucester, 19 of the 30 canons died. This mortality rate of over 60 per cent in a closed community was perhaps excessive, but indicates that the death-rate in Gloucester in 1349 was quite consistent with the one-third or more that is traditionally estimated.[4]

By means of immigration most of this population loss, and the loss due to subsequent outbreaks of plague in the 1360s, was replaced in the years to follow. There was, though, some permanent loss in population. The 300 or so built-up properties that Lanthony Priory held in Gloucester about 1350 would be only 240 a century later, the 20 per cent shortfall being mainly the result of cottages in poorer areas of the town becoming vacant and derelict in the years immediately after the Black Death.[5]

It is possible to estimate with some degree of accuracy the town's population level at this time. The returns of the Poll Tax of 1377 record 2239 taxpayers for Gloucester (compared with over 6000 for Bristol and 7000 for York, the largest provincial towns).[6] To allow for those under fourteen, those who evaded the tax, and those who were simply too poor to pay fourpence, this figure for taxpayers should be doubled, giving an estimated population figure of 4500. This was smaller than the pre-Black Death population, but by how much remains uncertain.

The catastrophe of the Black Death was not accompanied by economic decline. There are many small indicators of Gloucester's continued prosperity during these years, and in particular from the 1370s onwards there is evidence of a great deal of rebuilding. Whilst

2. R. B. Dobson, 'Urban Decline in Late Medieval England, *Trans. Royal Hist. Soc. (5th Ser)* 27 (1977), 1–22.
3. P. Ziegler, *The Black Death* (1969), 138.
4. P.R.O., C115 K2/6685, f. 12v.
5. P.R.O., C115 K1/6678, *passim*.
6. W. G. Hoskins, *Local History in England* (2nd edn. 1972), 238.

the number of poorer cottages had declined for want of tenants, houses in the better areas of town were being refurbished or replaced. It seems that many of the wealthier inhabitants between 1370 and 1430 built themselves new houses, which were often larger and grander than those they had previously possessed.[7] What was the basis of this prosperity? What was the part that Gloucester played within the feudal economy?

Situated on the River Severn, which was easily navigable to rafts, flat-bottomed trows and apparently larger ships as well, Gloucester in the medieval period functioned as an inland port, whilst Bristol controlled the seaborne trade of the river. The region at whose centre Gloucester lay was naturally a wealthy one. The Severn valley was a rich, grain-producing area, whilst to the east of the town lay the important wool-producing area of the Cotswolds. To the west lay the Forest of Dean which produced not only timber, charcoal and coal, but which was also medieval England's main source of iron.[8] As a river port and as the lowest bridging point on the Severn, Gloucester was a major market, indeed the commercial centre of its region, between Bristol 35 miles to the south and Worcester 25 miles to the north. As such, its marketing function was two-fold. Firstly, like any market it provided a place for the sale and exchange of the surplus produce of both peasants and demesne: and, secondly, it fulfilled the specialized role of distribution centre of luxury goods to the nobility and gentry of the county.

The surviving records make little mention of the many thousands of country people who came to Gloucester during this century to market their surplus crops. The vast number of small transactions by means of which the peasants acquired the cash to pay their rents, although the basic activity of every medieval market, can be perceived only dimly. However, something can be discovered about the traders or dealers who were based in villages or small towns, and who acted as a link between the large market and many of the agricultural producers. Unlike the peasants who marketed their produce infrequently, these men brought goods to Gloucester regularly, and so preferred, rather than pay tolls, to pay for an annual licence to trade in the town. From the surviving enrolments of the payments they made, for the years 1380, 1396, 1398 and 1423, much can be learnt about the trade of the region.[9]

The goods that these rural merchants brought into Gloucester were either raw materials for the town's craftsmen, or foodstuffs destined mainly for consumption within the town. So iron and honey came from the Forest of Dean; tanned leather from surrounding

7. P.R.O., C115 K1/6678, *passim.*
8. H. R. Schubert, *History of the British Iron and Steel Industry* (1957), 98.
9. Glos R. O., GBR 1295, 1296, 1297, 1298.

towns such as Ross-on-Wye, Newent and Painswick; wool from the Cotswolds and the Chilterns; fish from villages further down the Severn; and most importantly grain and malt from villages in the Severn and Avon valleys. In addition, from villages all around, men regularly brought in ale, whilst from villages and some towns rather further away – on average ten miles away – bread was brought in. The trade in ale was seemingly the larger of the two, with consignments coming in from practically every village within a six-mile radius. Such quantities of these two medieval staples were, of course, supplementary to the amounts produced within the town, a reminder of how difficult it was at all times to keep a large medieval town and its many visitors supplied with food and drink.

The grain that the rural merchants and the peasants brought to Gloucester was sold to the bakers and brewers of the town. A quantity of documentation relating to charges of illegal trading practices during the 1380s shows numbers of rural grain-sellers coming from the areas to the north and east of the town to sell wheat, barley and malt in quantities varying between a quarter and twelve quarters.[10] The bakers and brewers, when they bought grain, heaped up the measures, and so got more for their money than they should have done: there was, though, little that the rural salesmen could do about it, as they were faced with the same problem in the neighbouring grain markets of Tewkesbury and Cheltenham, and no doubt in other towns and markets too.[11]

Whilst this constant flow of small parcels of grain into the market was probably sufficient to satisfy Gloucester's own needs, it did not provide the quantities that the large grain dealers sought. Such a dealer of the latter years of the 14th century was Simon Broke, who was wealthy and influential within the town, being bailiff of Gloucester four times and the representative of the borough in four Parliaments, all between 1392 and 1408.[12] It was Broke's practice, certainly in his younger days in the 1380s, to frequent the unlicensed village market at Haw, on the Severn between Gloucester and Tewkesbury, and there and at Chipping Campden and elsewhere he bought large amounts of grain which he shipped down-river. The neighbouring town of Tewkesbury was also a grain market, though not such a large one as Gloucester, and the Tewkesbury bakers, brewers and corn dealers bought their grain from the same areas as did the Gloucester men. It seems that Broke and certain con-

10. P.R.O., KB 9/32 mm. 16, 20, 21. A quarter of grain was 64 gallons by volume, the equivalent probably of 400 lbs. weight.
11. Ibid., m. 20.
12. W. H. Stevenson, *Calendar of the Records of the Corporation of Gloucester* (Gloucester 1893), 1042, 1054; Gloucester Cathedral Library, *Register B of St Peter's Abbey*, 341; P.R.O., C115 L1/6687, f. 8v; *Members of Parliament* (House of Commons 1878), 244, 258, 263, 268.

federates of his were in the habit of illegally forestalling Tewkesbury market: on market days they would buy up grain on the roads leading into the town, and so take all Tewkesbury's business. Together they launched a particularly successful operation on the Saturday after Michaelmas 1386 -- a significant time of year, being soon after harvest when stocks would be high and prices would be low, but when the peasants would have to market grain to meet demands for rent. On this Saturday, 5 October, Simon Broke and his accomplices not only covered all the roads into Tewkesbury; they also managed to buy up all the grain coming in by river, seemingly along both the Severn and the Avon.[13]

Of the great quantities of grain that went down the river towards Bristol much was exported, particularly to the Bordeaux region. Exporting grain was a favourite occupation amongst the leading Gloucester merchants, and occasional surviving grants of royal licences show 14th-century Gloucester merchants obtaining permission to export 300, 500, and most often 1000 quarters of grain at a time.[14] In addition, there was illegal exporting; in February 1348 it was reported that grain was being daily sent down the Severn, loaded at sea into ships and taken over to France; and similar charges of widespread smuggling down the Severn were made in the 1380s.[15]

The grain trade was, then, a most lucrative one, and given the competition there obviously was for profits, we should not be surprised to find that whilst it was Simon Broke and his fellows from Gloucester who were forestalling Tewkesbury in 1386 and 1387, in 1401 the merchants of Tewkesbury and Worcester were successfully forestalling Gloucester market.[16] It was perhaps as a reaction to this that at about the same time the town authorities in Gloucester were said to be interfering with river-borne grain supplies to Bristol.[17] Competition in the grain trade was fierce, and town administrations, faced with the threat of high bread prices, and consequent unrest among the labour force, were quite prepared to pass the problem on to a neighbouring town.

When the wealthier people of the county frequented Gloucester it was usually for the purpose of purchasing the luxury goods of the Middle Ages, the most important of which being wine. The large quantities of wine that were sold in Gloucester were bought from merchants in the sea-ports, and although Bristol would have been the main supplier, Southampton also was important, and the Southampton records enable the trade to be seen in some detail. During the 15th century about 30 pipes of wine – that is, some 3000

13. P.R.O., KB 9/32 m. 20; KB 27/506, Justices m. 15.
14. *Calendar of Patent Rolls 1330–34*, 232, 509, 514; *1338–40*, 81; *1385–89*, 128.
15. *Cal. Pat. Rolls 1348–50*, 67; *Cal. Fine Rolls 1383–91*, 178.
16. *Cal. Pat. Rolls 1399–1401*, 516.
17. *Cal. Close Rolls 1399–1402*, 146.

gallons – were each year carted the 93 miles to Gloucester.[18] The Gloucester vintners and taverners sold most of this wine to the gentry and priests of the countryside. At least one of the vintners delivered to his customers in the 1380s; his carter was driving his wagon and eight horses and was delivering a pipe of wine when he was accidentally killed near Cirencester, seventeen miles from Gloucester.[19]

Other imported goods besides wine came into the town, and the Southampton records show Gloucester as the destination for regular consignments of almonds, oil, pepper, dates and raisins, as well as on average about 100 bales of woad each year, together with similarly large quantities of madder, alum and soap, all used in dyeing and finishing cloth.[20] As with the wine, these items were being carried to Gloucester as a centre of distribution rather than as a centre of consumption.

References to unpaid debts indicate a large volume of luxury goods coming to Gloucester from London. Between 1350 and 1450 there is evidence of 24 cases of Gloucester men owing money to Londoners, against only one of a Londoner not having paid a debt to a Gloucester burgess. [21] Amongst these 24 Londoners there were seven mercers, two grocers, a merchant, a haberdasher and a vintner; the Gloucester men they had had commercial dealings with all had similar mercantile interests. These are all examples of Gloucester mercers and other retailers of quality goods purchasing their stock from London suppliers.

Gloucester's distributive function is clearly observed through a similar examination of the credit relationships between Gloucester merchants and their customers. Whilst five Gloucester men in this century after 1350 owed money to men from Worcestershire, Bristol, Wiltshire and Herefordshire, there are references to 22 men from elsewhere who had clearly bought goods on credit from Gloucester merchants.[22] The places they came from included Bristol, Worcester, Cirencester, Hereford and Coventry, as well as some more distant places. Mercers from Newark and Hull owed £30 to a Gloucester mercer in 1419; and, less explicably, an Essex fisherman owed £3 to a Gloucester cutler in 1428. In 1442 a Devon chapman

18. O. Coleman (ed.), *The Brokage Book of Southampton 1443–44* 2 (Southampton Rec Ser 6, 1961), 325.
19. *Cal. Close Rolls* 1377–81, 455.
20. *Brokage Book of Southampton*, 322 and *passim*.
21. *Abstracts of Inquisitiones Post Mortem for Gloucestershire* 6 (The Index Library, British Record Society, 1912), 109, 187; the other references are all to be found in *Cal. Pat. Rolls* and *Cal. Close Rolls* between 1350 and 1450.
22. A. Beardwood (ed.), 'Statute Merchant Roll of Coventry 1392–1416', *Dugdale Soc* 17 (1939), 28; the other references are all to be found in the *Cal. Pat. Rolls* and *Cal. Close Rolls* between 1350 and 1450.

had seemingly obtained at least £8 worth of his stock from a Gloucester supplier.

The one-sided nature of the credit relationships denoting sellers and buyers is most clear, and illustrates well the process by which goods went from London to Gloucester, and were then sold over a very wide area. But the long distance nature of at least some of the transactions implies that the Gloucester merchants had more to sell than just the readily available items that could be obtained from London.

It was the manufacturing sector of Gloucester's economy that provided, probably, the goods that these merchants sold. Most of the population of Gloucester during this century were employed in the production of manufactured goods, working as craftsmen in the small workshops that were the units of production of the medieval period. In the rental of the town compiled in 1455, there were 204 named people with a given occupation, and although this is a small and somewhat unrepresentative sample, being biased towards the wealthier end of Gloucester society, yet it does indicate the occupational structure of Gloucester in the later medieval period.[23] Firstly, there was a great diversity of occupations – 51 in all, and this, it must be emphasized, is far from a complete list. Secondly, these separate occupations fell in the main into certain broad categories, with 38 people (19 per cent) involved in metalworking; 40 (20 per cent) in the provision of food and drink; and the largest group of all – 49 (24 per cent) – in the manufacturing of clothing and footwear. A further 18 (9 per cent) were occupied with the primary processes of the production of cloth and leather.

In this pattern of production, Gloucester was little different from other similar towns, with a large proportion of the labour force working to meet the simple needs of the town itself and the visitors to the market. Its proximity to the Forest of Dean, however, ensured that its iron industry was more prominent than would otherwise have been the case. For centuries the smiths of Gloucester had produced horseshoes, nails, arrow-heads, knives and other iron goods in large quantities, and much of this production had been destined for sale outside the region.[24] In the 1380s and 1390s the principal groups of ironworkers in Gloucester were the cutlers and the wiredrawers: the former making knives and all sorts of edged tools, and the bulk of the wiredrawers' production being used to make wool cards to comb wool prior to spinning. But there were also other ironworkers in the town; many farriers, of course, as well as sievemakers, locksmiths, armourers and bladesmiths (who made

23. W. H. Stevenson (ed.), *Rental of all the Houses in Gloucester A.D. 1455* (Gloucester 1890), *passim.*
24. Schubert, 94–98, 118.

swords). In addition, there were workers in the various copper alloys – pinners, bellmakers, lattoners, braziers and spurriers; and workers in lead or lead alloys, such as plumbers and pewterers.[25]

The years after 1350 saw a great increase in the amount of cloth made for export.[26] Clearly the cloth industry that Gloucester had possessed since at least the 12th century was thriving, and like the iron industry it produced for the wider market.[27] In 1363, 47 master weavers of the town were prosecuted for over-pricing, and we need not suppose that their workshops contained all of Gloucester's looms.[28] The cloth that they wove was finished elsewhere. In the 12th and 13th centuries there had been a Fullers' Street in the town; by 1300, however, the battle between the town fullers who 'walked' the cloth and the operators of the new rural fulling-mills had been lost, and there are no more references to fullers in Gloucester.[29] The dyers and other cloth finishers who continued to work in the town indicate that some cloth did return after fulling, but probably only a small proportion did so, as the aulnage returns of the 1390s, which record the tax paid on cloths when they were sold, seem to show Gloucester as only a minor cloth market. During 1397, for instance, 350 or so cloths were marketed in Gloucester, or on average only seven a week; and even allowing for the fact that these returns are generally reckoned to be inaccurate in under-estimating numbers of cloths, this figure is a low one for a major town.[30] The 134 people recorded as selling these cloths seem not to have been primarily occupied as cloth merchants, being recorded elsewhere as, for instance, brewers, bakers, dyers or even, in some cases, weavers. The merchants who were important figures in the industry appear only as minor cloth sellers: Richard Baret, for instance, amongst the wealthiest of the Gloucester drapers of the 1390s, marketed only three cloths in the town in 1397. It was through men like Baret, however, that the bulk of Gloucester's cloth production was marketed at places such as Cirencester, where it is known that Gloucester drapers were active, or was carried further afield, probably to be exported.[31]

Gloucester, then, functioned as a market only for cloth manufac-

---

25. Glos. R.O., GBR 1295, 1296, 1297, 1298.

26. H. L. Gray, 'The Production and Exportation of English Woollens in the Fourteenth Century', *Eng. Hist. Rev.* 39 (1924), 13–35.

27. During the reign of Stephen an annual payment to the Crown of 20s. from the weavers of Gloucester was granted to St Augustine's Abbey, Bristol: *Cal. Charter Rolls 1300–1326*, 378.

28. P.R.O., KB 27/411, Fines mm. 1, 2.

29. W. H. Stevenson (ed.), *Calendar of the Records of the Corporation of Gloucester* (Gloucester 1893), 119, 121, etc.

30. P.R.O., E101/339/2.

31. P.R.O., KB 27/429,, Rex m. 26d.

tured by small, independent producers; cloth which no doubt
supplied the needs of the town itself and its locality.

During the course of this brief survey of Gloucester's commercial
and industrial functions reference has already been made to some
of the merchants who were active in the town. As in all other
medieval towns, the merchants formed a social and economic élite
group, the top tier of urban society. They controlled the government
of the town, and through the offices of bailiff and Parliamentary
burgess they represented Gloucester's interests, or their own interests, to the outside world. Whilst it is not possible to define the
number and extent of this group, it is easy to identify the leading
members of the oligarchy simply by looking at who held these important public offices. The two bailiffs were elected annually, and
Gloucester sent two representatives to Parliament, which met almost
annually during the later Middle Ages: consequently these posts saw
a constant procession of occupants.

Perhaps the wealthiest of the Gloucester élite in the years around
1400 were the drapers. Richard Baret, who died childless in 1401,
made cash bequests totalling nearly £400, and bequeathed ten shops
and· tenements, in addition to the bulk of his cash and property
which he left to his widow.[32] Judging from the social position he
held – he served as member of Parliament for Gloucester five times,
and was four times bailiff between 1372 and 1401 – he was the leading Gloucester draper of his time.[33]

In terms of numbers the most important group of the oligarchy
were the retailers of luxury goods, such as the mercers and vintners.
Prominent amongst these men was William Crook who was bailiff
eleven times between 1361 and his death 40 years later, and four
times member of Parliament.[34] He was a vintner and, like at least
some others of his trade, also a brewer.[35] Amongst his many properties was a bakehouse, though it is not clear whether he baked
bread himself or rented it out.[36] By a judicious combination of
interests he prospered, though his pre-eminence in public office
clearly owed as much to his unusual longevity as it did to his social
position.

The craftsmen of Gloucester were represented in the ruling oligarchy only by those at the very top of their trades: those whose

32. P.R.O., PCC Wills, 1 Marche ff. 4–5v.
33. *Members of Parliament,* 195, 199, 252, 255, 258; P.R.O., KB 27/471; *Cal. Recs. Corp. Gloucester,* 1008, 1045; S. Rudder, *A New History of Gloucestershire* (Cirencester 1781), 139.
34. *Cal. Recs. Corp. Gloucester,* 978, 980, 1005, 1014, 1017, 1041; P.R.O., C115 L1/6687 f. 46v; SC 6/1271/1; *Abstracts of Gloucestershire Inquisitiones Post Mortem* 6 (The Index Library, 1912), 109; Rudder, 139; *Members of Parliament,* 182, 225, 228, 249.
35. P.R.O., KB 27/411, Fines m. 1 KB 9/29 m. 55.
36. P.R.O., C115 K2/6682 f. 143v; C115 K1/6678 f. 48v.

interests probably lay more in marketing goods than in making them. John Luke, who was bailiff in the 1430s and 1440s, was described as a brazier, but travelled in the Welsh Marches with goods worth £40 or more; and William Oliver, bailiff five times in the same period, was described as a chaloner, but presumably did not himself manufacture bedding.[37] John Pope, who was bailiff in the 1380s and 1390s, as a goldsmith was hardly typical of the artisan class.[38]

Brewers and bakers were prohibited by law from holding the chief offices in towns: their occupations were held to be incompatible with the exercise of powers to control the prices of basic victuals.[39] The regular enforcement of the Assizes of bread and ale, designed to hold down the cost of basic foodstuffs, was amongst the most important of the bailiffs' tasks. But brewers, at any rate, held office in Gloucester. Apart from vintners and others with a brewing interest, such as William Crook, there were several men described as brewers who served as bailiffs during this century; indeed in 1445 both of the bailiffs were brewers.[40] One can only assume that it was their wealth that secured their entrance to an office not legally theirs.

One other group of victuallers, in addition to the brewers, who held office was the fishmongers; at least three served as bailiff during this period.[41] Their trade was varied, as they dealt not only in preserved sea fish, but also in salmon, eels, shad and lampreys from the Severn.[42] A Gloucester lamprey could be worth as much as 10s. during Lent – perhaps six or eight weeks' wages for a labouring man – and the supply of such fish to the Court and to noble households was very profitable to the small group of Gloucester men who bought them from the Severn fishermen, or who themselves were able to rent fish-weirs from the Crown or the monasteries which owned them.[43]

Apart from the occupational groups already referred to, and those people like Simon Broke whose interests were too varied to allow of any occupational designation other than simply 'merchant',

37. P.R.O., C1/12/41; *Cal. Pat. Rolls 1441–46*, 8, 134; *Cal. Recs. Corp. Gloucester*, 52, 1100, 1108, 1121, 1123; *Cal. Pat. Rolls 1446–52*, 126.
38. *Cal. Recs. Corp. Gloucester*, 1005, 1025; *Cal. Inquisitions Miscellaneous*, 82; P.R.O., C115 K2/6684, f.29.
39. Statute of York (1318): *Statutes of the Realm* 1 (Records Commission, 1810), 178.
40. Walter Chauntrell and William Saundres: *Cal. Recs. Corp.. Gloucester*, 1125; *1455 Rental*, 17, 30.
41. Walter de Markeley in 1366–67, Thomas Hilley in 1447–48, and John Kylray in 1456–57: P.R.O., KB 27/429, Fines m. 2; KB 27/411, Fines m. 2; *Rudder*, 139; *1455 Rental*, 4; *Cal. Recs. Corp. Gloucester*, 1141; P.R.O., C115 K2/6685 f. 17.
42. P.R.O., KB 9/32 m. 18; KB 27/506 mm. 10d, 12; *Cal. Liberate Rolls 1226–1272*, (6 volumes), *passim*.
43. Ibid.; P.R.O. E101/559/26 mm. 1–5; C115 K2/6684 f.208.

only one other group seems to have filled the offices of bailiff of Parliamentary representative at this time, and that was the lawyers.

It is by the 1390s that it is possible to identify for the first time professional common lawyers resident in Gloucester. Their staple trade would have been to represent the legal interests of members of the local gentry, but they appear in the records usually when they acted in an official or semi-official capacity – when they served on a Commission of the Peace, or when they represented the borough of Gloucester in a legal dispute.[44] Gloucester lawyers served as stewards of nearby rural manors; and in the years after 1400 they are increasingly to be found filling the major public offices.[45] Indeed, they come to dominate the public offices, contributing after 1420 far and away more candidates for offices than the mercers, the second most numerous group. This leading role was the result of their wealth and influence, but a further factor was their enthusiasm for office. By serving as bailiff, and more importantly as Parliamentary representative, they could more easily bring themselves to the notice of the Crown, and thus secure the lucrative patronage in the sphere of local officialdom that they obviously prized. Collecting taxes or customs dues, supervising Gloucester's pavage revenues or repairs to the castle – these and similar tasks which had always been performed by leading members of the élite, now in the 15th century were being entrusted to the lawyers who had served as members of Parliament.[46] By 1450 there were at least seven or eight lawyers resident and working in Gloucester, together constituting the most influential and outward-looking section of the burgesses.

Socially, however, the lawyers were not full members of the borough community. They married outside the town, preferring the daughters of the rural gentry to those of their merchant neighbours.[47] In this they presumably showed their social ambitions as well as their social origins. But the other leading men of the town seemed content with the society in which they found themselves, and married within their group. All too often their wives were the widows of former member of the élite; their mortality rate was high, and often they died childless.[48] As a result those who lived and prospered sooner or later inherited, so that a combination of sickly, childless relatives, judicious marriage and long life was the surest formula for the accumulation of wealth.

44. For instance, *Cal. Pat. Rolls 1408–13, 373; 1413–16,* 177; P.R.O., C115 K2/6685 f. 17.
45. P.R.O., C115 K2/6682 ff. 121, 127v, 245; Glos. R.O., D621/M1 mm. 18, 27.
46. For example, *Cal. Pat. Rolls 1429–36,* 5, 442; *Cal. Fine Rolls 1430–37,* 67, 97; *1445–52* 58, 187.
47. For example, P.R.O., C1/39/101.
48. See, for instance, the family relationships and the rapid turnover in property as evidenced in P.R.O., C115 K1/6678, *passim.*

The transfer of such wealth from generation to generation can often be traced when it took the form of landed property. It was the practice of all the wealthier men of Gloucester to own some property in the town, which at the least would be the house they lived in, and at the other end of the scale could be a sizeable estate. The largest such holding around 1450 was that of Thomas Bisley, who owned over 30 houses of one sort or another; he was followed by Thomas Deerhurst with 28, and by about five others with ten or more houses.[49]

It is usually assumed that such investment in landed property by those with generally commercial interests did little to further their prosperity.[50] The rental value of such property was always, certainly in Gloucester, too small to be a very significant part of a merchant's income. But despite this, the ownership of land was still clearly of importance to these people. A well-documented example is that of William Griffyn, a Gloucester mercer whose business was failing in the 1370s. By 1379 he was unable to meet debts of £60 or more to merchants from London and elsewhere, and so his property was valued by the bailiffs as a preliminary to forced sale. He held five tenements and eight shops, with an annual rental value of £10, in addition to his own dwelling worth £1.[51] The five tenements and three of the shops were sold immediately for £67; two more shops were sold eighteen months later for £13.[52] His property, then, had been more than equal to his debts, and had in practice acted as security against which he had borrowed. This is not the only case of a Gloucester merchant having to sell property to meet a certain or probable debt, and it appears that the ownership of property was useful, or indeed necessary, in obtaining commercial credit. The rental value of property, then, whilst obviously of importance in insuring against old age and sickness, was to someone like William Griffyn of less importance than the capital value of his lands, which was a constant factor in his commercial dealings.

But there were those who deliberately accumulated property to obtain rental income, and who invested money to maximize that income. As stated above, of the individuals owning property in Gloucester about 1450, those with the largest holdings were Thomas Bisley with over 30 houses, and Thomas Deerhurst with 28. Both of these men were lawyers, as was John Gilbert, who held over 20 properties. Like their record in filling public office, this ownership

49. *1455 Rental, passim.*
50. R. H. Hilton, 'Rent and Capital Formation in Feudal Society', in R. H. Hilton, *The English Peasantry in the Later Middle Ages* (Oxford 1975), 209–12; A. F. Butcher, 'Rent and the Urban Economy: Oxford and Canterbury in the Later Middle Ages', *Southern Hist* 1 (1979), 12–18.
51. *Inquisitiones Post Mortem . . . Glos.* 6, 109.
52. P.R.O., CP 25(1) 78/79 mm. 1, 33.

of property by lawyers appears to have been the result of deliberate policy as much as an accidental concomitant of wealth. For instance, the properties of Thomas Deerhurst are the best documented, and reveal an attitude to property that was different from that of most of his peers. Firstly, he and his father John, also a lawyer, had purchased most and perhaps all of the property, rather than acquiring it by the usual methods of marriage and inheritance.[53] And, secondly, both of them followed a deliberate policy of developing their property. John Deerhurst had built a block of five houses or cottages on a vacant plot, and his son had similarly built a block of seven. One or the other of them had 'recently rebuilt' another such block. Several of Deerhurst's properties were clustered together in Southgate Street, and nearby were three vacant plots purchased by his father, clearly available for future development.[54] Of the 28 dwellings that Thomas Deerhurst owned, there is a known rental value for half: fourteen of his properties were rented out for £5 18s. 4d. This is, of course, in contrast to William Griffyn's thirteen properties worth £10 a year – roughly twice as much. And the difference arises from the type of property both men owned. Griffyn held houses and shops in the better retail quarter around the High Cross, let for large rents to lesser merchants or wealthier craftsmen.[55] Deerhurst's properties on the other hand, particularly the newer ones, were all aimed at the lower end of the housing market, so that whilst Griffyn's were let for rents varying from 10s. to over £2, many of Deerhurst's were let for only 6s. 8d. or 8s. One must assume that Deerhurst's concentration on cheaper properties was more profitable to him, and gave a better return than investment in more expensive properties would have done. Thomas Bisley's properties, too, although less can be said about them, were aimed at tenants from the lower social groups.[56] Yet, however profitable these holdings were in relative terms, they still must have been of marginal importance to these men whose incomes from other sources were many times greater than their incomes from rents.

Despite their wealth, and the pre-eminence that these merchants and lawyers enjoyed within their town, there were rivals to their power: institutions and officials determined to assert their own rights and privileges. The castle of Gloucester was the symbol of royal power in the region, the centre of the county administration; and the Church, in at least some of its various manifestations, maintained an aloof separateness that denied, or attempted to deny, the authority of the burgesses. During the years after 1350 the people

53. *1455 Rental, passim.*
54. *1455 Rental*, 8, 10, 12, 40.
55. *Inquisitiones Post Mortem . . . Glos.* 6, 109.
56. *1455 Rental, passim.*

of the town were becoming increasingly impatient with the claims of these extraneous establishments.

Since 1200 the burgesses of Gloucester had enjoyed the right of self government from the Crown. The elected reeves, and later bailiffs, had presided over the borough court, and had collected for their own use all Crown dues and rents from the town, paying over instead the fixed annual fee-farm of £65.[57] Such independence from royal authority was, however, limited. In the 1230s, despite the charter, the town was governed by a royal official – the Gloucester man, Richard the Burgess, who used the title 'Mayor of Gloucester' between 1228 and about 1240.[58] In 1264, during the Barons' War, Prince Edward, secure in the castle, drove de Montfort's supporters out of the town in a manner which was a stark reminder that the castle's function was as much to control the town as to protect it.[59] The unpopularity of the castle would have been heightened by the vestigial powers that the constable continued to wield in Gloucester, of which the most notable was 'castelcoule', a due of 3*d.* which he was entitled to collect each time a burgess brewed. In the 1320s, the only years for which figures are available, this yielded over £20 annually, and must have been a source of considerable annoyance to the large-scale professional brewers of the town, who would have been least able to evade it.[60] It is not surprising, then, that we find in the 1370s the town authorities adopting an air of studied indifference to the misfortunes suffered by the Crown servants who lived in the castle. Between the castle and the houses of the town lay the Bareland, an open space retained for military purposes, but on which the people of the town had taken to dumping ordure and general refuse. The stench inside the castle must have been appalling, but despite repeated demands from the Crown the bailiffs did nothing to stop the practice. In May 1381 the Earl of Buckingham, the King's uncle, was appointed to look into the matter, which was clearly by now giving great cause for concern.[61] Throughout the country the administration was unpopular, and disturbances which would culminate in the Peasants' Revolt of June and July 1381 were already occurring. At the beginning of the year the bailiffs of Shrewsbury had lost control of their town, and there must have been fears for Gloucester.[62] By the middle of July, Buckingham, having put down the rebellion in Essex, was back in Gloucester, and after

57. Cal. Recs, Corp. Gloucester, 6–9.
58. *Cal. Pat. Rolls 1225–1232, 182; Cal. Recs. Corp. Gloucester*, 2 (Rolls Series. 1887). 744.
59. W. A. Wright (ed.), *The Metrical Chronicle of Robert of Gloucester* 2 (Rolls Series, 1887), 744.
60. P.R.O., SC6/854/8.
61. *Cal. Pat. Rolls 1370–74*, 243, 293, *1381–85, 22.*
62. *Cal. Pat. Rolls 1377–81*, 631–2; *1381–85*, 1–2; H. Owen and J. B. Blakeway, *A History of Shrewsbury*, 1 (London 1825), 168–74.

a meeting of all the people of the town in the meadow now called Sudmede, ringleaders of the opposition to the Crown were singled out – Thomas Bisley, who had served as bailiff five times in the previous fourteen years; Thomas Compton, a young man who would be bailiff four times before his death in 1412; and several others. Charged with rebellious talk, they were all put in gaol. We are left to speculate as to the exact nature of the grievances they had been expressing, but a long-standing resentment of the castle had surely been a contributory factor.[63]

There were quarrels, too, with the Church, or rather with sections of it as the religious dimension of medieval urban life was expressed through many different forms. There were eleven parish churches in Gloucester, and most of these also accommodated private chantries for the dead, as well as parish gilds which maintained chantries, so that there were in 1363 over 60 chantry priests in the town.[64] The spiritual needs of the living community were perhaps better served by the three orders of friars who had houses in Gloucester, and who were everywhere renowned for the quality of their preaching and the relative poverty of their lifestyle. The physical needs of a proportion of the old and frail were met by the three hospitals of St Bartholomew, St Mary and St Margaret.[65]

The three major religious houses – St Peter's Abbey, Lanthony Priory and St Oswald's Priory – stood in yet another relationship to the townspeople. Dedicated to the monastic ideal, they did not by the 14th century play a very active role in either the religious or the social life of Gloucester. However, through their considerable holdings of urban land their relationship with many lay people was a close one: over half of the houses in Gloucester owed rent to them.[66] Under such circumstances it is clear that disputes over land or rent between the monks and the town would have been common, and indeed a list of such disputes between the Priory of Lanthony and the bailiffs of Gloucester survives from around 1450.[67] Interestingly, the nature of these points of disagreement, and the antiquity of many of them, indicate that the bailiffs had become openly defiant of Lanthony; in particular, they denied Lanthony's ancient rights of jurisdiction over many of their properties. The second half of the 14th century had seen the priors of Lanthony fighting to maintain their position; after about 1400 they seem to have ceased to do so

63. P.R.O., C115 K2/6685 ff. 12, 12v. For a more detailed consideration of this episode, and the full text of the reference to it in the Register of Prior Hayward, see R. A. Holt, 'Thomas of Woodstock and Events at Gloucester in 1381', *Bull. Inst. Hist. Res.* 58 (No. 138), 237–242.
64. L. E. W. O. Fullbrook-Leggatt, *Anglo-Saxon and Medieval Gloucester* (Gloucester 1952), 76–81; P.R.O., KB9/29 m. 38.
65. Fullbrook-Leggatt, 70–76.
66. *1455 Rental, passim.*
67. P.R.O. C115 K2/6685 ff. 10–16v.

face of the intransigence of the town authorities, so that in 1450 the bailiffs had still not paid to Lanthony £50 compensation they had been ordered by the courts to pay as long ago as 1391. The bailiffs were no longer paying rents of over £7 a year to the Priory, and, most importantly, they now exercised their authority over the suburb outside the South Gate, although most of it lay outside their area of jurisdiction, and was legally subject to Lanthony's authority.[68]

St Peter's Abbey, a major landowner in Gloucestershire and elsewhere, was the greatest of the representatives of the feudal order within Gloucester. Even so, like Lanthony Priory, it was by 1400 unable to withstand the growing assertiveness of the burgesses. Its own view of its relationship with the town was perhaps best expressed in 1305, when a great banquet given by the abbot was attended by the important local ecclesiastical personages as well as all the leading laymen of the county, whilst seemingly none of the townspeople had been invited.[69] Yet in 1414 the Abbey, in desperation, was to pay 40 marks to the Crown for a confirmation of its ancient rights of jurisdiction over its own precincts and its tenants within Gloucester: rights which, it was complained, the burgesses of the town were ignoring.[70] It would be surprising if such a confirmation had, in practice, any effect: without doubt the burgesses continued to exercise their own jurisdiction over all of the people and the area of Gloucester.

A considerable amount may be known about Gloucester at the end of the century after the Black Death through the most important single document to survive from the medieval town administration. The rental of the town that was compiled in 1455 lists each house or property with its owner, and often its occupant, and was designed apparently to facilitate the collection of the landgable or chief rents which were due to the bailiffs, although an unsuccessful attempt in the same year by the town authorities to secure an Act of Parliament compelling householders to pay for repairs to the streets probably provided an additional reason for undertaking the exercise.[71]

An unfortunate feature of the rental is that it is impossible to derive from it an exact figure for the number of houses in Gloucester, because of the many references to multiple holdings. The total of over 700 properties, however, may represent as many as 1000 dwellings, and clearly this enables an estimate to be made of Gloucester's population in 1455. Uncertainty about the size of the average household – if indeed such a concept is realistic for medieval towns – makes any such estimate a tentative one; how-

68. Ibid.
69. W. H. Hart (ed), *Historia et Cartularium Monasterii Sancti Petri Gloucesteriae* 1 (Rolls Series, 1863), 38.
70. *Cal. Charter Rolls 1341–1417*, 471.
71. *1455 Rental*; *Rotuli Parliamentorum* 5 (1783), 338a.

ever, if each of the 1000 dwellings housed four persons on average, the resultant population estimate is 4000. In comparing this with the population estimate of 4500 for 1377, it must be taken into account that the Poll Tax assessment included the suburbs outside the south and east gates which were omitted from the 1455 rental.[72] The southern suburb contained at least 100 dwellings, mainly cottages, in the 1440s; the eastern suburb was probably similar.[73] The estimate of the population in 1455 should, then, be augmented by around one-fifth.

There are too many uncertainties here to be able to state with any confidence that there were 5000 people in mid 15th-century Gloucester. The population was, though, apparently comparable with that in 1377, so that around 1450 Gloucester's population was very much what it had been in the years immediately following the outbreaks of plague a century before. It is very likely that the severe decline in population and prosperity that affected most other large towns at the end of the medieval period had already begun. And indeed there are signs of decline other than dubious population estimates. The 1455 rental itself is one such sign. The strenuous efforts of its compiler Robert Cole, the rent-collector of Lanthony Priory, to establish liability to pay landgable, coupled with internal indications that this rent had in fact not been paid on many properties for a great many years (in some cases 200 years), indicate this to have been a desperate attempt on the part of the bailiffs to collect a greater proportion of the notional £10 a year that the rent totalled, and so to increase town revenues.[74] The request to make owners of houses responsible for street repairs, unsuccessful in 1455 but granted at last in 1473, should be seen as a further indication that the revenues received by the bailiffs from tolls, rents and court profits were less than they had been.[75] Indeed only eight years before, in 1447, the men of the town had petitioned the Crown for some relief, claiming that the £65 for which they had to account each year to the Exchequer could be paid only if the bailiffs contributed £20 from their own pockets; a situation brought about, they said, by a reduction in the town's population due to epidemics, evidenced by the dereliction of many houses in the town.[76] The contents of the 1455 rental ought, of course, to throw more light on this claim; unfortunately, it is not a very clear light. In 1455, 48 properties in Gloucester were described as 'new', as opposed to only six which were 'decayed' or 'ruined'. It can be shown, though, that some at least of these 'new' buildings were perhaps 20 years old;

72. P.R.O., C115 K2/6685 f. 11v.
73. P.R.O., C115 K1/6678 ff. 2–17v.
74. *1455 Rental*, 10, 68, 112, etc.
75. *Rotuli Parliamentorum* 6 (1783), 49a.
76. *Cal. Pat. Rolls 1446–52*, 70.

and it is probable that derelict buildings would have been quickly demolished, as the timber of which they were built had a re-use value, if only as firewood.[77] In which case the existence of a large number of vacant plots could indicate a decline in the housing stock, and although comparison with Lanthony Priory records shows that the rental ignored most open ground, even so we are told of 24 vacant plots, as well as over 60 other pieces of land described as tofts or curtilages. Nevertheless the only certain sign in the rental of houses going out of use is the 20 or more former dwellings now being used as stables.

When in 1487 the town was again to petition the Crown for a reduction in its fee-farm, and it was claimed that the burgesses had fallen into such poverty that Gloucester now lay desolate, with more than 300 houses having fallen out of use in recent years because of the loss of population, we might feel that this was exaggeration; but there can be no doubt that by then Gloucester's decline had become acute.[78] In the 1520s, the returns of the Lay Subsidies show that the population of the town was now as low as 3000.[79]

The people of the 15th century saw the decline in the town's population as the cause of the deepening economic depression. They misunderstood what was happening to Gloucester, and to towns like it. As the population of medieval towns was maintained only by constant immigration from the countryside, the size of a town consequently depended on its ability to attract immigrants; so that when in the 15th century unprecedented prosperity came to the English peasantry, the economic need to leave the countryside lessened. Furthermore, the towns had become less attractive. The general reduction in upper-class spending power was passed on to those town merchants whose speciality lay in supplying luxury goods to the gentry; and lower down the urban social scale many craftsmen, particularly in the textile industry, saw their livelihoods slipping away in the face of competition from craftsmen based in villages and small towns.[80] Gloucester was simply becoming less important within the regional economy, and although it would maintain a level of economic activity commensurate with its status of market centre and county town, it would be many years before there was a return to the solid prosperity of the medieval period.

It is ironic that while in the midst of recession, with its population

77. Robert Cole described the New Inn as 'lately built' by John Twynnyng, a monk of St Peter's Abbey: *1455 Rental*, 84. However, Cole himself had described the New Inn in exactly the same terms in 1445: P.R.O. C115 K1/6678 f. 66, and furthermore John Twynnyng had not been a monk at Gloucester since at least 1441: *Cal. Pat. Rolls 1441–46*, 29.
78. *Cal. Recs. Corp. Gloucester*, 59.
79. In 1524 there were 390 taxpayers in Gloucester: P.R.O., E179/113/189.
80. Hatcher, 45–46.

falling away, and the income of the administration greatly reduced, Gloucester should have received an augmentation of its civic dignity with the charter of 1483. The bailiffs had long enjoyed every power they could realistically hope to wield; now they were to be joined by a mayor, aldermen, and a common council.[81] Despite the earlier complaints of the high cost of holding office, there seemed an eagerness to take on the extra expense that the inevitable increase in ceremonial entailed. With the cancellation in 1485 of the reduction in the fee-farm which had accompanied the charter, the finances of the administration must have been more uncertain than ever before.[82]

Hindsight makes it easy to be wise, and so the pretensions of the burgesses of the 1480s are most cruelly exposed. Yet they were not to know that their town was in a long-term decline, as part of a much wider phenomenon of change; they were not to know that the century that had followed the Black Death had seen the last flowering of medieval Gloucester.

Editorial suggestion for further reading

Britnell R. H., *Growth and Decline in Colchester, 1300–1525* (Cambridge, 1986).

81. *Cal. Recs. Corp. Gloucester,* 20.
82. Ibid., 21.

Chapter Nine

RALPH HOLLAND AND THE LONDON RADICALS, 1438–1444

Caroline M. Barron

from *A History of the North London Branch of the Historical Association, together with Essays in Honour of its Golden Jubilee* (London, 1970)

It is rare to find detailed records of a major factional dispute affecting the ruling body of a town. The relatively well-documented events which are lucidly presented in this article by Caroline Barron may usefully be compared with another celebrated case, of a generation later: that of Laurence Saunders in Coventry. It is perhaps significant that on both occasions popular discontent was channelled through a dissident member of the oligarchy. This would seem to reinforce Susan Reynolds's view that lesser burgesses everywhere saw the wealthy men of their town as a natural aristocracy. According to this theory, inferiors might question the particular judgement of their social betters, but never their right to govern. Alternatively, we may suspect that the mechanisms by which the oligarchy maintained its power were normally such as to stifle opposition from below. Only unusual circumstances – such as a charismatic leader, or a split in the oligarchy – could enable a serious protest movement to develop. In the case of Holland (as of Saunders) it would seem that these were precisely the circumstances that had arisen.

'The prosperity of the City of London depends not upon the merchants but upon the artisans.' So declared the tailor John Bale in 1443. He spoke for a large group of Londoners, many of whom were excluded from active participation in the government of the City and whose sense of injustice and grievance, while firmly rooted in the kind of company demarcation dispute which was common in the period, extended to the whole fabric of civic government.

The basic conflict arose between the Tailors and the Drapers and this was symptomatic of the fundamental rift in City life: the rift between the artisans and the merchants. The artisan companies might be ancient, but in wealth and power they lagged some considerable way behind the merchant companies who controlled the City government and so also gained the royal ear. The opposition which the ruling merchant oligarchy encountered in these years fed upon a variety of grievances, but its unity and driving force depended upon one man, a tailor called Ralph Holland. By his personal ability he articulated the artisans grievances, and out of the original dispute between the Tailors and Drapers there developed an organised opposition party in the city. This party first attacked the method of electing the Mayor and then, in 1443, resisted the new London charter which gave the Mayor and Aldermen powers as Justices, over and above their existing powers as Guardians of the Peace. When its attempts at reform within the existing framework of City government failed, the opposition party resorted to an attempt at an armed uprising. The failure of this in the autumn of 1443 marked the triumph of the conservative merchant elements but, during their brief period of agitation, Ralph Holland and his allies left behind them a record which helps to illuminate the actions and desires of that elusive being, the medieval common man.

The Tailors and Linen-Armourers of London had received letters patent from Edward III in 1327 whereby they were allowed to hold their guild once a year and to exercise the rights of search for defective work and correction of offenders, subject to the Mayor of London.[1] It was not until 1364 that the Drapers first received letters patent. By these they were granted a monopoly of buying and selling cloth in the City, and the power to elect four wardens to oversee and rule the mistery by aid of the Mayor and Sheriffs if need be.[2] In the fourteenth century there appears to have been no conflict between the two companies. Whereas the Tailors made up cloth, especially linen cloth, and did not act as retailers, the London Drapers were primarily concerned with the buying and selling of woollen cloth.[3]

In 1390 the Tailors received further letters patent from Richard II which granted them the right to elect a Master as well as their four Wardens and to make ordinances for the better government of the mistery.[4] Finally Henry IV incorporated the Tailors' Guild and authorized them to use a common seal and to hold land to the annual value of £100.[5] So it would appear that in the first part of the

1. F. M. Fry and R. T. D. Sayle, *Charters of the Merchant Tailors' Company* (1937), pp. 9–11.
2. A. E. Johnson, *The History of the Worshipful Company of the Drapers of London* (1914), vol. 1, pp. 204–8.
3. *Ibid.*, pp. 121–22.
4. 30 July 1390, Fry and Sayle, op. cit., pp. 13–15. Entered in the City's Letter Books, together with a writ from the King, dated 27 September 1392, instructing the Mayor to allow the Tailors to enjoy their gild and customs, *Calendar of the Letter Books of the City of London, Letter Book H* ed. R. R. Sharpe (1907) p. 384, (Hereafter cited as *L.B.H.*; so also *L.B.K.*)
5. 2 August 1408, Fry and Sayle, op. cit., pp. 15–18; P[ublic] R[ecord] O[ffice], Ancient Petition no. 12781; *C[alendar of] P[atent] R[olls] 1405–8*, p. 466.

fifteenth century the Tailors were the more established and the wealthier of the two companies. They had had a Master since 1390, they were incorporated in 1408 and there is evidence that they had a company hall as early as 1392, whereas the Drapers only began to build their hall in 1425.[6] Moreover in 1413 when the income from the London property of the Tailors' company stood at £44 3s. 7d. that of the Drapers was only £22 13s. 6d.[7]

Yet in spite of all this the Tailors appear to have occupied a relatively subordinate position in the government of the City. In the years between 1327 and 1435, when Ralph Holland became an Alderman, the Tailors provided no Aldermen, and consequently no Mayors, whereas the Drapers in the same period furnished 34 Aldermen, 14 of whom became Mayors. The other companies from whom nearly all the Aldermen were drawn in this period were the Mercers, Grocers, Fishmongers, Goldsmiths, Skinners and Vintners. What reason can be found for this subordinate position of the Tailors? Why did they not achieve civic office? The situation may, perhaps, be explained by the fact that the Tailors were an artisan guild, albeit a wealthy one. A Tailor worked with his hands; a Draper bought and sold. A Tailor could make no more money than his hands could earn; a Draper in this period of the expanding English cloth trade could become wealthy and a man of influence at home and abroad. The other great London companies of this period were also primarily merchant gilds. Merchant Drapers like John Hende, William Crowmer and Simon Eyre were rich men and generous benefactors, but there were no Tailors who stood out in this way. Furthermore, since the Drapers had the monopoly of buying and selling woollen cloth in London, the Tailors became dependent upon them for the means to carry on their own trade. Thus the London Draper had established himself securely as the indispensable middle man and the Tailor had no choice but to accept his dependent position.

In these circumstances an ambitious man, who had the necessary capital, would choose, if he could, to become a Draper. A few men appear to have belonged to both companies simultaneously, although this was unusual.[8] Ralph Holland was one of these. He appears first in the records of the Drapers' company for 1413–14 when he was sufficiently advanced in status to owe money for the

---

6. H. L. Hopkinson, *The History of the Merchant Tailors' Hall* (1931), chapters i and ii; Johnson, op. cit., vol. I, pp. 112–3.

7. 'Lay Subsidy temp. Henry IV', ed. J. C. L. Stahlschmidt, *Archaeological Journal*, vol. XLIV (1887), pp. 56–82; Johnson, op. cit., vol. I, p. 128.

8. John Derby was variously described as a Draper and as a Tailor, see A. B. Beaven, *The Aldermen of the City of London*, vol. I (1908), p. 330 n.1. In the early fifteenth century three men successfully petitioned to be allowed to transfer from the Tailors' to the Drapers' company, *L.B.K.*, pp. 39, 224, 309.

enrolment of his apprentice, Thomas Holme.[9] In 1414–16 he paid 20s. to enter the livery of the Tailors' company and even after he was Master of the Tailors two years later, he is still to be found in the Drapers' accounts contributing 40s. towards the new Drapers' Hall.[10] Indeed, even as late as 1441, when the Drapers' accounts end, Holland was still being assessed for Quarterage, although it is clear from other evidence that by this date he had fully identified himself with the interests of the Tailors' company.[11]

Ralph Holland may have come originally from Newington in Surrey in the early years of the fifteenth century.[12] By 1416 he was well established in London and was probably in his early twenties. Of his parents nothing is known, but sometime before 1419 he had married a wife Mathilda and by her had at least one son, also Ralph, who entered the livery of the Tailors' company in 1435/6 but appears to have died before his father.[13] In 1419 Ralph Holland was elected Master of the Tailors' company[14] and he appears first in the civic records when, on 5th September 1426, he was committed to prison, having criticised the Mayor for correcting the Tailors. This is the first hint of the outspoken radical who was to disturb the peace of the City at intervals over the next twenty years. On this occasion Holland was bound over with a caution, but he seems to have paid little attention to this.[15] In the court of Aldermen on 8th October John Olney, a Mercer, Thomas Cook, a Draper and Thomas Reynwell, a Grocer, gave evidence on oath against Holland. On that day the Mayor had reissued an ancient royal writ of 1315. This writ enjoined that only those citizens who had been summoned might attend the elections of the Sheriffs on 21st September and the Mayor

9. The surviving Drapers' accounts are printed by Johnson, op. cit., vol. I, Appendix no. 18, pp. 283–348, see esp. p. 287.

10. Merchant Tailors' Hall, Wardens' Accounts 1397–1445, Ms. A4 f.90. (Hereafter cited as Tailors' Accounts i).

11. Holland continues to appear in the Drapers' Accounts as a debtor until they end in 1442; otherwise the last description to be found of him as a Draper is in 1440, *C[alendar of] C[lose] R[olls] 1435–41*, p. 378. A deed enrolled in the Hustings Court 13 March 1444 suggests that Holland had severed his connection with the Drapers since he claimed that a London shop had been granted to him as 'Ralph Holland per nomen Radulphi Holland pannarii', G[uildhall] R[ecord] O[ffice], Hustings Roll 172 (21).

12. In his will Holland made a bequest to the poor there, and he also owned property in Surrey, see Sylvia M. Thrupp, *The Merchant Class of Medieval London 1300–1500* (Ann Arbor Paperback edn., Michigan, U.S.A., 1962), pp. 350, 381.

13. Mathilda, wife of Ralph Holland, entered the livery of the Tailors' Company 1419–20 and 'My mistress Holland' contributed 20/– for the chapel in 1438–39, Tailors' Accounts i f. 113, 304v. 26 March 1421 a licence to have a portable altar was granted to Ralph Holland and his wife Mathilda, *Calendar of Papal Registers: Petitions* vol. VII p. 333. Ralph Holland, junior, in his Will dated 24 October 1445, bequeathed tenements in the parish of St Dunstan in the East.

14. Tailors' Accounts i f. 112.

15. G.R.O. Journal ii, f. 82v.

on 13th October, and not the freemen of the City at large. It would seem that the practice of summoning citizens individually to these elections had lapsed, and that all interested freemen were accustomed to attend. By reverting to the older practice the Mayor and Aldermen were clearly intending to exercise some control over the composition of the electorate on these important occasions. Suspecting this motive, Holland had been heard to declare that the writs about the election of the Mayor were new, fabricated and untrue and were not to be found recorded in any of the City's ancient books. In fact Holland was mistaken on this point for the royal writ of 1315 was recorded in the City Letter Book and, as a result of his ill-judged words, Holland was sent to Ludgate prison.[16] The Sheriffs in their return to the royal writ of *habeas corpus* justified Holland's imprisonment on the grounds that he had not only 'wantonly declared that such ordinances were fabrications' but had also threatened the Draper, Thomas Cook, with violence.[17] Early, therefore, in his career Ralph Holland fought for a wide civic franchise and consequently fell foul of the ruling oligarchy. This problem of the civic franchise and of the right of the 'inferior' citizens to vote at civic elections was to become an important plank in Holland's later platform and, by tackling the problem of the constitutional basis of government, he showed a political awareness which raised him above his contemporaries. On this occasion Holland submitted and he was released on £100 bail provided by four men of whom three may be definitely identified as Tailors.[18]

By 1429 Ralph Holland had become a Common Councilman and in February of that year he was presented to the Court of Aldermen by the men of the ward of Baynard's Castle as one of their four candidates for the vacant Aldermanry. The other candidates were Ralph Skinnard, who had been one of Holland's sureties, the Vintner Thomas Walsingham and Thomas Duffhous who was a Fishmonger and, currently, one of the Sheriffs. The Aldermen unanimously chose Walsingham.[19] This rebuff did not make Holland more conformist. On 13th May 1429 Thomas Bradby, a Fishmonger, reported to the Court of Aldermen that in a meeting of Common Council held two days earlier, when the question of providing the King a loan had been discussed, Holland had said that the King's necessity was not as great as the Mayor and Aldermen represented.[20] Then, in September of the same year, Ralph Holland finally gained access to the 'establishment', for the Commonalty

16. Ibid. f. 85; for the 1315 writ see *L.B.D.* pp. 24–26.
17. *L.B.K.* pp. 55–56.
18. 10 October 1426, G.R.O. Journal ii, f. 85v.
19. Ibid. f. 131v.
20. Ibid. f. 133v.

elected him as their Sheriff for the succeeding year.[21]

Unfortunately the civic Journals are missing for the seven years following November 1429 so it is impossible to trace Holland's career in any detail.[22] In September 1434 he was elected one of the annual City auditors.[23] From the Tailors' company accounts it is clear that he was prospering and in July 1435 he was able to lend £100 to the King.[24] By October of that year he had been chosen as Alderman for the ward of Bread Street.[25] But by now the rivalry between the Tailors and Drapers had crystallised into a dispute over the rights of the two companies in searching for defective cloth in the City. In the year ending August 1435 the Tailors had spent £14 4s. 4d. on fees and entertainment for the lawyers who were helping them to construct their case against the Drapers.[26]

The dispute between the two companies was aggravated by the statute of 1437 which demanded that the rules and regulations of all gilds, fraternities and companies should be submitted for approval to the local Justices of the Peace or to the governors of the cities concerned.[27] In London it had always been necessary for gilds and companies to submit their regulations to the Mayor for approval, and, if the company wardens exercised rights of search for defective work they never did so absolutely, but as the Mayor's deputies. As a result of the statute many City companies sought a new royal confirmation of their charters. In November 1438 the Drapers received new letters patent incorporating them as a company and empowering them to elect a Master as well as their four Wardens.[28] The new charter did not specifically grant the Drapers the right to search for

---

21. *L.B.K.*, p. 102.
22. Although the civic records of the Court of Aldermen and Court of Common Council (Journals) are missing, the Tailors' Accounts reveal some of Holland's activities. He enrolled two apprentices in 1425–26; two in 1428–29; one in 1433–34; one in 1434–35; one in 1438–39; two in 1440–41; two in 1443–44, Tailors' Accounts i, f. 159v., 193v., 244., 303v., 329, 370. Holland was probably the wealthiest member of the Tailors' Company. His contributions to the new kitchen in 1425–26, 1430–31 and 1432–33 were larger than those of any other member of the Company, ibid., f. 161v., 237v. Holland's contribution of £4 towards the new charter in 1439–40 was larger than that of anyone else, and in 1433–34 he lent the Company £15 but took as security two silver gilt basins and two silver pottles. He was repaid 10 years later, ibid., f. 317v., 375.
23. *L.B.K.*, pp. 183–84.
24. 9 July 1435, *C.P.R. 1429–36* p. 467. P.R.O. Receipt Roll E 401/742. Holland also lent to the Crown in June 1437 (£100), April 1442 (£200), April 1445 (£200), July 1449 (£100), July 1449 (£500), April 1451 (£100), all recorded in the Receipt Rolls under the relevant term.
25. *L.B.K.*, p. 193.
26. Tailors' Accounts i, f. 258v.–259v.
27. *R[olls of] P[arliament]*, (1832), vol. IV, p. 507; see *L.B.K.*, p. xli.
28. Text of charter, Johnson, op. cit., vol. I, pp. 214–15.

defective cloth in the City, but the King appointed two Drapers as aulnagers in London, i.e. as collectors of the tax payable to the King on every piece of woollen cloth. No cloth could be sold, or made up, until it had been sealed by the aulnager to show that the tax had been paid and that the piece was of the correct width and length. Although the aulnagers were concerned with money, and not with defects of quality or workmanship, the grant of the office to two Drapers in February 1439 was regarded by their company as a considerable 'coup' and was greatly displeasing to the Tailors.[29]

But the Tailors were not to be outdone. They also received letters patent dated 24th February 1439 which confirmed their earlier royal grants but also added a new and important clause empowering the Master and Wardens to 'have and make full search in and of the misteries aforesaid and of all those persons who are or shall be privileged with the Tailors and Linen Armourers . . . and to correct and reform all defects found among them . . . by the survey of the Mayor of your said City . . .'.[30] By the considerable outlay of £79 18s. 3d. the Tailors had secured a signal advantage, for the search of members of their company was to be carried out either by the Mayor or their own Wardens.[31] The Mayor had, before this, always been entitled to choose those deputies he wished, although in practice he usually selected the Wardens of the company concerned. Thus the Tailors' new charter could be argued to have infringed the rights of the Mayor of London, and it was upon this ground that the Drapers chose to launch their attack.

Later in 1439 the Mayor ordered that both the Tailors and the Saddlers, whose new charter contained a similar search clause, should deposit their charters at Guildhall while it was decided whether they infringed the City's liberties.[32] The Drapers' accounts for the year ending August 1440 show that they were seriously worried by the search clause in the Tailors' new charter whereby they were completely excluded from any search of the artisan company. They paid 2s. for a Chancery copy of 'the newe article in the

---

29. The Drapers were Robert Shirborne and John Derby. Grant printed by Johnson, op. cit., pp. 216–20.
30. Fry and Sayle, op. cit., pp. 21–22.
31. Tailors' Accounts i f. 313v., 302. The largest items of expenditure were £30 for the Duke of Gloucester and £10 for the Bishop of Bath, the Lord Chancellor. Adam Moleyns, the Clerk of the Council, received £8 6s. 8d. and cloth worth £2. Most of the rest of the money was spent on dinners for important people, and fees for writing and enrolling the charter. See also C. M. Clode, *The Early History of the Guild of Merchant Tailors* (1888), part I, Appendix iii, pp. 345–46.
32. P. E. Jones, ed., *Calendar of Plea and Memoranda Rolls 1437–57* (Cambridge, 1954) p. 33. In 1439–40 the Tailors paid 1/8d. 'for a copy of the bill which the Mayor of London brought to our Lord the King and to the Council, for the charters of all the different mysteries of the City', Clode, op. cit., p. 346.

Taylours charter' and a further 2s. for the drafting and writing of two bills which they sent to the Mayor 'for the same article'.[33] The Tailors, however, spent a further £60 in this year for a royal confirmation of the new charter and other attendant expenses.[34]

During the early years of this dispute there is no evidence that Ralph Holland was promoting the Tailors' cause at the Court of Aldermen in a provocative or outspoken way.[35] Rather he would seem to have been taking steps to become accepted as a conventional Alderman and, hence, a candidate for the Mayoralty. He was appointed to committees and selected to put the City's case in the dispute with the Prior of Holy Trinity to the Duke of Gloucester.[36] This would suggest that Holland was known and liked by Duke Humphrey, and the Tailors' accounts indicate that their recent succes may have been due to his patronage, which would be of particular importance in this period of conciliar rule.[37] On 13th October 1439 the City Journals record for the first time the names of the two Aldermen whom the assembled freemen presented to the Court of Aldermen for their choice of Mayor for the following year. The candidates were Robert Large, a Mercer, and Ralph Holland. The Aldermen chose Robert Large.[38]

One rejection did not cause a constitutional crisis and Ralph Holland was content to bide his turn. The ill feeling between the Tailors and Drapers certainly continued. In November of that year John Pevenel was sent to prison for saying that he could prove six members of the Drapers' company to be false, when in fact he could not

33. Johnson, op. cit., vol. I, p. 337.
34. Tailors' Accounts i, f. 317v.–319v.; Clode, op. cit., pp. 345–46.
35. Holland had, of course, been involved in the activities of his Company. The Recorder of London in 1438–39 had been entertained at Holland's house when his advice was sought by the Company, and Holland had contributed £4 towards the cost of the new charter, Tailors' Accounts i, f. 203. 317v.
36. G.R.O. Journal iii, f. 7; *L.B.K.* p. 230. March 1439, Holland appointed to Committee to supervise City Aqueduct, G.R.O. Journal iii, f. 11.
37. The Duke entered the livery of the Company in 1414, and men were enfranchised as Tailors at his request in 1416, 1417 and 1436, Tailors' Accounts, f. 73v., 89v., 94v., 265v. Other men entered the livery of the Company at his instigation in 1425 and 1433, ibid. f. 150v., 237. Gloucester was given a hood in 1432, 1436, 1437, 1439, 1441–45, ibid. f. 229v., 272, 283, 309, 333, 346, 361, 376, 397. Eleanor, Duchess of Gloucester, was enrolled in the livery in 1434 and Richard Nedeham described as 'with my Lady of Gloucester' entered the livery in 1445, ibid. f. 246, 338. In 1431 Gloucester sold the 'Maison de Riall' to the Company for £40 and the sale was negotiated by Holland, ibid., f. 216v.–217v. When the trouble with the Drapers became serious the Tailors spent 36/8d. on cloth for Gloucester's confessor in 1435, in 1439 paid the Duke £30 (a bribe?) and at Christmas 1440 the Company paid his Mummers £6 13s. 4d. ibid., f. 259v., 313v., 332v. In July 1443 Holland acted as Gloucester's financial agent in receiving repayment of a loan for him, P.R.O. Issue Roll E 403/762.
38. G.R.O. Journal iii, f. 14v.

substantiate any of his charges.[39] Meanwhile Holland continued to be appointed to various committees of the Court of Aldermen[40] and, on 13th October 1440, the freemen again selected two candidates for the Mayoralty; John Paddesley, a Goldsmith, and Ralph Holland. The Aldermen chose Paddesley.[41]

It was during the Mayoralty of John Paddesley that the dispute between the Tailors and Drapers came to a head. Since 1439 both companies had been arguing their case before the Chancellor, and before the Court of Aldermen. Then on 5th August 1441 the Wardens of the Drapers' company complained to the Mayor and Aldermen that they did not have their customary scrutiny of lengths of cloth in the possession of Tailors. The particular reason for their concern was the forthcoming St Bartholomew's Fair which was held for three days around 24th August. On this occasion much cloth was bought and sold by both Tailors and Drapers and it had been customary for the Drapers to exercise the right of search. The Court postponed replying to this complaint until all the Aldermen who were absent at the time, including Holland, should have been consulted.[42] On 14th August 1441, the Mayor and Aldermen produced a compromise in time for the Fair. The Master and Wardens of the Draper's company were to exercise their general rights of search for defective woollen cloth as before. But as a temporary expedient to preserve the peace, and to give the Tailors a chance to present their case later, the Mayor himself would search the unmade-up woollen cloth displayed for sale by the Tailors at the Fair.[43] Clearly by this date the Tailors were acting as retailers of cloth and it would seem that the artisan company was attempting to encroach upon the trading activities of the Drapers. It was this desire on the part of the Tailors to upgrade themselves into a merchant company which lay at the root of the dispute, of which the trouble over the right of search was but the symptom.

While the Drapers had been busy furthering their cause at the Court of Aldermen, the Tailors had prevailed upon the King to send a letter to the Mayor instructing him to allow the Tailors to search and remedy defects in their mistery in accordance with the earlier royal letters patent of February 1439.[44] In spite of this regal com-

39. 27 November 1439, G.R.O. Journal iii, f. 30v.
40. In August 1440 Holland was appointed to oversee the work on the new bars at Smithfield, in September he was one of the Aldermen sent to the King to put the City's case about the abuse of the sanctuary of St Martin's-le-Grand, and he was on a second, smaller, committee set up to deal with the same problem later in the month; G.R.O. Journal iii, f. 52v., 59, 60.
41. G.R.O. Journal iii, f. 62v.
42. G.R.O. Journal iii, f. 93v.
43. *L.B.K.*, pp. 259–60.
44. 14th August 1441, *L.B.K.* p. 260. The Tailors spent a considerable amount of money 'upon divers men for the search of St Bartholomew's Fair'. They also

mand it would appear that the Mayor continued with his original plan of searching the Tailors at the Fair himself for, although four Drapers were sworn in Court to exercise the scrutiny, no Tailors were similarly sworn.[45]

The election of the Mayor on 13th October 1441 was, in these circumstances, of more than passing significance. Success or failure in the dispute over the rights of search would depend very largely upon the decisions of the Mayor in the coming year. Again there is little evidence to suggest that Ralph Holland had been acting in a way which his fellow-Aldermen might consider obnoxious. It is true that in March 1441 the Mayor's sergeant, John Russel, had been examined in Court about certain words which he had heard spoken by Holland,[46] but throughout the year he had continued to be appointed to arduous and important committees of the Court of Aldermen.[47] There would seem to be no grounds on which the Aldermen could reasonably reject Holland as Mayor if he were presented as a candidate for the third time.

The events of 13th October 1441 were of such an unusual nature that they even attracted the attention of contemporary chroniclers. The London freemen, gathered together in Guildhall, chose two candidates, the Tailor Ralph Holland and Robert Clopton, a Draper. Then, while the crowd waited breathlessly in the outer hall, the Aldermen deliberated in private. Finally John Paddesley, the current Mayor, emerged leading upon his right hand the Aldermen's choice – Robert Clopton, the Draper. Instantly a commotion broke out and the Tailors and other 'handycrafty' men called out 'nay, not that man but Raulyn Holland'. Nothing the Mayor could do nor his Sergeant's attempts at crying 'ozey' could quieten the incensed Tailors. Finally the Sheriffs had to round up the protesters and send them to prison. Indeed it appears that the Tailors not only rejected Clopton but even unofficially declared Holland to have been elected Mayor.[48]

paid 6/8d. to a secretary 'for devising and writing a letter from the King to the Mayor of London' (the letter of 14th August 1441), and other sums upon travelling expenses and suppers, amounting in all to £6 12s. 1d. Tailors' Accounts i, f. 351–351v.

45. G.R.O. Journal iii, f. 94v.
46. G.R.O. Journal iii, f. 80.
47. Holland had been appointed to the committees to supervise the new work on London Bridge, to deal with the Aqueduct accounts, and to arbitrate between the Bridge Wardens and the auditors of their accounts, G.R.O. Journal iii, f. 67, 67v., 76v.
48. C. L. Kingsford, ed., *Chronicles of London* (Oxford, 1905) pp. 154–55; F. W. Brie, ed., *The Brut, or the Chronicles of England* (early English Text Society, 1906) p. 508; A. H. Thomas and I. D. Thornley, eds., *The Great Chronicle of London* (1938), pp. 175–76; R. Flenley, ed., *Six Town Chronicles of England* (Oxford, 1911), p. 115.

The story in the chronicles is substantiated by the official version of the events of October 13th to be found in the City Journals.[49] An *ad hoc* jury of eighteen men declared that eleven men had been responsible for breaking the King's peace, six Tailors and five Skinners. These eleven were committed to prison and on the following day the Master and Wardens of the Tailors' Company asked to be allowed to go bail for the prisoners. This was refused on the grounds that a mandate from the King had instructed the Mayor that the Tailors were not to be released on bail. On 4th November the men were still in prison and the Court of Aldermen sent a deputation to the King's Council to discuss the matter. Three days later a further committee of more senior Aldermen was sent again to the Council to urge that the Tailors and Skinners should not be set free without the consent of the Mayor and Aldermen. A note was added in the Journal to state that the Aldermen had been graciously received and their petition heard.[50] On 8th November Shefuld, the warden of Newgate prison where the eleven men were kept, reported to the Court of Aldermen that the prisoners claimed that they were not guilty of the offences for which they were imprisoned and that they knew that their release depended not upon the Mayor but upon the Lords of the Council. Shefuld further informed the Court that Kent and White, who were Tailors, and Sherde and Palmer, who were Skinners, were the ring-leaders, and that Palmer and Kent had declared that even if they never left prison they would make no 'mediaciones' to the Mayor for their freedom. These were brave words.[51] Subsequently, however, the men were released by a writ of privy seal and were bound over to keep the peace, to appear before the Mayor's Court and the King's Council and to make reparation for their transgressions.[52]

With the troublesome Tailors and Skinners thus subdued, the new Mayor, the Draper Robert Clopton, turned his attention to achieving the suspension of the obnoxious scrutiny clause in the Tailors' charter. In this year the Drapers spent £10 2s. 11d. to some purpose for, on 21st August 1442, the King wrote to the Master and Wardens of the Tailors, withdrawing the exclusive right of search which had previously been granted to them and vesting this right once more in

49. G.R.O. Journal iii, f. 97v.
50. G.R.O. Journal iii, f. 98, 101v., 102. Holland did not attend the Court of Aldermen between 11 October 1441 and 31 January 1442, and his attendance after this date is very infrequent until July 1442.
51. G.R.O. Journal iii, f. 102v.
52. Only eight of the men appear to have been bound over in this way, in the sum of 100 marks each. They largely acted as mainpernors for each other, although Nicholas Toller, a Skinner who came into prominence as an artisan leader in 1442 (see p. 172) also acted in this capacity, G.R.O. Journal iii, f. 103v.–104. The Tailors paid 6/8d. to 'men of our craft and others that were at Newgate', Tailors' Accounts i, f. 351v.

the hands of the Mayor or those deputies whom he chose.[53] Another royal letter was sent to the Mayor confirming his right of search over all companies and misteries in London, in accordance with the City's ancient liberties and customs, notwithstanding the opposition of certain Tailors and other men in the City.[54] Thus the Tailors found themselves once more subject to the scrutiny of the Mayor or, what was worse, any deputy whom he chose to appoint. Currently, moreover, the Mayor was a Draper and he was always a representative of the merchant classes. The Tailors had spent a great deal of money in obtaining their new charter and now it was worthless and had to be returned to the King's Council before Michaelmas 1442. How differently might events have turned out for the Tailors if their man, Ralph Holland, had been chosen Mayor.

It is not surprising that in these circumstances the City governors feared renewed trouble at the election of the Mayor which was due to take place on 13th October 1442. Accordingly they obtained a royal writ instructing the Mayor and Sheriffs to proclaim that, because of recent disturbances, no one but the Aldermen and other discreet and powerful citizens were to attend the Mayor's election.[55] As early as 1426 Ralph Holland had protested at this limitation of the civic franchise, and for fear of protest, the Aldermen decided to proclaim not only the King's recent writ but also the ancient one of 1315, to show that this limitation was not an innovation.[56]

At the election on 13th October 1442 John Atherley, an Ironmonger, was chosen at a meeting consisting only of those who were summoned and whose names were checked off at the door of Guildhall.[57] The Journals do not record the election so that the name of the rejected candidate is unknown. Three days later a clergyman who was considered to have preached a seditious sermon at St Paul's Cross appeared before the Court and was asked to provide a written text of his sermon. On the following day the Court was informed that it was an Alderman who had provided the clergyman with his seditious material, namely that the first and the best Mayor whom the City had ever had was a Cordwainer named Walsh. No Cordwainer Walsh, nor indeed any Cordwainer, had ever filled the Mayor's office, but such an assertion was no doubt intended by the

53. Johnson, op. cit., vol. I, pp. 343–44. Their expenditure included £3 12s. 0d. to Lord Salisbury and 18/- to Adam Moleyns, the Clerk of the Council, and the costs of employing lawyers. Moleyns had also received money from the Tailors and gifts of cloth yearly to the value of 33/4d. p.a. since 1439, Tailors' Accounts i, f. 321, 333; *L.B.K.*, pp. 260–61; Sir H. Nicholas, ed., *Proceedings and Ordinances of the Privy Council of England* (1834), vol. v, p. 196.
54. *L.B.K.*, p. 260. 23 August 1442, these two letters were received and read in the Court of Aldermen, G.R.O. Journal iii, f. 150.
55. 10 October 1442, *L.B.K.*, pp. 274–75.
56. 11 October 1442, G.R.O. Journal iii, f. 152v.
57. *L.B.K.*, p. 275 and n. 1.

clergyman and his Alderman informant to be an incentive to the artisan classes to restore the ancient order of civic life when, in the golden age, the artisans ruled the City. The Court took the matter sufficiently seriously to require each Alderman to swear on the Gospels that he was innocent of providing such seditious information.[58] Nine Aldermen were absent from this meeting of whom Ralph Holland, the only artisan Alderman, was one. His guilt appears likely but not proven.

Even if Ralph Holland was not the ultimate source of the seditious sermon at St Paul's Cross, he was stirring up trouble elsewhere. On 26th October 1442 the Court questioned Holland about his statement that John Paddesley during his Mayoralty in the years 1440–41, had spent 1000 marks belonging to the City on his private concerns.[59] Holland's dislike of Paddesley is not difficult to explain for it was during his Mayoralty that the Mayor had taken back into his own hands the search of cloth exposed for sale by Tailors at Saint Bartholomew's Fair. Paddesley could also be held responsible not only for the choice of the Draper, Robert Clopton, to succeed him as Mayor, but also for the stern imprisonment of those Tailors and Skinners who raised their voices in protest at Clopton's election. The leader of the artisan Skinners in these years was Nicholas Toller who also criticised Paddesley. At Stourbridge Fair he had openly declared that Paddesley had been a false judge during his Mayoralty, had judged Toller himself unfairly and, in particular, had imprisoned men in Newgate unjustly. The Skinners' leader was here referring to Paddesley's imprisonment of the eleven Skinners and Tailors in October 1441. As a result of these injudicious words, the Court placed Toller under an obligation to keep the peace on penalty of paying £20 to the City Chamber.[60]

Meanwhile, although the Tailors' charter had been suspended since August 1442, it had not yet been finally quashed by the King's Council. The Court of Aldermen sent the Recorder to present the City's case and then engaged two sergeants at law to represent them before the Council.[61] The Tailors also employed legal counsel and

58. G.R.O. Journal iii, f. 153.

59. G.R.O. Journal iii, f. 154v.

60. 11 October 1442, Toller was bound over to abide by the decision of the Court; 29 October 1442, the £20 obligation was substituted for the earlier one, G.R.O. Journal iii, f. 153, 154v. Toller is first mentioned as a Skinner in 1426, J. J. Lambert, ed., *Records of the Skinners' Company* (1933), p. 94. He was a Master of Warden of the Company in 1438–39, *L.B.K.*, p. 222. It would seem that the artisan Skinners, as opposed to the merchant Skinners like Henry Barton, sided with the Tailors in their opposition to the City government in these years. Apart from the obvious community of interest, an explanation may lie in the fact that Nicholas Toller's brother, John, was a Tailor, *C.C.R. 1429–35*, p. 351. See n. 52 above.

61. 20 October, 5 November 1442, G.R.O. Journal iii, f. 153v., 156.

spent money on journeys to Westminster and on dinners for important people.[62] The Tailors' quandary was that their new charter *was*
contrary to the liberties of London since the right of search over all
misteries lay by customary right with the Mayor or the deputies
whom he appointed. Thus for companies like the Drapers, whose
influence in civic affairs was considerable, the Mayor's right of
search presented no problem. If the Mayor himself were not a
Draper, he could be easily persuaded to appoint Drapers as his
deputies. The Tailors, on the other hand, seemed unlikely to provide
a Mayor and could exercise no influence over his choice of deputies.
It was essential to them, therefore, to enjoy a right of search independent of the civic authority. There were two alternatives open to
the Tailors; either they must have their independent right of search
confirmed by the King, or they must achieve some influence in
civic government. It seemed now as if they were about to lose both
battles and so the situation between the artisans in the City who
sided with the Tailors and the merchant governors who supported
the Drapers, remained explosive. While the Tailors fought for their
hard-won charter, resentment seethed among the poorer classes in
the City. It is not surprising that the Draper, Robert Clopton, should
have thought it worthwhile to buy a charter of pardon from the
King for all trespasses and quarrels which had occurred during his
Mayoralty.[62a]

The final outburst of artisan discontent in these years was caused,
in part, by the City's new Commission of the Peace in 1443 which
was incorporated into the new charter in 1444. The text of the 1443
Commission was not enrolled in Chancery and has not survived
among the City's records. It was read out to the Court of Aldermen
on 13th August 1443 and appears to have regularised the judicial
powers of the Mayor and Aldermen, making them not simply Guardians of the Peace, but Justices with power to hear and terminate
cases.[63] Until this date the Mayor and Aldermen had always been
wary of acting as judges in criminal cases and had preferred to leave
such matters to the royal judges, especially where the City Companies were concerned. For example, when Paddesley, the Mayor,
in October 1441 had committed the eleven Tailors and Skinners to
Newgate prison for breaking the King's Peace, they had been

62. In 1442–43 the Tailors spent a total of £11 16s. 9d. on expenses for legal counsel
at Westminster and Guildhall, dinners and journeys to the King, Tailors' Accounts i. f. 365v.–366.

62a. *C.P.R. 1441–46*, p. 136

63. Journal iii ends 17 November 1442 and Journal iv does not begin until 13 August
1443. For the text of the new charter see G.R.O. Charter 55 and *Calendar of
Charter Rolls* vol. VI, pp. 41–44. The process whereby the Mayor and Aldermen
became fully integrated into the national system of local jurisdiction is discussed
by A. H. Thomas, ed., *Calendar of Plea and Memoranda Rolls 1323–64*,
pp. i–xxxiii.

released on bail by a royal judicial decision. It was, no doubt, the need for stronger measures to safeguard law and order in the City which had led the Court of Aldermen to seek for this regularisation of their powers. But in the prevailing atmosphere, it is not difficult to see why the new Commission of the Peace provoked such a violent reaction. As a contemporary chronicler wrote 'A commission was sued for the City of London which was called a charter, and the Commons were greatly aggrieved therewith'.[64]

The Aldermen may have particularly wanted the new Commission to be in operation before the St Bartholomew's Fair held in the middle of August, since the dispute between the Tailors and Drapers had not yet been finally settled by the King's Council, and the Court decided that the Mayor should search the woollen cloth sold by Tailors at the Fair as had been arranged during Paddesley's Mayoralty.[65] This compromise was known to be bitterly resented by the Tailors, but there is no evidence that they caused trouble during the Fair. Early in September, however, Ralph Holland launched a vehement attack upon the new Commission in the Court of Aldermen. He claimed that it would subvert the peace of the City and undermine its customary good rule to the detriment of the London artisans. Moreover he considered that the Recorder, Robert Danvers, and the Common Clerk, Richard Barnet, were particularly responsible for procuring the new Commission and he levelled other more scandalous charges against these two men which the Journal's clerk declined to record. Holland ended his attack upon a ringing note, 'This is a commission' he declared 'not of peace, but of war'. Indeed he was almost proved right.[66]

The storm broke on 21st September 1443, the customary day for the annual election by the freemen of London of the Chamberlain, and the two Sheriffs. While the Sheriffs changed every year, the Chamberlain was usually re-elected since the office required experience and skill. On this occasion a large crowd of 'inferior' citizens refused to agree that John Chichele, who had served the City as Chamberlain since 1434, should continue in office the following year. Instead they raised their hands and cried for 'Cottisbrook'. Chichele may have been singled out for attack in this way, because it was thought that by controlling the City's finances he was, in some sense, responsible for the purchase of the new Commission. But it may have been that, since the office of Chamberlain was one of the few important civic offices which the citizens controlled directly by annual election, their purpose was simply to exercise their powers rather than to attack Chichele. But they did not succeed, for the

64. R. Flenley, ed., *Six Town Chronicles of England* (Oxford, 1911), p. 117.
65. See p. 65 above. The Wardens of the Drapers' Company were sworn to exercise their scrunity, 21 August 1443, G.R.O. Journal iv, f. 1v.
66. G.R.O. Journal iv, f. 4v.

Mayor ordered that all those who had not been personally summoned should depart and the election take place again. The question was now put to the more select body of citizens and 'John
Chichele was nominated Chamberlain with the unanimous consent
of the Mayor and Aldermen'. The Journal's clerk added to his version of these events that Chichele was elected 'as a man faithful,
wise, diligent and prudent'.[67]

Who was Cottisbrook, the radicals' candidate? Before these
events it is not easy to identify him with the artisan cause. He was
a Grocer and a Common Councilman who had served the City as a
Member of Parliament in 1442.[68] He was not unqualified to act as
Chamberlain since he had already been one of the City's auditors.[69]
After his rejection as Chamberlain by the Mayor and Aldermen, he
became one of the more vocal and informed of the City radicals,
but he appears to have died in 1444 or 1445.[70]

The City governors now moved quickly. John Bakewell, a member of Christopher Water's houschold (a Skinner who was
subsequently associated with Holland's conspiracy) was imprisoned
for publicly cursing the authority of a City sergeant.[71] John Arcall,
a Tailor who had earlier insulted the Chamberlain, now declared in
court that even if he were offered £100 he would not want Chichele
as Chamberlain since he had been responsible for acquiring the new
Commission.[72] On 24th September 1443 the Masters and Wardens
of all the City companies were summoned to the court of Aldermen
and instructed to warn the men of their companies and the members
of their own households, to desist from spreading false rumours and
scandals about the Mayor and Aldermen. Three days later these
same men were again summoned before the Court to be informed
that the new Commission of the Peace was not contrary to the liberties of the City.[73] But this did not deter William Goldyngton, a
spirited Carpenter, from declaring to the Mayor's sergeant that he
had enough hurdles to draw all those traitors who had obtained the
new Commission of the Peace from the Tower to Tyburn. The new
Commission, he added, was contrived to bring the citizens of London into bondage.[74]

67. *L.B.K.*, pp. 286–87; G.R.O. Journal iv, f. 5v.–6v.
68. G.R.O. Journal iii, f. 76v., 115, 108v.
69. 21 September 1442, *L.B.K*, pp. 273–74. Cottisbrook was re-elected in 1443,
     ibid., pp. 287–88.
70. The last reference to Cottisbrook is to be found in July 1444, Thomas Rymer,
     comp., *Foedera* (3rd edn. 1739–45), vol. v., part i, p. 136.
71. G.R.O. Journal iv., f. 7.
72. G.R.O. Journal iv, f. 4v., 7. Arcall had been associated with Holland in April
     1441, P. E. Jones, ed., *Calendar of Plea and Memoranda Rolls 1437–57*, p. 165.
73. G.R.O. Journal iv., f. 7.
74. G.R.O. Journal iv, f. 7v. 5 October 1443, Goldyngton was released on bail of
     £100 to appear in the Mayor's Court, ibid., f. 9.

To add to the problems of the City governors, the date for the election of a new Mayor was fast approaching. In the circumstances the Mayor and Aldermen felt the need for the support of the whole body of Aldermen many of whom had not attended the Court since August. The absent Aldermen were sent letters drafted in English by the Journal's clerk in which they were asked to come and give their counsel and advice in 'diverse matters of great charge that be full peysaunt touching the governance of the City of London which remain in suspension and undetermined'.[75] Most of the Aldermen responded to these letters and returned from the country. Ralph Holland, not surprisingly, attended the Court only once between the Sheriff's election on 21st September and the Mayor's election on 13th October. As a further precaution the Court obtained from the King, as it had done in the previous October, a writ which restricted the electorate at the Mayor's election to those who had been personally summoned. This writ was made public in the City on 12th October, and the following day a Grocer, Thomas Catworth, was elected Mayor without any overt trouble.[76]

But, in fact, it is clear from evidence that was later heard by the Court of Aldermen, that some considerable show of artisan force had been planned for the day of the Mayor's election. The Tailors had men armed with swords, poleaxes and other weapons ready for the occasion.[77] There had been a series of secret meetings. John Bale, a Tailor, had urged Thomas Shrub to attend a meeting to discuss the new Commission.[78] A Draper, Clement Lyffýn, gave evidence at second hand that two thousand people were ready to rise in the City and that the insurrection would be led by Master William Clif.[79] But as Clif was a perfectly respectable surveyor who was subsequently employed by the City on a variety of projects, his connection with the radical cause is doubtful. A man named Fayrefeld gave evidence that there was a meeting of men from the Tailors', Saddlers', Skinners', Goldsmiths', and Brewers' companies, who were summoned by the beadles of the Tailors and met at the house of the Friars Minor.[80] Another Draper, Thomas Cook, who had earlier crossed swords with Ralph Holland, reported that in the house of a Pewterer named Lambe, the Tailor John Blake had uttered words which violently threatened the King's Peace. Lambe himself was examined and declared that Blake had said that

75. Letters dated 30 September 1443, G.R.O. Journal iv, f. 7v.–8.
76. Writ dated 8 October 1443, *L.B.K.*, p. 288.
77. G.R.O. Journal iv, f. 11v.
78. G.R.O. Journal iv, f. 7v.
79. G.R.O. Journal iv, f. 8.
80. G.R.O. Journal iv, f. 9v.

if the Commission remained in force the commons would rise, and if the commons rose there would then be great danger.[81]

The conspirators did not, however, confine themselves to planning an armed rising. William Cottisbrook, the Grocer whom the 'inferior' citizens had tried to make Chamberlain, had displayed a copy of the 'Great Charter of London' to his associates, and in the City at large. The 'Great Charter' of 1319 was so-called because it not only incorporated a large number of privileges which were important to the poorer freemen, but also because it had been confirmed in Parliament. Cottisbrook used this charter to try to undermine the authority of the Mayor and was heard to say that an elected Mayor is not the Mayor of those who had not elected him, hence those who had been excluded from the Mayor's election could withdraw their obedience to him. These were indeed radical doctrines about the basis of authority and must have appeared very novel to most contemporary Londoners. But in the end Cottisbrook denied that he had said any of these things.[82]

There was also a wide-spread belief among the artisan conspirators that the royal writ restricting the attendance at the Mayor's election to those who had been personally summoned, had not emanated from the royal Chancery but was, in fact, a fabrication by the Aldermen. Ralph Holland had attacked a similar royal writ in just these terms as early as 1426.[83] John Bale the Tailor who had already emerged as an agitator, and organiser of the movement, claimed that he heard the Lord Chancellor declare that the writ had not been recorded and that it had not passed through his hands nor come to his notice.[84] At some date around the middle of October the Tailors had come into contact with the Lord Chancellor since twelve of them had appeared before him. It would seem that they had been accused of making an armed – but obviously ineffective – rising or protest on the occasion of the Mayor's election. While Christopher Water, a Skinner of radical inclinations, had been attending a conspiratorial meeting at Ralph Holland's house on 15th October, a group of Tailors arrived with the news that the twelve Tailors who had appeared before the Lord Chancellor had been told by him that no writ about the Mayor's election had been sent by him.[85] Another Tailor named Henxton who, like John Bale must

---

81. See above p. 160. Blake himself subsequently claimed in the Court that he had said nothing, and was allowed bail, 16 October 1443, G.R.O. Journal iv, f. 9v., 10v.
82. For the 1319 charter see W. de G. Birch, ed., *The Historical Charters and Constitutional Documents of the City of London* (rev. edn. 1887), pp. 45–50; Gwyn Williams, *Medieval London* (1963), pp. 282–83; G.R.O. Journal iv, f. 10, 10v.
83. See pp. 163–4 above.
84. G.R.O. Journal iv, f. 10 and see p. 171 above.
85. G.R.O. Journal iv, f. 10.

have been one of the twelve accused, had declared that there was no writ to prevent any freemen from attending the Mayor's election, and that the Lord Chancellor had told him this and Adam Moleyns had confirmed it.[86] On the face of it, it would seem unlikely that the Lord Chancellor, or Adam Moleyns, would have taken rebellious Tailors into his confidence in this way. But Henxton further declared that, whether the King's writ were a fabrication or not, it was, in any case, not authoritative since the power and authority of Parliament lay behind the City Charter. Here Henxton was thinking about the same Great Charter of the City which William Cottisbrook had been displaying to support the radical cause.[87] It is of no little interest that as early as 1443 an ordinary workman was aware of the antithesis between the authority of Parliament and that of the Crown. Indeed Henxton, whoever he may have been, fits more closely into the pattern and ideas of seventeenth century history than fifteenth. A child born before his time. John Bale, the Tailors' organisation man, had more pressing matters at heart when he stoutly maintained in Court, that the prosperity of the City depended upon the artisans and not upon the merchants.[88]

Ralph Holland had lent his authority and his house to the conspirators. He was a Tailor and the ring-leaders in the movement were Tailors. The conspiracy, in its resort to force of arms, had clearly failed dismally, although it had also produced a brief flowering of ideas which could be dignified with the title of political thought. Although several men were involved in the movement, Ralph Holland was obviously the most powerful and the richest of the radical agitators.[89] Moreover the Court of Aldermen was informed that for the last six years, since 1437, Holland had had many deputies appointed to organise the opposition.[90] In these circumstances it is not

86. G.R.O. Journal iv, f. 11v.
87. G.R.O. Journal iv, f. 10.
88. G.R.O. Journal iv, f. 10.
89. On Holland's wealth see p. 165 and n. 22 and 24. When he died Holland was possessed of two considerable houses – Basset's Inn and Pembridge's Inn – and eight other tenements in seven London parishes. On the two Inns see C. L. Kingsford, 'Historical Notes on some Medieval London Houses', *London Topographical Record*, vol. X (1916), p. 56, vol. XI (1917), pp. 67–68. Holland left the two Inns to the Tailors' Company, the Rector of St. Margaret Patyns and the Priory of St. Leonard at Stratford, Middlesex, R. R. Sharpe, ed., *Calendar of Wills proved and enrolled in the Court of Husting, London, 1258–1688* (1889–90), vol. II, pp. 522, 525, 526, 563. Holland also bequeathed £80 to prisoners and £40 to hospitals (Rous P.C.C. 11). His property in London and Surrey was assessed as worth £24 p.a. in 1436, Thrupp, op. cit., p. 381. In 1454, Oxford University wrote to his executors asking for a bequest from the goods of that 'worshipful and notable man Raulyn Holand' for the work of the new Divinity Schools, H. Anstey, ed., *Epistolae Academicae Oxon.* (Oxford Hist. Soc., 1898) pp. 323, 326.
90. Thomas Thornton, a Draper, claimed that he heard Chantrell, a Tailor, declare this, G.R.O. Journal iv, f. 10v.

surprising that the failure of the movement should mark also the end of Ralph Holland's civic career.

The Court of Aldermen now turned its wrathful attention upon the radical leader, who prudently absented himself from its meetings. Thomas Catworth, the Mayor elect, and other Aldermen affirmed that they had been present when Ralph Holland had declared a number of objectionable things which were now listed by the Alderman John Reynwell for the benefit of the Court.[91] Holland had asserted that the control of St Bartholomew's Fair belonged, not to the City, but to the Prior of St Bartholomew's, which would mean that the Mayor was exceeding his rights in searching the cloth sold by Tailors at the Fair as he had done since 1441. In fact Holland's assertion was well-founded since the control of the Fair had been granted to the Prior by Henry I and the matter had been in dispute between the Prior and the City since 1428 although it only became serious (as a result, perhaps, of Holland's activities) in May 1444, and a compromise on the matter was finally negotiated in 1447.[92] In this case Holland was championing the partisan interests of the Tailors as against the general good of the City as a whole. Holland was also said to have declared openly that the King's writ, restricting the electorate at the Mayor's election in October 1443, had not been proclaimed in the City as it had been written under the King's seal.

The Court of Aldermen heard also of his scandalous words about certain individuals. Holland had said that the late Mayor John Paddesley was a brawler and always was and always would be, that the Common Clerk, Richard Barnet was out of his wits, that the Recorder John Danvers had been a disturber of the peace in his own part of the country and had come to spread discord in the City, and that Sir William Estfeld, the most venerable of the Aldermen, had an 'understanding' with Lord Cromwell, the King's Treasurer and had revealed to him the City's secrets.[93] Holland had further declared that the Court of Aldermen was under the sway of two or three of its members and, moreover, that he himself was the most able of its number to expedite City business when it was discussed by the King's Council. If Holland did, in fact, enjoy the confidence of the Duke of Gloucester this might well have been the case, although the conceit and condescension of Holland's attitude would not have endeared him to the rest of the Court.[94]

Apart from these statements the Court was told that Holland had

91. G.R.O. Journal iv, f. 11v.
92. August 1447, G.R.O. Journal iv, f. 188v. Further negotiations in March 1453 led to a more permanent agreement on 28 October 1553, G.R.O. Journal v, f. 106v., 107, *L.B.K.*, pp. 453–55.
93. See pp. 172, 174, and n. 102.
94. See p. 167 and n. 37.

advised the freemen of the City to present two bills to the Mayor and Aldermen to right their wrongs. In the first they were to demand that those who were party to a case should not act as judges, as had happened when the Court considered the dispute between the Tailors and Drapers. In the second bill they were to demand a restoration of their customary freedom to take part in the Mayor's election. Finally the Court was told that Holland had declared that he wished that all those who were in prison for love of him might be sustained. Indeed here spoke a man truly a forbear of John Wilkes. The fifteenth-century radical also knew how to play to his gallery.

In the light of these various declarations, and in view of the fact that Holland had supported the Tailors' case when it came up before the Council, although it threatened the City's liberties, the Mayor and Aldermen considered that it would be expedient if Holland were exonerated from his Aldermanry. But the Court wanted Holland to reply first to the charges against him. When Ralph Holland failed to appear on 23rd October 1443, John Combes, one of the sergeants, was sent to collect him. Combes, however, reported back to the Court that Holland had said that he could not come because his wife was lying gravely ill and so he had to go to Newgate to distribute money among the poor prisoners that they might pray for her recovery.[95] Holland continued to avoid an appearance in Court[96] and on 18th May 1444 he was finally exonerated from his Aldermanry, in the traditional formula, that he had sought to be dismissed and that the Court had found his reasons acceptable. A new Alderman was to be elected for Bread Street ward as soon as possible.[97] So ended the civic career of a premature radical and the movement to which he had given impetus, organisation and expression died with him.[98] As late as 1459 Holland's acts were cited as precedents,

95. G.R.O. Journal iv, f. 12.
96. 25 October 1443, Holland had still not appeared and he was appointed to answer on 28 October, G.R.O. Journal iv, f. 12. On 4 November 1443 he was given a day two weeks away. 6 November 1443 Holland received a royal exemption from holding any civic office such as the Mayoralty or Royal Escheatorship, but nothing is mentioned in the writ about the office of Alderman, *C.P.R. 1441–46*, p. 220.
97. G.R.O. Journal iv, f. 25.
98. There is no reference to Holland in the City Journals after May 1444, although he continues to appear in the Patent and Close rolls until June 1452, when he received two tenements in Watling Street from the King in recognition of his good services and personal kindness to the King and Henry V, *C.P.R. 1446–52*, p. 861. Holland died between 3 May 1452 (date of his last will) and 23 October 1452 (will enrolled). His executors appear to have had considerable trouble settling the estate and were not helped by the reckless behaviour of one of their number, Thomas Holland, the son of Ralph's brother, Robert. The other four executors had to petition Parliament to have Thomas's powers as an executor annulled, P.R.O. C49/File 32/15.

but the cause had been lost.[99] The radical movement had worked at first through the legitimate channels in its attempt to achieve the election of an artisan as Mayor. Then, thwarted in this, the movement had turned to conspiracy and attempted violence in October 1443.

But even after the failure of the rising and the eclipse of Ralph Holland the spirit of rebellion could be detected here and there. In January 1444 a man named John Farndon had to be sent to Newgate for presenting an unsuitable and scandalous bill against his Alderman in the wardmote of Bishopsgate, in which he had affirmed that Thomas Chalton, the Alderman, had perverted the course of justice by delay, favour and negligence.[100] Similar bills had been presented in the wardmotes of Bread Street, Broad Street, Queenhythe, Cornhill and elsewhere.[101] In these bills the Aldermen had been accused of being usurers as well as supporters of robbery and adultery. The Chamberlain was said to have appropriated the Common Soil of the City and the Recorder to have forced men into obligations of £20 to observe ordinances which they considered to be unjust. There was, it had been claimed in the bill, one law for the rich and another for the poor.[102] Resistance to the new Commission of the Peace continued also. A Dyer named William Haylyn was also sent to Newgate in January 1444 because he had protested at the spending of 2000 marks to buy a charter which was contrary to the liberties and franchises of the City and would destroy freedom.[103]

In general, however, the mood of the Londoners had softened. In September a meeting of the Common Council approved a revised draft of the charter which now included other new clauses which would be acceptable to the citizens, as well as the clause dealing with the powers of the Mayor and Aldermen as Justices of the Peace.[104] The City gained extensive rights in Southwark and the statement that nothing was to be done which would be to the detriment of the City's liberties, was reiterated constantly throughout the new Charter. Of course such a charter cost money, but the Common Council was sufficiently pleased with the new draft to agree that it should be paid for out of common funds, and even went so far as

99. 19 June 1459, G.R.O. Journal vi, f. 95v.
100. 16, 24 January 1444, G.R.O. Journal iv, f. 13.
101. G.R.O. Journal iv, f. 14, 16v.
102. 19 February 1444, evidence of John Farndon, G.R.O. Journal iv, f. 17v. The bills also claimed that William Estfeld, when Mayor (1437–38), had unjustly brought a case against Holland. This may explain Holland's attack upon Estfeld for collusion with Lord Cromwell, see p. 179 above.
103. Haylyn had been assessed to contribute 2/– towards the costs of the new charter, G.R.O. Journal iv, f. 14.
104. 21 August 1444 a draft of the new charter had been read to the Court of Aldermen which decided to continue negotiations with the King, and to consult the Commonalty, G.R.O. Journal iv, f. 39.

to vote great thanks to the Mayor and Aldermen for their efforts in obtaining it.[105] The new charter was finally sealed on 26th October 1444.[106]

The dispute between the Tailors and Drapers took somewhat longer to settle. In 1447 it was necessary to re-enact the compromise of 1441 whereby the Mayor was to search woollen cloth sold by Tailors at Saint Bartholomew's Fair.[107] Then, on 6th October 1447, the Drapers' right of search over all woollen cloths sold by retail in the City was confirmed by the Mayor and Aldermen. This confirmation was subsequently cut out of the Letter Book of the City – no doubt by the indignant Tailors.[108] In January 1448 John Lucock, a Tailor, protested at the Drapers' scrutiny and Richard Adkyns, one of the Wardens of the Tailors' Company, was examined in Court.[109] The Lord Chancellor considered the case again in April of that year[110] and in February 1450, the King himself reviewed the matter.[111] It would seem that a compromise, born of exhaustion, in the end prevailed in the City whereby the Tailors maintained their right to search woollen cloth in Tailors' shops whereas the general right to search unmade-up cloth in the City remained with the Drapers. The quarrel may also have died because of the need for joint action against the pretensions of the Shearmen.[112]

The opposition movement led by Ralph Holland was shortlived, primitive and unsuccessful; but it need not be disparaged for that. It showed what an able – and affluent – leader could do for a cause. Indeed there is more to admire in Ralph Holland than, perhaps, in either Wat Tyler or Jack Cade. The opposition which he formulated and nurtured was not simply a case of the 'have nots' against the 'haves'; there lay behind it a seriousness of purpose, and an awareness of the way in which civic government could function. It is surely of importance that in the years between 1438 and 1444 men of little

105. See p. 173 and n. 63. 7 September 1444, G.R.O. Journal iv, f. 47v.
106. The draft charter was again altered 18 September 1444, G.R.O. Journal iv, f. 42. 19 October 1444 a further levy of £3 from each Alderman was needed to buy the favour of the King's Council, and further discussions about paying for the charter took place in November 1444 and January 1445, G.R.O. Journal iv, f. 44v., 51, 57, 60v.
107. 23 August 1447, G.R.O. Journal iv, f. 189.
108. *L.B.K.*, pp. 321–22; Johnson, op. cit., vol. I, Appendix 14, pp. 233–35.
109. 12 January 1448, G.R.O. Journal iv, f. 205.
110. 19 April 1448, G.R.O. Journal iv, f. 216. The chronicler Robert Bale records in that year 'The Drapers and Tailors of London made great suit upon a truce between them but the Tailors obtained and recovered', R. Flenley, ed., *Six Town Chronicles of England* (Oxford, 1911), p. 122.
111. 4 February 1450, G.R.O. Journal v, f. 30.
112. In 1445 the Tailors had an iron yard made for measuring cloth, and the Company had its standard meter yard 'tynned' for 4d. in 1455, Tailors' Accounts vol. ii, f. 75. On the final compromise see Johnson, op. cit., vol. I, pp. 119–20, and Clode, op. cit., pp. 128–29.

learning, but much zeal, were formulating ideas which were to continue to be the backbone of the 'Good Old Cause' for centuries to come. The advocacy of a wide civic franchise; the belief that the authority of a governor rests upon a basis of conscious consent; the assertion of the greater authority of an act of Parliament than the sole act of a King; the consciousness of the well-being of the whole depending upon all its parts – in this case the artisans as well as the merchant governors; and, lastly, the determination that all men should be equal before the law; all these beliefs are important ones and, perhaps, especially so for being found so early and in such a humble context.

Editorial suggestions for further reading

M. D. Harris, (ed.), *The Coventry Leet Book*, vol. ii, Early English Text
  Society, orig. series 135 (1908), 430ff., 510ff., 574ff.
M. D. Harris, *The Story of Coventry* (London, 1911), 184–91, 197–8.
See also Chapter 10 of this volume.

Chapter Ten

THE COMMERCIAL DOMINANCE OF A MEDIEVAL PROVINCIAL OLIGARCHY: EXETER IN THE LATE FOURTEENTH CENTURY

Maryanne Kowaleski

Mediaeval Studies, 46 (1984)

This study of the commercial leaders of one of England's larger provincial cities demonstrates how the political structure of medieval towns reflected the economic ascendancy of the merchant class. The ruling group was not closed; rising families were readily recruited to replace those which had failed or left the town. Those citizens who reached the higher political ranks were rewarded with a range of economic and other benefits: civic contracts, lucrative public offices, legal influence in the city courts. The absence of recorded opposition to the oligarchy's authority may seem surprising. In fact, Kowaleski's conclusion that the evident lack of conflict was the result of Exeter's only moderate size and wealth may be questioned. Political tensions certainly existed in other towns, although they tend to be poorly recorded. It should be noted, however, that in documented cases (such as that described in the previous chapter) faction – the rivalry of 'ins' and 'outs' of roughly equivalent economic status – generally played a major part. The political views of the wider body of townspeople will not be understood until more work has been completed on the detailed practice of urban government, including the extent to which broader participation may have been fostered through petty officeholding.

Historians interested in the urban oligarchies of medieval England have tended either to focus on constitutional developments or to offer biographical sketches of exemplary members of the ruling elite.[1] While the two approaches have revealed much about the expansion of urban self-government, the evolution of civic offices, and

---

1. See, for example: Charles W. Colby. 'The Growth of Oligarchy in English Towns'. *English Historical Review* 5 (1890) 633–53; Alice S. Green, *Town life in the Fifteenth Century*, 2 vols. (London, 1894); James Tait, *The Medieval*

the prosopography of the burghal class, both have tended to concentrate on political issues to the exclusion of commercial developments. This excessive focus on the political powers of urban elites is inherently self-defeating: because local commercial clout and wealth usually formed the basis of municipal political power, commercial success was crucial for anyone who aspired to political office. By focusing on the political manifestations of urban oligarchies, historians have put the cart before the horse. To understand the tight civic control of town elites, we must first understand the commercial power that laid the foundation for political hegemony. Of course, the juncture of political and economic power did not move in only one direction; although political strength relied upon prior commercial success, it was also actively sought because control of civic offices enhanced the holders' commercial dealings. The interplay between politics and commerce can be clearly seen in late fourteenth-century Exeter when the men who dominated town government not only controlled a significant portion of Exeter's local trade, but also enjoyed extensive commercial influence in regional and international trade networks.

I

In the late fourteenth century, Exeter was a provincial town of moderate size inhabited by about 3000 people.[2] As the seat of a bishopric, an administrative center for the king's itinerant justices, a military stronghold with a royal castle, and a thriving seaport, Exeter served as the chief market town of the south western peninsula of England. Access to civic power in medieval Exeter was attained by admission into the 'freedom' of the city. Only members of this exclusive group were fully-fledged citizens and could vote or run for

English Borough. Studies on Its Origins and Constitutional History (Manchester, 1936); Susan Reynolds, *An Introduction to the History of English Medieval Towns* (Oxford, 1977). For the history of the oligarchy in individual towns, see *The Records of the City of Norwich*, ed. William Hudson and John Cottingham Tingey, 2 vols. (Norwich, 1906–10), introduction to vol. 1; Bertie Wilkinson, *The Mediaeval Council of Exeter* (History of Exeter Research Group 4; Manchester, 1931); Francis Hill, *Medieval Lincoln* (Cambridge, 1965); Colin Platt, *Medieval Southampton: The Port and Trading Community, 1000–1600* (London, 1973); Robert S. Gottfried, *Bury St. Edmunds and the Urban Crisis: 1270–1539* (Princeton, 1982), chaps. 4–6. The exception to this trend is Sylvia L. Thrupp, *The Merchant Class of Medieval London, 1300–1500* (Ann Arbor, 1948); however, London occupies a unique and atypical position in the urban history of medieval England as few provincial merchants reached the commercial or political positions enjoyed by many London merchants.

2. For the population estimate, see Maryanne Kowaleski, *Local Markets and Merchants in Late Fourteenth-Century Exeter* (Diss. Toronto, 1982), pp. 393–98.

high city office. In addition to political privileges, freedom members received numerous economic privileges, chief among them the right to trade at retail.[3] They also enjoyed monopolies in the cloth, wool, and woad trades, and in all trade in merchandise sold 'by weight' or 'by measure', except for victuals, and were free from the main market tolls in Exeter and in many other English towns. Freedom members also held certain legal rights within the local courts. Compared to similar freedom organizations in such other provincial towns as York, Norwich and Bristol, Exeter's freedom was highly selective; only 19 per cent of all the heads of household and a mere 3 per cent of the total population of 1377 Exeter actually enjoyed freedom membership.[4]

Entry into the freedom could be gained in a variety of ways: by patrimony, patronage, redemption, apprenticeship, and occasionally gift or service. From the fourteenth century onwards, however, entry into the Exeter freedom became increasingly restricted. For example, admittance by patrimony or succession was originally bestowed on all the sons of freemen, but, by the fourteenth century, only the eldest son was permitted to join upon the death of his father.[5] Younger sons enlisted either by apprenticeship or upon payment of a fine.

Concern about the excessive number of freedom members was probably the impetus behind the fourteenth-century restriction on the number of sons entering by succession. Complaints also arose in the 1340s over both the number and quality of men admitted.[6] The greatest outcry centered on the practice of nominating candidates 'at the instance of' prominent men who were often subsequently rewarded for their patronage. In 1308, for example, Walter Tauntefer, a one-time mayor of Exeter, received £3 in payment for sponsoring Thomas de Rewe's application for freedom member-

3. The rights and privileges of Exeter's freemen are detailed in *The Anglo-Norman Custumal of Exeter*, ed. J. W. Schopp (History of Exeter Research Group 2; Oxford, 1925). For later developments concerning their trading privileges, see the introduction to M. M. Rowe and Andrew Jackson, *Exeter Freemen, 1266–1967* (Devon and Cornwall Record Society, E. S. 1; Exeter, 1973), pp. xii–xiii.
4. For other freedom organizations, see Hill, *Medieval Lincoln*, pp. 302–303; R. B. Dobson, 'Admissions to the Freedom of the City of York in the Later Middle Ages', *Economic History Review*, 2nd Ser. 26 (1973) 1–22; *Records of the City* of Norwich 2.xxviii–xxxix; *The Great Red Book of Bristol*, ed. W. W. Veale (Bristol Record Society 2; Bristol, 1931), p. 21. See also D. M. Woodward, 'Freemen's Rolls', *Local Historian* 9 (1970) 89–95. In 1377 York, roughly 54 per cent of the heads of household became members of the town's freedom while only 32 per cent of Exeter's heads of household in 1377 joined their town's freedom. For the Exeter figure, see Kowaleski, *Local Markets*, pp. 37, 71–73 n. 15. For the York figures, see Jennifer I. Legett, 'The 1377 Poll Tax Return for the City of York', *Yorkshire Archaeological Journal* 43 (1972) 130.
5. Rowe and Jackson, *Exeter Freeman*, p. xiv.
6. For the text of the complaints, see Wilkinson, *Mediaeval Council*, pp. 71–74.

ship.[7] Another widespread patronage custom was to admit men to Exeter's freedom at the request of influential non-citizens, such as the countess of Devon, bishop of Exeter, and members of the local gentry.[8] Other men were also allowed entry in reward for service to the town. But all these practices were halted in response to the complaints of the 1340s: regulations passed in 1345 required the consent of the Council of Twelve before anyone was admitted by patronage or by redemption. As a result, entry by patronage practically ceased after 1345, while the number of men admitted 'by gift' or as a reward for service dropped also. In comparison to the fifty men who entered 'by gift' from 1299 to 1349, only eleven candidates entered the freedom by this method from 1350 to 1400 and almost all of these entries occurred in the earlier part of the period, as shown in Table 1.

TABLE 1 Freedom Entries in Exeter from 1299 to 1349 and 1350 to 1400 by Type of Entry

Type of Entry	Entrants 1299–1349		Entrants 1350–1400	
Redemption	229	(34%)	257	(80%)
Patronage	218	(32%)	0	–
Patrimony	139	(21%)	22	(7%)
By Gift	50	(8%)	11	(3%)
Service	27	(4%)	0	–
Apprenticeship	0	–	28	(9%)
Unknown	5	(1%)	3	(1%)
Total	668	(100%)	320	(100%)

Source: Rowe and Jackson, *Exeter Freemen*, pp. 5–38

The increased control over selection to the freedom was also evident in the fall in the number of men admitted after 1350. During the 1330s, 169 men entered the freedom; this was the highest number admitted in any one decade until the sixteenth century.[9] Indeed, as illustrated in Table 1, more than twice as many men entered the freedom in the first half of the fourteenth century as in the second half of the century. Declining population, as evidenced in the drastic reduction in the number of men entering by patrimony after 1350, was partially responsible for the decrease in freedom entrants. Nevertheless, the restriction on the number of sons entering the freedom by succession remained, although the citizenry was obviously experiencing difficulties in replacing itself after the damage

7. Rowe and Jackson, *Exeter Freeman*, p. xv.
8. ibid, pp. 1–27, *passim*.
9. ibid., p. xvii.

wrought by the plague. In addition, even though evidence suggests immigration to Exeter was quite plentiful in this period, immigrants rarely possessed the necessary wealth to gain admittance to the freedom.[10] Nor did the increasingly powerful Council of Twelve show any desire to welcome a greater number of entrants. Thus a reduced population, combined with more rigid control over the selection process, worked to make the freedom of late fourteenth-century Exeter an increasingly exclusive organization.

While entry by patrimony, patronage, service and gift declined greatly in the second half of the fourteenth century, entry by redemption and apprenticeship increased. The most popular method of entry into the freedom was by redemption or payment, and the preponderance of this type of entry during the period is illustrated in Table 1; 80 per cent of all freedom entries from 1350 to 1400 were made upon payment of a fine. This situation indicates both the replacement problems of the old citizenry following the plague and the still fledgling state of the apprenticeship and craft institutions in the second half of the century. In fact, the first recorded admission by apprenticeship occurred in 1358 and the next did not take place until 1380.[11] Only eight men entered the freedom by apprenticeship in the thirty-two year period from 1358 to 1390, but thereafter their numbers grew rapidly. In the following ten-year period alone (1390–1400) fourteen men entered by virtue of apprenticeship; moreover, all new members who entered by this method had served masters who were major merchants and were politically prominent in the borough. Only after the last decade of the fourteenth century, when the practice had become established, did apprentices serving craftsmen regularly enter the freedom. This rise in the number of men entering the freedom as apprentices to craftsmen reflects the growth of industry (especially the cloth trade) in Exeter and foreshadows the emergence of the craft guilds in the later fifteenth century.[12]

The increasingly selective nature of the Exeter freedom was consciously maintained by the town's ruling elite or oligarchy. Indeed, the economic institution of the freedom was intimately linked with

---

10. Kowaleski, *Local Markets*, pp. 40, 44.
11. But the practice of apprenticeship continued from 1350 to 1380; the Mayor's Court Roll (hereafter M.C.R. [unless noted otherwise, all documents cited here are deposited in the Devon Record Office, Exeter, hereafter D.R.O.]) recorded apprenticeship contracts in 22 November 1361 and 4 April 1362; neither of the apprentices was ever mentioned again in the records, however; they may have died or left Exeter before their terms were up.
12. For the growth of the cloth trade and craft guilds, see E. M. Carus-Wilson, *The Expansion of Exeter at the Close of the Middle Ages* (Exeter, 1963); Joyce Youings, *Tucker's Hall, Exeter: The Expansion of a Provincial City Company through Five Centuries* (Exeter, 1968).

political organization in medieval Exeter. Membership in the exclusive freedom of the city was a prerequisite for both commercial success and political power; only those belonging to the freedom could trade without restraint and were eligible to be elected to the higher municipal offices of mayor, steward, and councillor, or to be an elector for such offices. This system of restricting the full rights and privileges of citizenship to a select few was not unusual in medieval English boroughs. In discussing the freedom organization of York, R. B. Dobson notes that freedom admissions served as 'a mechanism deliberately designed to subserve the policies of city oligarchies'.[13] An oligarchy, composed of men who had served the city as mayor, steward, councillor or elector, also controlled admissions into the freedom of Exeter. Entry by patrimony ensured that the sons of the ruling elite inherited the privileges possessed by their fathers. More significantly, admission by apprenticeship or redemption introduced an element of choice and therefore control into the selection process. Potential candidates had to prove themselves not only to the members of the freedom, but also to those who exercised control over the freedom, the high officials or oligarchy of the town.

Occasional glimpses reveal how the oligarchy exercised its jurisdiction over the freedom. In 1340, while the thirty-six electors were absent on election day, 'by an impetuous clamor of many men inconsiderate of the profit and honor of the city, a burdensome multitude of men were elected to the freedom'.[14] As a result, the oligarchy passed a number of ordinances designed to reaffirm their power. In the future, no one was to be admitted to the freedom on election day in the absence of the more powerful men of the city. Moreover, no one could be elected mayor unless he had prior official experience (a minimum of one year's service as steward) and resided in the city with substantial property holdings.

The crisis of 1340 was not the last time the members of the freedom showed a desire to limit their numbers to a select few. In 1345 another civic crisis occasioned the promulgation of a new set of ordinances intended to reinforce the authority of the Council of Twelve which governed the town with the mayor and stewards.[15] Henceforth, no one was to be admitted to the freedom without the Council's consent, nor were any amercements or fines to be condoned without its permission. Those disagreeing with these and other ordinances passed at the time were deemed to be 'rebels and enemies of the city' and had to suffer expulsion from the freedom, never to hold office again. Thus, the higher ranking members of the

---

13. Dobson, 'Admissions to the Freedom', 18.
14. Misc. Roll 2. m. 54. For the printed text, see Wilkinson, *Mediaeval Council*, pp. 71–72.
15. Misc. Roll 2, item 32. For the printed text, see Wilkinson, ibid., pp. 72–74.

town government solidified their control over both entry into the freedom and the governing of the town.

Late fourteenth-century Exeter was governed by a mayor with the aid of four stewards, one of whom was the town receiver and, as such, was responsible for the city's annual accounts.[16] The mayor presided over the main borough court, called the Mayor's Court, while the stewards oversaw the Provosts' Court which primarily heard pleas of debt. The so-called 'common' Council of Twelve of the 'better and more discreet' men or *meliores* of the borough advised the mayor on all important business.[17] Originally the Council was designed to check the abuses of the mayor and stewards, but, in practice, the members of the common Council came from the same pool of citizens as did the mayor and steward; indeed, the interests of both groups were identical. The power of the Council grew considerably over the course of the late fourteenth and fifteenth centuries. No bonds, letters of pensions, or acquittances were to be sealed without its consent. After 1345, no one was admitted to the freedom without the Council's approval, nor were any fines or amercements condoned without its permission. The men who held the high-ranking offices in late fourteenth-century Exeter (mayor, four stewards, twelve councillors – hereafter called Rank A) represented only 1 per cent of Exeter's total population and were reelected year after year; in 1377, only 30 of a total 528 heads of household in Exeter (6 per cent) had ever served in one of these offices. Furthermore, their right to exercise this political power was linked with their personal wealth; a mayoral candidate, for example, had to own 100s. worth of property.[18] In the 1377 murage roll, which taxed all heads of household according to property wealth, fourteen out of the seventeen most highly assessed taxpayers had served as mayor, steward or councillor.[19] In view of their tight control over

16. The early history of Exeter's town government has been thoroughly discussed by Wilkinson, ibid. and by R. C. Easterling in her introduction to Wilkinson, pp. xi–xxxiv. For more on the duties of each official, see the work of the sixteenth-century Exeter historian, John Vowell alias Hoker, *The Description of the Citie of Excester*, ed. W. J. Harte, J. W. Schopp, H. Tapley-Soper, 3 parts (Exeter, 1919), 3.801–45.

17. Along with Bristol, Exeter possessed the first recorded common Council in medieval England; see Tait, *Medieval English Borough*, pp. 330–33. The 1345 ordinances established the Council permanently but such a group had appeared sporadically from the 1260s on: see Easterling, introduction to Wilkinson, *Mediaeval Council*, and Misc. Roll. 2, m. 54.

18. Misc. Roll 2, m. 54; Wilkinson, ibid., pp. 71–72.

19. These men paid from 4s. to 15s. in murage tax; see Misc. Roll 72. All the election returns were enrolled on the dorses of membranes 1 and 2 of each Mayor's Court Roll. Of the three who did not reach the highest offices, two served as electors, thereby placing them in the Rank B oligarchy. The third man, Stephen Boghewode, held no offices at all, perhaps because he was said to be 'in the service of the king' in M.C.R. 3 October 1373.

the freedom and civic government, their greater wealth, and their small numbers, this group can be justifiably be characterized as an oligarchy: 'government by the few'.

The mayor, stewards, and councillors were elected annually at Michaelmas by a body of thirty-six electors.[20] These electors were also chosen yearly by an elaborate selection process which favored the *meliores* or *maiores*. The first four electors, chosen from men who had already served in high office (Rank A men), nominated the remaining thirty-two electors. There is some evidence that the middling men of the town also had a hand in the election process: in 1267, for example, twelve of the electors selected were termed *mediocres*.[21] Indirect evidence also argues that electors were consciously drawn from among the middling men as well as the wealthier, higher-ranking citizens (see Table 2). Therefore, the Exeter 'oligarchy' was actually composed of two political groups: Rank A men and Rank B men – who attained the office of elector, but no higher, and who were separated from Rank A men by wealth, as well as by political standing.[22] In the 1377 murage tax, assessed according to wealth in property, Rank A members of the oligarchy paid an average of 4*s.* 6*d.* in tax, while Rank B men rendered on the average only 2*s.* 1*d.*

TABLE 2 Occupational Standing of Political Ranks A and B in 1377 Exeter

	Rank A	Rank B
Total	30	33
Occupations		
Merchants	21	8
Craftsmen	1	13
City Officials	0	4
Unknown	8	8
Average Murage Tax Paid*	4*s.* 6*d.*	2*s.* 1*d.*
No. in Overseas Trade	22	8

Sources: Misc. Roll 72: M.C.R. election returns, 1350–77; Exeter Port Customs Accounts, 1365–91.
* Does not include the three members of the oligarchy not listed in the murage roll.

20. See Hoker, *Description* 3.789–801 for a discussion of the election reforms of 1497 in which he cites the old way of electing city officials.
21. Easterling, introduction to Wilkinson, *Mediaeval Council*, pp. xxiv–xxxii.
22. These political ranks were assigned on the basis of the highest office achieved by 1377. Thus Rank A men often had previously held lower offices. Rank B includes all those who attained office no higher than elector, bridge-warden, bridge-elector, or warden of Magdalene Hospital.

Occupational standing also differed between the two groups: Rank A men tended to be merchants, many of whom regularly traded overseas, while Rank B men were generally craftsmen. There were some merchants in the lower ranking, but their commercial activities were inclined to be on a much smaller, more local basis than the mercantile dealings of Rank A citizens. Moreover, three of the eight Rank B merchants in 1377 eventually reached Rank A. Politically, the influence of Rank B citizens remained tenuous. While Rank A men appeared in office year after year, seventeen of the thirty-three members of Rank B in 1377 served in office only two years or less, which hardly represented continuous civic responsibility. But because Rank B men voted in the electoral process, could hold lower-level offices such as bridge warden, and were always members of the freedom, they had some political power and must be counted as members of the 'oligarchy'. Nevertheless, they were financially, socially and politically inferior to Rank A citizens who held the higher offices.

Below the Rank B offices of electors and wardens were a host of minor municipal offices, such as aldermen (who, in Exeter, were only wardsmen with few powers), gatekeepers, bailiffs and assorted market officials. These men formed a third group of officeholders (called Rank C) in medieval Exeter whose offices did not require freedom membership and who held no real political power because they had no say in either the city elections or the civic decision-making process. However, the duties of their offices, often crucial to the everyday functioning of the town (notably in terms of police control) endowed them with a certain measure of civic responsibility.

At the bottom of the scale of municipal power and responsibility were those residents who held no offices at all (called Rank D). Their only voice in town government came through occasional appearances as jury presentors in the town courts. But even these duties were more frequently carried out by the wealthier, more highly-placed citizens. Of the 528 heads of household in 1377 Exeter, 434 (82 per cent) never held any type of political office. Only thirty-nine of these Rank D men (9 per cent) belonged to the freedom and they tended to be wealthier than most other members of Rank D. The majority of Rank D taxpayers were very poor; their average murage rate in 1377 was only 8*d*., compared to 1*s*. for Rank C, 2*s*.1*d*. for Rank B, and 4*s*.6*d*. for Rank A taxpayers. Table 3 shows the high correlation between wealth, political office and commercial privilege (as represented by membership in the freedom) among Exeter heads of household in 1377. As one's personal wealth rose, so too rose one's chances of attaining economic and political privilege. In some few cases, economic privilege (i.e. freedom membership) could have preceded personal wealth, but this was unlikely considering the selective nature of admittances and the emphasis placed on ability to pay the entrance fee. More often than not, as Table 3 dramatically illustrates, political power, economic privilege and personal wealth went hand-in-hand in late fourteenth-century Exeter.

TABLE 3 Freedom Membership and Political Rank of Exeter Heads of Household in 1377 by Wealth (Property Tax Groups)

Tax Group	No. Taxed	In Freedom No. Row %		Rank A No. Row %		Rank B No. Row %		Rank C No. Row %		Rank D No. Row %	
2d.-3d.	26	0	–	0	–	0	–	1	4%	25	96%
4d.-6d.	202	12	6%	0	–	1	1%	9	4%	191	95%
7d.-18d.	122	39	32%	5	4%	11	9%	15	12%	91	75%
2s.-5s.	61	47	77%	17	26%	20	33%	3	5%	22	36%
7s.-15s.	6	6	100%	6	100%	0	–	0	–	0	–
Unknown or Unenumerated	111	6		2		1		3		105	
Total	528	110	21%	30	6%	33	6%	31	6%	434	82%

Sources: Misc. Roll 72; M.C.R. election returns, 1350–77; Rowe and Jackson, *Exeter Freemen*, pp. 22–33; for Unenumerated, see Kowaleski, *Local Markets*, Appendix 2.

II

The privileges of high political rank in Exeter worked to favor the commercial dealings of highly-placed civic officials in several ways. First, politically active citizens received preferential treatment in both financial assessment and in the allocation of borough business to private contractors. Second, such citizens were appointed ministers of the king both in the commercial sphere (e.g. as customs collectors or aulnagers) and in the political sphere (appointments to special inquisitions or juries). Third, they benefited from personal and business relationships with the king's officials, the local gentry, and the leading merchants of other towns.

The powers of political office were frequently manipulated for personal financial gain in medieval Exeter. The yearly City Receiver's Accounts regularly condoned the amercements and fines of the more powerful members of the oligarchy. Rents were excused for some of the wealthiest men of the town. For instance, the wardens of Exebridge noted in their 1381/82 account that John Talbot's rent of 40s. for a garden in Paulstreet 'could not be raised' even though Talbot ranked as the second wealthiest man in the 1377 murage tax.[23] Aside from escaping some of the basic costs of citizenship, the members of the oligarchy also enjoyed privileged access to town contracts. They habitually obtained first choice of the profitable farms of the customs of the city (for fish, meat and stallage, brewing and baking, etc.) and had first selection of the city-owned pastureland. From 1372 to 1392, a small group of forty-six people controlled all the customs farms in Exeter.[24] The oligarchy was responsible for 57 per cent of these farms even though it made up only 12 per cent of all the heads of household in 1377 Exeter. Business generated by civic activities frequently passed to the oligarchy. Wine and ale sent as gifts or bribes to influential officials were invariably purchased from members of the oligarchy as were most materials bought for the building or repair of city property.[25] The major merchants in town were undoubtedly the most likely candidates for such business, but their close association with the town government assured that all such trade was funnelled their way. Moreover, they were chosen, and paid handsomely, to supervise such civic projects as the building of the city wall and ditch, the repair of mill leats and weirs, and the construction of the city barge; usually, such activities were not directly related to the commercial dealings of the appointed merchants. Richard Bozoun, for example, a wealthy overseas merchant and four-time mayor of Exeter, received the princely sum of £20 for 'supervising' the new construction work on the city wall in 1387, the same year he was first elected mayor.[26] Such extra tasks greatly augmented the income of already wealthy and powerful men. In fact, the assignment of these positions undoubtly hinged on political rank.

The influence of the Exeter oligarchy was also substantially reinforced by frequent appointments to royal offices like controller,

23. Exebridge Wardens' Account (hereafter E.B.W.) 1381/82; see also E.B.W. 1385/86.
24. The customs were farmed out each year and were listed annually in the Mayor's Court Rolls immediately following the yearly municipal elections on the dorses of the first two membranes of each roll. This link between the customs and the elections suggests that the customs were bid upon or handed out when the town's most powerful political officials were present so that they could reserve the customs for themselves, or, at the very least, certainly influence who received the farms. From 1372 to 1392, there were 132 customs farmed out to only 46 people.
25. The purchases were enrolled each year in the City Receiver's Accounts (hereafter C.R.A.) under *Dona et Exhennia* and *Expensi necessari*. See also the Duryard manorial accounts under mill expenses; the Exebridge Wardens' Accounts under mill expenses and bridge repair work; the accounts for the city barge in Misc. Roll 6, mm. 17, 25 to 28; and for expenses on city weirs, walls, ditches, gates and the pillory, as well as a new Duryard mill built in 1377/78, see mm. 1–5, 8–12, 22–24, and 29–34.
26. C.R.A. 1386/87.

customer, havener, and aulnager.[27] The appointments, generally available only to Rank A members of the oligarchy, endowed their holders not only with political pull but also with additional opportunities for financial gain (either legal or illegal). Indeed, at least four former mayors of the city were indicted and convicted (although two were ultimately pardoned) of fraud in the collection of customs.[28] Members of the oligarchy served as both collectors and farmers of these port customs for years at a time. Their position as merchants, regularly engaged in the overseas and coastal trades, gave them the experience and knowledge to supervise port customs and subsidies, as well as the occasion to use their office and influence to profit financially. But it is important to note that the king was not simply passively supporting Exeter's oligarchic structure by siphoning all appointments in their direction. He was also building up a strong political base that often bore fruit. Several members of the oligarchy, such as Richard Bozoun and Walter Thomas, served the king on expeditions to such troublesome spots as Ireland.[29] Others, such as Robert Wilford, the richest man in 1377 Exeter, lent Edward III over £195 in assistance.[30]

Many members of both A and B Ranks of the oligarchy also served in minor royal offices, primarily at the county level. As tax collectors, commissioners on special inquisitions, coroners and escheators, the Exeter oligarchy participated in the political and economic life of the Devon county community, brushing shoulders with the local gentry who also served in these offices.[31] The royal and county appointments fostered the close ties that linked many of the highest ranking members of the oligarchy with the local aristocracy. Such powerful and wealthy citizens as John Grey, Robert Wilford, and John Webber numbered among the 'esquires' of the earl of

27. References to the appointment of Exeter citizens as port customs officials may be found in the relevant E 122 series of customs accounts in the Public Record Office, London (=P.R.O.) and scattered throughout the *Calendar of Fine Rolls* (=*Cal. F.R.*) and *Calendar of Patent Rolls* (=*Cal. P.R.*). Aulnager appointments are in E 101 338/11 and E358, 8 and 9. no. 8 in the P.R.O.

28. These men were Roger Plente, John Grey, Richard Bozoun and Robert Noble (*Cal. P.R.*, Edw. III, 14.52 and Rich. II, 8.234; *Cal. F.R.* 7.98).

29. *Cal. P.R.*, Rich II. 7.390 and Henry IV, 1.234.

30. *Issue Roll of Thomas de Brantingham*, ed. F. Devon (Publications of the Record Commissioners; London, 1835), p. 187. For other loans by oligarchic merchants of Exeter to the king, see *Cal. P.R.*, Edw. III, 9.143.

31. For such positions held by the Exeter oligarchy and local landed gentry, see for example: *Cal. P.R.*, Edw.II, 10.494 and Rich. II, 2.143, 3.392; *Cal.F.R.* 8.390, 9.55, and 9.231; Misc. Roll. 6, m. 17; J. J. Alexander, 'Exeter Members of Parliament. Part II. 1377 to 1537', *Transactions of the Devonshire Association* 60 (1928) 201–205, 213–14. See also Martin Cherry. 'The Courtenay Earls of Devon: The Formation and Disintegration of a Late Medieval Aristocratic Affinity', *Southern History* 1 (1979) 71–90.

Devon, Edward Courtenay's retinue, in 1384.[32] Robert Wilford provided for masses for the soul of Sir Hugh Courtenay, earl of Devon, in his 1397 will.[33] Other members of oligarchic families also remembered local gentry as friends in their wills, or even appointed them executors of their estates.[34] Men of the Exeter oligarchy stood as mainprise for the local gentry, and vice versa, in purchases of land or in debt suits.[35] Proximity and common interests, of course, influenced such social intercourse between gentry and oligarchy; ties with certain families were especially strong. The relationship between the Rank A oligarchy and the Courtenay family (which included the earls of Devon who resided at Tiverton and Powderham, both less than ten miles from Exeter) was close, if not always friendly.[36] City officials also formed fairly strong ties with John Holond, earl of Huntingdon and duke of Exeter; and even lent him money on several occasions.[37]

Members of Exeter's oligarchy, especially those of Rank A, formed similar strong relationships with the leading merchants of other towns. Prominent merchants of other Devon towns, such as the one-time mayors of Plymouth and Dartmouth (Humphrey Passour and John Hawley respectively), possessed commercial ties with Exeter merchants of the Rank A oligarchy, stood as mainprise for these same merchants, and served with them on county commissions, as members of Parliament, and as port customs officials.[38] Other Exeter merchants formed business and even personal relationships with merchants from as far away as London, appointing these

32. Additional Charter 64320 in the British Library, London. See also Cherry, ibid., 73, 82, 85–87.
33. M.C.R. 8 January 1387.
34. See, for example, the wills in M.C.R. 21 July 1371, 7 May 1375. 17 December 1403.
35. See, for example, *Cal. F.R.* 9.368–69 and 10.54, 62, 121–22; Book 53A, fol. 28v; ED/M/501.
36. Andrew Jackson, 'Medieval Exeter, the Exe and the Earldom of Devon', *Transactions of the Devonshire Association* 104 (1972) 57–79: A. G. Little and R. C. Easterling, *The Franciscans and Dominicans of Exeter* (History of Exeter Research Group 3; Exeter, 1927), pp. 39–44; *Powderham Castle Muniments, Précis of Leases, etc. . . . . 1271–1724*, ed. Oliver Moger, no. 80 (manuscript deposited in the D.R.O.): D.R.O. Court Rolls and Account Rolls, nos. 534, 543. See also Cherry, 'Courtenay Earls of Devon', 71–90.
37. C. J. Tyldesly, The *County and Local Community in Devon and Cornwall from 1377 to 1422* (Diss. Exeter, 1978), pp. 168. 190. See also *Cal. Inq. Misc 7*, nos. 65 and 137; C. R. A. 1390/91. In 1400, an armed uprising on Holond's behalf occurred in Exeter but the oligarchy's role in this short-lived rebellion is unclear.
38. Passour: Provosts' Court Roll (hereafter P.C.R.) 19 September 1381, 5 October 1385; *Cal.F.R.* 10. 121–22; E 122 158/28 in the P. R. O.; R. N. Worth, *A History of Plymouth* (Plymouth, 1931), p. 277. Hawley: P.C.R. 4 November 1385, 27 June 1387; Cherry, 'Courtenay Earls of Devon', 85, 91, 94; Stephen P. Pistano, 'Henry IV and John Hawley, Privateer, 1399–1408', *Transactions of the Devonshire Association* 111 (1979) 145–63.

outsiders as executors of their estates, or joining their families through marriage.[39] These relationships, as well as those between Exeter merchants and the local gentry, were facilitated by Exeter's pre-eminent position in the South West as a regional market town, port, merchant staple, ecclesiastical center and administrative center (county courts, for example, were held at the local Rougemont Castle). Indeed, many of the gentry and even some of the non-Exeter merchants such as Humphrey Passour owned land or tenements in Exeter.[40] Thus personal relationships, fostered through common interests, political ties, commercial connections, and even intermarriage, built associations between the three groups, which bolstered the already high status of Exeter's ruling elite.[41]

The upper oligarchy's connections with the central government also appeared in their frequent election (or appointment) as representatives to Parliament. As specified in the first writ summoning Exeter and other towns to Parliament in 1268, the parliamentary representatives of Exeter were always from among the 'better, richer, more discreet and more powerful men of the city'.[42] Exeter members of Parliament tended to be either prosperous landowners from the Exeter area, wealthy merchants of the oligarchy, or professional lawyers from Exeter. The remuneration paid to members of Parliament was very small, and the inconvenience of travelling was very great, but merchants probably used such trips to London for business purposes; they predominated among Exeter parliamentary representatives throughout the fourteenth century.[43]

In the late fourteenth and fifteenth centuries, professional lawyers increasingly appeared as parliamentary representatives for Exeter and other Devon towns. The movement coincided with much pluralism, especially in the West Country where the hardships of

---

39. See, for example: M.C.R. 31 December 1380, 24 August 1383, 7 September 1388, 18 November 1392, 17 June 1398, 29 March 1423 and ED/M/484.

40. Gentry holdings in Exeter were numerous; see the various Exeter deed collections. For Passour, see M.C.R. 26 October 1360. For other non-Exeter merchants' property in Exeter, see M.C.R. 9 May 1379, 6 March 1396 and ED/M/460.

41. For intermarriage between the gentry and oligarchy, see Alexander, 'Part II', 203–207. Only the richest and most powerful of the oligarchic families, such as the Wilfords and Talbots, formed such alliances. For instances of the oligarchy benefiting from their ties with the local gentry, see M.C.R. 4 November 1387 and Tyldesly *County and Local Community*, pp. 17–18.

42. May McKisack, *Parliamentary Representation of English Boroughs in the Later Middle Ages* (London 1932), p. 3.

43. For the small pay awarded to Exeter M.P.s, McKisack, ibid., pp. 91–92 and the City Receiver's Accounts. Both Exeter and Dartmouth tended to send mainly merchants to Parliament; see Tyldesley, *County and Local Community*, pp. 38, 41, 43.

travel to London were not taken lightly.[44] Members of the oligarchy often considered parliamentary representation to be an onerous responsibility because representatives had to be absent from Exeter for as long as seventy-five days at a time.[45] In fact, while municipal, county or royal office offered opportunities for political power and financial gain, the duties were, nonetheless, sometimes considered an unwelcome burden by potential officeholders. Like other towns, Exeter occasionally had to use borough regulations, threats, fines and ultimately imprisonment to convince some burgesses to perform more onerous and less profitable civic duties.[46]

The reluctance of some Exeter citizens to fulfill all their civic responsibilities points out some of the disadvantages of high political rank. In the first place, the demands of office took time, distracting the merchant or craftsman from his regular business. Much time and effort were expended on elections, council meetings, civic expeditions to London or other towns on city business, entertainment of visiting justices, and the innumerable arrangements required for the repair and upkeep of city property. Moreover, the oligarchy's most important and time-consuming task consisted in keeping the peace and administering justice in the town. The mayor and stewards spent at least one day a week presiding in court, the receiver and wardens of Exebridge collected rents and compiled annual accounts, and all members of the oligarchy frequently served as jurors in the city courts. High-ranking officials were also subject to financial liabilities by virtue of their civic office. The outgoing mayor, for example, was required to give a feast for all the most prominent town officers at his own expense on election day.[47] Special expenses, such as the construction of a barge for the king's service or rebuilding of a burned city mill could only be met by loans from wealthy citizens. For instance, in the mid-1360s, seven leading citizens, six of whom had served as mayor of Exeter, each lent the city from £1 to £8 to subsidize the repair of the city wall.[48]

44. J. J. Alexander, ' Exeter Members of Parliament, Part 1: 1295–1377', *Transactions of the Devonshire Association* 59 (1927) 185 and Tyldesley, ibid., pp. 43–44 and his 'Summary'.

45. *Calendar of Close Rolls (=Cal. C.R.)*, Rich. II. 1.498 and 2.134, 300: Henry IV. 1.331; and C.R.A. 1389/90.

46. Exeter men were reluctant on occasion to serve in such minor offices as gatekeeper or market warden; see, for example, M.C.R. 3 October 1373, 13 October 1376, 13 October 1404. Others also tried to avoid constant appointments on country commissions and juries; see, for example, *Cal.P.R.*, Rich II, 1.598. But no men ever tried to escape serving in any of the major Rank A or B offices. For a recent discussion of this problem, see Jennifer I. Kermode, 'Urban Decline: The Flight from Office in Late Medieval York', *Economic History Review*, 2nd Ser., 35 (1982) 179–98.

47. Hoker, *Description*, 3.914.

48. Misc. Roll 6, m. 16. For other loans to the city by members of the oligarchy, see mm. 16 and 20 in Misc. Roll 6 and C.R.A. 1393/94, 1396/97.

The oligarchy's sense of civic responsibility extended even to bequests. The testaments of members of the oligarchy often included grants to the city for public projects such as the upkeep of Exebridge, the construction of a water conduit 'for the easement of the whole community' or the foundation of almhouses and hospitals for the poor and sick of the community.[49] In Exeter and other medieval towns, civic responsibility and wealth were inextricably intertwined. Oligarchic rule by a wealthy merchant elite was often considered the best possible means of government since that class was the best equipped to bear the burdens of public office. Members of the oligarchy considered themselves the best qualified directors of borough affairs not only because their leading role as merchants in the town's economy gave them the right to govern the town, but also because their wealth enabled them to meet the often excessive demands of town government.[50]

III

The pre-eminence of the oligarchy within the local markets of Exeter can be illustrated through an analysis of 4526 debt cases in the local courts over a ten year period from 1378 to 1388.[51] In the absence of notarial contracts such as exist for continental Europe, debt cases provide the best reflection of the commercial world of medieval English towns. About 70 per cent of the debts concerned purely commercial matters such as credit purchases, loans, custom payments and cash transactions. The remaining 30 per cent were roughly divided between salary disputes, unpaid rent or relief disputes, and cases concerning unpaid legal and pledging costs. Supplemented by information on occupations and political ranks from the voluminous and detailed Exeter records of this period, the type and extent of commercial participation by individuals in Exeter's local markets can be broadly measured by the frequency and nature of their appearances in debt cases in the local courts. The dominance of the oligarchy in the local markets, especially by

49. E.B.W. 1369/70, 1391/92; M.C.R. 22 September 1421; Hoker, *Description*, 3.858–59

50. Exeter's oligarchy expressed this sentiment in the regulations of 1345; see Wilkinson, *Mediaeval Council*, p. 71. For an excellent discussion of class distinctions in medieval London and the right of the merchant oligarchy to rule, see Thrupp, *Merchant Class of London*, pp. 14–27.

51. There were 4,629 creditors and 4,702 debtors involved in these 4,526 debt cases. See Kowaleski, *Local Markets*, Appendix 3, for a full rationale and explanation of this project. Except for Table 4, all further tables will exclude data on women, clergy and non-Exeter residents since they were all ineligible to run for office.

those of Rank A, can be illustrated, first of all, by a comparison of both the creditors' and debtors' political rank.

TABLE 4 Creditors and Debtors in Exeter by Political Rank, 1378–88

Political Rank	% of Heads of Household in 1377 (N = 528)	Creditors (N = 4629)	Debtors (N = 4702)
A	6%	21%	3%
B	6%	12%	5%
C	6%	10%	9%
D	75%	36%	46%
Women	7%	4%	8%
Clergy		3%	4%
Non-Exeter Residents		14%	25%
Total	100%	100%	100%

Sources: Misc. Roll 72: M.C.R. election returns, 1350–1400; M.C.R. and P.C.R. debt cases, 1378–88.

As Table 4 shows, members of the oligarchy, who accounted for only a very small percentage of the total population, nonetheless were responsible for a much larger proportion of the local trade (as reflected in their appearances in debt cases in the Exeter courts). Furthermore, their more frequent appearance as creditors (they were about seven times more likely to come into court as creditors than as debtors) emphasizes their financial solvency in the community. In contrast, members of Ranks C and D, who exercised little or no political influence and who were unlikely to enjoy the privileges of freedom membership, were more often at a disadvantage in their commercial dealings as evidenced by the regularity of their appearance as debtors. In addition, their less frequent appearances overall in debt cases (in proportion to their numbers within the town's population) indicates their less commercially active position as artisans and laborers.

Indeed, the economic strength of the oligarchy largely resulted from their wealth and occupational status. As Table 5 illustrates, Rank A men overwhelmingly operated as distributor/retailers and were rarely involved in the actual manufacture of goods, while those of lower political rank were more likely to work either as artisan/retailers (both manufacturing and selling their own products, such as bakers, skinners and weavers), or as mere processors or laborers (such as fullers, millwards or carpenters).

As distributors, members of the Exeter oligarchy, like the grocers of medieval London studied by Sylvia Thrupp, functioned as both wholesalers and retailers.[52] Retail trading by Exeter's oligarchy

TABLE 5 Political Ranks of Exeter Creditors and Debtors by
Occupational Function 1378–88 (N = 5662)

Occupational Function	Rank A	Rank B	Rank C	Rank D
Distributor and/or Retailer	76%	50%	34%	16%
Artisan/Retailer	23%	49%	55%	64%
Processor	1%	1%	11%	17%
Servant	0	0	0	3%
Total	100%	100%	100%	100%

Sources: M.C.R. election returns, 1350–1400; M.C.R. and P.C.R. debt
cases, 1378–88.

provided a valuable addition to wholesaling activities. Compared to
the merchants of the larger market towns of London, Bristol and
Southampton, Exeter merchants operated on a smaller, more
provincial scale, suffering from smaller amounts of capital and fewer
national commercial connections. Nevertheless, in Exeter's own
local markets the oligarchy served as the most important middlemen, selling either to a retailer or directly to a consumer. For
example, Richard Bozoun imported large quantities of wine, herring, figs, oil, iron, bowstaves, boards, wainscot and other goods,
while exporting primarily cloth and small amounts of wool and
hides. He sold lead *in grosso,* as well as consignments of madder
and woad. He also retailed smaller amounts of goods such as malt,
oats, ale, wine and building stone.[53] Other members of the oligarchy
specialized in certain commodities. John Aisshe, termed both
'vitner' and 'merchant' in the records, regularly imported and sold
large quantities of wine to retailers while he also directly retailed
wine, as well as ale, mead and wood. Like many other members of
the oligarchy, he also exported cloth, acting as middleman between
textile producer and overseas retailer.[54]

Members of the oligarchy were distinguished occupationally from

52. S. Thrupp. 'The Grocers of London: A Study of Distributive Trade', in *Studies in English Trade in the Fifteenth Century.* ed. Eileen Power and M. M. Postan (London, 1933), pp. 247–92.
53. Exeter Port Customs Accounts (hereafter P.C.A.) 1371/72, 1372/73, 1382/83, 1383/84, 1385/86, 1386/87; E 122 158/31, 158/34, 193/23, 40/8, 40/6, 40/18 in the P.R.O. Wholesale activities: M.C.R. 20 September 1389; P.C.R. 5 May 1386, 12 May 1386; E 101 338/11. no. 6 in the P.R.O. Retail activities: C.R.A. 1380/81, 1386/87; P.C.R. 6 October 1384; South Quarter Mayor's Tourn 1374 to 1388. The amount of individual debts also serves as a rough guide to retailing and wholesaling activities; Bozoun's debts ranged from 8 marks to 2*s.* 6*d.*
54. M.C.R. 3 August 1377, 2 February 1383, 21 November 1390; P.C.R. 15 January 1379, 30 June 1384; North Quarter Mayor's Tourn 1373–74–76–83–86; C.R.A. 1386/87; P.C.A. 1365/66 to 1372/73, 1381/82, 1383/84, 1384/85; E 122 158/24, 40/8, 193/23 in the P.R.O.

the rest of the local working population not only by their occupational function, but also by their involvement in the trade by sea. Overseas trade required large amounts of capital, the ability to take financial risks, and good commercial connections. Membership in the freedom was also helpful since non-freedom members had to pay port customs and were barred from certain types of retail and wholesale activity in the cloth and woad trades. As a result, only thirty Exeter citizens, twenty-two (73 per cent) of the A Rank and eight (24 per cent) of the B Rank, were engaged in some aspect of the port trade in 1377; they represented slightly more than 5 per cent of all the Exeter heads of household. Furthermore, this small group of prominent merchants controlled roughly one third of all trade through the port of Exeter.[55] Their overseas (and coastal) commercial activities must have proved extraordinarily profitable since these few men enjoyed a local monopoly on such crucial imports as wine, iron, salt, woad, and a variety of foodstuffs. Moreover, the oligarchy's predominance as distributors made them the natural middlemen for other importers who wanted to wholesale their goods in Exeter. Obviously control of the profitable and commercially prestigious port trade contributed to the ruling elite's domination of the local markets through the wealth such trade generated.

Within the port trade, two activities, linked to one another, predominated: the exportation of cloth and the importation of wine. As the chief export of the region, cloth was the basis for the growing wealth of Devon in the late fourteenth century.[56] On the other hand, wine was always the major product imported through the port of Exeter; from 1381 to 1391, for example, 60 per cent of all importers at the port of Exeter imported wine.[57] During this period, Exeter merchants controlled 38 per cent of the total volume of wine imported at Exeter.[58] While similar precise figures on oligarchic participation in cloth exporting are unavailable because the cloth customs were farmed in the 1370s and 1380s, our scattered references do indicate that exports through Exeter were almost always local cloth.[59] Many Exeter merchants were heavily involved in the town's cloth industry, contracting with weavers, fullers and dyers to perform various manufacturing processes on wool, yarn, and cloth which the merchants then sold or exported.[60] Licences granted

55. P.C.A. 1381/82 to 1391/92; Exeter merchants accounted for 289 of a total 954 importers at the port of Exeter during this period.
56. Carus-Wilson, *Expansion of Exeter.*
57. P.C.A. 1381/82 to 1391/92; 574 of the total 954 importers imported wine.
58. P.C.A. 1381/82 to 1391/92; Exeter merchants imported 1832.25 tuns of a total 4861.25 tuns imported at Exeter during this period.
59. E 122 158/24, 158/32, 158/31, 40/8, 193/23, 102/14, 102/14A, and 158/34 in the P.R.O.
60. For a full discussion of the oligarchy's influence in the local cloth trade and industry, see Kowaleski, *Local Markets*, pp. 111–18.

to Exeter merchants to trade overseas usually stipulated that the merchants take local cloth to France (Gascony) in exchange for wine or, occasionally, for other merchandise such as woad.[61] Even oligarchic distributors such as John Nymet, a 'cutler' who supplied iron and coal to local smiths, or Thomas Smytheghes, a 'ferrour' who also sold iron, marketed wine and cloth.[62] Thus, regardless of specialization, the common occupational characteristics of the ruling elite of late fourteenth-century Exeter were: (1) their function as distributors (and, to a lesser extent, as retailers) within particular trades; (2) their local monopoly of Exeter's port trade; and (3) their focus upon the profitable cloth and wine trades. Even though members of political Ranks C and D dominated numerically all but the occupation of general merchant, they were spread more evenly throughout the various occupations and tended to hold inferior positions as artisans and processors.[63]

The concentration and dominance of the oligarchy in the town's local markets may also be seen in the cash value of the debts contracted. As Tables 6 and 7 point out, members of the oligarchy,

TABLE 6 Debt Amounts of Exeter Creditors and Debtors by Political Rank, 1378–88

Political Rank	Debt Amount						Total
	1d.–1s.	1s.–5s.	5s.–10s.	10s.–£1	£1–£5	£5–£50	
Creditors							
Oligarchy (N = 624)	7%	48%	20%	13%	9%	3%	=100%
Ranks C and D (N = 863)	16%	52%	16%	9%	6%	1%	=100%
Debtors							
Oligarchy (N = 135)	7%	32%	21%	16%	16%	8%	=100%
Ranks C and D (N = 1297)	11%	51%	20%	10%	7%	1%	=100%

Sources: M.C.R. election returns, 1350–1400; M.C.R. amd P.C.R. debt cases, 1378–88. Note: The oligarchy includes Ranks A and B.

61. See, for example, *Cal.P.R.*, Edw. III, 12.510, 521.
62. Nymet: Rowe and Jackson, *Exeter Freemen*, p. 30; P.C.R. 19 November 1381, 10 October 1387; M.C.R. 15 December 1382, 13 June 1390, 26 June 1391; C.R.A. 1386/87; P.C.A. 1369/70 to 1371/72, 1387/88 to 1389/90; E 122 158/34, 40/8, 193/23 in the P.R.O. Smythesheghes: P.C.R. 2 August 1382, 15 October 1383, 22 March 1386, 27 June 1387, 9 January 1388, 15 February 1388; M.C.R. 13 May 1387.
63. For an examination of the occupational status of non-oligarchic Exeter residents, see Kowaleski, *Local Markets*, pp. 110, 168–93.

TABLE 7 Average Amount of Debt of Exeter Creditors and Debtors
by Political Rank, 1378–88

Political Rank	Average Debt of Creditors	Average Debt of Debtors
Oligarchy	17s. 8d.	37s. 6d.
(Creditors = 624)		
(Debtors = 135)		
Ranks C and D	8s. 9d.	9s. 1d.
(Creditors = 863)		
(Debtors = 1297)		

Sources: M.C.R. election returns, 1350–1400; M.C.R. and P.C.R. debt cases, 1378–88. Note: The oligarchy includes Ranks A and B.

whether creditors or debtors, were more likely to become entangled in large debts. The fact that oligarchic debtors owed the largest cash amounts emphasizes the premier place occupied by the oligarchy in the town's commercial sphere. While men of lower political rank outnumbered men of Ranks A and B in the local markets, the oligarchy compensated for its small numbers by controlling most of the major trade in these markets. Furthermore, major trade required major expenditures; high debts were the natural offshoot of such ventures. Such heavy debts stress the risky nature of some of the oligarchy's commercial ventures. Although members of the oligarchy could expect higher returns on their greater investments, so too they had to accept potentially greater losses.

The high risks undertaken by the merchants of the oligarchy were revealed most dramatically in overseas and coastal trade. The dangers of such trade were well known to Exeter merchants; storms at sea, pirates, and the constant threat of war (especially in the late fourteenth century) all combined to present real hazards to the merchant willing to embark on such ventures.[64] The capital needed to finance the overseas enterprises could be furnished only by the wealthier merchants. Thus, participation in the shipping trade was closely connected to wealth, high political office and occupation. For example, of the nine wealthiest men in 1377 Exeter, all belonged to the Rank A oligarchy, functioned as a merchant wholesaler, and possessed interests in the sea trade through the port of Exeter.[65]

The financial risks and cash flow problems associated with both overseas and wholesale trade were often eased by forming financial

---

64. For the hazards of sea trade experienced by Exeter merchants and others trading off the south Devon coast during this period, see *Cal.P.R.*, Edw. III, 12.83 and Rich. II, 1.356, 6.584–85; *Cal.C.R.*, Edw. III, 10.32, 83, 87.
65. The one exception was Robert Dene, an artisan/retailer in the leather and skin trade who paid 5s. in murage tax and achieved no higher than B political rank.

partnerships.[66] The Exeter evidence suggests that partnerships in the seagoing trade were particularly beneficial to those beginning a commercial career who lacked the requisite capital (or experience). For example, both John Talbot and Thomas Estoun began their sea-trade activities by importing wine in partnership with well-established merchants.[67] Although Talbot and Estoun began their commercial ventures without benefit of freedom membership or high political office, both men went on to attain entry into the freedom, Rank A status in the oligarchy, and great wealth. While their success underlines the important role that investment in overseas trade played in attaining commercial and political power, it was necessary to mitigate the high risks of their initial forays into overseas trade by forming partnerships with wealthier, established merchants.

Even established merchants who frequently traded overseas occasionally formed importing partnerships with others. The partnerships were almost always made with fellow citizens who were also wealthy merchants of the oligarchy.[68] On less frequent occasions, Exeter merchants entered into partnerships with shipmasters who used Exeter as a home base. Men such as John Bole and John Trote, both members of the Exeter oligarchy, not only mastered ships sailing along the coast and overseas but also shared investments in the cargoes as well.[69] The commercial partnerships between merchants or between merchants and shipmasters considerably alleviated the financial and organizational problems of both sea and inland trade and were undoubtedly facilitated by the networks formed in Exeter by family, friendship, neighborhood, and public office.

Exeter merchants pooled resources not only in their overseas commercial enterprises, but also in domestic and coastal trade. For example, a theft recorded in 1403 reveals that John Talbot and Simon Grendon (both members of the Exeter oligarchy) jointly purchased large quantities of oil, almonds and figs from a Dartmouth merchant.[70] Unhappily, the goods turned out to be stolen. Grendon and Talbot had pooled their resources on other occasions as well. In 1398 and 1402 they bought several parcels of land in Exeter from

---

66. M. M. Postan, 'Partnership in English Medieval Commerce' in *Medieval Trade and Finance* (Cambridge, 1973), pp. 65–91; M. K. James, 'A London Merchant of the Fourteenth Century', *Economic History Review*, 2nd Ser., 8 (1956) 369–70; Thrupp, *Merchant Class of Medieval London*, pp. 104, 108, III.

67. Talbot: P.C.A. 1372/73; Estoun: P.C.A. 1384/85.

68. See, for example, P.C.A. 1367/68, 1369/70, 1370/71, 1372/73, 1386/87, 1388/89.

69. Bole: P.C.A. 1365/66, 1366/67, 1367/68, 1369/70, 1372/73; Misc. Roll 72; E 122 40/8, 193/23 in the P.R.O.; Rowe and Jackson, *Exeter Freemen*, p. 31. Trote: P.C.A. 1369/70; M.C.R. 29 May 1374, 17 August 1383; East Quarter Mayor's Tourn 1372; Rowe and Jackson, *Exeter Freemen*, p. 33.

70. *Cal. Ing. Misc.* 7, no. 251.

various sellers, one of which cost the substantial sum of £40.[71] Their partnership was eased by their common service in public office and shared commercial interests. Both served as mayors of Exeter: Grendon in 1395 and Talbot a year later in 1396. For at least fourteen years, they both held seats in the powerful city Council and for eight years served together as electors. Both also exported cloth and imported wine (although Talbot's trade was more diversified and included dealings in salt, herring and iron).[72] The advantages of partnership to both men (despite the unhappy theft of 1403) resulted in frequent trading ventures.

As indicated in the property acquisitions of Talbot and Grendon, landed wealth was an important economic resource for members of Exeter's oligarchy. A large proportion of the oligarchy's commercial income was funnelled into property investments. As a general rule, the wealthier the man, the more intense his participation in the land market. Robert Wilford, the richest resident of Exeter in 1377, owned dozens of properties scattered throughout the town, including shops, houses, messuages, gardens, pastureland, cellars, and solars; he leased many of these properties.[73] The investment represented by the properties must have been considerable. For example, in 1384, Wilford and his wife Elizabeth paid £40 for just one tenement in Exeter.[74] All but one of the references to Wilford's property transactions concern acquisitions. Similarly, all eleven property transactions of Richard Bozoun, another well-to-do merchant and landowner of the oligarchy, involved either the acquisition or leasing of property.[75] The types of debts contracted by members of the oligarchy reflect the tendency for the governing elite to act as buyers

71. M.C.R. 23 September 1398; ED/M/599. It was not unusual for members of the Exeter oligarchy to own or to lease property together. In many cases (although not in Grendon and Talbot's) this was due to (1) the joint action of executors of estates who were responsible for selling off lands of the deceased, or (2) those who inherited land together, usually executors. At any rate, these practices established joint property ownership patterns among the oligarchy.
72. M.C.R. 22 December 1382, 22 January 1392; P.C.A. 1383/84, 1388/89, 1390/91 to 1411/12; E101 338/11, nos. 6 and 7 and E 122 40/18, 158/34, 40/8 in the P.R.O.
73. C.R.A. 1376/77, 1377/78; Book 53A, fols. 29, 63, 75; E.B.W. 1390/91, 1386/87; Misc. Roll 4, m. 3v; ED/M/520; M.C.R. 27 March 1378, 24 June 1381, 1 July 1381, 6 October 1382; Duryard Court Roll (hereafter D.C.R.) 21 October 1396; St. Sidwell's Court Roll (hereafter S.C.R.) 20 April 1390; Dean and Chapter Accounts of Collectors of Rents in Exeter 5155–5156 and Dean and Chapter Deeds, nos. 119, 121 in the Exeter Cathedral Library; Ethel Lega-Weekes, 'An Account of the Hospitium de le Egle, Some Ancient Chapels in the Close, and Some Persons Connected Therewith', *Transactions of the Devonshire Association* 44 (1912) 484. 490, 505–507.
74. M.C.R. 12 December 1384. For the one property Wilford sold, see ED/M/546.
75. M.C.R. 16 April 1375, 4 June 1380, 15 December 1382, 6 October 1382, 9 December 1409; D.C.R. 13 October 1383, 13 May 1389 and 1382/83, m. 13; S.C.R. 20 April 1382; Book 53A, fols. 55, 76; *Cal. P.R.*, Rich. II, 3.522.

and landlords in the town's property market. After sales debts, the oligarchy's most frequent debts occurred in property and rent disputes. The oligarchy appeared much more often as creditors in such disputes (48 creditors, 15 debtors). This trend was especially noticeable among the Rank A oligarchy; three times as many Rank A as Rank B citizens prosecuted renters for debt. The degree of the oligarchy's involvement in the local land market suggests that property investment assured a steady income, part of which provided further capital for the landlord's riskier commercial or industrial activities.[76]

An examination of the other types of debts contracted by oligarchic litigants sheds additional light on their presence in the local markets.[77] Half of all debts tried centered around sales; oligarchic creditors were slightly more likely to be involved in sales debts than were non-oligarchic creditors (52 per cent compared to 47 per cent). Among debtors, however, the differences were greater; only 34 per cent of the oligarchy (and 23 per cent of Rank A alone) owed money on previous purchases while 50 per cent of the men of Ranks C and D incurred such debts. Instead, oligarchic debtors appeared in cases concerning rents (22 per cent), *obligationes* (10 per cent), and service (9 per cent). Oligarchic creditors also prosecuted more often cases concerning rents (22 per cent) and cash loans (6 per cent). Such data corroborate the patterns already established for the oligarchy. Its weightier representation in sale cases as creditors rather than debtors bespeaks the commercially dominating role of distributor in the local markets. As employers rather than employees, members of the oligarchy naturally appeared more frequently as debtors in cases concerning unpaid wages or stipends. As the major landowners in the town, with heavy investments in property, they were also more likely to become entangled in rent disputes. As the wealthiest men in the borough, the oligarchic citizens were also the natural moneylenders, and thus were more likely to appear in litigation concerning unpaid loans. Finally, as the leaders in the commercial sector of the town, with personal and business connections overseas and throughout Devon, they more frequently appeared in cases regarding *obligationes* (the formal, court-enrolled legal promise to pay usually large amounts of money to a creditor).

The immense power and influence of the Exeter oligarchy affected even the administration of justice in the community. As illustrated in Table 8, oligarchic creditors in debt cases were more

---

76. Derek Keene noted a similar trend in medieval Winchester; see his *Some Aspects of the History, Topography and Archaeology of the North-East Part of the City of Winchester with Special Reference to the Brooks Area* (D. Phil. thesis Oxford, 1972), pp. 154–55.
77. Information on the type of debt is based on responses for 794 creditors and 816 debtors.

TABLE 8 Court Decisions for Exeter Creditors and Debtors by Political Rank, 1378–88

Political Rank	Court Decisions						Total
	Guilty	Plea Not Pursued	Licence of Concord	False Query	Failure to Wage Law	No Information	
Creditors							
Oligarchy							
(N = 1515)	31%	23%	15%	4%	2%	25%	=100%
Ranks C and D							
(N = 2153)	25%	34%	14%	7%	4%	16%	=100%
Debtors							
Oligarchy							
(N =381)	18%	34%	15%	8%	2%	23%	=100%
Ranks C and D							
(N = 2594)	34%	25%	14%	6%	4%	17%	=100%

Sources: M.C.R. election returns, 1350–1400; M.C.R. and P.C.R. debt cases, 1378–88. Note: The oligarchy includes political Ranks A and B.

likely to receive a favourable decision than were creditors of lower political rank. The same principle applied when oligarchic citizens were sued as debtors; they were less likely to receive unfavorable verdicts than were men of Ranks C or D. For example, oligarchic debtors were less often judged guilty ('in mercy') than debtors of lower political ranks while oligarchic creditors more often won guilty verdicts against their debtors. Similarly, members of the oligarchy obtained *non prosequitur* verdicts (in which the creditor was fined for failing to pursue the case) less frequently as creditors, but more frequently as debtors when this decision became advantageous. The same trends occur in the false query decisions. Little difference, however, exists for the licence of concord decision or the failure to wage law. Members of the oligarchy generally possessed a distinct advantage in the local courts; their wealth and power encouraged them to pursue suits at the same time that such advantages discouraged their opponents.[78] In most cases, those of the highest group of the oligarchy, Rank A, received better verdicts than any other group. Only 14 per cent of Rank A debtors, for instance, were convicted of debt and only 3 per cent of Rank A creditors were

---

78. Similar trends were evident in rural England; Barbara Hanawalt, *Crime and Conflict in English Communities, 1300–1348* (Cambridge, Mass., 1979), p. 53 notes that primary villagers were convicted less often than poorer villagers of lesser status in criminal cases.

found guilty of pleading a false query. The wealth, commercial status, and public offices enjoyed by the Rank A litigants obviously influenced the court (run by the same oligarchic group) in handing down its decisions.[79]

IV

'Oligarchy' has not only denoted 'government by the few' but has also frequently been interpreted as a closed system of government that recruited new members from among the families already in power. Thus this type of government has been viewed as confining public power and prestige, year after year, to a small, privileged group of prominent families or individuals. This outlook ignores the social mobility characteristic of medieval urban life. The vicissitudes of commercial life, the failure to produce heirs, and the occasional drain of the wealthy urban elite to the rural gentry, combined with the constant flow of immigration to the town, entrepreneurship, simple good fortune, and advantageous marriages to ensure that the town's oligarchy was not restricted to the same pool of oligarchic families; the oligarchic pool remained small but not stagnant.

In Exeter, demographic failure to produce heirs dealt the most devastating blow to oligarchic fortunes. The inability to produce an adequate number of male heirs (aggravated by high infant mortality) cut short the rise of many oligarchic families in medieval English towns.[80] Moreover, there was no assurance that sons would follow their fathers into commerce (or have any talent for such a career). Thus the only son of Roger atte Wille, a prosperous member of the Rank A oligarchy with interests in the local cloth industry, became a Franciscan monk. After Roger and his wife died, his land escheated to the king because the clerical status of his son made him ineligible to inherit the property.[81]

Other members of the oligarchy, such as Henry Scam, William Oke, and Simon Grendon, left no heirs at all, and their goods and properties were sold off by their executors.[82] A different solution was found by Richard Goldsmith of Rank A whose two marriages had produced two daughters who both predeceased him. Rather

---

79. The mayor presided over the Mayor's Court, the stewards ran the Provosts' Court and jurors in both courts were usually chosen from among members of the oligarchy.
80. Thrupp, *Merchant Class of Medieval London*, pp. 191–206; Colin Platt, *The English Medieval Town* (London, 1976), pp. 98–102.
81. Little and Easterling, *Franciscans and Dominicians*, pp. 23–24. Thrupp found that barely two thirds of aldermen's sons in medieval London followed their fathers into trade (ibid., p. 205).
82. M.C.R. 9 June 1382, 22 June 1416, 9 January 1413.

than dissolving his estate, he bequeathed all his goods, properties, and tools of his goldsmith trade to his servant, John Russell, another goldsmith. Only a year after Goldsmith's death, John Russell was already well-established in his trade and paid 2*s*. in the 1377 murage tax. In 1378 he entered the freedom, paying a higher than usual entry fine. Russell went on to serve in municipal office as well, attaining Rank B oligarchic status.[83]

Of course, some families endured and retained oligarchic status for more than two or three generations. The Gerveys family, for example, was active in Exeter from the early thirteenth into the fifteenth century.[84] The Wilfords also produced several generations of extremely successful and wealthy merchants who served the town as mayors and members of Parliament in the fourteenth and fifteenth centuries.[85] Other members of the late fourteenth-century oligarchy also produced adequate heirs: John Gist left seven heirs, Adam Golde had three daughters, a son and a grandson when he died, and Ralph Swan left behind two sons and a daughter.[86] Although no precise figures are available for Exeter, it appears that the town's oligarchic families followed a pattern observed in other medieval towns. Some families endured for several generations without any lack of male heirs, but few survived past three or four generations.[87]

Besides the failure to produce adequate heirs, financial and commercial risks weakened the ability of some oligarchic families to survive.[88] The accumulation of misfortune by certain members of the oligarchy certainly suggests that commercial failure was not uncommon. For example, Walter Fouke, an oligarchic merchant of Rank A who participated in both local and overseas trade, was never as wealthy as other members of the elite; he paid only 18*d*. in the 1377 murage, far below the 4*s*. 6*d*. average for other Rank

---

83. Goldsmith: M.C.R. 22 December 1382, 12 March 1380; ED/M/464. Russell: Misc. Roll 72; Rowe and Jackson, *Exeter Freemen*, p. 34; Russell paid a £1 6*s*. 8*d*. entry fine to the freedom, i.e. more than the usual fine of £1.

84. Rowe and Jackson, ibid., pp. 4, 8, 13, 23, 30; M.C.R. 16 February 1400; *Mayors of Exeter from the 13th Century to the Present Day*, comp. M. M. Rowe and J. Cochlin (Exeter, 1964). pp. 2, 5. The Gerveys (or Gervase) family was responsible for the first stone bridge over the Exe River outside the west gate of the city; see W. G. Hoskins, *Two Thousand Years in Exeter* (Chichester, 1960; rpt. 1969), pp. 28–31.

85. M.C.R. 8 January 1397, 9 July 1414; Tyldesley, *County and Local Community*, pp. 37–38

86. M.C.R. 18 March 1381, 14 August 1396, 21 October 1415.

87. Étienne Fournial, *Les villes et l'économie d'échange en Forez au XIIIᵉ et XIVᵉ siècles* (Paris, 1967), p. 259 notes that 93 per cent of families in the Forez region towns disappeared in less than three centuries; most families died out within three generations.

88. See, for example, James, 'London Merchant', 369–74.

A citizens.[89] Fouke, quite simply, did not enjoy the commercial successes experienced by other Rank A merchants. He was frequently sued in the courts for large sums; in 1375, he owed Henry Martyn of Chumleigh 16 marks; in 1376, he was prosecuted by John Seyneet, a spicer, for 50*s*.; in 1379, he acknowledged a debt of over 36*s*. to Thomas Canon, and in the same year Robert Wilford successfully sued him for £16.[90] His own actions as a creditor were equally unfortunate. For example, Thomas Webber had incurred a debt to Fouke of £10, which he failed to pay. After Webber died, Fouke went to Webber's widow, Helewisia, for payment but she put him off since she had decided to marry again. After the wedding, Fouke tried to claim the debt but Helewisia and her new husband stalled again. To complicate matters, Webber had died intestate and his affairs took years to settle, so Fouke was required to pursue the case in the Exeter courts over a course of many years; unfortunately, no verdict was ever recorded.[91] Other misfortunes also befell Fouke. His house was burglarized in 1375 and goods valued at 26*s*. were taken. In 1378 several malefactors forcibly entered his house and set it afire to the damage of £20. He also failed to meet a custom payment and suffered the distraint of his goods to cover the cost of the custom debt.[92] When Fouke died in 1381, his widow Christine was immediately sued by numerous creditors, including at least one former business partner of her husband.[93] This postmortem debt litigation continued to plague Christine for nearly a decade; as late as 1390 a Lamport merchant claimed she owed him 5 marks as Fouke's widow and executor.[94] All this must have been too much for Christine; in 1393 the City Receiver pardoned her court fines with the comment 'because she is a pauper'.[95] Whether Fouke's misfortunes were due to a lack of business acumen, an unpleasant personality, personal tragedy, or just plain bad luck, we will never know. While his continuous financial difficulties underline dramatically the problems and risks that faced Exeter's merchants, the wealthiest merchants of Exeter rarely suffered such unrelenting financial disasters. Secure in their business dealings and landed wealth, and acknowledged as the governors of their town, the more

89. P.C.A. 1365/66 to 1371/72. Fouke was elected steward in 1371 and 1375 and served as an elector twelve times from 1366 to 1381. See Misc. Roll 72 for his murage payment.
90. M.C.R. 12 March 1375, 15 September 1376; P.C.R. 28 April 1379, 8 October 1379.
91. P.C.R. 14 October 1378; M.C.R. 30 May 1379, 6 June 1379.
92. P.C.R. 8 May 1382; M.C.R. 23 July 1375, 8 November 1378.
93. M.C.R. 16 February 1383. For his previous dealings with Aisshe, see P.C.R. 19 September 1381.
94. M.C.R. 5 December 1390. For other debts of Fouke she had to deal with, see M.C.R. 12 January 1383, 6 August 1386.
95. C.R.A. 1392/93.

prosperous members of the Exeter oligarchy reigned supreme within their provincial setting. In London, the urban oligarchy had to deal with much more intense competition for both trade and political influence. Therefore, the risks undertaken by London's merchants were necessarily greater, as were the corresponding successes and failures.

Although several historians have argued that the wealthy urban elite escaped as soon as possible from their commercial origins and established gentry pretensions in the countryside, this pattern did not exist in Exeter.[96] A few Exeter merchants certainly owned property outside of Exeter and sometimes such holdings were quite considerable, bringing in substantial rents each year.[97] Their rural holdings, however, did not transform urban merchants into landed gentry, nor did they create urban exploitation of the countryside.[98] There is no evidence that members of the Exeter oligarchy either worked for or desired the life of a country gentleman. The disinterest of Exeter merchants in gentry living could reflect the relatively modest means of a provincial urban elite compared to the greater towns of London, Bristol, or York. But reports of such transformations may well be exaggerated. Although some moves from wealthy town merchant to country squire undoubtedly took place, they probably involved an extremely small (albeit highly visible) proportion of any town's oligarchy. The traditional view of wealthy burgesses scrambling to escape to the life of country gentlemen may well be overstated.

The weaknesses in the oligarchic class (threats of commercial and financial disaster, failure of heirs, and the occasional elevation of wealthy merchants to the landed gentry) required that the ranks of the ruling elite be bolstered periodically with new members. Those born into a lower political rank, as well as new immigrants to the town, could still hope to climb the urban ladder to commercial, political and social success. Opportunities came in several different forms. Some, like goldsmith John Russell, received money, property, and a head start in his chosen occupation as a reward for faithful service to a childless master. Others, like John Talbot and Thomas

96. Thrupp, *Merchant Class of Medieval London*, pp. 279–87; Platt, *Medieval Southampton*, p. 63; Platt, *English Medieval Town*, pp. 102–103.
97. *Cal. Inq. P.M.* 13, no. 18.
98. Historians of continental Europe have dwelt more on the exploitation of the town, led by the landed interests of the oligarchy or 'patriciate', than have historians of English towns. This may be due to the greater size of many continental cities, as well as the evolution of city-state systems there. See, for example, David Nicholas, *Town and Countryside: Social, Economic and Political Tensions in Fourteenth-Century Flanders* (Bruges, 1971), pp. 267–330; Richard Hoffmann, 'Wroclaw Citizens as Rural Landholders' in *The Medieval City*, ed. Harry A. Miskimin, David Herlihy, and A. L. Udovitch (New Haven, 1977), pp. 293–312.

Estoun (see above, p. 205) appear to have succeeded through commercial risk-taking and business acumen. Other members of the Rank A oligarchy, such as Adam Golde, Ralph Swan, and John Piers, also took part in the risky business of overseas trade before they gained either entry into the freedom or high political office.[99] This scenario suggests that participation in sea trade, combined with some element of 'entrepreneurship' or plain luck, may have served as an avenue to greater wealth and political power. It is also significant that examples of this type of upward mobility are found mostly in the decades immediately following the Black Death when the deaths of many townspeople created more opportunities for immigrants and less well-off inhabitants. Finally, marriage to a wealthy woman often provided access to the merchant elite as well. For example, Philip Seys, John Holm, and Richard Kenrigg all attained entry to the Exeter freedom the same year they married wealthy widows of the oligarchy.[100] All three men also went on to obtain oligarchic status.

Although such examples show that upward social mobility was certainly possible in medieval Exeter, the combination of wealth, commercial success, and political power necessary for entry into the higher echelons of the oligarchy was not attained easily or frequently. Birth was still the best path to success in medieval town life and the families of the Exeter oligarchy tried at all times to maintain their status in the borough. Moreover, the oligarchic class always remained a small, tightly-knit community united by wealth and common occupational backgrounds. For instance, only 40 of the 472 non-oligarchic heads of household in 1377 went on to join the oligarchy.[101] Their average murage was 1s. 6d. compared to the 1s. 1d. average. The distinction between Ranks A and B also remained firm. Of those reaching Rank A, 53 per cent functioned as distributor/retailers while only 22 per cent of the future Rank B citizens belonged to this group, and most of these men were more active in the retail trade than as wholesalers. The vast majority (70 per cent) of the men who eventually attained Rank B were artisan/retailers (i.e. craftsmen).

99. Golde: P.C.A. 1365/66 to 1372/73, 1381/82 to 1383/84, 1386/87, 1388/89; M.C.R. 1 October 1369, 2 October 1374; E 122 40/8, 193/23; Rowe and Jackson, *Exeter Freemen*, p. 31; Golde entered the freedom in 1362, achieved Rank B in 1369 and Rank A in 1374. Swan: P.C.A. 1381/82 to 1383/84, 1385/86, 1387/88, 1388/89; M.C.R. 2 October 1385, 30 September 1398; E 122 40/8, 193/23, 40/26, 40/15; Rowe and Jackson, *Exeter Freemen*, p. 34; Swan entered the freedom in 1374, Rank B in 1385 and Rank A in 1398. Piers: P.C.A. 1372/73; Rowe and Jackson, *Exeter Freemen*, p. 33; he joined the freedom in 1374, was elected to Rank B in 1377 and Rank A in 1381.
100. Rowe and Jackson, ibid, pp. 34–35; M.C.R. election returns, 1378–90; P.C.R. 14 October 1378; M.C.R. 14 July 1382, 12 January 1383.
101. Kowaleski, *Local Markets,* Appendix 4.

Rank A always remained more selective; only 17 of the heads of household in 1377 (who were not already in Rank A) went on to join Rank A and six of these men had already reached Rank B by 1377. Twenty-three of the non-oligarchic citizens in 1377 went on to join Rank B of the oligarchy. Thus, Exeter inhabitants certainly realized that the chances of boosting themselves into the oligarchy were slim without a background of wealth. This wealth could be gained through family connections (whether by inheritance or marriage) or through commercial success or luck. Yet to attain high political rank and its commercial privileges, and to maintain this status, wealth was the overriding factor. Wealth delineated the sectors of the Exeter community, and determined political rank, occupational function, and social status.

There is little doubt that the less privileged inhabitants of Exeter noted the immense gap which separated them from the oligarchy. Reports of abuses of power by the oligarchy and of the resulting resentment of the lower classes were not uncommon in the town. This resentment, however, rarely went beyond the stage of heated words and accusations, and usually the trouble-makers were successfully prosecuted by the oligarchy in court. For example, Robert Plomer, a craftsman and a marginal member of Rank B (he served as elector once), was presented by twelve sworn men in the city court because he 'maliciously and falsely said openly that Robert Wilford, recently mayor of Exeter, had sealed a charter of Felicia Kirton with the seal of the mayor against her will'.[102] John Cole, a skinner who held no political offices, was sued by William Rok, a wealthy merchant of Rank A, for calling William a false juror in the city court.[103] Still other accusations of fraud and deceit in town government came from men such as Robert Coble who accused John Talbot, then mayor of Exeter, of unjustly fining a woman in the Mayor's Court when she was not present. Apparently Coble accompanied this accusation with a rude gesture, for Talbot became angry and cautioned Coble that as mayor he should not be insulted since he sat in court in place of the king. Coble answered back that the office of mayor stood for nothing since Talbot maintained prostitutes and other *lurdicos* in the city, as well as forestalling and regrating wine, herring, and other merchandise. Talbot promptly called Coble a liar, arrested him and threw him into prison.[104]

These incidents underline contemporary awareness that members of the Exeter oligarchy could and did manipulate public office to their own advantage. But the oligarchy's firm grip on municipal government and justice prevented most malcontents from expressing

102. M.C.R. 8 November 1389.
103. M.C.R. 12 January 1383.
104. M.C.R. July 1397.

this awareness or proffering accusations openly. Moreover, the Exeter oligarchy never experienced overt challenges to its authority, nor did 'class' disputes in Exeter ever reach the level of bitterness seen in other English towns.[105]

The lack of such virulent quarrels between the privileged and less privileged groups of society in Exeter was most likely due to the small size and moderate wealth of the town, as well as to the absence of a strong local lord. The gap between wealthy and poor, enfranchised and disenfranchised was not as large in Exeter as in the bigger, more prosperous towns of Bristol and London. Moreover, Exeter's electoral system, which allowed men of more moderate means to have some say in local government, and which created a buffer zone or 'middle class' (Rank B) between the truly wealthy and the poorer majority, may have also eased social and political tensions within the town. But as the economy of fifteenth- and sixteenth-century Exeter grew more vigorous and the town emerged as a major market center, the authority of the oligarchy expanded.[106] Similar movements occurred in other English towns as trade grew more complex and profitable and the wealth of individual merchants increased, town governments became more elaborate and subject to the control of a select few.[107]

Editorial suggestions for further reading

Reynolds, S. 'Medieval urban history and the history of political thought', *Urban History Yearbook* 1982, 14–23.

Rigby, S. H. 'Urban "oligarchy" in late medieval England', in J. A. F. Thomson (ed.), *Towns and Townspeople in the Fifteenth Century* (Gloucester, 1988), 62–86.

105. In Bristol, for example, fourteen members of the oligarchy were forced to flee the city for over a year following a riot by the townspeople angry with the way the fourteen had coopted the customs of the port and market for themselves; see Green, *Town Life* (n. 1 above), pp. 266–68.
106. Wilkinson, *Mediaeval Council*, pp. 24–29.
107. Green, *Town Life*, pp. 280–87; Reynolds, *English Towns*, pp. 175–77.

Chapter Eleven

THE ESSENCE OF MEDIEVAL URBAN COMMUNITIES: THE VILL OF WESTMINSTER, 1200–1540

Gervase Rosser

Transactions of the Royal Historical Society, 34 (1984)

In view of the social and factional violence present in all medieval towns, it is remarkable that these did not in fact destroy urban life altogether. This essay ventures a preliminary explanation of the ways in which a shared sense of identity might, at particular moments, be generated among the inhabitants of a town: an awareness of communal interests which could intermittently bring together the diverse body of the townspeople in a collective ritual or practical endeavour. For most of the time, the allegiance and behaviour of town dwellers were determined by the sectional interests of their respective social groups. But on occasion the collective need to maintain public works, or a general desire to participate in an inclusive ritual event, transcended the social differences which prevailed at other times and established the idea of the town as a community. The need for spontaneously created mechanisms of this kind was the greater in an unincorporated town, such as Westminster, which lacked formal structures of urban administration. It was true of all towns, however, that the elites which dominated urban government in the Middle Ages commanded very limited resources whereby to impose order. The occasional realization of a widely shared sense of civic community, though it could not remove social inequalities nor occasions for dispute, was arguably crucial to the survival of the medieval town.

The modern study of urban history began in the nineteenth century, and has since continued to reflect the preoccupations of its founders. For these historians, the towns of the European Middle Ages nurtured the seeds of political democracy and economic liberalism. Consequently, two great historians of the late nineteenth century, Charles Gross and F. W. Maitland, laid down criteria for the definition of towns which stressed above all the theme of administrative independence.[1] It was declared that fundamental legal differences

1. C. Gross, *The Gild Merchant* (Oxford, 1890); F. W. Maitland, *Township and*

216

distinguished the borough from other forms of community, in particular the village. 'Burghal status' and the features associated with it – such as the existence of a civil constitution, the right to representation in parliament, and the free tenure of property – have been exhaustively analysed by subsequent writers, notably James Tait.[2] This emphasis upon the legal autonomy of towns has been strengthened by the prestige of the great medieval cities of Flanders, Germany and Italy, which repeatedly exemplify the trade centre fighting or bargaining to achieve communal independence from feudal overlords and control over the surrounding countryside.[3] In accordance with this pattern of urban development, historians have tended to seek, as a necessary first stage of growth, evidence of such a struggle for self-governing independence.

Recently, however, this approach has been criticised. A fundamental weakness in the legal conception of the borough is exposed by Susan Reynolds, who argues that, after all, 'there was no particular legal capacity, or degree of legal capacity, which attached to boroughs as such'.[4] Whether it possessed a charter or not, a town commanded neither more nor fewer legal rights than any other collectivity, be it a village, a kingdom or a university. The received image of the medieval town, as an island of privileged autonomy set in a feudal sea, has been further undermined by Professor Rodney Hilton, who has re-emphasised, with a fresh significance, the common features of experience shared by both town and country. Without denying their particular respective qualities, Hilton insists that the social and economic links which bound the two require that they be seen as inseparable parts of the same society.[5]

The orthodox definitions of the medieval town thus appear, at

Borough (Cambridge, 1898). I should like to thank Dr Caroline Barron for the generous encouragement which she gave me in the writing of this essay.

2. J. Tait, *The Medieval English Borough* (Manchester, 1936); M. Weinbaum, *The Incorporation of Boroughs* (Manchester, 1936). For the continuing debate about boroughs, see M. W. Beresford and H. P. R. Finberg, *English Medieval Boroughs: a Handlist* (Newton Abbot, 1973), introduction. The compilers explain that they 'resisted the temptation to include a place simply because it is known to have had an urban character in the Middle Ages. "Urban", on analysis, turns out to be an even more elusive concept than burghality' (25–6). But this does not make burghality a more useful or important question than the concept of what is urban.
3. A theme developed by Henri Pirenne in particular; see *Medieval Cities: their Origins and the Revival of Trade* (Princeton, 1925), chap. vii.
4. S. Reynolds, 'Medieval history and the history of political thought', *Urban History Yearbook* (1982), 14–23, esp. 17. Madox himself assembled voluminous materials to demonstrate the rights which unincorporated communities shared with corporate boroughs. T. Madox, *Firma Burgi* (1726), *passim*.
5. R. H. Hilton, 'Towns in societies – medieval England', *Urban History Yearbook* (1982), 7–13. The agricultural aspect of medieval urban life was a theme of Maitland's *Township and Borough*.

least in emphasis, unsatisfactory, and the question arises, can better ones be found? In seeking an answer, it may be helpful to consider one of the very numerous English centres of population whose small size and 'unfree' status have hitherto disqualified them from the attention of urban historians. These small towns exhibited great variety, but a single, richly documented example can offer some general insights into medieval urban life. The case to be considered here is the settlement which gathered during the Middle Ages around the abbey and palace of Westminster, to the west of the City of London.

The district of Westminster was throughout the medieval period, until the Dissolution, a dependency of its single lord, the abbot of St Peter's monastery there. As such, its framework of seigneurial jurisdiction continued essentially unaltered before the sixteenth century; not until 1585 was the 'cyttie or burroughe of Westmynster' legally established by a parliamentary Act.[6] It was an assumption of the Whiggish historians who first charted the progressive accumulation of English urban liberties that, although some towns, such as St Albans, owed their origins to the traffic generated by religious institutions, the development of urban life properly so-called was impossible under the secular control of the Church. This, indeed, was a principle to which many medieval burgesses themselves subscribed. The medieval history of Bury St Edmunds provides the classic case of a protracted struggle between monks and townsmen over the control of jurisdiction and, more fundamentally, of economic resources.[7] Nevertheless it is possible to identify, even in a place which neither attained nor yet strove for self-governing independence, other characteristics which distinguish the small town from the village. The secular inhabitants of medieval Westminster evolved no elaborate set of institutions of their own to compete with those of the abbot. On the contrary, they lived under monastic rule without recorded protest. Yet despite their apparently restrictive circumstances, they developed, in response to neighbourhood issues of a markedly urban character, a large measure of corporate self-determination. Their achievement can be appreciated in two well

---

6. 'An Acte for the good Government of the Cyttie or Burroughe of Westmynster', 27 Eliz. cap. 31, *Statutes of the Realm*, iv (1819), 763–64. The situation in the early sixteenth century is conveniently described in a draft of a petition to parliament on this very subject, composed by the then abbot. Westminster Abbey Muniment (WAM) 6576.

7. M. D. Lobel, *The Borough of Bury St. Edmunds* (Oxford, 1935), 59–60, 123 and chapter iii, *passim*. See also, R. S. Gottfried, *Bury St. Edmunds and the Urban Crisis: 1290–1539* (Princeton, 1982), 167–80. For other examples of conflict, at Coventry, Reading and elsewhere, see N. M. Trenholme, *The English Monastic Boroughs* (University of Missouri Studies, ii(3), Columbia, 1927), *passim*.

recorded spheres of activity; the manorial system of local government, and the parish.

Before these two dimensions of local life are considered, a brief
characterisation of the district will explain what would appear, from
the traditional urbanists' point of view, to be its arrested constitutional development. First, the power of the lords was considerable.
The manor of Westminster had been given to the monks by King
Edgar in *c.* 960.[8] The territory granted stretched from the abbey
almost as far as the walls of London, and between the line of the
present Oxford Street and the River Thames.[9] After the settlement
of a dispute in 1222, this estate was reduced at its eastern limit; but
the area remaining to the abbey – the 'liberty' of Westminster – was
declared exempt from the ecclesiastical jurisdiction of the bishops
of London.[10] From the crown the abbots also acquired extensive
rights of secular government within the manor, in addition to those
attaching to lordship. Consequently by 1293 the abbot could claim
to exercise such royal prerogatives as judgement of pleas of the
crown, the view of frankpledge and the assize of bread and ale.[11]
On the other hand, by the thirteenth century at the latest all tenants
of the manor were enfranchised, a feature attractive to settlers which
the manor of Westminster shared, for example, with the City of
London.[12] But such institutions of local government as existed in
medieval Westminster belonged solely to the abbot, either as feudal
lord or else as the recipient of royal grants of power within his
demesne.

The concern of this essay is not, however, with the whole of the
manor but with its heart, the immediate vicinity of the abbey and
palace. From the late twelfth century, the period of the earliest surviving records, this area was distinguished from the rest of the estate
by its intensive development as a centre of accommodation both for

---

8. P. H. Sawyer, *Anglo-Saxon Charters. An Annotated List and Bibliography* (Royal
   Historical Society, London, 1968), no. 670. There accepted as a Saxon copy of
   a more or less genuine original. The impossible date it bears, 951, is usually
   corrected to 959, within Edgar's reign, on the grounds that Dunstan was bishop
   of London in that year. But Dunstan is in fact referred to in the charter as
   archbishop; so a date of 960 or later could be argued.
9. Cf. M. Gelling, 'The boundaries of the the Westminster charters', *Transactions
   of the London and Middlesex Archaeological Society*, new ser., xi (1953), 101–4.
10. *Acta Stephani Langton . . . 1207–1228*, ed. K. Major (Canterbury and York
    Society, I, 1950) 69–73; and see G. Saunders, 'Results of an enquiry concerning
    the situation and extent of Westminster, at various periods', *Archaeologia*, xxvi
    (1836), 223–41.
11. Sawyer, op. cit., no. 1127; *Calendar of Charter Rolls, 1226–57*, 208–9; ibid.,
    1257–1300, 238–39; *Placita de Quo Warranto* (Record Commission, 1818), 479.
12. There are no more than one or two references to tenurial services in the
    Westminster deeds of the thirteenth century (see n. 14), and none in the manor
    court rolls of the later period, discussed below.

employees of the departments of royal government which became gradually stabilised in the palace, and for the attendant community of victuallers and other suppliers.[13] The district was defined topographically by the two axes of King Street (the present Whitehall) and Tothill Street (still extant), which led respectively to the north and west from the abbey. The rentals and leases of the monastic landlords show how this area became densely built up.[14] Rapid settlement took place throughout the thirteenth century. A further busy phase of house building was concentrated in the 1370s and 1380s and was financed largely by the monks; but the fifteenth century records tell of decline, apparent in falling rents and empty properties. Towards 1500, however, these symptoms were reversed, and the activities of lay building speculators imply renewed pressure on housing. This impression of late medieval growth is strengthened by approximate population figures for the late fourteenth and for the mid sixteenth centuries. A total in 1377 of about 500 rose sixfold by 1548, to about 3000.[15] The evidence on which these figures are

13. On the centralisation of government in Westminster, see R. A. Brown, '"The treasury" of the later twelfth century', *Studies Presented to Sir Hilary Jenkinson*, ed. J. Conway Davies (1957), 35–49; T. F. Tout, 'The beginnings of a modern capital: London and Westminster in the fourteenth century', *Proceedings of the British Academy*, x (1923), 487–511.

14. There is a space here only for a summary account of the development of property in the vill, which is based upon a thorough study of rich materials among the Westminster Abbey Muniments. Among these are some two thousand deeds and leases relating to the vill, and dating from between the late twelfth and the early sixteenth centuries. They survive either as originals or, for the earlier period, transcribed into the fourteenth century cartulary known as the Westminster Domesday. The other invaluable source is the series of account rolls of the various monastic obedientiaries, of whom six derived a significant portion of their respective incomes from the lease of properties in the vill of Westminster. These were the sacrist, almoner and cellarer, and the wardens of the Lady chapel, of the 'new work' and of the 'rents of new purchase'. The earliest of these annual accounts date from the late thirteenth century; from the late fourteenth century until the Dissolution, the survival rate is good: approximately two-thirds in each case. The accounts contain both rentals and tallies of expenditure on the construction or maintenance of properties. By correlating these two sources, it has been possible to compile detailed tenement histories, and so to perceive general trends of settlement and occupation. For these various classes of documents, see the calendar of manuscripts in the Muniment Room.

15. The Middlesex (Ossulstone Hundred) poll tax return for 1377 is at Public Record Office (PRO), E179/141/23. Those taxed in the vill of Westminster, as distinct from other parts of the manor, numbered 280; this was supposed to be the total lay population aged fourteen or over. The chantry return is printed in *London and Middlesex Chantry Certificate 1548*, ed. C. J. Kitching (London Record Society, xvi, 1980), no. 139. The number of communicants entered in the return – supposedly the total population of St Margaret's parish (for which see below) aged fourteen and above – is 2500. Even if, as is very possible, the former figure is an under-assessment and the latter rounded up, the difference between the two is striking. *Author's additional note* (1990). The late fourteenth-century figure

based is subject to controversy, but the ratio between the two is valid as a broad indicator of a remarkable increase. The signs of recession during much of the fifteenth century suggest that the increase must have been largely concentrated in the late fifteenth and early sixteenth centuries. This expansion, moreover, far outstripped the contemporary growth of neighbouring parts of Middlesex (such as the district of the Strand, which also lay within the manor of Westminster), measured by the same evidence.[16] At the Dissolution the monks, whose vast estates made their house the second richest in the country, derived as much as twelve per cent of their total income from their rents collected in this part of the manor of Westminster alone.[17] Furthermore, this sector coincided in the later Middle Ages with the parish of St Margaret, which was itself sometimes defined, in contradistinction to the other parishes of the manor, as the 'vill' of Westminster.[18] Yet for all this, the neighbourhood possessed no jurisdictional rights of its own.

The second factor which operated against political change was the character of Westminster's economy. The settlement which grew up around the twin focus of the royal abbey and palace was almost entirely dependent upon the patronage of this dual market. A conspectus of the resident population can be compiled from the abbey's estate records and, at the end of the period, from wills.[19] Among the occupations named there is an overwhelming preponderance of such 'service' industries as hostelling and the retail of food and drink, tailoring, the building trades, and luxury crafts such as goldsmithing and book production. All relied upon a market whose peculiar characteristic was its unpredictability. For they catered not only to the monastery and to resident bureaucrats, but also to short-term visitors: pilgrims, lawyers and their clients, members of parliament and of the royal court. The cycles of the seasons and of markets affected all towns; but in this case the alternation between

proposed here is too low. In G. Rosser, *Medieval Westminster 1200–1540* (Oxford, 1989), pp. 167–8, the basis of the poll tax is shown to be misleading. On the basis of different evidence, a population estimate is advanced for 1407–8 of approximately 2000.

16. The comparative figures are set out in J. C. Russell, *British Medieval Population* (Albuquerque, 1948), 274–75.
17. B. F. Harvey, *Westminster Abbey and its Estates in the Middle Ages* (Oxford, 1977), 68–69, 332.
18. E.g. in a charter of 1393 cited by Saunders, 'Results', 236, 239. This document has since been lost, see E. P. Bailey, 'Notes upon the boundaries and jurisdictions of the city and liberties of Westminster' (1973), typescript circulated by the Executive Committee of the *Victoria County History of Middlesex*, n. 8. On the parish *per se*, see below.
19. See n. 14. About 150 Westminster wills of the period 1504–1540, registered in the Peculiar Court of Westminster, are preserved in the Westminster Public Library, Archives Department, in named volumes.

brief periods of prosperity and hardship was irregular, and the contrast more extreme. The dependence upon rich but erratic consumers hampered the development even of those 'service' industries which alone could survive in this economy. But having no reason to quarrel with their best customers, the local suppliers found no economic impulse to rebel against the seigneurial government. The diversity of trades represented in Westminster was greater than would be found in an agricultural village, by any definition of that term.[20] Yet there was no large-scale commerce or industrial specialisation, and no trade gilds evolved such as in other places generated their own momentum towards policy-making and local administration.[21] 'Les liges gentz de la ville de Weymonster' expressed their dependence in a petition of 1337 prompted by Edward III's removal of his administration to York:

> 'Come la dite ville', they protested, 'ne est citee, burgh (ne ville) marchaunde, et lour principal gayn et sustenance soleit estre del commun Bank et del Escheker et des altres places lorsque ils furent a Westmonstre . . . il soient del tut anyentiz et enpoveriz puis le departir la court de iloek.'[22]

Yet this plaint has also a more positive significance. The petition itself is a sign that the inhabitants of Westminster were capable of reaching and acting upon a collective decision on an issue which affected the neighbourhood as a whole. It indicates an awareness, on the part of its authors, of Westminster's peculiar status; neither a self-sufficient agrarian village, nor a permanent centre of trade or industry. This intermediate condition gave rise, in the course of the later Middle Ages, to a number of social problems with which the existing manorial system of jurisdiction was ill-equipped to deal. The situation was not unusual. Professor Hilton has described, as a common phenomenon, the manorial village disrupted by the appearance of urban features, which the traditional structure proved inadequate to control.[23] The proceedings of the manor court of Westminster largely exemplify this pattern. The records of the Westminster court also show, however, that in the later medieval period this assembly

20. Occupations in Westminster were, indeed, more varied than in many of the small towns discussed by Professor Hilton. R. H. Hilton, 'The small town as part of peasant society', *The English Peasantry in the Later Middle Ages* (Oxford, 1975), 76–94, esp. 80.
21. Trenholme, *Monastic Boroughs*, 91–2; Tait, *Medieval Borough*, 225–6; S. Reynolds, *An Introduction to the History of English Medieval Towns* (Oxford, 1977), 164–7.
22. PRO, SC 8/78/3889. The subsequent inquisition confirmed the justice of the claims that the vill relied heavily upon rents, and that it possessed hardly any arable land. PRO, C145/132/7.
23. Hilton, 'The small town', esp. 91.

was significantly modified, to admit of a degree of self-determination by the inhabitants.

As there were no servile tenants all were free of the court, which was convened annually, in June, by the seneschal or bailiff of the abbot.[24] The presentment of cases before these officers was made by a body of twelve tenants known as the 'chief pledges' (*capitales plegii*) of the vill. Although in theory appointed by the abbot, the chief pledges were far from being mere ciphers. The fact that their names begin to be fully recorded in the late fourteenth century, shortly after the series of extant court rolls begins, may indicate that their importance was growing at this period.[25] By the early sixteenth century at the latest – but probably from a much earlier date – they had become self-electing, to the abbot's expressed indignation.[26] On the basis of 126 names of chief pledges recorded between 1364 and 1514, they may be characterised as a distinguished body of local residents, always men of substance, though not confined to any particular trade or interest group. Royal courtiers and lawyers, innkeepers and bakers, carpenters, masons, chandlers and tailors all sat together on the court, which represented a fair cross-section of the activities pursued in medieval Westminster.[27] The chief pledges' official function was to indict transgressors against the customs of the manor and, so far as had been granted, the laws of the crown. But while they continued, under the lord's supervision, to impose and collect the amercements which were his usual profits of justice, the chief pledges began, of their own accord, to develop new means of law enforcement, and even to issue their own injunctions with regard to issues of general concern.

In the late fourteenth century, the chief pledges began to create

---

24. About 70 court rolls are extant from the period 1364–1514. A very small proportion of these rolls relates to meetings held around 1 November, which were similar to the evidently more important sessions of June. WAM 50699–777; and a stray at PRO, SC 2/191/66.
25. WAM 50705 *seq*.
26. See WAM 6576.
27. In a sample year, 1505 (WAM 50770), the jury was made up as follows (in order of seniority): Thomas Bough, gentleman usher of the king's exchequer (cf. Peculiar Court of Westminster (PCW), Wyks, pp. 220–2); Robert Stowell, master mason (see below, n. 71); Thomas Eton, innkeeper (cf. WAM 50770–6); Thomas Hogan, baker (cf. PCW, Wyks, pp. 242–8); William Yonge, victualler (cf. WAM 50760–70); Robert Morley, citizen and clothier of London (cf. PCW, Wyks, pp. 84–92); William Baynard, brewer (cf. WAM, Register Book 1, f. 141–141v); John Norreis, yeoman of Eybury (cf. WAM, Register Book I, ff. 64v–65); William Waller, brewer (cf. PCW Wyks, pp. 24–5); William Bate, stainer or butcher – or both (cf. WAM, Register Book 1, f. 150v; 50770); Quentin Poulet, librarian to King Henry VII (cf. PCW, Wyks, pp. 65–8); John Attwell, gentleman, chandler and groom of the cellar of Westminster Abbey (cf. PCW, Bracy, ff. 12v–15; WAM, Register Book II, ff. 199v, 264v).

new functionaries to assist in local administration. These minor officers, like the chief pledges themselves, were apparently unsalaried, and their proliferation testifies to a growing desire among the inhabitants to be involved in the running of local affairs. Pairs of ale-tasters are recorded from 1375, while constables, who also appear at about this date, multiplied during the following century until they numbered between twenty and thirty. Groups of these constables were allocated specific 'beats' within the manor, one being designated 'chief constable'.[28] In 1508 another department of local government was set up, that of the scavengers. Half a dozen of these 'city cleaning officers' were appointed annually, exclusively for the King Street and Tothill Street area.[29] This emerging system clearly reflects the influence of that which operated from a much earlier date within the City of London. There, the surviving wardmote returns for 1422 record an officialdom in each ward usually composed of a beadle, constables, scavengers and ale-conners; a hierarchy which was already old by the early fifteenth century.[30] The later-developing structure at Westminster remained more haphazard during the medieval period, but fulfilled some of the same functions.

From the early fifteenth century onwards, the court also occasionally instituted positive measures to order and improve the environment of the vill. A vital issue was that of drainage. The scouring of ditches is a pungent theme encountered in many medieval court records, but at Westminster, where the ground was low-lying and predominantly marshy, the subject was of fundamental importance. Every year's record contains a long list of blocked runnels, rivulets and pipes, causing 'annoyance' or worse, to be cleared on pain of fine. In 1491 the more positive step was taken to appoint a local commission of 'supervisors of the ditches of Westminster'.[31] A few years later eight of the chief pledges of the vill (describing themselves importantly as 'headboroughs' – latent 'burgesses'), in collaboration with the bailiff, jointly hired a ditcher to clean the watercourses of the neighbourhood. The Lambeth man who undertook the job complained of not receiving due payment; but the

28. WAM 50706 *seq.*
29. WAM 50773 *seq.*
30. *Calendar of Plea and Memoranda Rolls . . . of the City of London, 1413–37*, ed. A. H. Thomas (Cambridge, 1943), 116 and cf. p. xxx *seq.* C. M. Barron, 'The government of London and its relations with the crown 1400–1450' (Ph.D. thesis, London Univ., 1970), 40–8. Compare with Westminster the case of the unincorporated monastic town of Reading, where in the late fifteenth century the townspeople, complaining of bad government by the abbot's officers, unconstitutionally elected their own. Trenholme, *Monastic Boroughs*, 72–3.
31. WAM 50764.

significant fact here is the co-operative measure taken by the leading townsmen to maintain essential public works.[32]

Another recurrent topic of these summer meetings in Westminster was the control of local butchers. Butchers, like drains, were ubiquitous; but again, the scale of the problem at Westminster was unusual. Comparison may be made, for example, with the enrolled City of London wardmote presentments of 1422–23, or with the surviving original returns of a few decades later for Portsoken ward in London.[33] The sources of concern to these London courts were in general similar to those which preoccupied the chief pledges of Westminster. Worries about butchering, however, stand out in the Westminster records as a distinctive feature. The Westminster butchering trade was promoted by the London ordinance, passed in 1361, which banished slaughterhouses from the City; and it may have received further encouragement from the increased personal standards of living of those Londoners, greatly reduced in numbers, who survived the Black Death.[34] Each year, from the 1370s onwards, some half-dozen Westminster butchers were presented for the sale of unwholesome or overpriced meat.[35] Large-scale graziers were regularly summonsed for overcrowding the common pasture on Tothill with their animals, as was John Waryn in the 1380s; at this period Waryn bought fifty-seven oxen from the cellarer of Westminster Abbey, and he also held a lease on a flock of three hundred sheep belonging to the abbot.[36] Many other inhabitants of Westminster, whatever their primary occupations, invested in the meat market by keeping pigs, in quantities surely beyond the requirement of local consumption, and often beyond the tolerance of their neighbours. In 1407, for instance, nineteen individuals were charged with owning stray pigs which had been destroying gardens

32. PRO, C1/326/87. Datable to the chancellorship of Archbishop Wareham, 1504–15. The term 'hedborowis' was also used to describe the chief pledges by the early sixteenth century abbot who drafted the document cited in n. 6. The significance of this term, which is found elsewhere, was pointed out to me by Dr G. H. Martin.
33. *Cal. Plea and Mem. Rolls, 1413–37,* 115 *seq.,* 150 *seq.*; Corporation of London Record Office, Ward Presentments, Portsoken Ward, 5–22 Edw. IV, 23 Hen. VII (loc. ref. 242A).
34. See E. L. Sabine, 'Butchering in medieval London', *Speculum,* vii (1933), 335–53; C. M. Barron, 'The quarrel of Richard II with London 1392–7', *The Reign of Richard II,* ed. F. R. H. Du Boulay and C. M. Barron (1971), 173–201, esp. 175–6.
35. WAM 50712 *seq.*
36. WAM 50718; 18866–7, 18869; 5984. A notice of proceedings in 1523, at the end of the period, lists seven butchers and others who had overcharged the common, in each case, with between four and twenty-three beasts. WAM 50778.

and purportedly devouring geese and other poultry; one of the accused, Simon Bellringer, kept as many as twenty pigs, as well as two
sheep.[37] Butchering was, moreover, associated with offensive sub-
sidiary processes and with related industries which, although never
practised extensively in Westminster, could be noxious. A tailor was
fined in 1422 for having sub-let his land to butchers who were using
it as a tip for their offal.[38] In the same year one of a number of
local tanners was accused of fouling the Clowson stream, which ran
through the vill, with rotting skins.[39] In the absence of gild controls,
the chief pledges of the court coped with these environmental
problems as best they could. From about 1400, there begin to appear
at the foot of some of the court rolls the texts of innovative ordinances drawn up and agreed by those attending. A number of these
injunctions relate to butchering. The careful penning of animals was
the subject of decrees issued in 1422 and twice more in the 1480s.[40]
In 1505, the times were stipulated when butchers might dispose of
offal and carcasses; this was only to be allowed between 8 p.m. and
6 a.m. in winter, and 10 p.m. and 3 a.m. in summer.[41]

Other matters of concern to the court were less peculiar to
Westminster, but were also problems associated with a distinctively
urban, not a rural, environment. Housing regulations, for example,
became increasingly necessary as the vill was more densely built up.
Encroachments upon the street or upon the common pasture were
a frequent source of complaint.[42] So too were dangerous premises,
roofed with straw or containing a wooden chimney.[43] The hostelling
and related trades which were particularly characteristic of medieval
Westminster also received constant attention. In addition to the
large numbers of innkeepers, brewers and bakers presented in the
Westminster court, there were many cooks, some of whom cluttered
King Street with their stalls and open hearths.[44] Another profession
which troubled the court was the prostitution which clearly
flourished in this particularly male-dominated neighbourhood of
royal officers, parliament-men and clerics. The business was not

---

37. WAM 50738.
38. WAM 50745.
39. Ibid.
40. WAM 50745, 50760–1.
41. WAM 50770. Fishmongers were to be subject to the same restrictions.
42. E.g. WAM 50758, 50760.
43. E.g. WAM 50760.
44. E.g. WAM 50718 (1386); 50745 (1422, William Cros obstructed the street with
a 'rostyngherthe'). See *London Lickpenny*, verse 8, ed. E. P. Hammond, *English
Verse between Chaucer and Surrey* (Durham, N. Carolina, 1927), 238–9. The
court also made stipulations about the quality of bread in 1488, and about the
price of victuals in 1494. WAM 50761, 50767.

regulated here as it was in the Bankside stews of Southwark.[45] The Westminster authorities' only resort, apart from the usual innocuous fine, was to expel undesirables from the vill, a measure employed in periodic bouts of reforming zeal.[46]

There are, therefore, ample indications that the leading residents of Westminster were conscious of some of the specific problems arising from their changing environment, as, indeed, it was only natural that they should be. Their positive attempts to regulate public amenities, trades and the social order reflect a developing sense of communal interests and purpose. They managed to introduce new measures, appropriate to developments taking place in the late medieval town, into the customary jurisdiction of the manor. At the same time, however, the endless repetition of charges which characterises the series of court records demonstrates the limitations of the authorities' powers to enforce their injunctions. By the same token there was no system of local taxation, and therefore no common fund. For this reason local pride did not find expression in major public works, such as the construction of a town hall. But there were other means, outside the framework of the manorial administration, by which a sense of communal urban identity could be realised. A separate context for sociable activity was found in the organisation of the parish.

St Margaret's parish originally encompassed the entire manor of Westminster.[47] Its size was reduced, however, by the creation of new parishes, and from *c.* 1300 onwards it coincided in area with the central portion of the manor here under discussion.[48] The parish church was probably first built, within the precinct of the abbey, in the late eleventh century.[49] But in the decades around 1200, the abbey church of St Peter seems still to have represented the spiritual focus of the neighbourhood. The monastery's popularity at that time is shown by the donations made during the first phase of the Gothic rebuilding of the abbey. Of the many recorded benefactions, a large proportion came from local residents in return for the prayers of the monks.[50] The parishioners abruptly withdrew their support, how-

45. J. B. Post, 'A fifteenth-century customary of the Southwark stews', *Journal of the Society of Archivists*, v (1974–7), 418–28.

46. Thirty-one people said to be 'ill-governed of their bodies' were thus driven out from the franchise in 1508. WAM 50773.

47. See the decree of 1222 cited in n. 10.

48. Saunders, 'Results', 236–9. St Martin-in-the-Fields parish was in existence by *c.* 1300. See Westminster Domesday (WAM, Book 11), ff. 562v–563.

49. The earliest reference to the church occurs in a grant of Abbot Herbert (1121 – *c.* 1136). WAM 3435; British Library, Cart. Harl. 84 F.46. But there was a fourteenth-century tradition at Westminster that a church had been built by Edward the Confessor. Westminster Liber Niger (WAM, Book I), f.76v; and see H. F. Westlake, *St Margaret's, Westminster* (1914), 3–4.

50. Copies of these donations fill many pages of the Westminster Domesday. They included numerous gifts of land and rents in the vicinity of the abbey.

ever, after the project was taken over by King Henry III in 1245.[51] The royal connection, which hereafter tended to exclude more humble contributors, may have encouraged a shift of popular interest to the parish church. This change of affections was also related to a general transference of patronage away from the old Benedictine houses.[52] When, in the late fourteenth century, the Westminster monks resumed the reconstruction of the nave of their abbey church at their own expense, they were able to raise intermittent contributions from the crown, but practically none from the local community; consequently the work dragged on for a century and a half.[53] The great rebuilding of the parish church of St Margaret around 1500 presents a vivid contrast.[54] The church which stands today was begun in *c.* 1487 and was complete by 1523. The cost was divided unequally between the parish, which initiated the work and paid for the new nave and two aisles in their entirety, and the monks who, as rector, financed the completion of the choir. The abbey's expenses amounted to £160; those of the parishioners to some £2000.[55] The methods by which this vast sum was raised show how efficiently the parishioners could co-operate in such a major undertaking.

Whereas the ordinary annual receipts of the churchwardens, from offerings and bequests, were about £25 in this period, the most active years of the rebuilding produced dramatic increases in the parochial income. The average annual total doubled once in 1498–1502 to *c.* £50, and again in the following two years to £110. During the rebuilding of the tower, between 1516 and 1522, the yearly re-

51. An impression derived from a reading of the Westminster Domesday, and confirmed by the historian of the royal work, who remarks, 'of private benefaction there is very little evidence'. H. M. Colvin, ed., *The History of the King's Works*, i (H.M.S.O, 1963), 130, 135.

52. Cf. Harvey, *Estates*, 42. The changing trend of patronage in an urban environment, that of Norwich, has been described by Alan Carter in a paper read to the Conference on Pre-Modern Urban History held at the Institute of Historical Research, London, on 5 Dec. 1981. The great period of benefaction and building of the religious houses of Norwich was over by 1380; after that date the direction of lay patronage shifted almost entirely to the parish churches.

53. R. B. Rackham, 'The nave of Westminster', *Proceedings of the British Academy*, iv (1909–10), 33–96; the overall distribution of the cost is set out on p. 91. Non-royal secular contributions supplied barely 1.5% of the total.

54. The major source is the churchwardens' accounts (CWA) 1460–1540 (of which period 14 years' accounts are missing), Westminster Public Library, Archives Department, MSS E.1 (1460 *seq.*), E.2 (1510 *seq.*), E.3 (1530 *seq.*). (Only the first volume is paginated.) On the present fabric, see *Royal Commission on Historical Monuments: London*, ii (H.M.S.O., 1925), 99–104 and pls. 149–52; N. Pevsner, *The Building of England: London*, i (1973 edn.), 493–5.

55. For the former figure, see WAM 23602. The latter is an estimate; the incompleteness of the accounts for a few busy years of the rebuilding prevents an exact addition of the expenses.

venue fluctuated between £110 and the impressive peak of £190.[56] Every single parishioner was a benefactor of 'the church work', from a waterman, who gave 20d., to a London clothier living at Westminster, who contributed 20s.[57] The donors included many of the craftsmen employed on the site. The master mason of the tower, Henry Redman, each year returned his entire wage to the church-wardens, as also did the local brewer who organised the carriage of building materials.[58] Fund-raising activities were arranged, such as parish lotteries and a children's 'May game'.[59] But the most telling scene was occasioned in 1522–23, by the finding of the new steeple bells. After three bells had been cast out of the old set, and a fourth had been presented collectively by a fraternity maintained within the parish, dedicated to the Virgin Mary's Assumption, there still lacked one to complete the peal. To provide this, the churchwardens made a collection, 'in goyng abowhgt the paryshe', of a great number of pewter pots, latten basins and the like, which were then delivered to the founder for casting. So much potential bell-metal was accumulated that the surplus was sold for cash. When the new bells were hung at last, in 1527–28, the first peal to be rung upon them, from the gleaming white tower in the heart of the vill, celebrated a genuinely communal achievement.[60]

Another manifestation of this spirit of community was the formation by the parishioners of religious gilds. An early Westminster gild, recorded in the thirteenth century, was responsible for ringing the bells in the abbey; but the weight of the evidence suggests that this form of neighbourhood fellowship grew in popularity *pari passu* with the parish church itself, towards the end of the Middle Ages.[61] One such gild was founded in the late fourteenth century, and eight more made their first recorded appearance before 1520.[62] Of course, religious fraternities were not an exclusively urban phenomenon.

56. CWA *sub annis*.
57. CWA (1460–1510), pp. 308, 548.
58. CWA (1510–30), *passim*. The brewer, John Pomfrett, rented the Lamb Inn in King Street. WAM 19768–807; Register Book II, f. 26–26v.
59. CWA, *sub annis* 1502–3, 1503–4, 1516–17, 1518–19; see also Westlake, *St Margaret's*, 168.
60. CWA, *sub annis* 1522–23, 1527–28.
61. For the bell-ringers' gild, see WAM 3455; Westminster Domesday, f. 183; *Calendar of Patent Rolls, 1247–58*, 403. Lack of evidence may conceal the existence of other such early gilds.
62. The nine gilds recorded after 1385 were dedicated, respectively, to St Mary of Rounceval, the Assumption of the Virgin Mary, the Holy Trinity, St Cornelius, St George, St John the Baptist, St Christopher, St Anne and Corpus Christi. For the first two, see below. For the last, see notebook accounts of the curate of St Margeret's *c.* 1514; 'Item payd to corpus xp̄i brethered. 4d.'; it seems probable that the brotherhood mentioned was based in Westminster. WAM 33300, f. 18 For the remainder, see CWA, *passim*.

They may, however, have had particular relevance to a society which faltered at a stage between that of an agricultural village and that of a self-governing town, and which therefore lacked constitutional means of self-definition. This suggestion can be considered in the light of some rare accounts relating to two of the Westminster gilds.

The leading Westminster gild was that of the Assumption of the Virgin Mary. This, 'the great brotherhood of Our Blessed Lady', is first documented in 1431, evidently not long after its foundation.[63] The motives of the founders are unrecorded, but the extant accounts, of the late fifteenth and early sixteenth centuries, provide evidence of its nature and activities.[64] The price of admission to the gild was 6s. 8d., and subscription thereafter was probably, as in other gilds, about 1s. a year.[65] Membership figures are not provided in the records, but if the rate of quarterage was typical, the total annual sums collected of £8 or £10 would indicate a body of subscribers approaching two hundred; a sizeable association in a parish of three thousand souls.[66] Its social range was limited; the membership fee was inevitably a restricting factor. But the gild officers fairly reflected the spectrum of careers pursued in the vill; and the gild as a whole included humbler, if not the very humblest, representatives of all these activities. Women, too, who were excluded from the trade gilds which existed in some towns, could belong to religious fraternities, and their participation was natural in a gild of the Virgin Mary. Sisters of the gild watched over the body of a departed member; sewed liveries and prepared dishes for the triennial gild feast; made or donated vestments for use at gild services; or simply left money 'to be prayed for' by their fellow members.[67] Indeed, the primary advantage of membership, for the initiates of this as of all parish gilds, was the benefit of intercessory masses, celebrated in the gild chapel in the parish church, for the souls of departed brethren, and the prospect of a speedier release from Purgatory into

63. WAM 18890: the reference is to a quitrent owing from the gild. Royal licence for the constitution of the gild was obtained in 1440. *Calendar of Palent Rolls, 1436–41*, 448. Richard Willy, gentleman of Westminster and yeoman of the crown, who died between 1468 and 1471, was later said to have been 'one of the founders' of the gild, which could not, in that case, have been instituted long before 1431. *Calendar of Close Rolls, 1468–76*, 33; *Calendar of Palent Rolls, 1467–77*, 281; CWA (1460–1510), 555.

64. Accounts of the gild 1474–77, 1487–90, 1505–8, 1518–21, bound together with records of the gild of St Mary Rounceval, are in Westminster Abbey Muniment Room, unnumbered.

65. *Parish Fraternity Register, Fraternity of the Holy Trinity and SS. Fabian and Sebastian in the Parish Church of St Botolph without Aldersgate* ed. P. Basing (London Record Society, xviii, 1982), xvii.

66. See n. 15.

67. Gild accounts, *passim*; will of Cecily Selly, 1472, PRO, 16 Wattys.

Heaven.[68] But while the religious inspiration of the gilds undoubtedly remained fundamental, their social role has perhaps not yet been fully appreciated.[69]

The importance of the Westminster gild of St Mary's Assumption is reflected in the distinction of its rulers. The appointment of a master and two wardens took place at intervals of three years.[70] From the period between 1440 and 1545, the names of sixty-one different masters and wardens of the gild are recorded. These officers were invariably drawn from the élite of local society. The mastership itself was never reached except via preceding stages of public life, which commonly included a term as warden. Moreover, almost every known master or warden was a member of the jury of chief pledges in the court of Westminster. For example, the master in 1499–1502 was Robert Stowell, a celebrated mason who had been master of the works at Westminster Abbey since 1471, and who was almost certainly responsible for the design of the new parish church of Westminster, then in process of building. In addition to a term as warden of St Mary's gild in 1490–93, Stowell's credentials included his membership of the local court since 1488 and experience as chief constable of Westminster in 1489–90. He had also invested extensively in local property, and himself apparently resided in a large house within the abbey sanctuary called 'St Albans'. The gild mastership, conferred shortly before Stowell's death in 1505, was the climax of a distinguished public career in the town.[71] Another typical case was George Lorde, the master in 1521–24; an usher of the royal exchequer and a purveyor of the king's works. Lorde's property at this period was valued at £40. He had been a local constable for King Street in 1509, and was subsequently a chief pledge of the court from 1513. Thereafter, he was prominent not only in the great gild of Our Lady but also in the Westminster gild of St Mary of Rounceval, of which he was a warden in 1520–22. He survived until 1533, when he was buried in the gild chapel of the Virgin's Assumption in the parish church , 'before my pewe there'.[72]

---

68. The gild employed no less than three permanent chantry priests.
69. The existing general accounts are *English Gilds*, ed. Toulmin Smith (Early English Text Society, xl, 1870), introduction by L. Brentano; H. F. Westlake, *The Parish Gilds of Mediaeval England* (1919); G. Unwin, *The Gilds and Companies of London* (1908, 3rd edn. 1983), chapter ix. See most recently Basing, *Parish Fraternity Register*.
70. Probably 'the old masters chose the new'; compare ibid., 3 (no. 15).
71. Gild accounts; WAM 50761–70; 17809; 23535–47; 19720–49; PCW, Wyks, pp. 14b, 43–5. See also J. H. Harvey, *English Medieval Architects. A Biographical Dictionary down to 1550* (1954), 153; E. Roberts, 'Robert Stowell', *Journal of the British Archaeological Association*, 3rd ser., xxxv (1972), 24–38.
72. Gild accounts; WAM 12366; *King's Works*, iii (I), 407; PRO, E179/238/98; WAM 50774, 50776; PCW, Bracy, ff. 28v, 35–35v; CWA, *sub anno* 1533–4, week 14.

These instances could readily be multiplied. Their common pattern shows that the mastership of the gild represented the peak of advancement in the secular society of the vill. The important standing of the gild in the neighbourhood may be compared with that of such prominent urban gilds of the period as those of the Holy Trinity at Coventry and of St George at Norwich.[73] Indeed, in the sphere of local politics, a proportionately greater importance attached to the Westminster fraternity in the absence of a sophisticated system of local government such as existed in those other towns. A closer parallel with Westminster is found at Cirencester, where the townsmen, frustrated in an abortive attempt to gain independence from the abbot's jurisdiction in 1343, created an alternative forum for the expression of communal feeling in the new gild of Holy Trinity.[74] Like their counterparts in Cirencester, the leading officers of the gild of St Mary of Westminster were precisely those individuals and families who, in an independent borough, would have occupied the chief posts in the ruling council.

A further comparison may be drawn with the gilds of sixteenth-century Venice.[75] Like the English parish gilds, the five or six *Scuole Grandi* at Venice were lay associations, whose religious practices closely resemble those of their smaller English counterparts. But these institutions also, in the first half of the sixteenth century, provided an arena for the playing of politics by citizens who were constitutionally debarred from such activities in the oligarchical Venetian government.[76] The opportunities for political factionalising were equally limited, although for different reasons, in late medieval Westminster. Yet, as the governmental capital of the realm, Westminster was hardly a political backwater, and the royal officers and lawyers who were so prominent in the neighbourhood were not such men as would be indifferent to the advantages of status and its concomitant influence. The gild of the Virgin's Assumption, to judge from the composition of its leadership, functioned as an outlet for such aspirations.

The gild commanded considerable wealth. From 1474, the year of the earliest surviving account, its income amounted to some £80

---

73. C. V. Phythian-Adams, *Desolation of a City: Coventry and the Urban Crisis of the Late Middle Ages* (Cambridge, 1979), 120; *Records of the Gild of St George in Norwich, 1389–1547*, ed. M. Grace (Norfolk Record Society, ix, 1937), esp. 12–13.
74. E. A. Fuller, 'Cirencester; the manor and the town', *Transactions of the Bristol and Gloucestershire Archaeological Society*, ix (1884–5), 298–344, esp. 329. A similar role was performed by the parish gilds of Bury St Edmunds. Gottfried, *Bury St Edmunds*, 186–92.
75. B. Pullan, *Rich and Poor in Renaissance Venice. The Social Institutions of a Catholic State, to 1620* (Oxford, 1971).
76. Ibid., 99–131.

a year. Half of this sum was composed of revenues from lands and about ten tenements in Westminster; the remainder was made up of offerings and membership fees. In addition to the commemoration of the dead, subscribers participated in regular social events, the details of which go far to explain the gild's popularity. The chief of these occurred just once in every three years, on the anniversary of the Virgin's Assumption (15 August), when all members of the gild assembled at the great house in King Street of the archbishop of York, which was graciously made available for the occasion, for a spectacular 'general feast'. The hall was hung with decorations, and servants were dressed in liveries of Our Lady, bearing Her Lily. Members of the gild were provided with gilt badges of the fraternity to wear, and with garlands made of crimson velvet, lined with blue silk. Music was supplied by a band of minstrels, and actors performed 'a play'. The food and drink, as at any successful medieval banquet, surpassed description.[77]

Meanwhile, the fraternity did not restrict all its benefits to its own members. The distribution of alms at gild obits was standard practice; but of more particular interest is the society's maintenance of a small row of almshouses in Westminster, in a lane opening off King Street known as Our Lady's Alley.[78] Throughout the period for which records are extant, four cottages here were reserved for poor people of the parish, who were not members of the gild. In addition to their lodgings, these individuals received an allowance of 6s.8d. each quarter from gild funds. Both men and woman were helped in this way. Those whose effects were recorded at their deaths were certainly poor; in 1505, the gild beadle sold the belongings of Joan Margery, late an 'almesse woman of our lady', for 7s.; and in 1515–18 Margaret Rogers and Mother Laurence, 'bedewomen', left sums of 12s. 2½d. and 43s. 4d., respectively.[79] Unlike the similar, and often much larger, institutions supported elsewhere by private benefactors or (as in London) by livery companies, the interest of the cottages in Our Lady's Alley is that they were a community concern, organised by members of the parish acting as a body.[80]

Further evidence of this kind is provided by another of the Westminster gilds, which ran the small 'hospital', or almshouse, of St Mary Rounceval beside Charing Cross. The hospital had been

77. Westlake, *St Margaret's*, 54–7, prints in part the expenses of the feast of 1490 (*sic*).
78. The alley belonged to the gild as early as 1431, although the name is not given at that date. Cf. n. 63.
79. Gild accounts, *sub annis*.
80. Contrast, for example, the Whittington almshouse in London, the collaborative foundation of a rich individual and the Company of Mercers. J. Imray, *The Charity of Richard Whittington* (1968).

founded, as the dependency of a Spanish priory, in the thirteenth century.[81] As an alien house, however, it fell victim to royal appropriation in 1379.[82] In 1385, by a dramatic turn of fortune, it was adopted by the local inhabitants, who formed within it a religious fraternity.[83] By the early sixteenth century, this had become almost as popular and active a gild as that of the Virgin's Assumption. Records extant from the 1520s and 1530s testify to a membership of two hundred or more, served by two full-time chantry priests, and to an income of about £45 a year.[84] The masters and wardens of the Rounceval gild were drawn from the same local élite as were those of the fraternity of the Virgin's Assumption; and it was characteristic of their self-esteem that the leading lights of the Rounceval association formed a 'head council' of twenty-four.[85] The establishment which they supported might best be described as a hostel for the infirm or dying, especially those who were destitute. Of elaborate medical care there is no evidence; but inmates were provided with a bed (there were nine or ten in all), clean linen, basic hygienic facilities and maintenance at a standard rate of 1d. a day.[86] The numbers of those taken in to the hospital in the years recorded were small; a total of ten, for example, in the whole accounting year 1521–22. Moreover, it seems that only men were admitted. A large proportion were already at death's door when they arrived, and after a few days were duly buried in the churchyard of the Rounceval hospital. Those admitted in the early 1520s included 'John Foster that lay in the street', who lay sick for two days; two priests, one of whom was ill and remained for three weeks; a Scotsman called Thomas a Ley, who died after two days; an anonymous Dutchman; and an equally unknown soldier.[87] The poor clerics, the migrant foreigners and the discharged soldier may be taken to represent three elements in the drifting population of sixteenth century London, each of which found this small portion of relief at the Rounceval gild hospital in Westminster.

At least one of the remaining seven parish gilds, that of St Cor-

81. *Calendar of Charter Rolls, 1226–57*, 167–8.
82. See PRO, C 44/11/8. See also J. Galloway, *The Hospital and Chapel of Saint Mary Roncevall at Charing Cross* (1913). The gild records were unknown to Galloway.
83. See PRO, C 47/42/212. A fresh charter of foundation was secured in 1475. *Calendar of Patent Rolls, 1467–77*, 542.
84. Accounts of the gild 1520–4, 1538–40 (see n. 64).
85. See expenses for the year 1521–2. Also described as the 'stablisshers' (1523–4).
86. Nine tapestry-work bed-covers were bought in 1523–24: ten pairs of sheets were disposed of at the Dissolution in 1539–40. Other facilities included a 'buckyng tub' (for washing linen), a 'rinsing tub' and a 'pissing tub'. Gild accounts, *passim*. Among bequests to the house was that of Anthony Leigh, who in 1518 left 66s. 8d. for the purchase of sheets, blankets and shirts. PCW, Wyks, pp. 260–5.
87. Gild accounts, *sub annis* 1520–2.

nelius, was likewise endowed with local property whereby it maintained its own hospital. This institution, whose existence is recorded in Cardinal Wolsey's time, was more specialised than the last-mentioned, being 'an hospytall for the relyef of them that have ye fallynge sykenes' (i.e. epilepsy). Twice in the early sixteenth century, the churchwardens of St Margaret's recorded the burial of former inmates of St Cornelius' hospital at the parish church.[88]

It has been said that medieval methods of charitable welfare failed and 'withered', long before the Reformation ended them.[89] This was evidently not, however, the case in Westminster. The social relief provided by the gilds suggests potential developments along communal lines, which were arguably cut off prematurely by the Dissolution of the chantries.[90] Natalie Zemon Davis has described how, in the Catholic city of Lyon in the 1530s, a centralised and efficient welfare organisation was first set up by some of the citizens. Their action parallels that of the inhabitants of Westminster who founded, on a proportionately reduced scale, the various almshouses there.[91] This development, as Professor Davis shows, had little to do with contemporary changes in religious attitudes towards poverty and alms-giving associated with the Protestant conscience, but was rather a practical response to the challenges of a growing population, food supplies and communal health.[92] Even more than some of the relief programmes of great medieval city governments, the Westminster almshouses exhibit a *communal* approach to social problems.

The community of Westminster at the end of the Middle Ages was evidently prosperous, expanding and increasingly self-confident. The rebuilt parish church is standing testimony to this wealth and vitality, while the little almshouses represent a collective attempt to relieve some of the harsher consequences of a growing population. Moreover, economic conditions apart, this was a sophisticated neighbourhood, whose proximity to the royal court and London gave it a cultivated and cosmopolitan air. For example, residents of Westminster were among the first to own some of the new printed

---

88. For the property, see PRO, C 1/807/41–3. For the hospital, see Oxford, Bodleian Library, Gough Gen. Top. 364, p. 661; CWA, *sub annis* 1526 ('Joan of St Cornelius' house'), 1531 ('Philip at St Cornelius' hospital'). See also *Calendar of Letters and Papers, Henry VIII,* i, no. 5101.
89. W. K. Jordan, *Philanthropy in England, 1480–1660* (1959), 55–6, 146–7.
90. After the Reformation, the development of effective poor relief in Westminster was delayed until the seventeenth century. See the forthcoming Oxford Univ. D. Phil. thesis of T. V. Hitchcock on poor relief in general.
91. N. Z. Davis, 'Poor relief, humanism and heresy', *Society and Culture in Early Modern France* (1975), 17–64.
92. Ibid., 59. Compare S. Brigden, 'The early Reformation in London, 1520–47: the conflict in the parishes' (Ph.D. thesis, Cambridge Univ., 1978), 354–63.

books, produced on William Caxton's Westminster press from 1476.[93] The music which accompanied services in St Margaret's church was equally modern, due to the innovatory influence of the royal chapel choir. The singers of St Stephen's chapel made regular visits to the parish church, no doubt performing there some of the new polyphonic music composed by its members.[94] An interest in education, anticipating by several decades the Protestant emphasis upon learned preaching, was evinced by a prosperous tailor of Westminster, William Jarden, who in 1482 gave to Queen's College, Oxford, his Tothill Street inn called the Catherine Wheel.[95] By one of the conditions of this bequest, the provost and masters of the college undertook to find a scholar priest who would pray perpetually for the souls of William Jarden and his wife, and who would travel to Westminster once a year, to 'preach to the people the word of God' in St Margaret's church. Such general, not merely individual, exposure to and interest in books, contemporary music and learned sermons bears further witness to the liveliness of the community. This picture of Westminster in the late Middle Ages differs markedly from accounts of certain other English towns, which appear to have been simultaneously suffering deep decline.[96] Amid the current debate on English urban fortunes in this period, the case of Westminster may suggest a principle that every town was unique, and deserves particular study before comparisons are drawn.[97]

Westminster does, however, raise interesting questions about the nature of medieval towns in general. Historians, starting from legal criteria, have preferred to talk about those places classified as 'boroughs' in the documents, and have been led into extensive debate as to the precise definition of 'borough status'.[98] The evidence of Westminster, however, suggests that excessive importance

---

93. H. M. Nixon, 'Caxton, his contemporaries and successors in the book trade from Westminster documents', *The Library*, 5th ser., xxxi (1976), 305–26.

94. CWA, *passim*; H. C. Baillie, 'London churches, their music and musicians, 1485–1560' (Ph.D. thesis Cambridge Univ., 1958), 17 and *passim*.

95. Oxford, Bodleian Library, MS. D. D. Queen's Coll. 1766.

96. See, for instance, Phythian-Adams, *Coventry*; D. M. Palliser, *Tudor York* (Oxford, 1979), 201–25.

97. For example, in the Cheapside area of the nearby City of London, recovery from a fifteenth-century recession was not felt until the later sixteenth century, according to the initial findings of Dr Derek Keene's Social and Economic Study of Medieval London (personal communication). For the historical debate, see, notably, R. B. Dobson, 'Urban decline in late medieval England', *Transactions of the Royal Historical Society*, 5th ser., 27 (1977), 1–22; S. H. Rigby, 'Urban decline in the later Middle Ages', *Urban History Yearbook* (1979), 46–59; A. Dyer, 'Growth and decay in English towns, 1500–1700', ibid., 60–72; S. Reynolds, 'Decline and decay in late medieval towns', *Urban History Yearbook* (1980), 76–8.

98. See n. 2.

has been attached to constitutional definitions, and not enough to other aspects of urban life. Crowded, heterogeneous and cosmopolitan, by the thirteenth century the society of Westminster had lost, if it had ever enjoyed, the innate solidarity of the village. During the later Middle Ages the vill contained elements widely diverse in wealth and occupation and yet did not, for reasons which have been indicated, produce a constitutional system of government whereby this large and disparate population might be organised. But the development of a sense of community was not dependent upon the existence of such administrative structures. The inhabitants of Westminster, as has been seen, found other means to express their common interest in neighbourhood issues. Though they lacked wide powers of legislation, they partially adapted the manor court to serve their own public ends. Meanwhile, they created more effective means of collective action, and at the same time satisfied a need for mutual support in a changing environment, by the formation of parochial fraternities. Their determination to co-operate was illustrated most impressively in the total rebuilding of their parish church, at the enormous and shared cost of all. It was shown once again when in 1549 Protector Somerset attempted to pull the church down, to provide stone for the building of Somerset House in the Strand:

> The workmen had no sooner advanced their scaffolds when the parishioners gathered together in great multitudes, with bows and arrows, staves and clubs, and other such offensive weapons, which so terrified the workmen that they ran away in great amazement, and never could be brought again upon that employment.[99]

The parish church, indeed, seems to have occupied that central place in the life and affections of the vill which was held in other communities by a town hall. More than any institutional feature, it is the sense of community reflected in these various activities which distinguishes successful town life. If nineteenth century historians were naturally and legitimately concerned with constitutional aspects, their successors of the present day might well choose to focus attention upon the qualities of community which were of the essence of medieval urban society.

Editorial suggestion for further reading

Rosser, G. *Medieval Westminster 1200–1540* (Oxford, 1989).

99. P. Heylyn, *The History of the Reformation* (1661; Cambridge, 1849 edn.), i, 151.

Chapter Twelve

CEREMONY AND THE CITIZEN: THE COMMUNAL YEAR AT COVENTRY, 1450–1550

Charles Phythian-Adams

from P. Clark and P. Slack (eds), *Crisis and Order in English Towns*, 1500–1700 (London, 1972)

This was the first serious study of urban ritual in medieval England. It was of the greatest significance that its author brought to the subject a knowledge of the literature and methodology both of folklore studies and of anthropology. The former emphasized the rural roots of many urban ceremonies and festivities; the latter provided, from comparative studies of different cultures, model explanations of the ways in which public ritual may operate to defuse tension and to reaffirm the rightness of the existing order. A feature of the approach adopted here is the assumption that formalized behaviour of this kind serves the function of perpetuating the society in which it is observed; that, indeed, ritual is designed to preserve the status quo. *There exists, however, room for debate on this question. Although civic ceremonial in the Middle Ages was orchestrated by town rulers, they could not effectively claim a monopoly on the interpretation of public processions, games or plays: the meaning of such events might appear differently to different participants. Though these occasions were designed to flatter the self-importance of the ruling group, their often explicit celebration of the urban 'community' publicised a less elitist view of town society. Moreover, the ritual cycle of late medieval Coventry was perhaps not so completely subordinated to the requirements of the city government as is implied by the hypothesis of a division of the year into 'ritual' and 'secular' halves. While the hypothesis is clearly correct in parts, so important a communal feast as All Saints fell (on 1 November) squarely into the allegedly 'secular' half of the year. The importance of ritual was, arguably, not that it operated as a safety mechanism to protect the urban hierarchy, but that it brought together the different members of town society in events which provided a focus and a common language for debate about the true identity of the town. Charles Phythian-Adams has himself shown, in a more extended study of Coventry, that the ritual hierarchy observed in processions could be adjusted as a result of changes in the relative economic status of different groups within the city. Ceremony was not exclusively a conservative force in medieval urban society.*

For urban communities in particular, the middle and later years of the sixteenth century represented a more abrupt break with the past than any period since the era of the Black Death or before the age of industrialization. Not only were specific customs and institutions brusquely changed or abolished, but a whole, vigorous variegated popular culture, the matrix of everyday life, was eroded and began to perish. At the very heart of social activity, before these changes were effected, lay the repetitive annual pattern of ceremonies and cognate observances peculiar to each local community. An enquiry into the contemporary relevance of such practices as a whole for a particular urban society may, therefore, help to promote a wider acknowledgement of the magnitude of the subsequent shift in the social and cultural environment.

Accordingly, this exploratory analysis will seek first to demonstrate some simple congruities between Coventry's late medieval social structure (that relatively enduring but adaptable framework of institutionalized positions and connective relationships) and its ceremonial or ritualized expression in action, in time – with respect to the local calendar – and on the ground. It will then become possible, secondly, to establish the extent and nature (rather than the social effects) of the subsequent change by briefly charting the rapid disintegration of what had once evidently formed a coherent ceremonial pattern.

Methodologically, such an approach is only possible if the evidence for unquestionably perennial customs may be extracted from a wide period. Here, however, in that minority of cases where the documentation is not contemporary, the evidence of survivals has not been trusted after 1640, and earlier justification for its use has always been sought where possible. While this reconstruction seems broadly appropriate to the century from 1450 to 1550, known structural modifications therein have had to be sacrificed at the altar of brevity. The picture probably remains truest for the generation living between 1490 and 1520 when the surviving evidence is peculiarly rich, and before the tempo of social change had been accelerated by the final collapse of the city's medieval economy.[1]

1. I am particularly grateful to Professor W. G. Hoskins under whose sympathetic aegis this investigation was begun while the author was Research Fellow in English Local History at the University of Leicester between 1966 and 1968; to Messrs A. A. Dibben, D. J. H. Smith and colleagues for multifarious assistance far in excess of their statutory duties; and to the Company of Cappers and Feltmakers of Coventry for permission to study their earliest account book. A

Since the citizens of Coventry themselves were convinced that ceremonial proceedings like the Corpus Christi procession and plays contributed to 'the wealth & worship of the hole body', it is first necessary to establish the composition of this entity whose welfare and dignity were thus promoted. That it included only those persons who shared the expense of attaining these ends, the members of craft fellowships, is put beyond dispute by the same and similar contexts. At this period, only the crafts had the power to admit those who would later be called Freemen; the city could merely register new apprentices and swear them to the franchise. Hence 'to be discomyned oute of this Cite' involved *inter alia* estrangement from a man's craft. Exclusion from the fellowships of building workers or journeymen dyers automatically meant the stigma of inferior status as 'only comen laborers' or mere servants. When all masters and journeymen annually processed in their respective companies at Corpus Christi-tide and on the eves of Midsummer and St Peter, therefore, the community in its entirety was literally defining itself for all to see.[2]

There can be little doubt that practically every ceremony hereinafter to be discussed related to this restricted communal membership. In a total population of between 8000 and 9000 in 1500, all unqualified adult males, possibly 20 per cent of all householders to judge from extrapolating craft records, were excluded. So too, in effect, were all single females under forty. For all such women, whether or not they had served an apprenticeship, were specifically debarred from keeping house by themselves; in-service evidently being felt to be preferable even to their possession of a chamber, let alone a shop. Surviving lists of journeymen, moreover, contain no women's names. Marriage thus remained the only realistic avenue of admission to the community for females. It was therefore no accident that the wedding ceremonies of masters or journeymen were compulsorily attended by the groom's particular fellowship. In the case of the tanners, indeed, the journeymen were accustomed to attend the marriages of masters. But communal recognition clearly did not mean immediate occupational privileges even for a newly married woman. These probably had to await her (first)

full-scale study of Coventry society between 1480 and 1660 on social anthropological lines, which will amplify matters only touched on here, is currently in preparation. Unless otherwise specified all MS. references relate to the Coventry Record Office.
2. M. D. Harris, ed., *The Coventry Leet Book* (*LB*) (Early English Text Society, 1907–13), p. 556; ibid., p. 558; ibid., pp. 655, 560; ibid., p. 294; ibid., pp. 653, 694; ibid., p. 417; T. Sharp, *A Dissertation on the Pageants or Dramatic Mysteries Anciently Performed at Coventry (Dissertation)* (Coventry, 1825), pp. 22, 79–80, 161, n.f, 182–3; accession 241, original fols 2v., 4; cf. p. 262, below.

husband's demise – a fact which, no doubt, added a further level of meaning to the craft's attendance at his funeral.[3]

Ceremonial occasions repeatedly underlined this peripheral status of wives. Men or boys played the female parts in the Corpus Christi plays and there is some evidence, at least from 1565, that the women sat separately in St Michael's, the larger of the two parish churches. Certainly it was unusual for them to be present at either gild or craft banquets with their menfolk. Master Cappers' wives rarely attended craft meetings until they were widows. Even 'the Mairasse & hir Sisters', the other civic officers' wives, dined apart from their husbands when the Queen sent a present of venison in 1474. An early seventeenth century description of the mayoral inauguration, which evidently fossilized traditional practice, moreover, makes it clear that these ladies did not even attend the civic oath-taking. Instead, 'Old Mistress Maioris', the other officers' wives and the town sergeant, separately escorted the new Mayoress to the church where they awaited the arrival of their husbands after the ceremony was over.[4]

To all those outside or on the edge of the community, therefore, ceremonies must have been a constant reminder of its discrete and predominantly masculine identity. For those inside it, on the other hand, they were the visible means of relating individuals to the social structure. The sequence of oath-taking ceremonies, in particular, regularly punctuated the life cycle of the successful citizen from the moment he pledged himself to his city, his craft or his gild, to that later period in life when similar *rites de passage* admitted him to the authority which was the reward of advanced years. Initiation to the annually held senior craft office, some thirteen or fourteen years after joining, in the case of the Cappers for example, had a special significance in this last respect. For by the mid-sixteenth century, ex-officers were being termed 'the Auncente' or 'the moost auncient persones' of a craft – designations that implied more than official seniority when 60 per cent of the members of even a prosperous

3. See my forthcoming *Coventry in Crisis 1518–1525* (Department of English Local History Occasional Papers, second series, Leicester); accession 100: Weavers 11 (unfol.), quarterage payments and journeymen's groats 1523–1537; A5, fols 152r., 164r., 173r.; Cappers and Feltmakers' Company MSS, first account book (Cappers' accs), fols 67v., 68r., 70v., 71r.; *LB*, pp. 568, 545; ibid., p. 249; Cappers' accs fols 68r., 71r.; A5, loc. cit.; Weavers 2a, fol. 2v.; Weavers 2c, journeymen's orders; A99, fol. 2r.; accession 241, original fols 2v.–3r.; Weavers 2a, fol. 4r.; A5, fol. 1r.; cf. L. Fox, 'The Coventry Guilds and Trading Companies with Special Reference to the Position of Women', in *Essays in Honour of Philip B. Chatwin* (Oxford, 1962), pp. 13–26.
4. Accession 100: Weavers 11, 1524; A166 (with acknowledgment to Professor R. W. Ingram), extracts from S. Michael's vestry book; cf. A98, 'For comyng to the Churche'; A6, *passim*; A5, *passim*; Cappers' accs *passim*; *LB*, pp. 405–6; A34, fol. 269r.

craft like the Cappers do not seem to have survived twenty years of membership, and at a period in which 'the best age' was considered over at forty. The civic sequence of office, furthermore, usually seems to have succeeded that of the craft except in the cases of the richest companies like the Drapers whose head masters appear to have been at least ex-sheriffs. Even though potential civic office holders often reached the top of their fellowships more rapidly than normal, it still took a further seventeen years on average to reach the appropriately designated position of 'alderman' from junior civic office.[5]

The relevance of age to the oath-taking ceremonies, which accompanied every step on this ladder, was emphasized by the apparent timing of the citizen's progress through the two religious and social gilds of Corpus Christi and Holy Trinity. Usually within four years or so of being sworn to their fellowships, potential office-holders from the middling to wealthy crafts were pledging themselves to the junior gild of Corpus Christi. The composition of this fraternity seems to have been strongly biased to the less aged office-holders, a characteristic which was underlined by the admission of dependent young offspring of the city's élite. Despite the destruction of the Trinity Gild's register, there are indications that in mid-career, the successful citizen transferred from the junior to the senior fraternity. Certainly regular attendance at the former seems to have ceased at about the time a man assumed the shrievalty. Out of fifteen cappers, moreover, who had held craft office prior to 1520, only six were still attending Corpus Christi gild banquets in or after that year, though all were yet alive. Since both fraternities were ostensibly focused on eternity, it seems reasonable to suggest that in such cases the same need was being met by the only alternative organization available, the Trinity Gild. There remains, therefore, the strong implication that the senior fraternity was dominated by the ageing élite of the city – certainly the aldermen and probably the more elderly ancients of at least the wealthiest crafts.[6]

The importance of this broad but basic age categorization was

5. *LB*, p. 560; Bodl. MS. Top Warwick c. 7 (Reader), fol. 118r.; A5, fol. 2r.; G. Templeman, ed., *The Records of the Guild of the Holy Trinity, St Mary, St John the Baptist and St Katherine of Coventry* (Dugdale Society, XIX, 1944), p. 31. Calculations from Cappers' accs have been made on the basis of 'New Brethren' up to 1513. Weavers 2a, fol. 6r.; A98, rules 6 and 3; A110, rules 11, 13, 28; *LB*, p. 792; Reader 92v.; Bodl. MS. Top Warwick d. 4, fol. 19v.; accession 154, *passim*; Cappers' accs, *passim*; *LB*, calculated from all those serving as warden or chamberlain between 1490 and 1520. Coventry's gerontocracy will be fully discussed in the larger work mentioned in n. 1.
6. Calculated for all cappers in A6 between 1515 and 1524; Cappers' accs *passim*; A6, fols 206r. *et seq*. A microscopic examination of gild membership has yet to be completed.

brought out in inaugural ceremonies. In many crafts, authority was clearly conferred on new officers by the most senior members on behalf of the whole, the choice being made as with the Smiths by 'xij of the Eldest & discretest of the feliship'. In a rather more complex manner, the mayor and junior civic officers were secretly elected and sounded in mid-January by the aldermen, whose choice was formally rubber-stamped on the 25th at a purely ceremonial meeting of twenty-four men. Here, however, in those cases where it can be checked, attendance was divided between a contingent of more junior civic officers, particularly ex-sheriffs, headed by the Master of the Corpus Christi Gild who would himself be about to undertake the mayoralty within a year or two; and the ex-mayors, preceded by the Master of the Trinity Gild, who, by the early sixteenth century, was assuming his office immediately after relinquishing the mayoralty. When the civic oath-taking itself took place a week later, the ceremony heavily underlined the accountability of the new mayor to his senior colleagues. The incoming officers processed into St Mary's Hall where the retiring officers and aldermen were already symbolically in possession. At the culmination of the ceremony the new mayor was obliged to doff his hat, in the presence of the people, as a public gesture of deference to the old mayor and aldermen, 'intreating their loves and assistances'. Of the sheriffs and the coroner, on the other hand, he simply entreated assistance, while the junior civic officers and the rest were more tersely 'required' to do their duties.[7]

Oath-taking ceremonies were thus of wider significance than purely technical exercises which related only to the specific institutions concerned; by following an established sequence, they also helped each time to transfer the initiate to another broad social age category. In a number of further ways, too, they invested office with solemn and social attributes over and above the practical demands of annual executive position. A corporate act of worship by all the participants, for example, seems to have been the normal custom at both craft and civic levels. In the early fifteenth century, the Tilers were accustomed to offer at High Mass in the White Friars before their election. The Mercers, on the other hand, were 'after election, to bring the new Maister to churche' in Elizabeth's reign. The mayoral oath-taking ceremony, by the seventeenth century, was actually sandwiched between the first lesson and the sermon during morning prayer at the adjacent parish church of St Michael.[8]

Such observances were not irrelevant in view of the officers' obligations. Medieval head masters of the Weavers were sworn, indeed, not only to be good and true to their craft but also to its

7. *LB*, p. 743; *LP*, XII, 108; e.g. *LB*, pp. 604–5; A6, fol. 148r.; A34, fol. 269r.
8. Reader, fol. 217r.; A99, fol. 16v.; A34, fol. 269r.; cf. Reader, fol. 100r.

chapel of St James the apostle. The Mayor and his retinue were expected to attend church daily before the Reformation. As in other societies, furthermore, office was hedged with taboos. If even the job of town gaoler could be put at risk because its holder succumbed to the temptations of fornication, senior civic officers were specifically debarred in 1492 from adultery and usury as well. Regular worship and theoretically high standards of morality thus helped to legitimate authority in ways which transcended the group concerned.[9]

Another seemingly supernumerary facet of inauguration ceremonies was the Choice Dinner. Either before the election as in the case of the Drapers, or after, like the Weavers and the Dyers (who in fact held a breakfast), it was customary for the old and/or new masters to bear at least a substantial proportion of the cost of a dinner for their company. After his oath-taking on Candlemas day, the Mayor likewise had to throw a huge banquet at his own very considerable expense. Whether it was largely furnished by the incoming or the outgoing office-holder such an occasion was either the first or last formal exercise of his position. Despite subsidization, however, it was also clearly meant to be an act of 'hospitality' and as such was an expression more of social than of official obligation and status.[10]

The culminating procedure of inaugural ceremonies ensured that the citizen's new official status was unquestionably established outside the confines of his specific group in his own home neighbourhood. Most crafts probably observed the same custom as the Mercers who processed with the new masters 'from churche to the head-maisteres' houses'. Certainly the same effect was achieved when the master Dyers obeyed the order to fetch their under-master before the marching of the watch on Midsummer and St Peter's eves 'at hys howse, And from thence to goe to the head master's howse'. Likewise after the Mayor's inaugural banquet, the civic body was accustomed to attend on the new and old Mayors; first to the former's home, where the civic insignia, the sword and the mace, were symbolically deposited, and thence for the last time to the house of the retiring Mayor. By making an officer's home a focus for this group, a man's social status outside it was also inevitably enhanced.[11]

And indeed it was by the spectacular advertisement of specific

9. Weavers 2a, fol. 7v.; *LB*, p. 662; ibid., pp. 279, 544; M. Fortes, 'Ritual and Office in Tribal Society', in M. Gluckman, ed., *Essays on the Ritual of Social Relations* (Manchester, 1962), pp. 82–3.
10. Phrase used in 1615, A98 (unfol.); Reader, fol. 92r.; Weavers 2a, fols 5v., 6; Reader, fol. 117r.; LP, XIV (1), 77; cf. Reader, fol. 100.
11. A99, fol. 16v.; Sharp, op. cit., p. 183; A34, fol. 269v.

status in general contexts that ceremony made its most vital contribution to the viability of the city's late medieval social structure. For office was otherwise unremunerative. Unpaid or underpaid and greedy of time, it was unpopular and hence compulsory on pain of fine for those elected. Apart from the possibility of future promotion and the actuality of present influence, therefore, the exaggerated social precedence of ceremonial occasions was an office-holder's basic reward. 'In every procession and all other Congregacions for Worschipp of the Citte and Welth of the seyd Crafte,' the Weavers ordained in 1452–3, 'every man shall goo & sytt in order as he hath byn put in Rule of the seyd crafte'. Significantly, the worst punishment that could befall a contumacious ex-mayor after fine and imprisonment, was to be 'utterly abiect from the Counsell of the Citee & the Company of theym in all theire comen processions, ffestes, and all other assembles & from weryng of his cloke or skerlet in theire companyes'. In magnifying and publicizing the importance of annually held offices, the ceremony completed the transformation of wealth ownership into class standing for the upper levels of society.[12]

It is therefore notable that the order of march laid down in 1445 for the massive processions at Corpus Christi and Midsummer was based not on a system of precedence reflecting some *economic* class division of society (which might, for example, have allotted an inferior position to the handicraftsmen), but on occupational groupings whose order was determined apparently by the contribution of each to civic office-holding. Leaving aside two misfits in this scheme – the combined fellowship of pinners, tilers and wrights, and the craft of weavers, who may have been the occasion of the ordinance – the order of precedence was simple. It began, in the junior position, with the victuallers, all of whom, despite their wealth, were theoretically banned by parliamentary statute (even after 1512 at Coventry) from holding civic offices unless they suspended their occupations. Next came the leather and metal trades (though the identity of the latter grouping was somewhat blurred by the amalgamation of miscellaneous crafts with the fellowship of Cardmakers), neither of which were overly conspicuous for their tenure of offices. Last were the wool and textile occupations on which the prosperity of the city depended, culminating in the places of honour with the Dyers, Drapers and Mercers in that order. Not only were these the wealthiest companies in the city; they also furnished a disproportionate quota of its officers.[13]

12. *LB*, p. 107; Templeman, op. cit., p. 173; *LB*, pp. 619–21, 676–7; Weavers 2a, fol. 2v.; *LB*, pp. 670, 743; Weavers 2a, fol. 3v.; *LB*, p. 648.
13. *LB*, p. 220; *Statutes of the Realm*, 3 Hen. VIII c. 8; *LB*, p. 533; Templeman, op. cit., p. 6, n. 5, the Mercers' Craft included Grocers, Merchants and perhaps Vintners.

Civic office consequently lent prestige even to the crafts whose representatives held it, and though the order of march did not apparently vary with the occupation of the mayor, his own fellowship would often find a means of advertising its temporary prominence. As from 1533 the parvenu craft of Cappers aped a custom of the London companies by bearing a carnival-type giant, with illuminated eyes, through the dusky streets at Midsummer and St Peter's, on the increasingly numerous years in which their fellowship could boast any civic officer or Master of the Trinity Gild. Not to be outdone, the established company of Drapers in later years provided this titan with a spouse, though 'when Master Norton was mere' in 1554, they blasted off 12 lb. of gunpowder.[14]

Thus although ceremony obviously helped to transform the formal constitution of the city into some sort of reality, conversely it was also a valued instrument through which the basic divisions of humanity, by sex, age and wealth, could be related to the structure of the community. In addition, ceremonial occasions often provided at least the opportunities for bringing together in celebratory circumstances those who might otherwise be opposed or separated in their respective spheres.

In this connection, little needs to be added to the preceding discussion of those almost wholly ceremonious institutions, the two gilds, whose formal non-charitable activities were restricted to the observance of obits and religious festivals, public processions, civic or gild inaugurations and regular sumptuous banquets. For the office-holding class, their membership cut horizontally, as it were, across those major vertical subdivisions of the community, the individual crafts, since there was no restriction by occupation. Even the seeming division into broad social age categories was significantly blurred within the junior fraternity. Only a minority of officers from the humbler crafts could afford to join it – between 1515 and 1524, for example, there were only five carpenters as members – and fewer still could have found the £5 admission fine to the Trinity Gild. As a result, elderly ancients, like the carpenter Robert Hammond, were to be found rubbing shoulders with the adolescent sons of aldermen at the proceedings of the Corpus Christi Gild.[15]

The gulf between the senior civic officers and the current craft officers, whether or not they were gild members, was bridged at least twice during the year. It would seem that prior to 1545, the

14. G. Unwin, *The Gilds and Companies of London* (fourth edition, 1963), p. 269; Cappers' accs fols 45v. *et seq.*; *LB*, *passim*, and A7(a), *passim* – in a minority of years the junior civic officers cannot be ascertained; Sharp, op. cit., pp. 203–5; accession 154, p. 34; the Drapers' possession of a male giant cannot be proved.
15. Templeman, op. cit., pp. 152–9, 179–84; A6 and A5, *passim*; Templeman, op. cit., p. 178; A6, fols 226r., 225r.; A5, fols 38v., 60r., 106v.

mayor at Midsummer and the two sheriffs at St Peter's were respectively accustomed to entertain at least the officers of the crafts after the marchings of the watch. The composition of the guests at these established 'drynkynges' is suggested in the craft accounts by gifts from the Mayor of money for wine and cakes 'that we shold have had at Medssomer nyght' as from about that date: 'my wyn' as the head master of the Weavers once described it. There is, however, the further interesting possibility that whole fellowships were the beneficiaries of this largesse. The quantity of drink – three gallons or its equivalent cost was usual for the Weavers – would seem somewhat excessive even when, as in this instance, there may have been two rent-gatherers as well as the two keepers to help consume it. In fifteenth-century Bristol, all those 'persones of Craftes' who had actually attended the watch were to 'send ther own servantes and ther own pottes for the seide wyn', which was issued in quantities varying from two to ten gallons. Since some face-to-face contact does seem to be implied at Coventry, however, it is possible that the craft officers attended in person on their civic hosts in order to supervise the transfer of the bulk of the liquor for their members to imbibe elsewhere.[16]

Evidence for structurally integrative commensality lower down the social scale is inevitably harder to find. But it is not impossible that other crafts practised the same custom as the Weavers, whose masters partook of a communal meal and drinking with their journeymen once a year in the early fifteenth century. Both Dyers and Smiths at least provided ale or wine for their journeymen at Corpus Christi, Midsummer and St Peter's.[17]

On certain fixed occasions, however, commensality did express those topographical arrangements of the population which cut across formal social groups or groupings. For while in 1522–4 there was no mistaking the geographical concentration of some occupations in certain quarters of the city, even in the most extreme cases, the butchers and the cappers, there was considerable overlapping into different areas. To judge from ranking the wards by mean household sizes, other neighbourhoods, especially near the heart of the city, were similarly biased towards the wealthier levels of society, though none was totally exclusive. Taken as a whole, the social topography of Coventry was remarkable chiefly for the evident intermixture of all types of person.[18]

It was this which gave significance to the social activities of the

---

16. *LB*, p. 779; accession 100: Weavers 11 (unfol.) 1544, 1550, 1557; A5, fol. 140r.; E. W. W. Veale, ed., *The Great Red Book of Bristol* (Bristol Record Society, 1933), I, 125–6.
17. *LB*, p. 94; Sharp, op. cit., p. 181, n.p.
18. A96; E 179/192/125; 1523 census; Phythian-Adams, op. cit.

two huge parishes into which the city was divided. As elsewhere, the Holy Cake, for example, was consumed together in church by the parishioners after the celebration of Mass even in times of famine. On other occasions, in accordance with the instructions laid down for him in 1462, the first deacon of Holy Trinity was to serve the parishioners with 'bred & alle, and other thengs', at Mylborne's, Meynley's and other *diriges* 'made of the churche cost'. This is to say nothing of Whitsun ales and wakes at the feasts of dedication for which local evidence has yet to come to light.[19]

A rather different kind of observance was the informal gathering around each of the bonfires that are known to have blazed on the streets during Midsummer and St Peter's nights. These occasions were widely acknowledged celebrations of neighbourliness. 'At Baptis-day with Ale and cakes bout bon-fires neighbours stood' carolled William Warner in his *Albion's England,* while at nearby Warwick, money was specifically bequeathed to the 'neyhboures of the other thre bonfyres' within a ward 'to make merry withall'. Stow stated quite categorically that in London, 'These were called Bone-fires, as well of amity amongst neighbours, that being before at controversie, were there by the labour of others reconciled, and made of bitter enemies, loving friends'. Topographical groupings when expressed in such convivial ways must have helped at least to encourage cross-cutting ties within the social structure.[20]

Just as customary commensality served to promote cohesion within the community, so tensions stemming from rigidities within the social structure seem to have been provided with institutionalized outlets. The most clear-cut example of what amounted to periodic relaxations of the social order was the Coventry Hock Tuesday play. The structural implications of this are perhaps best revealed by comparison with the practices of May Day, since these two occasions involved distinctly contrasted social age categories. May Day everywhere was, of course, primarily a festival of unmarried young people, the 'Maides and their Makes', as Ben Jonson characterized the Coventry participants; while Hock Tuesday concerned the women or the wives. In view of the markedly inferior status with regard to the opposite sex which females incurred as a consequence of the oath-taking ceremony of marriage, it is hardly surprising that the contrast between these two traditional observances was complete.[21]

19. J. C. Cox, *Churchwardens' Accounts* (1913), p. 58; *LB*, p. 669; T. Sharp, *Illustrative Papers on the History and Antiquities of the City of Coventry (Antiquities)* (corrected by W. G. Fretton, Birmingham, 1871), p. 123.
20. *LB*, p. 233; G. C. Homans, *English Villagers of the Thirteenth Century* (New York, 1960), p. 375; Sharp, *Dissertation*, pp. 175–6.
21. B. C. H. H. Percy and E. Simpson, eds, *Ben Jonson* (Oxford, 1941), VII, 785; Cox, op. cit., pp. 64–5, 261–3.

On May Day the relationship was one of equality expressed in friendly dance. The preoccupation with courtship and love-making hardly needs emphasizing, but it is worth drawing attention to an aspect of popular symbolism which lay at the core of that seasonal rite. This was the widespread custom whereby yearning maidens on May Day in particular, and at other relevant moments in their lives, sported articles of clothing conspicuously embroidered with blue thread, for blue was the universal symbol of constant love. This simple practice, to which Coventry's dyeing industry traditionally catered and lent the term 'Coventry blue' because of its appropriate permanence, underlines what was probably a basic feature of May Day: the deliberate pairing-off by couples for the holiday as opposed to the unselective promiscuity implied in the more fevered castigations of certain Puritans.[22]

By contrast, the Hock Tuesday play used the anonymity of a *generalized* division of the sexes to reverse temporarily the *in*equalities existing between married men and women through the medium of conflict. This play-cum-mock-battle, in celebrating the putative historic overthrow of the Danish yoke by the citizens of Coventry in particular, culminated in a much diluted dramatization (with no doubt a reduced number of participants) of the rural custom by which the wives of the parish were accustomed to bind and/or heave the menfolk before releasing them on payment of a ransom. At Coventry after the men had fought out the battle, the play harped on 'how valiantly our English women for loove of their cuntree behaved themselvez', and how the Danish warriors having been beaten down 'many [were] led captive for triumph by our English weemen'. For once there is no doubt that women did take part; references to feminine costume hire amongst the expenses of special performances of this play before Queen Elizabeth are conspicuously absent.[23]

If relationships between the sexes concerned everyone in the community at an informal level, the position of mayor was the keystone in the formal structure of office-holding. It is, therefore, notable that at Christmas-time the mayoral dignity probably fell victim to institutionalized ridicule. Coventry then seems to have emulated that annual custom of a Lord of Misrule which was also to be found at Court, in great households, university colleges and the Inns of Court.[24]

22. Percy and Simpson, op. cit., p. 785; J. Brand, *Observations on the Popular Antiquities of Great Britain* (1841), II, 69, 59, 75, 80; B. Poole, *Coventry – its History and Antiquities* (Coventry, 1870), p. 358; Brand, op. cit. (1859 edition), I, 213.
23. E. K. Chambers, *The Mediaeval Stage* (Oxford, 1903), I, 155; Poole, op. cit., pp. 51–2; Sharp, *Dissertation*, p. 128.
24. Chambers, op. cit., pp. 403, 407, 418.

Now it may be that this personage represented or came eventually to represent no other function than that of 'Master of Merry Disports' or superintendent of the revels, a purely prestigious adjunct to the seasonal festivities and hence to the standing of the host. Yet there are a number of pointers which suggest that there may have been more to it than this. The very title, for example, indicates that he was Lord not of *un*ruliness and licence, though this may have been and indeed possibly was a consequence of his activities, but of *mis*-rule or misgovernment. Early commentators like Polydore Vergil and Selden, moreover, were emphatic that Christmas was a season when the master of the house abdicated his position in order to obey or wait upon his own servants, one of whom would act as the Christmas Lord during the festivities. In the restricted context of a great man's home, some connection between misrule at Christmas and the normal sway of the household head (whether in a public or private capacity) during the rest of the year could hardly have been avoided.[25]

It is in these circumstances that the urban version of this custom must be judged. For it is evident that Lords of Misrule pertained only to civic governors and not to other rich merchants or tradesmen. At Coventry and Chester they were associated with the mayor; at London with both the mayor and the sheriffs. It may also be significant that at Coventry in 1517 the Lord himself was one of the civic sergeants. Since mayors' sergeants were to be found at this time in the Corpus Christi Gild they clearly belonged to the office-holding class, and so may have been considered suitably dependable candidates for the festive post. Alternatively, there may even have been some form of deliberate status elevation within the body of civic officers for the duration of the holiday. Either way, the indications are that within the confines of his household or even elsewhere, the civic ruler had to be seen or known to put temporarily aside his formal status, in order to become, instead, the subject of satirical government: hence perhaps in part, the open house kept by the mayor for the whole twelve days at Coventry, at least in 1517, and the public processions of the London sheriffs with their respective Lords of Misrule through the streets of the capital.[26]

The only other time of the year at which the social barriers were lowered was the period of early summer. In this instance it was the classic antipathy between town and country which was expressed,

25. Ibid., p. 403; Thomas Langley, *An Abridgemente of the Notable Worke of Polidore Virgile* (?1570), fol. Cr.; Sir F. Pollock, ed., *Table Talk of John Selden* (1927), p. 28.
26. BM. Harl. MS. 6388, fol. 28v.; Chambers, op. cit., p. 418; A6, fols 216r., 217v., 218r., 221v., 223r.; J. G. Nichols, ed., *The Diary of Henry Machyn* (Camden Society, XLII, 1848), pp. 28, 274.

the sanctity of private property that was annually violated and the privileged immunity of the local land-owning class which was breached. For the festivities of Midsummer, St Peter's and probably May Day required the lavish decoration of houses, halls and streets with birch boughs and blossoms, quite apart from Maypoles, all of which were most conveniently procured without permission or payment from nearby estates. Thus, when in 1480 the Prior of Coventry complained that every summer his underwood was being taken, the mayor had to invoke a widespread custom in answering the charge, 'remembryng that the people of every gret Cite, as London & other Citeez, yerely in somur doon harme to divers lordes & gentyles havyng wodes & Groves nygh to such Citees be takyng of boughes & treez, and yit the lordes & gentils suffren sych dedes ofte tymes of theire goode will'. In like manner the citizens of Leicester hacked down timber for use on May Day in the woods of Sir Henry Hastings in 1603, while the gardens of the gentry in the neighbourhood of Nottingham were being ransacked for flowers at Midsummer up to the reign of Charles I. It seems that at such times everyday rules did not apply, while the privileged class, whose interests normally ensured their preservation, was expected to acquiesce passively in their flagrant transgression.[27]

The significance of all these practices lay not in the ways in which social tensions were haphazardly released but in the methods by which they were controlled. In the first place, such observances appear to have been the means of canalizing traditional periods of licence – a process which seems to have been completed at Coventry during the fifteenth century. The Hock Tuesday play, created in 1416, for example, was clearly a deliberate urban rationalization of contemporary bawdy practice in the rural Midlands generally. Accordingly Hock Monday, when the men usually bound the women in the country, withered away completely in an urban environment to become merely the Monday before Hock Tuesday. Local evidence for Christmas licence does not survive, but it is worth noting in passing that if Lords of Misrule did not originate during the fifteenth century, they only seem to have become generally popular towards its end. Midsummer and St Peter's were, however, indubitably times of extreme disorder and even riot. It was as a necessary response to this that the Prior of Coventry and other worried ecclesiastical dignitaries had suggested the inception of a special watch in 1421 to control 'the grett multytude of peopull' and to

---

27. *LB*, p. 233; Sharp, *Dissertation*, pp. 179–80; *LB*, p. 455; W. Kelly, *Notices Illustrative of the Drama and other Popular Amusements chiefly in the sixteenth and Seventeenth Centuries, . . . Extracted from . . . Manuscripts of the Borough of Leicester* (1865), pp. 102, 72, 99; C. Deering, *Nottinghamia Vetus et Nova* (Nottingham, 1751), p. 124.

avoid the 'grett debate and man-slaughter and othure perels and synnes that myght fall, and late have fallen'. There is no evidence before 1445, however, that their recommendations were accepted.[28]

These customs, secondly, had built into them, as it were, certain safeguards for the preservation of the structure. In all cases those in subordinate roles encroached in some way only on certain *attributes* of socially superior positions. At Hocktide representatives of the women overcame the menfolk in their unaccustomed masculine role as warriors and not as husbands or householders. In summertime the townspeople did not specifically attack the gentry class: they merely appropriated its property. Even at Christmas, the Lord of Misrule seems to have been a bad ruler rather than a 'mock mayor' or 'mayor of misrule'. If such customs deliberately distorted certain aspects of the social order, there was no question of altering the whole: in disfiguring the structure temporarily, the participants were in fact accepting the *status quo* in the long run.[29]

And it was perhaps this emphasis on preserving and enhancing the wholeness of the social order which most distinguished the ceremonies of this late medieval urban community. In a close-knit structure composed of overlapping groups or groupings, where a change of status in one sphere so often could affect standing in another, ceremony performed a crucial clarifying role. It was a societal mechanism ensuring continuity within the structure, promoting cohesion and controlling some of its inherent conflicts, which was not only valued as contributing to the 'worship' of the city, but also enjoyed by contemporaries. Even in times of crisis the plays were performed and the watches marched. If anything, before 1545 the tendency was not to cut back on over-costly trappings but to preserve and elaborate them. A reforming mayor in the 1530s was quite unable to stop accustomed drinkings even when craftsmen were being ruined by the expense. Feelings in favour of the Hock Tuesday and Corpus Christi plays, or some substitute for them, survived their formal abolition, and some way of observing Midsummer and St Peter's evidently outlived the watches. But the real significance which contemporaries attached to such practices may be

28. F. Bliss Burbidge, *Old Coventry and Lady Godiva* (Birmingham, n.d.), p. 218; n. 23, above; Brand, op. cit., pp. 184–91; Cappers' accs fol. 68v.; cf. J. Latimer, *Sixteenth Century Bristol* (Bristol, 1908), p. 10 and Brand, op. cit., p. 377; most early references to Lords of Misrule are sixteenth century: Chambers, op. cit., pp. 403–18, cf. p. 173; *LB*, pp. 35, 220.

29. M. Gluckman, *Order and Rebellion in Tribal Africa* (1963), chap. III; E. Norbeck, 'African Rituals of conflict', *American Anthropologist*, LXV (1963), 1254–75; P. Rigby, 'Some Gogo Rituals of "Purification" – an Essay on social and Moral Categories', in E. R. Leach, ed., *Dialectic in Practical Religion* (Cambridge, 1968), pp. 153–78; V. W. Turner, *The Ritual Process* (1969), pp. 170–8, 183–5.

better gauged by turning now to the cultural, temporal and spatial contexts in which they took place.[30]

The citizen's year was marked by rather different seasonal quarterings to those which, according to Homans, characterized the open-field husbandman's calendar. At Coventry, the beginning of the year seems to have been determined by the long-standing tradition by which the city's Lammas pastures reverted to private hands on 2 February, the date at which the mayoral inauguration had also come to take place and from which the mayoral year accordingly began. It is more than probable that, as elsewhere, May Day was accepted as the start of summer, and the re-opening of the Lammas lands to common pasturing on 1 August as the beginning of autumn. Judging from lighting regulations, winter was thought to lie between 1 November and 2 February. It seems indeed to have been a function of the city waits to emphasize this seasonal and predominantly pastoral framework. With the exception of the first quarter when they played from the first week in Clean Lent through to Easter, the waits performed nightly during the first part of each of these quarters, up to Midsummer, Michaelmas and Christmas respectively.[31]

Cutting clean through this seasonal sectionalization of the calendar, however, was another division of the year. In this instance, subdivision was by halves: a bisection made possible by that evident unity of the six months between 24–5 December and 24 June inclusively ($182\frac{1}{2}$ days), which stemmed from an oft-noted coincidence of Christian and archaic native practice. In the case of the church, the outcome was to cram all the major observances connected with the birth, life, death and resurrection of Christ into these six months, the unity of which is still roughly expressed when reference is made to Christmas, Easter and Whitsun in preference to a strictly calendrical ordering. Even the movable feasts were tied in a way to Christmas: Lent could begin as early as 4 February, only two days after the feast of the Purification, logically the last rite of Christmas. Similarly, at the latter end of the moiety when Easter fell at its latest, the feast of Corpus Christi, the culminating festival of the cycle, coincided with Midsummer Day. Whatever the date of Easter, it seems reasonable to suggest that the very movability of the greatest feasts of the Church, and the universal custom of relational dating thereto, helped to invest the whole of this period with an appreciable quality of its own.[32]

30. Phythian-Adams, op. cit.; Cappers' accs fols 24r., 26v., 29v.; accession 100: Weavers 11, 1523; cf. Cappers' accs fols 24r. and 94r.; *LP*, XIV, 1, 77; A14(a), p. 216.
31. Homans, op. cit., p. 354; E. O. James, *Seasonal Feasts and Festivals* (1961), p. 309; *LB*, p. 777; Sharp, *Dissertation*, p. 211.
32. James, op. cit., pp. 291, 230, 225–6, 207–25.

Through their origins and practice, moreover, native popular observances served to emphasize this unity. The widespread acceptance of the end of December as pertaining more logically to the succeeding than to the current year, for example, had its origins in remote antiquity: according to Bede, the heathen year, which also broke down into two halves, had begun on 25 December. In later times, the twelve days, of course, remained inseparable from Christmas itself and so acted as the connecting link with the following year. Events on each of these days were commonly seen as predictive of the weather or fortunes of the succeeding twelve months.[33]

Such popular attitudes served also to bridge the gap between Christian observances. At Norwich, Lent was ushered in by the King of Christmas on Shrove Tuesday 'in the last ende of Cristemesse', 'as hath ben accustomed in ony Cite or Burgh thrugh al this reame'. In like fashion did native customs span the interval, when there was one, between the end of the movable Church cycle and Midsummer. There are indications, for example, that May games were played in London up to 24 June (though a command performance was once held on the following day before Queen Elizabeth). It may be significant in this connexion that at the Coventry Midsummer watch in the 1550s, the Dyers' contingent was attended by a herdsman blowing his horn and someone 'carrying the tree before the hartt' – probably a reference to a 'company' of morris dancers with a maypole and other props. A relevant confusion in popular thought was also criticized by one puritan preacher who claimed that 'What offences soever happened from that tyme [Rogation] to Midsommer, the fumes of the fiers dedicated to John, Peter, and [though uncelebrated at Coventry] Thomas Becket the traytor, consumed them.' Any attempt at analysing popular culture has to take into consideration the ways in which religious and vulgar symbolism thus complemented each other and often merged into one.[34]

Particularly notable in this respect was the manner in which the contrasted symbols of fire and vegetation were accepted in Coventry, as elsewhere, by both Church and layman alike during this temporal moiety. If at Christmas time, Holy Trinity church was ablaze with extra candles, the Smiths' craft also specifically employed 'iij tapers at Crystmas & a candle ageynst xij day', while both Church and craft sported the obvious evergreens, holly and ivy.

33. M. P. Nilsson, *Primitive Time-Reckoning* (Lund, 1920), pp. 294–5; Chambers, op. cit., pp. 247 n. 3, 269; Brand, op. cit., pp. 478–80.
34. W. Hudson and J. C. Tingey, eds, *The Records of the City of Norwich* (1906), I, p. 345, n. 2, and unconvincing assertions, p. xc; Nichols, op. cit., pp. 20, 89, 137, 201; cf. J. Godber, *History of Bedfordshire* (Luton, 1969), p. 170; Sharp, *Dissertation*, pp. 200–1; Brand, op. cit., p. 308.

There is no need to dwell on the relevance of Candlemas, the ritual-ized burning of 'palm' leaves on Ash Wednesday, the bearing of 'palms' on Palm Sunday, nor on the hallowing of fire in church at Easter. The use of fresh foliage to decorate the city at the summer feasts has already been indicated as have the Midsummer bonfires. It is worth emphasizing, however, that half the point of the marching watch seems to have been literally to carry fire through the streets. Each craft had its own special cresset bearers for this purpose, probably an urban echo of that rural custom of rolling burning wheels down hills to mark the summer solstice.[35]

Also to be found in these six months were the extremes of sacred and profane drama with their common themes of birth, death and re-birth, and their corollary sexual relationships. Though Christmas mummers are not evidenced, the parish churches dramatized Palm Sunday with the unveiling of the Rood and Easter Day with the resurrection from the Easter sepulchre, while the crafts performed their plays at Corpus Christi. The inter-sex dramas or ritualized games of Hocktide and May Day have already been discussed, but as at Leicester and Stratford-upon-Avon, it is likely that the proces-sion which marked St George's Day (23 April) was also enlivened by some representation of the traditional fight with the dragon. A courtly version of what would probably have been stock practice was the highlight of Prince Edward's visit to Coventry on 28 April 1474 to observe a late St George's feast. This showed a King and a Queen 'beholdyng seint George savyng theire doughter from the dragon', a very similar tableau being presented before Prince Arthur in 1498.[36]

This temporal unit was further characterized by pronounced polarities in everyday activities and behaviour. On the one hand were the long period of Lenten diet, the accompanying civic en-forcement of personal morality – the aldermen were specifically ordered to punish 'bawdry' during Clean Lent – and, more often than not, the eight-day Corpus Christi fair, that annual apogee of the city's economic endeavour. On the other were the traditional periods of licence and the only major extended holidays in the year. An obviously pre-Reformation ruling in a later sixteenth-century recension of the Cardmakers' ordinances was probably rep-resentative in permitting neither

> Cutinge, prickyng, doublyng, Crooking, nor Settinge, within the xij
> dayes at Christmas neyther at any Satterday, at after noone, after one

35. Sharp, *Antiquities*, pp. 123–4; Reader, fol. 84r.; accession 154, p. 41; cf. Brand, op. cit., p. 305; Sharp, *Dissertation*, p. 184; Homans, op. cit., pp. 369–70.
36. James, op. cit., p. 272; cf. *LB*, p. lii, n. 12; Sharp, *Antiquities*, pp. 122, 124; Kelly, op. cit., p. 47; E. I. Fripp, ed., *Minutes and Accounts of the Corporation of Stratford-upon-Avon* (Dugdale Society, I, 1921), p. xix; *LB*, pp. 393, 590–1.

of the clock, neyther on any Vygill Even after the same houre, . . . neyther shall they woork at any of the poynts above specyfyed in Easter weeke, neither in Whitsune week . . .[37]

The contrast with the six months between 25 June and about mid-day on the vigil of Christmas (182½ days) was absolute. In this period there was no religious or popular symbolic coherence, there were no institutionalized extremes of behaviour and there were no extended holidays. Essentially this was a time for uninterrupted, normal economic activities, some of which, even in a city the size of Coventry, were still dependent on rural rhythms. The Lammas pastures could only have been free for use on 1 August if, as elsewhere, the hay harvest began at Midsummer, while the grain harvest made the few Michaelmas lands similarly available. More germane were the completion of sheep shearing by mid-June and the wool sales which followed: new supplies may have been reaching the army of wool and textile workers soon after Midsummer. Similarly, if somewhat later in the year there was no early winter slaughtering in the locality to bring supplies of meat into the city, there were, very probably, sales of surplus stock well before Christmas. The importance of this generally drier season for travel, finally, emphasizes the conspicuous number of fairs which at least the merchants might have wanted to attend. Coventry seems to have belonged to a minority in holding its own fair before Midsummer in nearly all years.[38]

It is thus difficult to doubt the existence of a marked pre-Reformation dichotomy of the year, the two halves of which it is surely no exaggeration to denominate for convenience as respectively 'ritualistic' and 'secular'. It must be stressed, however, that this is to suggest not that the former necessarily saw a general slowing down of economic activity, but rather that the same routines continued to be carried out against an abnormal background. When ceremonies occurred in this half, they did so in a heightened context which was wholly absent in the secular moiety. It is therefore relevant to enquire into what sorts of ceremonies were most usually associated with each, leaving aside those largely administrative occasions which recurred half yearly or quarterly like the ordinary

37. *LP*, IV(3), Appendix I; J. C. Jeaffreson, *Coventry Charters and Manuscripts* (Coventry, 1896), B48; Reader, fol. 95v.
38. Homans, op. cit., p. 370; P. J. Bowden, *The Wool Trade in Tudor and Stuart England* (1962), p. 22 and cf. pp. 86–7, 91; P. J. Bowden, 'Agricultural Prices, Farm Profits, and Rents', in J. Thirsk, ed., *The Agrarian History of England and Wales* (Cambridge, 1967), p. 621; Alan Everitt, 'The Marketing of Agricultural Produce', ibid., p. 533; F. Emery, 'The Farming Regions of Wales', ibid., p. 121; H. P. R. Finberg, 'The Genesis of the Gloucestershire Towns', in H. P. R. Finberg, ed., *Gloucestershire Studies* (Leicester, 1957), pp. 86–8.

meetings of crafts or the court leet, and arbitrarily fixed events like obits.

With this obvious proviso it is an interesting comment on the value attached to the ideal of local community, that the ritualistic half embraced every major public ceremony (St Peter's eve excepted) which formally interrelated separate whole groups or groupings of the social structure. Even as late as the seventeenth century, all the festival days on which the aldermen were to wear their scarlet fell in this period with the only exceptions of two post-medieval additions, 1 November and 5 November.[39]

This emphasis on the ritualistic half was further brought out by the frequency of processions and occasions which, in so far as separate ceremonies pertained to similar structural relationships, seem to have been concentrated into sometimes overlapping temporal blocs. The half began by expressing the relation of the civic body to the community. If the retiring mayor was burlesqued over Christmas, his successor and junior colleagues were chosen and then approved in January prior to their inauguration before the citizens at Candlemas in, appropriately, St Mary's Hall. On the morrow of Lenten mortification, it was the turn of those socially cohesive topographical groupings, the parishes, which, from as early as the Palm Sunday processions through the entire Easter celebrations, seem to have been the unrivalled foci of ceremonial activity. It is even conceivable that the two sides in the Hock Tuesday play (ten days after Easter) originally represented the two parishes which, in any case, came into their own again with the normal Rogationtide processions. Hock Tuesday, however, could fall on any day between 6 April and 3 May, only two days after that other celebration of inter-sex relationships, May Day itself.[40]

At this juncture the gilds and probably the civic body began to dominate the scene. There is some evidence to suggest that both gilds processed with their cross-bearers on St George's Day (23 April), Ascension (which fell between 30 April and 3 June), and Whit Sunday (10 May to 13 June). It is more than probable that the mayor and his brethren were associated with the first and, certainly in company with the commonalty, the last, which was indeed still an official festival day for aldermen in 1640. Not that the parishes were excluded – Holy Trinity, at least, also fielded its cross, banner and streamers on all three days.[41]

---

39. A14(b), p. 6.
40. Above, pp. 242–3, 249–51; *Sharp, Antiquities*, pp. 120, 122–3; cf. James, op. cit., pp. 300–4.
41. Sharp, *Dissertation*, p. 161; Templeman, op. cit., p. 158; Poole, op. cit., p. 211; A6, fol. 322r.; *LB*, pp. 588–9, 299–300; A14(b), p. 6; Sharp, *Antiquities*, p. 120. The evidence seems to be against a number of separate processions on each day.

The ceremonial activities of this ritualistic half reached a spectacular climax with four processions: on Corpus Christi day (21 May to 24 June), the following day – Fair Friday-Midsummer eve, and (for the sake of analytical continuity, though it belonged strictly to the secular half) five days later on St Peter's eve. In all of these, of course, the civic body was accompanied by the craft fellowships or, in the case of Fair Friday alone, two or three accoutred representatives.[42]

In a very real sense the community thus ceremonialized itself *vis-à-vis* all its major activies, with a changing emphasis on worship, work and particularly authority. The ritualistic half may have begun with a parody of government, but it ended with the mayor processing as the king's representative backed by a token armed force provided by each company. In more general fashion the frequent ultra-formalization of group interrelationships throughout this half was conspicuously balanced by the structurally distortive customs of Christmas, Hocktide and Midsummer, which fell broadly at the beginning, middle and end of the period in question. It is thus tempting to see such practices as representing in this instance, not the exact opposite of everyday life, as has been suggested on general grounds by Dr Leach, but rather of communal ceremonialization. For *both* ceremony *and* structural distortion operated on an exaggerated plane which was quite distinct from normality: the former idealized and the latter inverted social norms. Conceptually they complemented each other.[43]

Whereas during the ritualistic half the component groups of the community were ceremonially interrelated in public, throughout the secular period the parts, on the whole, ceremonialized themselves in private. Perhaps to avoid the interruption of the next ceremonial 'season', this half was primarily concerned with the election of those officers who, unlike the mayor, could not be regarded as symbols of the community as a whole. Both gilds, for example, then elected their masters; the Trinity Gild on 18 October and the Corpus Christi Gild on 8 December. Ten out of the fourteen fellowships for which information survives or can be inferred, furthermore, also elected

At Whitsun, for example, the gilds would hardly have segregated themselves from the Mayor's procession which contained their two Masters.

42. Above, p. 63; Reader, fol. 33. The Corpus Christi Gild may have processed as a separate entity on its major feast day, but no provision was made for this in Craft ordinances (e.g. accession 241, original fol. 2v.). There is evidence for processional activity by the Gild on the vigil: A6, fol. 325r.

43. Sharp, *Dissertation*, pp. 182–3, 192–5; Turner, op. cit., pp. 168–9, 176–7; E. R. Leach, *Rethinking Anthropology* (1966), p. 135; E. R. Leach, *Political Systems of Highland Burma* (Boston, 1965), p. 286. The logical opposite of everyday behaviour in Dr Leach's schema should surely be disguise or masquerade – even holiday as opposed to work.

their officers in the secular half. There even remains, in some cases, traces of an occupational pattern. The elections of the 'textile' crafts, for instance, seem to have been fairly closely bunched. The Cappers who began in 1496 with 26 July, later changed to 7 August in 1520, while both the Weavers and apparently the Fullers favoured 25 July. The accounts of the latter were usually rendered on 23 November, a popular date for this, and the same day as the Dyers, the date of whose elections may thus be broadly inferred. By contrast, the Cordwainers and Tanners elected on or near 9 October and 16 October respectively, while the new master of the Butchers held his inaugural dinner on the 18th of the same month.[44]

All the four fellowships whose elections overlapped into the ritualistic half chose their officers between Christmas and New Year's Day. The Tilers, who elected on 26 December (although the St Stephen's Day in question could conceivably have been 2 August), represent the only serious aberration in an otherwise remarkable overall pattern. The leet ordinance on the hybrid character of the fellowship of Cardmakers, Saddlers, Masons and Painters probably explains their date (29 December) during the holiday period when either disputes might in theory, perhaps, have been more easily avoided, or a mutually convenient date on which to meet, most readily found. Clearly the Mercers and Drapers, on the other hand, whose dates fell on 27 December and 31 December, had to fall in line with the elections to civic office which were due to take place during the succeeding month.[45]

Differences between the two halves of the year were not restricted to the varying ceremonialization of social structure, however; there were also significant contrasts in the actual territory over which open-air ceremonies took place. This was partly due to the peculiar topography of Coventry. For, firstly, at its heart lay what was virtually a single vast churchyard containing not only the two parish churches, but also the Cathedral priory. Flanking it were the Bishop's palace, and halls for priests, as well as the major civic administrative buildings like St Mary's Hall and the gaol, and finally the huge covered cloth-market, the Drapery. Since the approach to the Cathedral and the circuits around the parish churches were mostly if not all known as 'procession ways', it is clear that this whole consecrated area constituted a ritual centre for the city. It is therefore noteworthy that the ceremonies in the earlier part of the

44. Cf. Templeman, op. cit., p. 157; ibid., pp. 159, 152; A6, fols 332v., 347.; *LB*, pp. 573, 670; Weavers 2a, fol. 6 and cf. fol. 5v. and accession 100: Weavers 11 (unfol.) 1523 expenses; accession 30, pp. 10, 17; Reader, fol. 117r.; A98, rule 3; accession 241, original fol. 4r.; Reader, fol. 100r.; *LB*, p. 743; A110, rules 22 and 20; A5, fol. 21r.
45. Reader, fol. 217r.; *LB*, p. 205; A99, fol. 2r.; Reader, fol. 92r.

ritualistic period were mainly confined to it. The mayoral inauguration was focused on St Michael's Church and St Mary's Hall, while the parochial processions around the churchyard on Palm Sunday, the Easter celebrations and quite possibly rather more elaborate occasions, as at Whitsuntide, were likewise restricted.[46]

The city, secondly, was triangulated by gild chapels: the chapel of St Nicholas which belonged to the Corpus Christi Gild lay just outside Bishop Gate to the north-west; that of the Trinity Gild, St John Bablake, was situated just inside the Spon Gate at the western end of the city; and the unique craft-cum-gild chapel of St George which pertained to the Shermen and Tailors was attached to Gosford Gate itself, on the eastern side. Most probably, each of these was the departure point or destination of a major procession in the latter part of the ritualistic half. That at Corpus Christi must have started from St Nicholas chapel, where the host would have been consecrated, before proceeding through the streets until it reached what seems to have been the first pageant station at Gosford Gate where the plays were to begin. Since the Feast of the Nativity of St John the Baptist was the dedication day of the Trinity Gild chapel, and since the mayor who presided over the procession was accustomed to visit Bablake 'overnight' for *dirige*, 'dyvers consideracions & other great busynes', it is very possible that the riding on Midsummer's eve began there. (It will be recalled that following the watch, which evidently did not start until after dark, he was engaged in entertaining at least the craft officers.) More probably still, the St George's Day procession, after leaving Bailey Lane which skirted the churchyard centre, would have included a visit to the only chapel dedicated to that saint in the city and to an area customarily connected, at second-hand, with the chivalrous slaughter of monsters. A bone of the fabulous boar slain by Guy of Warwick hung at Gosford Gate, while a few hundred yards up the hill outside was a chapel dedicated to yet another dragon dispatcher, whose fame was locally celebrated, St Margaret.[47]

During the ritualistic half, therefore, there seems to have been a movement of formal ceremony from the centre outwards to the limits of the city but no further. Nearly every other observance during this moiety was similarly confined. Hocktide games took

---

46. *LP*, XIII (2), 674; *VCH, Warwickshire*, VIII, 329; J. Speed, *Theatre of the Empire of Great Britaine* (1611), fols 49v.–50; Poole, op. cit., p. 203; A24, pp. 33, 32, 29; *LB*, pp. 460–1, 264, 299, 588; Sharp, *Antiquities*, pp. 122, 120; Cox, op. cit., pp. 253–8; *LB*, p. 299.

47. Hardin Craig, ed., *Two Coventry Corpus Christi Plays* (Early English Text Society, E.S. 87, 1957), pp. xiii–xiv, 84–5; *LB*, p. 558: significantly, a number of 'pageant houses' were conveniently sited nearby, e.g. ibid., p. xiii, n. 2, A24, p. 8; Poole op. cit., p. 211; above, p. 64; *LB*, p. 589; Speed, op. cit., fol. 49r.; *LB*, pp. 738, 291–2.

place 'in' the city and not on adjacent waste ground; maypoles stood over the streets; bonfires burnt on them; 'pageants' trundled through them. The one part-exception would have been the Rogationtide processions which traced the parish boundaries outside as well as within the city. Such practices are not only a reminder that medieval streets were as important for recreation and marketing as for communication; rites and processions, like the carriage through the streets of the Corpus Christi host or the Midsummer fire, periodically added a mystical dimension to this utilitarian valuation of the immediate topographical context. While doing so, they underlined further the physical inescapability of communal involvement.[48]

Though somewhat mitigated by the fewness of the occasions, a contrast was provided, once again, by the secular half. Here the emphasis was on the surrounding countryside, the city's fields and the *County* of Coventry. Communal participation, moreover, was attenuated. Attendance on the Chamberlains' annual Lammas ride (1 August), to oversee the renewal of common access to pasture land, for example, was restricted as from 1474 to those appointed, and after 1495 to representatives from each ward. What theoretically became a triennial activity as from 1469, the riding of the metes and bounds of the County of Coventry, also seems to have taken place in the secular half. If the intention to ride before the Michaelmas leet was sometimes announced at its Easter predecessor, the only surviving exact dates indicate that the execution was left to the last possible moment: 4 October in 1509 and 26–7 September in 1581. On the latter occasion, the party included not only a number of aldermen, sheriffs, other civic officers, and 'yonge men appoynted', no doubt as guardians of the future, but also 'dyvers others of everie Townshipp sommune within the forrens'.[49]

The correlation between town and country, which seems to have been associated with this moiety, was emphasized in another way. For to accommodate the demands of the Exchequer year, the sheriffs for the county were sworn and so designated at the Michaelmas Leet in the secular half. When the same men appeared at the following Easter Leet in the ritualistic half, however, they did so only in their *civic* capacities as 'bailiffs'. It may not be too far-fetched to suggest, therefore, that the marching of the watch on St Peter's eve in the first week of the secular half may have had an extra-urban bias. It was conducted by the sheriffs and not by the mayor; fines for non-attendance by craftsmen were, at least in one instance, less severe than at Midsummer; the city Weavers do not even seem to have participated; and there appears to have been no formally defined order of march by crafts. It is thus just possible either that

---

48. Poole, op. cit., p. 90; A14(a), p. 216; *LB*, p. 233.
49. *LB*, pp. 843, 565; ibid., pp. 348, 571, 622, 628, 821 – a special survey.

there may have been some progression from township to township or, more likely, that county representatives joined the civic procession. Such an explanation might help to account for the overlap of this ritualistic activity into the secular half of the year.[50]

Taken as a whole, however, Coventry's calendar seems to betray a conspicuous correspondence between social structure and its ceremonialization in time and space. That observances occasionally overlapped their temporal contexts cannot be denied, but by and large the intricate regularity of the pattern is remarkably clear. Reconstructed, it bears mute witness both to the communal quality of a late medieval urban society, particularly the evident subordination of the parts to the working of the whole, and to the pervasive role of the pre-Reformation Church and its practices in that community. Such a reconstitution also highlights the extent of the subsequent change: the destructive impact of the events of the mid-sixteenth century and the consequent obliteration of the established rhythm of life itself.

The modernization of this late medieval framework was characterized by the triumph of the secular half over its ritualistic counterpart as, one after another, the principal ceremonies vanished. The important processions of St George's Day, Ascension, Whitsun and Corpus Christi were either unrecognizably altered or later abolished by the amalgamation of the Corpus Christi Gild in 1535 with the Trinity Gild, and their subsequent dissolution in 1547. At the same time, St George's chapel was probably abandoned though the Shermen and Tailors survived as a craft fellowship. Like London and Bristol, Coventry then also secured some respite from the summer watches, officially relinquishing that on St Peter's in 1549, though the last riding at Midsummer does not seem to have taken place until some fourteen or fifteen years later. Meanwhile, in 1552, a new October fair had been granted, and during the very year that the Queen had foisted a Catholic mayor on the city (1556), the mayoral inauguration had been moved from Candlemas to 1 November, a date with fewer papistical overtones. A first attempt at abolishing the Hock Tuesday play seems to date from 1561, but the insistence of the citizenry ensured its spasmodic resurrection thereafter. Thirty years later it was finally moved out of context to St Peter's eve, when its performance was theoretically to be restricted by confinement to the stages of the Corpus Christi 'pageants'. The sacred plays, for which these theatrical waggons had originally been designed, were last acted in 1579. For a few years, however, they were replaced by a safe Protestant substitute which, in 1591 at least, seems to have been performed at Midsummer. With

---

50. Ibid., pp. 271–2 *passim*; ibid., p. 791; Sharp, *Dissertation*, p. 182; accession 100: Weavers 11, Expenses 1523, *passim*; *LB*, p. 220; cf. Brand, op. cit., pp. 337–8.

the removal, finally, of all maypoles from the city in the same year, the ritualistic half no longer existed as a recognizable unit for both church and society.[51]

The changing venue of ceremony was itself indicative of the nature of this momentous alteration in the yearly round. The only open-air ceremonies to survive, for example, were now justifiable on technical grounds alone: to proclaim the fair or to perpetuate the boundaries, of parish, field or county. With the emasculation of popular practices at May Day, Hock Tuesday or Midsummer, profane rites and even a recreation, like football in 1595, were banished from the streets. The Queen's highway was left to its purely materialistic functions. If the opportunity for popular participation in public rituals was consequently largely removed, that especial meaning which sacred ceremonies and popular rites had periodically conferred on the citizens' tangible environment also fell victim to the new 'secular' order. Ceremony and religion together withdrew indoors from the vulgar gaze. The formalization of social structure was now passively restricted accordingly to the hierarchical seating arrangements within the parish churches. As a result, that unknown proportion of the population which bothered to attend them was automatically divided.[52]

For, most significantly, formal communal processions had totally disappeared. The nearest the later sixteenth century could come to former practices was the Fair Friday display with its minimal craft representation. Indeed, until the days of the later Godiva procession (which in origin bore all the hallmarks of an advertising stunt), formal communal involvement of any sort was restricted to the annual mayoral inauguration, a largely indoor affair. The civic body may have ceremonially observed certain church festivals, but there is no evidence that anyone else took part.[53]

The leading representatives of that simultaneously adjusting social structure, who had helped to bring about all these changes, may have belonged to a wider cultural and economic environment than their predecessors, but at least in one respect their societal horizons were narrower. By the seventeenth century the claims of the community, at this level, were yielding first place to class loyalties. With

51. *LB*, pp. 722–3; cf. A99, fol. 2 (pre-1551: ibid., fol. 2v.); *VCH*, op. cit., p. 332; *APC*, New Series, I, pp. 447, 422, and cf. Cappers' accs fol. 72; *LB*, p. 791; Sharp, *Dissertation*, p. 201 and cf. accession 100: Weavers 11, fols 53 *et seq.*; A5, fols 185r., 187r.; *CPR, Edward VI*, IV, 380; *APC*, New Series, V, p. 218; Bodl. MS. Top Warwick d. 4, fol. 20; Craig, op. cit., pp. xxi–xxii; A14(a), p. 216; *VCH, Warwickshire*, VIII, 218.
52. A3(b), p. 13; Bodl. MS. Top Warwick d. 4, fol. 36; A98 (unfol.) 'For comynge to the Churche'; Poole, op. cit., p. 157.
53. Cf. accession 100: Weavers 9 (unfol.), 1622; Bliss Burbidge, op. cit., p. 256; Cappers' accs fol. 208v.; A14(b), p. 6.

this development, the annihilation of what had evolved into a ceremonial system in the late medieval period, was closely connected. It was no accident that the elaborate official inaugurations which had characterized the old secular moiety alone survived untarnished, in the post-Reformation world, to dominate the altered and abbreviated ceremonial calendar of the Coventry citizen.

Editorial suggestions for further reading

Phythian-Adams, C. V. *Desolation of a City: Coventry and the Urban Crisis of the Later Middle Ages* (Cambridge, 1979).
James, M. 'Ritual, drama and the social body in the late medieval English town', *Past and Present*, 98 (1983), 3–29.

Chapter Thirteen

URBAN DECLINE IN LATE MEDIEVAL ENGLAND

R. B. Dobson

Transactions of the Royal Historical Society, 27 (1977)

> *The debate on the condition of England in the late Middle Ages goes back to the nineteenth century. In the 1950s it seemed to be resolved in Postan's authoritative, pessimistic account of the late medieval economy. But then the gloomy orthodoxy was challenged by the appearance in 1962 of Bridbury's* Economic Growth: England in the Late Middle Ages. *This made the case that, within a contracted economy (the inevitable result of severe population losses from 1348 onwards), new enterprise flourished at this period on all fronts, the urban sector included. While agrarian historians now generally agree that fifteenth-century conditions permitted an expansive, even proto-capitalist, approach to peasant farming, Bridbury's claim that towns were prospering even more than the countryside remains controversial. Dobson's article on the question has been chosen for inclusion here because it inaugurated a spate of subsequent discussion, and because in its wide-ranging review of the sources it represents a broad approach to the issue of prosperity, which can never be reduced to such crudely quantifiable measures as population size and tax assessments. Even so, Dobson's catalogue and analysis of economic indices is not exhaustive. His hint as to the usefulness of urban property values as a guide to economic change has since been taken much further, above all by Keene's work in Winchester and London. A major omission from Dobson's discussion is the theme of urban crafts and manufactures, on which recent work has begun to provide some pointers. Not 'the decline of towns', but shifts of emphasis, both within the economy as a whole and within the urban sector in particular, may prove to have characterized the late Middle Ages.*

For so moche as dyvers and many Howses Mesuages and Tenementis of Habitacions in the Townys of Notingham, Shrewesbury, Ludlowe, Brydgenorth, Quynborowe, Northampton and Gloucester nowe are and of long tyme have been in greate ruyne and decaye . . . specially

in the chief stretes . . . desolate and void groundys, with pittys,
sellers and vaultes lying open and uncovereyd, very peryllous for
people to go by in the nyght without jeopardy of lyfe.[1]

More than four centuries have passed since the famous preambles
to the various Tudor acts for the re-edifying of English towns
generalized with such unnerving confidence about the lamentable
state of provincial urban communities in the early sixteenth century;
but no historian today who has the temerity to walk through those
still perilous streets can be under any illusion as to the continued
hazards of such an expedition. Yet that this journey, despite its
dangers and frustrations, deserves to be undertaken more frequently
and more urgently than ever before seems very clear. Even the most
optimistic historian must occasionally suffer some qualms at a situation in which the single most important issue in pre-industrial
English urban history – the exact contribution of the late medieval
and early modern town to the society and economy of the nation as
a whole – seems to be becoming more rather than less mysterious
with every detailed monograph and every new methodological problem. For here of course, much more in 1976 than in 1894, we are
in the presence of one of those 'burning questions in which impetuous economists have outrun the historians, and have not found
it premature to set in order by the help of accepted theories the
obscure chaos of social history in the Middle Ages'.[2]

It could, and indeed has, nevertheless been argued that the question of late medieval urban decline is in the last resort unanswerable.
Characteristically wise in his time, F. W. Maitland was long ago 'far
from thinking that any one history should be told of all our
boroughs'; while as recently as last year it has been argued that 'the
town as such, and possibly even the type of town, is not, beyond
the most preliminary stage, a useful or appropriate object of social
analysis'.[3] It is certainly already clear that the analytical problem
which has tended to obsess the medieval historian more than any
other, the definition and the categorization of the urban com-

---

1. *Statutes of the Realm* (London, 1810–28), iii, 531–32; cf. ibid., pp. 127, 176–77,
   768–69, 875, and the recent discussion of these statutes in G. R. Elton, *Reform
   and Renewal: Thomas Cromwell and the Common Weal* (Cambridge, 1973),
   pp. 106–9.
2. A. S. Green, *Town Life in the Fifteenth Century* (London, 1894), i, p. xii. For
   the first, and still one of the best, attempts to reconcile what were already 'strangely conflicting opinions' on the fortunes of the later medieval English town, see
   W. Cunningham, *The Growth of English Industry and Commerce during the
   Early and Middle Ages* (Cambridge, 4th edn., 1905), pp. 369–80, 452–56, 506–21.
3. F. W. Maitland, *Township and Borough* (Cambridge, 1898), p. 36; P. Abrams,
   'Towns and economic growth: some theories and problems', *Towns and
   Economic Growth* (Proceedings of Past and Present Society, Annual Conference,
   1975), p. 4.

munities of provincial England, is never likely to lead to any
positively illuminating general conclusion. Even the admirably prag-
matic solution of 'three tiers of urban society' recently suggested for
the early modern period rests so heavily on the criterion of numeri-
cal size that it can rarely be applied with confidence to a medieval
England so notoriously devoid of reliable population statistics.[4] That
said, it ought to be pointed out that the primary concern of this
paper is the economic fortunes of those forty or so English towns,
not including London, known to have had a tax-paying population
of 1000 or more at the time of the 1377 Poll Tax.[5] Such concentration on the major urban centres has its obvious dangers; and
naturally 'not even the strictest stagnationist denies the growth of
craft industry in the countryside'.[6] What remains profoundly uncertain is whether the development of that rural industry and such
spectacular consequential successes as those of Totnes and Tiverton,
Lavenham and Lewes should be interpreted as symptoms of general
urban strength rather than of weakness. In the case of England's
largest and oldest towns the problem can be posed at least a little
more simply. 'Sethen the makyng of which statute and ordinaunce',
declared a statute of 1512 referring to a period almost two centuries
earlier, 'many and the most partie of all the cities, bouroughes and
townes corporate wythin this realme of Englonde be fallen in ruyne
and decaye and not inhabited with marchauntes and men of such
substaunce as they were at the tyme of makyng of the foreseid
statute and ordinaunce'.[7] Is that melancholy judgement likely to be
more right than wrong?

On Maitland's own familiar principle that all students of the
medieval town must be prepared to think themselves 'back into a
twilight',[8] it would in any case seem proper to preface any investigation of late medieval urban decline with the comments of those
Tudor observers who first posed the problem for posterity. Familiar
though so many of these lamentations are, their cumulative effect
can leave one in no doubt of contemporary bewilderment at a

4. *Crisis and Order in English Towns, 1500–1700*, ed. P. Clark and P. Slack (London, 1972), pp. 4–5.
5. J. C. Russell, *British Medieval Population* (Albuquerque, 1948), pp. 140–43. All
   but seven of these towns figure among the forty wealthiest urban contributors to
   the Lay Subsidy of 1334; and similarly all but seven (not the same seven) occur
   among the forty English towns most heavily assessed in the Tudor subsidies of
   the 1520s: see *The Lay Subsidy of 1334*, ed. R. E. Glasscock (London, 1975),
   passim; W. G. Hoskins, *Local History in England* (London, 1959), pp. 176–77;
   A New Historical Geography of England, ed. H. C. Darby (Cambridge, 1973),
   pp. 179–85, 241–43.
6. R. H. Hilton, *The English Peasantry in the Later Middle Ages* (Oxford, 1975),
   pp. 37–38.
7. *Statutes of the Realm*, iii, 30.
8. Maitland, *Township and Borough*, p. 11.

The Medieval Town 1200–1540

society which had allegedly 'let fal into ruyn and dekey al theyr cytes, castelys, and townys'.[9] Undoubtedly a safer guide to social thinking than to social realities in the sixteenth century, such jeremiads themselves need to be placed as firmly in a historical context as the conditions they purport to describe. What they do not deserve is the fate of casual dismissal out of hand. Even polemical literature reveals its unintended secrets; and perhaps the most remarkable feature of the great Tudor debate on the nature of the Commonweal is the way in which 'the great plentie of povertie in all the cities great townes and other inferior market townes in England and Wales' is so rarely regarded as anything but self-evident.[10] Less dramatic but certainly unenthusiastic were the comments on provincial English towns made by the first Italians to leave on record their impressions of this country. For experienced and no doubt blasé travellers like these, not only was Canterbury, its cathedral apart, a town 'about which there seems to be nothing to be said'; but it could even be broadly asserted, in a particularly famous dismissal of 1496–97, that 'there are scarcely any towns of importance in the kingdom' except for London, Bristol and York.[11] Although so sweeping a judgement was perhaps the product of a carefully cultivated ignorance, even Polydore Vergil, that Italian who must have known early sixteenth-century England better than most of its natives, combined conventional tributes to the more famous English cities with the rhetorical but probably considered view that the English 'do not so greatlie affecte citties as the commodious neareness of dales and brookes'.[12]

Needless to say, Polydore Vergil's elementary generalization pales into complete insignificance by comparison with the voluminous results of 'the Laboriouse Journey and Serche of Johan

9. *England in Henry VIII's Time : A Dialogue between Cardinal Pole and Lupset by Thomas Starkey,* ed. J. M. Cowper (Early English Text Society, Extra Series, xii, 1871), p. 93.
10. Bodleian Library, Oxford, Jones MS. 17 (Thomas Lupton's proposals to ameliorate the conditions of the poor in London, York, Canterbury and Lincoln), fo 6; cf. W. R. D. Jones, *The Tudor Commonwealth, 1529–1559* (London, 1970), pp. 108–32.
11. *A Relation, or rather a True Account, of the Island of England . . . about the Year 1500,* ed. C. A. Sneyd (Camden Society, xxxvii, 1847), p. 41; cf. *English Historical Documents,* iv *1485–1558,* ed. C. H. Williams (London, 1967), pp. 188, 200.
12. *Polydore Vergil's English History from an Early Translation . . . containing the first eight books,* ed. H. Ellis (Camden Society, xxxvi, 1846), p. 4; cf. D. Hay, *Polydore Vergil* (Oxford, 1952), pp. 116, 121. Similarly, John Major paid due respects to the distinction of Coventry, Norwich and Bristol but seems to have been well aware of the decline of Lincoln ('of renown in old days') and of York ('In circuit it is great but not in population or in wealth'): *A History of Greater Britain . . . by John Major,* trans. and ed. by A. Constable (Scottish History Society, x, 1892), p. 22.

Leylande for Englandes Antiquitees'.[13] Naturally Leland was neither an impartial nor indeed an unemotional guide; and it may not be too fanciful to suggest that for him, as for Dr Johnson in the university city of St Andrews in 1773, the sight of a town 'pining in decay and struggling for life, fills the mind with mournful images and ineffectual wishes'.[14] However, Leland certainly did have an appreciative eye for a 'praty market' like Leeds, for 'the fair streates' of Exeter and even for the remarkable new 'bewty' of Birmingham; and it is precisely because he was such an observant as well as 'totally enflamed' traveller that one can never ignore his melancholy verdicts on those once prosperous towns, like Boston, Carlisle and Coventry, where 'the old glory and riches' had departed.[15] For Leland, and for those who came after him, it was within the smaller urban communities that physical decay was most immediately apparent. What the reader of the *Itinerary* is likely to remember most vividly are the sorrowful images of places which were no longer towns at all: Reculver in Kent, which 'at this time is but village like'; Hedon in the East Riding, with 'but a few botes'; and Brougham in Westmorland, 'now very bare, and very yll buylded: yet yt hathe bene some very notable thinge'.[16] No doubt, as befits the bible of the English local historian, Leland's *Itinerary* provides innumerable different texts to support a variety of different interpretations. What certainly needs no urging is that Leland not only encountered numerous examples of urban decay but was often prepared to explain that decay – usually as a consequence of the decline of cloth-making in the case of the larger towns, and of the reduction or abolition of markets in the case of their smaller counterparts – in terms still acceptable to the modern local historian.[17]

From the pages of Leland's *Itinerary* even more specific themes unmistakably emerge. Most obvious and familiar of these is the decay of the urban castle, a phenomenon for which there is also copious documentary evidence from most parts of the country. All allowances made for Leland's obsessive interest in the ruined castle and also for the obvious exceptions, like Carlisle, Durham and Pon-

---

13. *The Itinerary of John Leland in or about the years 1535–43,* ed. L. Toulmin Smith (London, 1907–10), i, p. xxxvii.

14. *Johnson's Journey to the Western Islands of Scotland and Boswell's Journal of a Tour to the Hebrides,* ed. R. W. Chapman (Oxford, 1924), p. 8.

15. *Itinerary of Leland,* v, 39; i, 227–28; ii, 96–97; iv, 114, 181–82; v, 52–53; ii, 106–08.

16. Ibid., iv, 59; i, 61–62; v, 147.

17. 'What we do know is that, by about 1640, the 1500 or 2000 medieval markets of England had shrunk to fewer than 800': A. Everitt, *New Avenues in English Local History* (Leicester, 1970) p. 10. For an especially illuminating regional study of this decline see D. M. Palliser and A. C. Pinnock, 'The markets of medieval Staffordshire', *North Staffordshire Journal of Field Studies,* 11 (1971), pp. 49–59.

tefract, which prove the rule, there can be no reasonable doubt that from Richmond to Leicester and from Hereford to Southampton most of the great urban fortresses of medieval England now 'tendith towards ruine'.[18] At Gloucester the king's castle had been positively 'thrown down' by 1489; at Bristol 'the great hall and other elegant buildings designed for the reception of royalty were crumbling into ruin'; and even at York what had once been the most important centre of royal authority in the north never recovered from the 'takyng doune of youre Castell thar by King Richard [III]', a monarch who had originally intended to undertake its reconstruction.[19] Better interpreted as a symptom of governmental financial stringency than of increased royal confidence in either gunpowder or the prospects for internal peace, the gradual dilapidation of the urban castle towards the end of the middle ages must naturally be interpreted within the context of the decay of late medieval English fortifications as a whole. Nevertheless it is unlikely to have been a matter of complete indifference to the citizens of the adjacent town: at the least it was often alleged to have helped to promote that much lamented development, perhaps only partly reversed during the course of the sixteenth century, whereby 'Every gentylman flyth into the cuntrey. Few that inhabyt cytes or townys'.[20] A much more direct index of an urban corporation's economic fortunes and financial priorities was however likely to be afforded by the state of its own defences, its walls and gates.

Now that medieval historians have at last been forcibly reminded that few English towns 'of importance were without walls by the end of the fifteenth century', they can be under no doubt that capital expenditure on the maintenance and repair of those walls was one of the most common and most burdensome financial commitments undertaken by the burgesses of the later middle ages. Quite how voluntary and sustained a commitment that was remains a much more open question: perhaps the greatest single revelation to emerge from Dr Hilary Turner's preliminary exploration of the sub-

18. *Itinerary of Leland*, i, 7, 15; ii, 64, 105; iv, 25; v, 19.
19. *Calendar of Patent Rolls, 1485–94* (London, 1914), p. 298; M. D. Lobel and E. M. Carus-Wilson, 'Bristol' (*Atlas of Historic Towns*, ed. M. D. Lobel, ii, London, 1975), p. 13; York City Archives, House Book 6, fo 83; *An Inventory of the Historical Monuments in the City of York*, ii: *The Defences* (Royal Commission on Historical Monuments, 1972), pp. 19, 67.
20. *Dialogue between Pole and Lupset*, p. 93. It needs no urging that a high proportion of successful sixteenth-century merchants were, like their medieval predecessors, of gentry origin; but the direct evidence for the alleged 'return to the towns' of the Tudor gentry themselves still seems much less than conclusive: see, for example, W. T. MacCaffrey, *Exeter, 1540–1640, The Growth of an English County Town* (Cambridge, Mass., 1958), pp. 247–63; A. D. Dyer, *The City of Worcester in the Sixteenth Century* (Leicester, 1973), pp. 181–88; C. Platt, *The English Medieval Town* (London, 1976), pp. 188–90.

ject is the extent to which the initiatives in this field derived from the royal government rather than from within the cities and towns themselves.[21] More generally, it is now clear that the golden age for the building of stone walls around medieval towns lay in the late thirteenth and early fourteenth centuries. Of the hundred or so walled towns of medieval England, apparently only the defences of Alnwick can be confidently dated, in their entirety, to the period after 1400.[22] How many towns would have been able to preserve substantial sections of their walls into the early Tudor period without the national government's willingness to supplement its local murage grants with remissions of the fee-farm and assignments on the national customs revenues is bound to be a debatable matter; but, as it was, several smaller towns, like Richmond and Warwick, gradually lost their defences altogether and even more substantial urban communities found the financial strains of maintaining their walls almost insupportable.[23] In 1460 the walls on the landward side of Southampton were 'so feble that they may not resiste ayenst any gonnes shotte, and so thynne that no man may well stond upon them to make eny resistance or defence'; by 1486 the walls of Chester were also alleged to have fallen into ruin and decay; while for the modern visitor to York a comparison between the handsome limestone ashlar Walmgate Bar and barbican of the fourteenth century and the prosaically humble brick 'Red Tower' built three hundred yards away in the early 1490s conveys its own dispiriting message.[24] On the increasingly popular assumption that medieval town walls should be interpreted as conscious symbols of municipal independence and civic pride, the condition of those walls in the late fifteenth century is often bound to raise disquieting questions about

21. H. L. Turner, *Town Defences in England and Wales* (London, 1971), pp. 13–16, 25, 30–44, 90–91; M. W. Barley, 'Town defences in England and Wales after 1066', *The Plans and Topography of Medieval Towns in England and Wales*, ed. M. W. Barley (Council for British Archaeology, Research Report No. 14, 1976) pp. 57–71.
22. G. Tate, *The History of the Borough, Castle and Barony of Alnwick* (Alnwick, 1866–69), pp. 238–41. The stone wall of Coventry is perhaps the major exception to prove the rule: built at erratic intervals during the long period from 1356 to 1534, 'it is perhaps remarkable that the campaign was eventually completed' (Barley, 'Town Defences', p. 68; E. Gooder, *Coventry's Town Wall* (Coventry and North Warwickshire History Pamphlet, No. 4), 1971 pp. 3–37).
23. E.g. *Calendar of Patent Rolls 1377–81* (London, 1895), p. 76; *Itinerary of Leland*, i, 79; v, 147; M. W. Barley and I. F. Straw, 'Nottingham' (*Atlas of Historic Towns*, i, 1969), p. 5; *Victoria History of the County of Warwick*, viii (London, 1969), p. 420.
24. C. Platt, *Medieval Southampton* (London, 1973), p. 172; K. P. Wilson, 'The port of Chester in the fifteenth century', *Transactions of the Historic Society of Lancashire and Cheshire*, cxvii (1966), p. 2; T. P. Cooper, *York: The Story of its Walls, Bars and Castles* (London, 1904), pp. 291–304, 328–30; *Inventory of Historical Monuments in York, The Defences*, pp. 19–20. 139–40, 142–49.

the state of that independence and of that pride at the end of the middle ages.

A much simpler and less complicated physical manifestation of these qualities in the medieval urban community is likely to be afforded by municipal buildings proper, and above all by a borough's Common or Guild Hall. It may well be that the history of the town halls of medieval England can never be written, partly because so few of them survive intact and partly because the medieval archives of individual towns, in this case even those of London, usually preserve such fragmentary and inadequate references to their very existence before the late fourteenth century. Nevertheless it seems worth emphasizing that most of the evidence at present available points to the first fifty or sixty years of the fifteenth century as a time of a veritable boom in the building or rebuilding of town halls within the largest England boroughs, a boom which was apparently over by the 1470s.[25] The correct interpretation of this fashionable phenomenon, especially as so little is usually known about the sources of revenue from which these guildhalls were financed, is once again an exceptionally delicate matter; but it seems impossible not to see the new town halls of the early fifteenth century as the material expression of that late medieval transition from urban community to urban corporation which caused Maitland to characterize the fourteenth century as 'the golden age of the boroughs'.[26] Such a judgement can still afford to stand, provided that the achievement of corporate or (for a select dozen late medieval towns) county status is not automatically interpreted as a consequence of economic confidence on the part of mayors, bailiffs and aldermen. At Lincoln, for example, the royal creation of a 'county of the city' in 1409 was evidently desired as a political cure for economic ills. Not surprisingly the cure in this and several other cases proved inefficacious. As the Lincoln citizens' inability to rebuild the Guildhall they had pulled down in the late fourteenth century demonstrates, corporate ambitions could easily outstrip economic resources.[27] By definition the building of a municipal common hall was an enterprise likely to be restricted to those larger towns with the financial means to con-

25. E.g. at Cambridge, Canterbury, Coventry, Hull, Ipswich, King's Lynn and Norwich as well as York and London: see J. Harvey, *English Medieval Architects* (London, 1954), pp. 260, 299; M. D. Lobel, 'Cambridge' (*Atlas of Historic Towns*, ii), pp. 15–16; *V. C. H., Warwickshire*, viii (1969), pp. 141–42; *V. C. H., Yorkshire, East Riding*, i (1969), p. 398; V. Parker, *The Making of King's Lynn* (London, 1971), pp. 140–48; J. Campbell, 'Norwich' (*Atlas of Historic Towns*, ii), p. 15.

26. Maitland, *Township and Borough*, p. 85; cf. M. Weinbaum, *The Incorporation of Boroughs* (Manchester, 1937), pp. 45–96.

27. *Calendar of Close Rolls 1389–92* (London, 1922), p. 135; J. W. F. Hill, *Medieval Lincoln* (Cambridge, 1948), pp. 254, 270–71.

vert their corporate ambitions into stone and mortar; and after the completion of the stone fabric of York's Guildhall in the late 1450s it becomes increasingly difficult to find many examples of urban communities which decided that heavy expenditure on such a cause was either justifiable or indeed economically practicable.[28]

But 'What do the perpendicular churches prove?' Nearly forty years since that familiar problem was posed it is not a little remarkable that the historian's response remains so tentative. Professor Postan's own reply to his own question, that 'their architectural excellence has nothing to do with either the growth or the decline of English industry, agriculture or trade' has never commended itself to all; and despite the additional and often unconvincing complications more recently introduced by the advocates of a coincidence between 'hard times' and periods of heavy investment in art and architecture, there still remains room for William Cunningham's simpler view: 'there is hardly any token of general prosperity on which we may rely with more confidence than the fact that many people are able and willing to expend money in building'.[29] It might be sugggested that the real problem now facing the late medieval urban historian is less the general validity of that principle than the practical difficulties of applying it. Most of those difficulties are obvious enough: it is, for instance, dangerously easy to generalize on the basis of the fifteenth-century churches which survive, at the expense not only of those earlier medieval churches which preceded them but of those which were dismantled or reconstructed in a later age. At a more practical level, the perpendicular churches of medieval England are often notoriously difficult to date at all precisely. More serious still is our ignorance of who actually paid for the rebuilding and refurbishing of most late medieval parish churches. Failure to at least consider that question has often led to the making of many unjustified assumptions about the wealth of particular provincial towns: it apparently still needs to be pointed out – to take a very special case – that the multiplication of academic colleges in fourteenth- and fifteenth-century Oxford and Cambridge is so far from supporting a thesis of urban prosperity that it could be seen by the burgesses of both those two university towns as an objectionable symptom of their own decay.[30]

28. Of the various exceptions, perhaps the most significant is the Guildhall at Exeter which was substantially rebuilt from a ruinous state in 1468, on the eve (as Professor Joyce Youings kindly informs me) of that late fifteenth-century period of expansion 'which made Exeter one of the wealthiest and most populous cities in the land': E. M. Carus-Wilson, *The Expansion of Exeter at the Close of the Middle Ages* (University of Exeter, 1963), p. 31.

29. M. M. Postan, *Essays on Medieval Agriculture and General Problems of the Medieval Economy* (Cambridge, 1973), p. 46; Cunningham, *Growth of English Industry and Commerce,* p. 294.

30. 'Parliamentary Petitions relating to Oxford', ed. L. Toulmin Smith, *Collectanea*

For these and many other reasons, the time has certainly not yet come to generalize with confidence as to the economic and social implications of late medieval ecclesiastical building in the English town. However, the recent intensive if highly localized researches of the Royal Commission on Historical Monuments have done little as yet to rebut the traditional view that the third quarter of the fifteenth century was a period of comparative building inactivity.[31] By the 1450s the fabric of the four largest urban parish churches of medieval England, Boston, Yarmouth, Hull and St Michael's Coventry, seems to have been substantially complete; and it is of course to Lavenham and Long Melford, to Cullompton and Cirencester rather than to the older corporate English towns that one must turn to see the best urban or quasi-urban examples of the great *floraison* of late Perpendicular Gothic. So crude and perhaps over-familiar a contrast certainly admits of several exceptions, most obviously at Norwich, and tends to ignore the gradual processes of piecemeal accretion which characterize the architectural history of most English parish churches. But those who believe that the foundation and construction of chantry chapels may be a safer guide to the wealth of a city's richest inhabitants than the general architectural history of the parish churches to which they were annexed, can give but little comfort to the advocates of urban prosperity. In several of the largest English towns – quite how many future research has yet to reveal – the foundation of new perpetual chantries by laymen in urban parish churches seems after 1450 to be in full decline, a decline most readily explicable in terms of economic rather than 'liturgical bankruptcy'.[32] Nor can the copious evidence for the increasing poverty of existing late fifteenth-century perpetual chantries and urban parish churches be readily discounted. As the notorious petition of the mayor, bailiffs and commonalty of Winchester to the government of Henry VI bears witness, a petition which conveyed the alarming information that by 1450 no fewer than seventeen named parish churches in the city 'ben fallen downe', the

iii (Oxford Historical Society, xxxii, 1896), pp. 139–59; H. E. Salter, *Medieval Oxford* (Oxford Historical Society, 1936), pp. 87–89; R. H. C. Davis, 'The Ford, the River and the City', *Oxoniensia*, xxxviii (1973), pp. 258–68; *Rotuli Parliamentorum* (Record Commission, 1783), iii, 185, 254, 260, 515; v, 432; vi, 436; M. D. Lobel, 'Cambridge' (*Atlas of Historic Towns*, ii), p. 13.

31. P. Kidson, P. Murray and P. Thompson, *A History of English Architecture* (revised edition, London, 1965), pp. 128–32; *An Inventory of the Historical Monuments in the City of Oxford* (R.C.H.M., 1939), pp. 125–47; *An Inventory of the Historical Monuments in the City of York*, iii: *South-West of the Ouse* (R.C.H.M., 1972), pp. xlii–xlv, 3–5, 10–11, 16–17, 20–22, 26–27.

32. R. B. Dobson, 'The Foundation of Perpetual Chantries by the Citizens of Medieval York', *Studies in Church History,* iv, ed. G. J. Cuming (Leiden, 1967), pp. 22–38; cf A. G. Dickens, 'A Municipal Dissolution of Chantries, 1536', *Yorkshire Archaeological Journal*, xxxvi (1944–47), pp. 164–73.

inhabitants of late medieval English towns undoubtedly did see a close connection between the prosperity of their community and the welfare of its churches.[33] Without taking this type of evidence further than it is at present legitimate for it to go, it remains necessary to consider not only why more town churches disappeared in the century between 1450 and 1550 than ever before or since but also why the modern visitor to England's oldest towns will find so comparatively few physical memorials to the achievements of that particular hundred years.

If, after all, the perpendicular churches may in time produce revelations of interest to the urban historian, what about that most notorious evidence of all – petitions to the crown for remission of a borough's fee-farm or its exemption from parliamentary subsidies? So numerous are these plaintive documents that they can certainly never be ignored; but here again the late medieval urban historian is faced with one of those antiquated controversies whose final resolution must nevertheless still be delayed until the exchequer records of the fifteenth century have been made to disclose the detailed consequences of such petitions on governmental principles and practice. No medievalist in his senses would wish to take these lamentations, usually presented within the comparatively conventional format of a parliamentary petition, entirely at their face value. Indeed the very fact that so many of these petitions were presented in parliament clearly encouraged borough representatives there to emulate each other in the art of producing a convincing plea of poverty: as it happens, perhaps the single most eloquent petition to survive, the articles of 'the causez of the ruyne of youre Cite of Lincoln' presented to Richard III is to be found in the municipal archives not of Lincoln but of Grimsby.[34] Nevertheless, as Professor Postan was the first to emphasize, what is at stake here is less the veracity of the petitioners than the vigilance of the English government. Occasionally perhaps, and most notably in the short and chequered reign of Richard III, a king may have been unusually generous in his response to such petitions, less because he was moved to commiseration by the woes of his burgesses than because he was prepared to sacrifice long-term financial resources for immediate political and military assistance. But throughout most of the fifteenth century the readiness of a financially embarrassed monarchy to make such substantial fiscal concessions (amounting to over £60 000 in the case of remissions on tenths and fifteenths alone be-

---

33. 'A petition of the City of Winchester to Henry VI, 1450', *Archaeologia*, i (1770), p. 94; cf. *Calendar of Patent Rolls, 1436–41*, p. 400; ibid, *1441–46*, p. 84.
34. Grimsby Borough Archives, Petition of Citizens of Lincoln; *Historical Manuscripts Commission 14th Report*, Appendix viii (1895), pp. 263–65.

tween 1433 and 1472)[35] is best interpreted as a reluctant recognition of reality, an acknowledgement that any attempt to enforce payment would produce 'no profit to yor gode grace'.[36]

Towards the lowest end of the economic spectrum there can, in any case, be no doubt of genuine civic destitution. At Wallingford, where only forty-four householders (*lares foventes*) survived by 1439, the only possible solution to the problem of the fee-farm was the taking of the borough into the king's hands.[37] A few years later the city of Winchester, 'which in ancient times was chosen out for the coronations and burials of kings' was similarly in such decay 'that, withoute gracious conforte of the Kyng our soverayn lord, the mair and bailiffs must of necessitee cesse and deliver uppe the citee and the kayes into the Kynges hands'.[38] Moreover, when such petitions contain specific corroborative detail, the information provided (whether the 'scarce two hundred citizens' still resident at Lincoln in 1447, or the decay of '300 and more dwelling places' at Gloucester in 1487-88, or even the '987 messuages in ruin' at Winchester in the 1440s)[39] rarely seems to be beyond the bounds of possibility. Similarly, the allegation of the burgesses of Great Yarmouth in 1471 that their previous fleet of '80 ships with *fore castellis* and 140 others' had shrunk to only 24 *'naves vocati ffishers'* is by no means out of line with the results of modern research.[40] Somewhat ironically, a recent attempt to apply critical scrutiny to a genuinely suspect series of petitions for relief of fee-farm ends by conceding that the citizens of Chester between 1445 and 1486 do in fact 'appear to have had some justification'.[41] Nor for the fortunate historian who is able to test the veracity of a borough's representations to the crown by the evidence of the matters discussed at its council meetings can the conclusion be very different. No one who pursues the tortuous course of the campaign for tax remission waged by the mayor and aldermen of York from 1482 onwards through the folios of the con-

35. *Rotuli Parliamentorum*, iv, 425; v, 5, 37, 68–69, 142, 228, 497; vi, 40 (usefully calendared in Cunningham, *Growth of English Industry*, pp. 454–55).
36. *Historical Manuscripts Commission, 14th Report*, p. 264, and cf. pp. 10–12; Hill, *Medieval Lincoln*, pp. 285–88.
37. Public Record Office, Patent Roll 17 Henry VI, ii (C.66/444), memb. 11d; *Calendar of Patent Rolls, 1436–41*, pp. 317–18.
38. 'Petition of the City of Winchester, 1450', op. cit., pp. 94–95.
39. *Calendar of Patent Rolls, 1436–41, p. 400; 1446–52*, p. 80; *Calendar of Records of the Corporation of Gloucester*, ed. W. H. Stevenson (Gloucester, 1893), nos. 58–59.
40. P. R. O., Patent Roll 49 Henry VI (C.66/491), memb. 17d; *Calendar of Patent Rolls, 1467–77*, pp. 250, 393; cf. *Materials for the Reign of Henry VII*, i (Rolls Series, 1873), pp. 326–27, 330; G. V. Scammell, 'English Merchant Shipping at the end of the Middle Ages: some east coast evidence', *Economic History Review*, 2nd series xiii (1961), pp. 327–41.
41. Wilson, 'The Port of Chester', op. cit, p. 10.

temporary civic 'house books' can seriously doubt the gravity of a crisis evident even to 'the blessed Trinite'. When on 17 September 1483, the new king Richard III summoned before him in the chapter-house of the Minster 'the said Mair, hys brethyr the Aldermen, and many othir of the comuns of the said Cite' to rehearse 'the dikey and the great poverte of the said Cite', he may have been anxious to reward a group of exceptionally loyal adherents for their services during an unprecedently tumultuous summer; but it is inconceivable that such poverty and decay did not exist.[42]

Nor need even the most sceptical historian be unduly perturbed by the revelation that many and perhaps most towns assigned the payment of their fee-farms to a particular category of their total revenues.[43] Given the antiquity of the *firma burgi* and the almost universal rigid separation between its constituent resources and those of the separately administered civic chamber, it would be surprising if such were not the case. In practice most of the larger English towns seem to have paid their fee-farms from what the citizens of Lincoln called their sheriffs' 'tollez, courtes, finez and amerciaments', forms of revenue which – like property rents themselves – often did tend to dwindle and atrophy during the course of the fifteenth century.[44] Not for nothing, after all, did the inhabitants of late medieval English towns apply to their general economic plight a word most familiar to them, as to us, in context of *'Decasus Reddituum'* within an annual civic account roll. But to what other sources of income could the financially embarrassed municipal corporations of the late fifteenth century have turned? At the risk of making yet one more premature generalization, it seems clear enough that the supposed 'immense wealth' of late medieval urban corporations is largely chimerical: what is remarkable, especially by continental standards, is how few English cities – at any period of the middle ages – enjoyed annual net incomes comparable to those,

42. York City Archives, MS. A/Y, appendix fo 14; cf. *York Civic Records*, ed. A. Raine (Yorkshire Archaeological Society, Record Series, 1939–53), i, 65–66, 71, 73, 82, 135–37, 165–67; ii, 36–37, 70, 81, 83; and cf. British Library, Harley MS 433, fos 38, 81.
43. Green, *Town Life in the Fifteenth Century,* ii, 216–17, 332, 406, 410–11; A. R. Bridbury, *Economic Growth: England in the later Middle Ages* (London, 1962), pp 75–76. By contrast, the discussion of these issues in A. P. M. Wright, 'The Relations between the King's Government and the English Cities and Boroughs in the Fifteenth Century' (University of Oxford, D. Phil. thesis, 1965), pp. 173–230, suggests that even when urban claims for tax exemption on grounds of insufficiency were specious in detail they were often well founded in substance.
44. E.g., York City Archives, Chamberlains' Accounts, 1397–1502 (C.1–C.5); *V. C. H., Yorkshire, City of York* (1961), pp. 72–73; *V. C. H., Yorkshire, East Riding,* i, 40–42; E. Gillett, *A History of Grimsby* (London, 1970), pp. 55–56, 66–67; M. D. Lobel and J. Tann, 'Gloucester' (*Atlas of Historic Towns,* i), pp. 10–11.

of, say, the major religious houses in their vicinity. The real problem, and an exceptionally difficult one, is the extent to which the poverty of a civic chamber could co-exist with the presence in the urban community of individually wealthy citizens. On grounds of psychological probability alone, is it likely that the comparatively small and introspective urban community of the later middle ages would tolerate great wealth without great responsibility?

To that particular question the records of a very large number of fifteenth-century English towns do indeed seem to offer a partial answer by their revelation of an often obsessive preoccupation with the notorious problem of the withdrawal of labour from civic office-holding. As distraint of knighthood will always remind us, ambivalence of attitude towards the heavy burdens that went with the high status of administrative office was a familiar feature of medieval society at every level. Certainly a disinclination to undertake these burdens was not a novel development in the fifteenth-century town. Nevertheless, and all due allowances made for the extent to which individual cases of exemption from office-holding are much better documented in late medieval rather than earlier civic records, it is during the period after 1450 that the evidence for massive evasion of civic office becomes almost universally conspicuous. To a problem that was continuously discussed in the council meetings of every late fifteenth and early sixteenth-century town where records survive there was clearly no easy solution. A gradual increase in the number of civic chamberlains 'to bere such great charges' was one of the more common responses; and so too was the imposition of increasingly stringent financial and other penalties on the recalcitrant citizens who refused to serve. At York, the especially copious evidence for widescale attempts to evade office suggests a remarkably close chronological correlation with the process of general urban decline.[45] Similarly, at Bristol in 1518, in a particularly informative *cause célèbre*, William Dale responded to his election as sheriff by an appeal to the Star Chamber against the mayor and aldermen of that city, men who had themselves allegedly only 'passed the daungeour of the said office by the great substance that they hadd before gottyn'.[46] Other examples, derived from published town records alone, could be multiplied *ad nauseam*; and it is for each historian to decide at what point the accumulation of

45. *Statutes of the Realm*, ii, 359; *York Civic Records*, i, 135–37; *V. C. H., Yorkshire, City of York*, pp. 74–75, 139. The refusal of civic office in early sixteenth-century York is to be discussed at length in Dr David Palliser's forthcoming history of the Tudor city: I am most grateful to him for his generous assistance on these and other issues.
46. *Select cases before the King's Council in the Star Chamber*, ii, ed. I. S. Leadam (Selden Society, xxv, 1911), pp. cii–cxviii, 142–65.

isolated instances of evasion from office signifies for him a general crisis. For the citizens of Lincoln in the 1480s there could be little doubt: their analysis of their own plight ended with the claim that it was the expenses of office-holding which 'causeth many men that hath beene brought upp in thys Cite by prentishode, service, or oder wyse, to avoyed and goo forth thereof, and to inhabett theime in oder placez; and there ys nedere craft man ne soiourner that wille come too a bide or dwelle here, for fere of the seyd office; and thus this Cite dissolatez and fallith in grete decaye'.[47]

Evidence for the reluctance or inability of late fifteenth-century burgesses to take up office has moreover long been familiar to English medievalists in a very different and especially intriguing field. The invasion of the borough constituencies of the English parliament by members of the county gentry is usually interpreted in terms of the increasing aggressiveness of the fifteenth-century magnate and his affinity.[48] Yet the implications of that 'revolution in the personnel of parliament' for the victims of this process are surely quite as thought-provoking. The revelations of the Paston Letters and other sources have made it abundantly clear that by the 1450s the landed aristocracy and gentry were highly interested in the possibilities of influencing the results of parliamentary elections at Norwich and Exeter, let alone Yarmouth and Maldon. It has recently been suggested that 'representation by a respectable gentleman might well increase the effective volume of the urban voice', an argument which concedes the main point and was in fact anticipated by Ralph Neville, second Earl of Westmorland, in the famous letter whereby he asked the mayor and burgesses of Grimsby to return 'ii of my counsale to be Burgessis for youre seid towne'.[49] By the later fifteenth century, as Dr Alan Rogers has amply demonstrated in the case of Stamford, there is no doubt that many of the smaller boroughs elected country gentlemen and royal officials on their own initiative.[50] Can one seriously interpret such a ubiquitous and important phenomenon except in terms of a comparative lack of power or of confidence, or of both, on the part of the burgesses them-

---

47. *Historical Manuscripts Commission, 14th Report,* Appendix viii, p. 264.

48. *The Paston Letters,* ed. J. Gairdner (London, 1904), i. 152; iii, 53–55; M. Mc-Kisack, *The Parliamentary Representation of English Boroughs during the Middle Ages* (Oxford, 1932), pp. 60–64, 100–18; cf. P. Jalland, 'The Revolution in Northern Borough Representation in Mid-Fifteenth-Century England', *Northern History,* xi (1976 for 1975), pp. 27–51.

49. Grimsby Borough Archives, HMC. OL 2/21; *Historical Manuscripts Commission, 14th Report,* Appendix viii, p. 252; cf. A. Rogers, 'Parliamentary Elections in Grimsby in the Fifteenth Century', *Bulletin of Institute of Historical Research,* xlii (1969), pp. 212–20; *Clark and Slack, Crisis and Order in English Towns,* pp. 9–10.

50. A. Rogers, 'Late Medieval Stamford: A Study of the Town Council, 1465–92', *Perspectives in English Urban History,* ed. A. Everitt (London, 1973), pp. 28–29.

selves? The truth is that the incursus of the county gentry into the borough seats may be seen as merely one of the many manifestations of the obsessive search for 'good lords' which characterized the policies of most late fifteenth-century towns. This is obviously not the place to enlarge upon the various ways in which civic politics of the late fifteenth century became embroiled in the national factionalism of the period; but it may still need to be said that a study of any reasonably informative civic archive to survive rapidly dispels the curiously persistent myth that English towns found it easy to remain uninvolved and unaffected by the civil wars of the period. Such admittedly exceptional catastrophes as the 1461 siege of Carlisle and sack of Stamford apart, there is much evidence to suggest that, as one would expect, the major protagonists of the Wars of the Roses were no respecters of urban persons. Reading, Coventry, Leicester, Nottingham and Salisbury, to mention only five examples at random, were all compelled to make substantial contributions to Edward IV's war effort; and Professor Storey has recently shown how easy it was for Lord Egremont to recruit men in the streets of York itself during the 1450s.[51] Indeed in a not too incredible piece of special pleading to Henry VII in December 1485, the York corporation attributed the origins of their 'povertie, decay and ruyn' to Edward IV's indignation that so many men of the city had fought on the Lancastrian side at the battles of Wakefield, St Albans and Towton.[52] Nor can the single most famous example of urban involvement in fifteenth-century national politics, the 'special relationship' between Richard of Gloucester and the aldermen of York, be made to seem intelligible unless one supposes that the civic oligarchy saw that particular *dominus specialissimus* as the saviour who might lead them out of their current economic wilderness.

No doubt such emotive language, though considerably less melodramatic than that often used by the inhabitants of English towns themselves, should be out of place in any investigation of late medieval urban decline; and it must certainly be conceded that most of the evidence so far adduced in this paper has been highly impressionistic. Are there any alternatives? To the urban historian brave enough to wrestle with statistical material there are indeed, most obviously in the form of figures arising from the annual admission

---

51. *Reading Records: Diary of the Corporation, 1431–1654,* ed. J. M. Guilding (London, 1892–96), i, 52; *Coventry Leet Book, 1420–1555,* ed. M. D. Harris (Early English Text Society, 1907–13), pp. 313–19, 353–58; *Records of the Borough of Leicester, 1103–1603,* ed. M. Bateson (Cambridge, 1899–1905), ii, 279, 315–16; *Records of the Borough of Nottingham,* ed. W. H. Stevenson (London, 1882–1900), ii, 257; *English Historical Documents, 1327–1485,* ed. A. R. Myers (London, 1969), pp. 507–508; R. L. Storey, *The End of the House of Lancaster* (London, 1966), pp. 125–32, 142.
52. *York Civic Records,* i, 135–37.

of freemen into a city's liberty; from the fluctuations of overseas trade in the Enrolled and Particular accounts of the national customs; from the rise and fall of rent values within particular towns; and finally from comparisons between a highly heterogeneous collection of surviving taxation assessments. Perhaps there will always be a division between those historians who, to adapt a phrase of Professor Postan, approach these sources 'in the hope of finding general causes, and others who do the same in the hope of losing them.'[53] As it is, research in these increasingly technical spheres is still genuinely in its infancy; and one can only hope that the present state of confusion, whereby the two most forceful and influential historians of the subject have at times used exactly the same statistical evidence to come to opposite conclusions, may not be indefinitely prolonged.[54] In the case of surviving freemen's registers, some reservations have already been expressed about their limitations as an absolutely reliable guide to both total demographic trends and to occupational distribution within the late medieval town.[55] Nevertheless, and at the risk of seeming to want to leave the cake and yet to eat it, one may still suspect that whereas the high rates of freemen admission so often encountered in the years immediately after the first outbreak of bubonic plague in 1348–49 are largely attributable to heavy mortality within the existing citizenry, the comparatively low rates of recruitment characteristic of the years around 1500 may sometimes reflect a provincial town's genuine inability to attract an adequate supply of new freemen at that time.[56]

Analogous problems of interpretation lie in wait for those who would wish to utilize statistical material from other sources. Precisely because the evidence of the national customs accounts has so often, and so skilfully, been exploited to support the case for economic growth in certain areas of late medieval England, it was salutary to be reminded a few years ago by one of the editors of *England's Export Trade, 1275–1547* that at least in Southampton

53. Postan, *Medieval Agriculture and General Problems*, p. 274.
54. Ibid, pp. 44–46; M. M. Postan, 'Medieval Agrarian Society in its Prime: England', *Cambridge Economic History,* i (1966 edn), p. 568; Bridbury, *Economic Growth*, pp. 56–64.
55. R. B. Dobson, 'Admissions to the Freedom of the City of York in the Later Middle Ages', *Economic History Review*, 2nd series, xxvi (1973), pp. 1–22; cf. D. M. Woodward, 'Freemen's Rolls', *The Local Historian*, ix (1970), pp. 89–95.
56. *The Records of the City of Norwich*, ed. W. Hudson and J. C. Tingey (Norwich, 1906–10), ii, pp. xxx–xxxii, cxvii–cxxii; *A Calendar of the Freemen of Lynn, 1292–1836* (Norfolk and Norwich Archaeological Society, 1913), pp. 1–42; *V. C. H.*, *Yorkshire, East Riding*, i, 56; *Register of the Freemen of the City of York*, i (Surtees Society, xcvi, 1897), pp. 213–52; Bridbury, *Economic Growth*, pp. 65–69; *Exeter Freemen, 1266–1967*, ed. M. M. Rowe and A. M. Jackson (Devon and Cornwall Record Society, Extra Series i, 1973), pp. xiv, 54–69.

flourishing commercial activity could co-exist with a 'miserably poor' civic body.[57] Sometimes, no doubt, conclusions based on too simple an interpretation of the customs accounts may err in the opposite direction; in addition to the familiar problems created by royal licences to export free of subsidy and by an unascertainable amount of smuggling, Mr James Campbell has recently suggested that economic historians hitherto may have seriously under-estimated the value of the late fourteenth-century export trade in worsteds from Norwich and Great Yarmouth.[58] And whereas the 'unprecedented boom' in cloth exports from Exeter must be directly related to the commercial 'vitality' of much of south-western England at the end of the fifteenth century, even a sympathetic observer of the progress of English merchant shipping on the east coast has concluded that 'it was not until about 1550 . . . that the numbers, and probably the tonnage of c. 1340–1440 were re-attained and surpassed'.[59] However, the difficulties of coming to a balanced view in that long cultivated field pale into insignificance when compared with those which will one day confront the analyst of urban rent values. At this early stage of investigation on so important a topic it would be dangerously facile to offer any general verdict on the basis of the declining rent-rolls of so many fifteenth-century urban corporations and religious bodies. For the greater landlords themselves, some compensation may have been forthcoming during a period when 'the main trend after the building expansion of the thirteenth century seems to have been towards institutional ownership of the bigger blocks of urban property'; but for that reason among many others it still seems unlikely that historians will ever be able to interpret the acquisition and management of real property in the fifteenth-century English town as a genuinely dynamic feature of its economy.[60]

In the case of taxation records, whether those of the early fourteenth-century Lay Subsidies, the poll taxes of 1377–81 or the sixteenth-century Tudor subsidies, their limitations as an index of either the population or the absolute wealth of individual English towns are currently under such heavily critical scrutiny that one might hesitate to do more than suggest that they can sometimes be a guide to the more dramatic rises and falls of particular urban fortunes. Unfortunately demographic historians have not yet been able

57. O. Coleman, 'Trade and Prosperity in the Fifteenth Century: Some Aspects of the Trade of Southampton', *Economic History Review*, 2nd series, xvi (1963), p. 21; cf. the less melancholy verdict of Platt, *Medieval Southampton*, pp. 141–63.
58. J. Campbell, 'Norwich' (*Atlas of Historic Towns*, ii), p. 16.
59. Scammell, op. cit, p. 339.
60. R. H. Hilton, 'Some Problems of Urban Real Property in the Middle Ages', *Socialism, Capitalism and Economic Growth*, ed. C. H. Feinstein (Cambridge, 1967), p. 337; cf. Platt, *English Medieval Town*, pp. 181–

to consider the general implications of Dr Neville Bartlett's startling
discovery that at least 'part of the 1381 York Poll Tax Returns was
a deliberate fraud based on the Lay Subsidy Rolls of twenty-three
years earlier'.[61] Nor, perhaps, does an especially learned and influential attempt to utilize a comparison between the Lay Subsidy
of 1334 and the Tudor Subsidy of 1525 to suggest that at the latter
date 'urban wealth constituted a far larger proportion of total lay
wealth' than previously emancipate us from similar problems. Not
only does extensive suburban development complicate the already
difficult task of distinguishing between town and country but the use
of different categories of wealth as the basis for the taxes in question
introduces the possibility of almost unpredictable distortion.[62] There
are also some grounds for believing that in the early fourteenth and
early sixteenth centuries alike the assessment of taxation in towns
could differ quite markedly in practice from that in the country. The
extraordinary variation in the number of tax-payers recorded on the
several surviving subsidy returns for the early sixteenth-century city
of York is hardly likely to enhance one's confidence in any one
urban assessment.[63] More alarming still is the possibility that the
early fourteenth-century wealth of the English towns was consistent-
ly under-valued by the taxers of the lay subsidies, themselves usually
leading citizens of the communities they were assessing. Professor
Beresford has already pointed out that the decision, first taken in
1294, to levy the subsidy at a higher rate in the towns than the
country 'is an interesting comment on economic development' at the
time.[64] Indeed it is, but (when one considers all the complications
of classifying taxation boroughs that ensued) may it not also be a
decision prompted by the Edwardian government's awareness that
there was no more subtle method available of trying to correct the
imbalance of the comparative under-assessment of the real wealth
of the English towns?

61. N. Bartlett, 'The Lay Poll Tax Returns for the city of York in 1381', *Transactions
    of the East Riding of Yorkshire Antiquarian Society*, xxx, p. 7. Dr Bartlett's edi-
    tion of these returns remains, most regrettably, unpublished; but an offprint is
    included in his 'Some Aspects of the Economy of York in the Later Middle
    Ages, 1300–1550' (University of London, Ph.D. thesis, 1958). Cf. J. I. Leggett's
    'The 1377 Poll Tax Return for the City of York', *Yorkshire Archaeological Jour-
    nal*, xliii (1971), pp. 128–46.
62. R. S. Schofield, 'The geographical distribution of wealth in England, 1334–1649',
    Economic History Review, 2nd series, xviii (1965), pp. 483–510; Bridbury,
    Economic Growth, pp. 78–82; and cf. D. J. Keene, 'Suburban Growth', *Plans
    and Topography of Medieval Towns* (1976), pp. 71–82.
63. *V. C. H., Yorkshire, City of York*, p. 121.
64. M. W. Beresford, *The Lay Subsidies and the Poll Taxes* (Canterbury, 1963), p. 3;
    cf. the differentiated lists of items exempted from taxation as summarized in J. F.
    Willard, 'The Taxes upon Movables of the Reign of Edward I', *Eng. Hist. Rev.*,
    xxviii (1913), pp. 517–18.

The extent to which such reservations may or may not be justified only much current research is likely to reveal. It would, in any case, be folly to imagine that the economic development of all English urban communities can be easily 'fitted into any pre-conceived pattern'.[65] Some towns, like Grimsby and Dunwich, Northampton and Winchester, manifest symptoms of decline long before the end of the thirteenth century; others, like Salisbury and Reading, Exeter and Ipswich, may well have been positively prospering at the end of the fifteenth century; and in the case of many cities and boroughs, most obviously Newcastle-upon-Tyne, the most mysterious as well as the most successful of all the 'new towns' of post-conquest England, the sparsity of the evidence makes it almost pointless to put the question. Nevertheless, all due allowances made for important chronological and regional vicissitudes, that there is a common if not universal story to be told seems undeniable. What that story was the abundant records of late fifteenth-century York, a city whose economic fortunes were much more representative of those of other major English towns than has usually been recognized, tell only too clearly. By the 1460s and 1470s signs of York's economic distress are visible in every conceivable quarter. As always, it is the merchant and aldermanic classes who have left the most abundant evidence of their own reduction from a previously proud state to that of self-styled 'hevie creatours'. From the mid-century onwards they moved into an increasingly desolate era of contracting personal fortunes; an era when an ever-growing proportion of those fortunes appear to have been invested in rural rather than urban property or trade; when several of their members are known to have migrated to London and elsewhere; when one mayor (John Tonge, 1477–78) could be defamed as 'bot a beggar' by a local parish priest, and another distinguished ex-mayor (Thomas Gray, 1497–98) eventually had to resign his aldermanic gown because of his great 'decay and poverty'; and when the dominant figures in York politics and society, like Sir Richard York and Sir George Lawson, owed much of their ascendancy to their connections with the Yorkist and the Tudor courts.[66] To the aldermen of York the nature of their disaster was clear enough: in the words of a petition to Henry VII on St George's Day 1487, a petition to whose premises the king himself explicitly assented, 'ther is not half the nombre of

---

65. E. M. Carus-Wilson, *The Expansion of Exeter at the Close of the Middle Ages*, p. 5.
66. *York Civic Records*, i, 32; J. C. Wedgwood, *History of Parliament: Biographies of Members of the Commons House, 1439–1509* (London, 1936), p. 389; *Testamenta Eboracensia* (Surtees Society, 1836–1902), iv, 134–37; D. M. Palliser, *The Reformation in York, 1534–1553* (Borthwick Paper No. 40, York, 1971), pp. 1–2, 5; *V. C. H., Yorkshire, City of York*, pp. 89–91, 105–06, 110–13, 117, 122–26.

good men within your said citie as ther hath beene in tymes past'.[67]

To that particular problem not even a modern government can provide an easy solution; and that it was the fundamental problem for the town councils of the vast majority of all late medieval corporate towns their own words testify. Too often the manifestations of severe population decline within and indeed without the fifteenth-century provincial town – the supposed 'restrictive practices' forced on so many urban craft guilds by the decline of consumer demand for their products, the drift of the textile industry into rural areas, the gradual usurpation of regional trading functions by the merchants of London – have been interpreted as the primary causes of urban decay. But only the existence of prolonged and remorseless demographic attrition in England as a whole, an attrition emphatically not generally reversed at some unascertainable point in the fifteenth century, seems capable of explaining the ubiquity of the urban malaise. This was a process which, by very definition, was likely to cripple the smaller cities, like Lincoln and Winchester, at an early stage of its course; whereas the largest English towns might, like York, be presented with the temporary consolation of an Indian summer of remarkable affluence before they too succumbed. That in time almost every large English city did succumb, dependent as they all were on regularly sustained immigration for their very survival, there can be no reasonable doubt. Perhaps the single most dramatic and well-attested example of decline and fall is that provided by the so-called Coventry 'censuses' of 1520 and 1523.[68] But it can certainly be regarded as no coincidence that of the three leading English provincial towns, York and Bristol both welcomed the person of the first Tudor king in 1486 with pageants which bemoaned their desolation and decay; while a few years later the third, Norwich, secured statutory relief on the grounds that 'an auncient Citie is greatly decaied'.[69] Until such decay began to be arrested, at various dates in different centres but usually at a comparatively late point in the sixteenth century, English provincial towns are most notable for how little and not for how much they contributed to the cultural and social life of their age, an age whose most meaningful dichotomy long remained one of court and country rather than of town and country. Nor is the failure of its towns to

67. *York Civic Records,* ii, 9.
68. See C. Phythian-Adams's forthcoming *Coventry in crisis, 1518–25*; cf. *V. C. H., Warwickshire,* viii, 4–5; J. C. Lancaster, 'Coventry' (*Atlas of Historic Towns,* ii), p. 9. I am most grateful to Mr Phythian-Adams for permission to consult two unpublished papers which argue the case for the persistence of general urban decline in early sixteenth-century England at considerable length.
69. *Statutes of the Realm,* ii, 577; *York Civic Records,* i, 158; S. Seyer, *Memoirs, historical and topographical, of Bristol and its Neighbourhood* (Bristol, 1821–23), ii, 206.

act, in Braudel's words, as the 'transformers' and 'accelerators' of early modern English society necessarily quite as inexplicable as it has sometimes seemed to the present generation of economic theorists. Whether or not the concept of an 'autonomous death-rate' should be seen as an admission of defeat on the part of modern economic historians, to the late medieval historian it can only prove a liberating influence, emancipating him from the sterile and indeed ultimately impossible task of attempting to construct hypothetical population trends from scattered references to plague and disease. Quite when the process of demographic regeneration began is fortunately not the concern of this paper; but perhaps it is still worth listening to the advice offered to Cardinal Pole by Master Lupset as late as the 1530s: 'Sir, indede, when I loke to the cytes and townys and vyllagys in the cuntrey, I can not deny but ther hath byn more pepul here in our cuntrey than there ys now. Wherfor, wythout ferther cauyllatyon, agreying apon thys, let us go forward.'[70] Neither the medieval nor the Tudor historian is likely to want to go forward anything like so quickly in the company of so committed a controversialist as Thomas Starkey; but it could be both interesting and illuminating to consider what might happen if they did.[71]

Editorial suggestions for further reading

Phythian-Adams, C. V. 'Urban decay in late medieval England', in P. Abrams and E. A. Wrigley (eds), *Towns in Societies* (Cambridge, 1978), 159–85.

Rigby, S. H. 'Urban decline in the later middle ages: some problems in interpreting the statistical data', *Urban History Yearbook* (1979), 46–59.

Keene, D. J. *Survey of Medieval Winchester,* Winchester Studies, 2 (Oxford, 1985).

Palliser, D. M. 'Urban decay revisited', in J. A. F. Thomson (ed.), *Towns and Townspeople in the Fifteenth Century* (Gloucester, 1988), 1–21. Provides further references to the literature.

70. *Dialogue between Pole and Lupset,* op. cit., p. 76; cf. I. Blanchard, 'Population change, enclosure, and the Early Tudor economy', *Econ. Hist. Rev.,* 2nd series, xxiii (1970), p. 435.

71. I am heavily indebted to Professor Joyce Youings, Dr David Palliser and Dr Paul Slack for their invaluable criticisms and comments on an earlier version of this paper.

Index